THE OPEN COURT
LIBRARY OF PHILOSOPHY
Edited by
EUGENE FREEMAN

CREATIVE SYNTHESIS
AND PHILOSOPHIC METHOD

CREATIVE SYNTHESIS AND PHILOSOPHIC METHOD

CHARLES HARTSHORNE

THE OPEN COURT PUBLISHING CO.
La Salle, Illinois

To Paul Weiss

ever-delightful and helpful friend;
ingenious, skilful and versatile author and editor;
theoretical, practical, organizational, pedagogical,
indefatigable and astute protagonist of philosophy
or the search for comprehensive ideas and ideals
which can give our judgments perspective
and our endeavours nobility.

CONTENTS

CONTENTS

ACKNOWLEDGMENTS

PARTS of Chapter I are adapted from *The Unitarian Register and The Universalist Leader* 141 (1962), pp. 9–11; the *Journal of Philosophy* 55 (1958), pp. 944–53; *Darshana* 2 (1962), pp. 47–52. (A Spanish version of much of the chapter appeared in *Revista de la Universidad de Costa Rica* 3 (1962), pp. 237–44). Much of Chapter II is from the *Journal of Karnatak University* (Dharwar, India) – Social Sciences 3 (1967), pp. 1–15. Chapter III is largely from *The Monist* 47 (1963), pp. 188–210. Chapter XIV is also from *The Monist* 54 (1970). Chapter VII employs parts of two essays, one in *Foundations of Language* 2 (1961), pp. 20–32, the other in *The Anglican Theological Review* 43 (1961), pp. 35–47. Chapter VIII is from the *Review of Metaphysics* 12 (1958), pp. 35–47. Two pages near the end of Chapter XVI are from *The Daily Texan*, June 20, 1969.

I also thank the University of Chicago Press for permission to use the quotation from the translation of Fechner which appears in *Philosophers Speak of God*, pp. 252f.; The Macmillan Company and the Cambridge University Press for permission to use the quotation from A. N. Whitehead, *Process and Reality: an Essay in Cosmology* (1929), p. 32; and The Belknap Press of Harvard University Press for permission to use material from Charles Hartshorne and Paul Weiss, editors, *Collected Papers of Charles Sanders Peirce* (1931–5), Vol. VI, ch. 7.

Some Thoughts from the Past

O God, who himself fashioned himself. *Ikhnaton of Egypt*

Thou, creator of all, art creator of thyself.
 Nezahualcóyotl, pre-Columbian poet of Mexico

The self-moving . . . is the source of motion to all that moves besides.
The self-moved is the same as that which has the name soul. . . .
The movements of soul are will . . . deliberation . . . joy, sorrow, confidence, fear, hatred, love and other primary movements which again receive the secondary movements of corporeal substances and guide all things. *Plato*

The soul is in a manner all things. *Aristotle*

Thou hast created me creator of myself. *Jules Lequier*

Should God's soul consist of nothing save a supreme will? Should there be in his consciousness nothing which for him is involuntary (though for itself perhaps voluntary)? Then indeed there could be no individual beings in God; for this alone makes them particular creatures in him, that his higher will can be stimulated in particular ways through their inferior wills.
 The perfection of God . . . is not in reaching a definite or limited maximum but in seeking an unlimited progress. Such a progress, however, that God in each time is the maximum not only of all the present, but also of all the past; he alone can surpass himself, and does it continually. *Fechner*

Mind . . . the sole self-intelligible thing, is entitled [to be regarded] as the fountain of existence. *Peirce*

The ultimate metaphysical principle is the advance from disjunction to conjunction, creating a novel entity other than the entities given in disjunction. The novel entity is at once the togetherness of the entities which it finds, and also it is one among the disjunctive 'many' which it leaves. . . . The many become one and are increased by one.   *Whitehead*

Mich wunderts dass es mir ein Wunder wollte sein
    Gott selbst zu eigen haben auf der Erde.   *Mörike*

We are such stuff as dreams are made on; and our little life is rounded with a sleep.   *Shakespeare*

PREFACE

PHILOSOPHY aspires to impersonal truth, but a personal element stubbornly persists. I can most easily suggest what the reader may expect from this book by being somewhat autobiographical. Unlike most philosophical writings of our time, this is an essay in systematic metaphysics. In so far it resembles Paul Weiss's *Modes of Being* and John Findlay's Gifford Lectures. With these writers (and with A. N. Whitehead and Paul Tillich) I share a generous – some would say extravagant – view of the scope of philosophy. Brilliant, humane, and wise as the men just mentioned are, they do not exhaust the speculative possibilities now open to us; nor, I think, do they explore quite the most promising of these.

My philosophy is simpler than Weiss's, and – if I am not deceived – it has a more lucid and coherent structure, in ways which will be explained later (especially in Chapter VI). However this may be, I salute Weiss for the inclusiveness of his vision of life and the world.

Findlay's philosophy leans heavily, though cleverly, upon Plotinus, Hegel, and Husserl. I think our English inheritance of critical caution and concern for clarity should play a larger part in his procedure; also that we should learn more from Leibniz, the most lucid metaphysician in the early modern period, as well as from Bergson, Peirce, James, Dewey, and Whitehead, five philosophers of process of great genius and immense knowledge of the intellectual and spiritual resources of this century. I largely share Findlay's appreciation of Buddhism, though we emphasize different factors in this tradition. I also share with him a conviction that idealism (here taking Ewing's definition: the belief that reality can be explained in terms of mind) has more to teach us than most contemporaries realize. But I distrust the Hegelian method, and though, like Findlay, I was once Husserl's (post-doctoral) student (also Heidegger's), the exposure scarcely 'took'. I think Leibniz, as modified by Peirce and Whitehead – three mathematician-logician-metaphysicians – can better show us *how* to explain reality (including 'matter') in terms of mind. Though closer than Findlay to the Gospel view of the Eminent or Divine reality, I am farther than he is from conventional beliefs in personal immortality, whether Christian or East Indian. I am happy to agree with him that the eminent reality exists necessarily, beyond the reach of empirical argument pro or con, but necessarily with some contingent features or other.

From Stephen Pepper, another writer of comprehensive interests, I differ partly in seeing logical structure, rather than favourite metaphor, as the basic difference between systems, partly in not sharing Pepper's anti-theistic bias, and partly in that, whereas Pepper regards his entire enterprise as empirical, I hold that an empirical world-view is at best either science outrunning its empirical warrant, or a self-critical fusion of *a priori* first principles and the conclusions of science. Philosophy has two primary responsibilities: to clarify the non-empirical principles and to use them, together with relevant empirical facts, to illuminate value problems of personal and social life. Pepper is helpful on values, especially in aesthetics, but hampered, in my judgment, by his attempt to dispense with the *a priori*.

In this book, more than in others, I have attempted to find common ground with linguistic analysts, and to meet the demand of our time to use no technical philosophical or theological terms without taking care to explain them in words with standard non-philosophical uses. I have tried hard to say things sufficiently definite so that they could at least be right or wrong, and then if possible to eliminate what is wrong. If I seem not to have learned much from Wittgenstein, Austin, Bouwsma, Wisdom, or Lazerowitz, it is partly because the mistakes they are at pains to correct seldom seem ones committed by the philosophers I take most seriously, and also because except in the case of Wisdom, the questions they discuss are rarely those with which I wish to deal. I wonder, too, if there is no justice, with reference to some of the authors mentioned (and others omitted), in the remark of Kreisel, that the accumulation of trifling details is by no means sure to add up to something significant.

In conclusions, though scarcely in method, I have some

sympathy with Berdyaev and Teilhard de Chardin, since they show how a positive philosophy of religion can dispense with certain traditional dogmas of Western metaphysics, including the priority of being over becoming, the reduction of creaturely freedom to the mere reiteration of items in the divine fiat to create the world, the denial of chance or randomness in the world, the complete immutability of deity. In such matters I have been encouraged, but probably not otherwise influenced, by these men.

Undoubtedly the closest parallel to, and probably the strongest influence upon, my philosophy is Whitehead's. However, the doctrine of 'eternal objects' has always seemed to me, for reasons explained in Chapter IV, an extravagant kind of Platonism, a needless complication in the philosophy of process. Then, too, I question if God can be a single 'actual entity', another doctrine which appears out of place in this philosophy. I am puzzled also by talk of 'earlier' and 'later' phases in the becoming of entities said to be devoid of actual succession. Finally, I explain – some would say, explain away – Whitehead's concept (or metaphor) of 'perishing' very differently than some leading expositors do.

With these considerable reservations I am not far from Whitehead, particularly in his views of memory, perception, and causality, summed up in the doctrine of 'creative synthesis' or 'creativity' as the 'ultimate' abstract principle of existence. This can be viewed as a clarification – but a brilliant and momentous one – of Bergson's notion of experiencing (human and non-human) as at once creative and preservative, and as in its becoming *la réalité même*. Dewey, except with reference to the lowest levels of nature, had a similar idea, partly derived from the great Frenchman. As a philosopher of process Whitehead was anticipated, particularly in regard to the idea of God, by the Socinian theologians centuries earlier, then by J. Lequier, G. T. Fechner, Varisco, several English theologians, William James, W. P. Montague, Brightman, and my teacher W. E. Hocking. Perhaps none of these except James influenced Whitehead, but some of them blazed a path for me to the process view of deity.

The 'neoclassical' metaphysics, 'surrelativism', or 'creationism' – labels I have used for my kind of philosophy – can be viewed as Peircean, if Peirce's 'neo-Pythagorean categories' are purified of certain ambiguities and applied, as he largely refused to apply them, to God as well as everything else, and if the one-sided emphasis upon continuity (his 'synechism'), which I think inconsistent or confused, is corrected. From Peirce and James I accept a basic pragmatism (it is also a kind of existentialism): ideas must be expressible in living and behaviour or they are merely verbal. Or, as Whitehead put it, 'Rationalism is the search for the coherence of the presuppositions of civilized living.' I agree with James that neither the 'absolute idealism' of his day nor any mere materialism can meet this test. However, the same holds of some of James's own doctrines, though not of his form of indeterminism.

I call my system 'neo-classical' because, while it is not an example of what most people mean by 'the great tradition', or 'the perennial philosophy', it has been thought out in intimate relation to the great metaphysical systems. The ideal, at least, has been to avoid indulgence in mere personal whim or contemporary fashion. The problem is to find or create a view of first principles that is livable and rationally defensible. In arguing with others, the aim is not so much to persuade them to think as one does oneself as to explore with them the possibility of so thinking, in spite of more or less plausible objections. It is a philosopher's business above all to warn against bad or insufficient arguments or unjustified restrictions upon ways of interpreting the world, so that as people choose their world-views they will be given a chance to know what they are doing, and to have good rather than poor reasons for their decisions. An example of the 'poor' reasons is the way many persons have been determinists because they thought 'science' required this doctrine, in spite of the contrary testimony of men of great scientific experience and acumen, from Maxwell and Peirce to Heisenberg and Norbert Wiener. Again, how many have been atheists because of arguments which, according to many theologians and philosophers, misconceive the nature of the theistic question! People should not be forced to deny or neglect their own intuitions by clever sophistries, or intellectual fashions resting on no thorough, careful survey of the speculative possibilities and the thereto relevant evidence. This is a vicious narrowing of a valuable form of freedom in an advanced society.

A basic methodological conviction, to which my practice only partly corresponds (I should have learned more from my former colleague Rudolf Carnap, my present colleagues Norman Martin and Paul Lorenzen, or my former student Lucio Chiaraviglio, my friend Richard Martin, or my son-in-law, Nicolas Goodman), a conviction first acquired from two teachers, Lewis and Sheffer, and then strengthened by reading Russell, Peirce, and Whitehead, is that, as May Sinclair put it, 'logic is the backbone of philosophy', and also that nothing is quite clear logically unless it can be put mathematically. Ideally at least, a philosopher should be a mathematician and logician as well as metaphysician. Perhaps this could be said of Plato, certainly of Leibniz, Peirce, and Whitehead – scarcely of Descartes or of Kant, certainly not of Hegel, and not, in an emphatic sense, of Husserl or Wittgenstein.

A philosopher, however, should also have a sense for the non-logical side of awareness. Ideally he should have more in common with poets than even Aristotle, Leibniz, Husserl, or Russell have had. Here James and Bergson were great and so was Whitehead – who, however, learned from the other two. It was so long ago that I can barely recall how it was, but I may have learned more metaphysically from Emerson's Essays (illogical as they are) and Wordsworth's and Shelley's meta-physical poetry (from which Whitehead also profited) than by reading and hearing Whitehead. And as a college sophomore I learned from Royce's great essay on 'Community' (in *The Problem of Christianity*) the most essential metaphysical lesson of all, perhaps, a lesson the Buddhists had learned long before. This was to detect the element of illusion (or, if you prefer, confusion) in the idea of a plurality of selves mutually external to each other. (There are some mutually external experiences – this Royce failed to see clearly – but not selves or persons, unless very short-lived or remote from each other in space.) During the year following this reading of Royce, it became clear to me, and is so to this day, that any form, however subtle, of self-interest theory of motivation is the erroneous erection into a first principle of what is merely one chief expression of the truly first principle – the participation of experiences in other experiences, i.e., 'sympathy' or, in terms of its higher and happier forms, 'love'. Whitehead's taking 'society' as more

basic than 'substance' was for me the technically sharp version
of what I had firmly believed for ten years. Such also, only less
clear, was Peirce's 'Agapism'.

In the centrality of the social structure of experience, I find
the key to cosmology and epistemology, as well as ethics and
religion. From an early pious – yet rather liberal – Christian
training, my dogmatic slumber in which was rudely and once
for all interrupted by Matthew Arnold's *Literature and Dogma*,
the firmest residuum is summed up in the phrase *Deus est caritas*,
together with the two 'Great Commandments': total love for
God, and love for neighbour comparable to love for self. But
at least something like these principles is in certain forms of
Hinduism, Buddhism, Judaism, Islam, Zoroastrianism, and even
in the two-thousand-year-old hymns of Ikhnaton. If there are
central intuitive convictions back of my acceptance or rejection
of philosophical doctrines, these may be the ones. But I dare to
declare that, in the fifty years during which I have been medi-
tating and writing upon metaphysical problems, I have paid
careful heed to as many objections and alternative positions as
I could find. I have read, and enjoyed reading, agnostics,
atheists, positivists, phenomenalists, existentialists, analysts,
materialists, phenomenologists. I have had close discussions
with philosophers of these persuasions and also with representative philosophers of India and Japan. Similarly, if I reject
what I call 'classical theism', it is not because of unfamili-
arity with the works, arguments, or people favouring this position.

Since technical logic alone cannot establish a metaphysics,
intuitions being also needed, and since these, at least as put into
words and conceptualized, are not infallible or invariable from
person to person, how far philosophers can ever agree is deeply
problematical. As Popper says, all we can require is that the
thinker hold himself open to and cordially invite criticism,
above all by making as clear as possible what it is that he
believes. With Popper I agree also that there are legitimate
metaphysical questions which observation could not answer.
Critical rationalism, not empiricism, is the arbiter here. The
prestige of science is misused if it is taken as establishing the
universal competence of empirical methods. In this conviction,
so far as it goes, Popper, Weiss, Findlay, Whitehead, and I

stand not too far from Descartes and Leibniz, though of course
we are much more aware of the vast scope of problems that do
come under empirical methods, and also far more acutely aware
of the difficulty of making our rationalism genuinely critical.
I am not sure that Kant is as much help here as Hume, and I
find James at least as enlightening as Moore.

As early as 1924 I was wrestling with Heidegger's critique of
metaphysics. Where I can appreciate his insights they usually
seem to me as well or better put by Bergson, Peirce, James,
Dewey, or others, including the Buddhists.

It may strike some readers that (in Strawson's terms) I am
doing 'revisionist' rather than 'descriptive' metaphysics. However, they will be right to this extent only: ordinary ways of
speaking, for very good reasons, greatly simplify the complexities
of life and the universe, with the result that philosophers who
are too passive and unsuspecting in the face of these simplifications will not be describing human thought in its full range.
Rather, by implication, they will be doing the very thing for
which some revisionists are justly blamed, that is, denying as
'unreal' some aspects of experience: those which are normally
glossed over in our speech because the purposes that make them
important are somewhat unusual ones, such as arise in microphysics, cosmology, ethics, aesthetics, or high religion. Thus, as
prime example, the idea of substance, or individual thing or
person, taken as not further analysable or reducible, does quite
well in ordinary practical discourse, but it has broken down in
microphysics, and is dispensable in cosmology; moreover, the
Buddhists discovered two thousand years ago that it is inadequate in ethics and religion. It has been cogently argued that
it has seriously hampered Christian theology. The idea is so
central to our one-sided and in so far dangerous western individualism that deep shocks may be needed to teach us what
we miss at this point. Alas, the shocks seem only too probable.
One hopes, because one must, that the shocks will cure rather
than kill.

For me it is virtually self-evident that neither individual nor
national self interest can be *the* principle of action for a truly
rational animal. Not even sub-rational animals in fact derive
all their other-regarding behaviour from self-concern; rather
they directly (though naïvely) seek, now to protect or help

themselves, now to protect or help offspring, mates, or fellow group members. The notion that self-preservation is *the* law of nature is poor biology. Species-preservation is closer to the true law. Animals with power to reflect pervert this power and deceive themselves if they use it to justify altruism by reference to self interest. Before the bar of reason altruism does not need this justification, and cannot without sophistry be given it (in spite of Michael Scriven's brilliant attempt in *Primary Philosophy*).

Why is one interested in oneself? Because (*a*) like other selves one is an interesting, complex, and more or less harmonious or beautiful reality; (*b*) one is intimately acquainted with this reality; (*c*) one has power to change, guide, protect, and help it in its successive adventures. (To do this is satisfying in the doing, but this – the only essential – 'reward' of virtuous action is in the action, right now, not in the future). One may add (*d*) that social customs expect and inculcate a measure of self-concern. But all these reasons 'justify' being interested in, valuing, wanting to help, various other persons. The degree may differ (often tragically so), not the principle. True, only one's own bodily injuries are felt as painful; those of others, like their physical pleasures, must be imagined. But the same is true of one's own future pains and pleasures. Even memories of one's past sensations are fast fading. It is imagined experiences that chiefly motivate us, as Santayana knew; and imagination may, yet need not, be preoccupied with one's own future weal or woe. For metaphysics to canonize the former option is a sad but common misuse of speculative reason. It is the opposite of rationality, and a kind of stupidity, with which we are all more or less afflicted, to be unwilling or unable to find and respond to values and needs in the lives of others. Moreover, the own self is but one, the others are many, and some of them will indefinitely outlive oneself. So collectively they have the stronger rational claim.

The basic motivation, however, is neither the appeal of a self for that same self; nor even the appeal of other selves for the own self. Rather, it is something more general and yet, in its instances, more specific or concrete: the appeal of life for life – thus my past or future life (or self) for my present life or self and also the appeal of your past or future life (or the lives of birds, or the cosmic life) for your or my present life, reality, or self. Apparently it was Buddha who discovered this, centuries before Christ, if I may so speak, rediscovered it.

Although the foregoing half-open secret of motivation has been known to some for close to twenty-five centuries, technical philosophy has mostly made rather a mess of the job of finding metaphysical concepts to express it. Even Royce sadly failed here. Enormous ingenuity has gone and is going into finding some key to the motivation problem other than love, sympathy, social participation, whose subjects are momentary selves, not substances. (The latter are objects, not subjects.) No such key, I hold, has been found, apart from fairy tales of Heaven and Hell, Karma, or of the partly imaginary and partly diseased human being calculating every future advantage for self and permitting or encouraging self to care about others only as a result of such calculations. The prerequisite for clarity in this matter is close attention to the temporal structure of experience. 'Philosophies of process' have been paying this attention – since long ago in parts of Asia, chiefly in the last eighty years in the West. To contribute to this inquiry is the principal aim of this work, which is more systematic and comprehensive than my previous books. In some chapters it is not even roughly anticipated by them.

Chapter I tries to put the reader into the intuitive centre of the philosophy with a minimum of technicalities. Chapters II–IV introduce some of the technicalities, Chapter III in a partly historical way. Chapter V outlines the method, Chapter VI summarizes and Chapters VII–XIII explicate the logic of the system. Chapter XIV gives my revision of the theistic proofs. Chapter XV sketches the basic idea of my first book, *The Philosophy and Psychology of Sensation*, relating the idea to current preoccupations with language. Chapter XVI gives a theory of aesthetic, ethical, and cognitive good.

Ten chapters – IV–VI, IX–XIII, XV, XVI – have not previously been published.

I am as always indebted to Dorothy Hartshorne, my wife, for her skilful editing. Also to my colleague, I. C. Lieb, for suggesting Chapter IV and for some other helpful pieces of advice.

I

A PHILOSOPHY OF
SHARED CREATIVE EXPERIENCE

VARIOUS ideas have been taken by philosophers as fundamental. Substance, matter, form, being, are examples. Prior to
the twentieth century, scarcely any philosopher (at least in the
West) saw in the idea of creativity a fundamental principle, a
category applicable to all reality. True, theologians had talked
much about the divine 'creation' of the world, and also about
human artistic creation. But they generally supposed that there
were simply uncreative sub-human creatures. Also divine
creation was generally thought to be entirely different from ours,
since it is creation out of nothing, and ours, out of something
already there. Finally if creativity is a first principle, not only
must every being be capable of creating, but every being must
actually create. However, God was said by most theologians to
have faced the option of creating or not creating. Suppose he
had not created: then creativity would have had no illustration
whatever; there would have been no such thing. This shows that
creativity was not, in such doctrines, treated as an ultimate
principle. At most its possibility was so treated. Yet it is arguable
that possibility presupposes creativity as already, though
inexhaustively, exercised.

In our century there have been philosophers who take
creativity as ultimate, for instance Bergson, Berdyaev, and
Whitehead, most explicitly the last. They think that there is a
sense in which every individual creates and could not fail to do
so while existing at all. *To be is to create.* According to this view,
when we praise certain individuals as 'creative', we can properly
mean only that what they create is important or extensive,
while what others create is trivial or slight. But what they
create cannot be zero, so long as the individuals exist.

Why would anyone hold such a view? And what is it to create? Let us consult experience.

In every moment each of us accomplishes a remarkable creative act. What do we create? Our own experience at that moment. But, you may say, this experience is not of our own making, since it is produced in us by various causes. But, please note, they are many causes, not one. This is enough to show that the causes alone cannot fully determine the result. For the experience is one, not many. What causal law could prescribe in advance just how the many factors are to fuse together into a new single entity, an experience? There is no psychology text-book which seriously attempts such a thing, or sensibly could attempt it. By no logic can many entities, through law, exhaustively define a single new entity which is to result from them all.

A person experiences, at a given moment, many things at once, objects perceived, past experiences remembered. That he perceives certain objects and remembers certain things, we can more or less explain: the objects are there, the experiences are recent and connected by associations with the objects, and so on. But an experience is not fully described in its total unitary quality merely by specifying what it perceives and remembers. There is the question of how, with just what accent, in just what perspective of relative vividness and emotional colouring, the perceiving and remembering are done. And no matter how we deduce requirements for these aspects from the causes, we still have omitted the *unity* of all the factors and aspects. There is the togetherness of them all, in a unity of feeling which gives each perception and each memory its unique place and value in *this* experience, such as it could have in no other. Causal explanation is incurably pluralistic: on the basis of many past events, it has to explain a single present event or experience. It is, then, simple logic that something is missed by the causal account. Not because of our ignorance of causes: if we knew them all, the multiplicity of causal factors would only be the more obvious, and so would the jump from the many to the new unity. From $a, b, c, d \ldots$ one is to derive the *experience* of $a, b, c, d \ldots$, and not just *an* experience of them, but precisely *this* experience of them. There can be no logic for such a derivation. The step is not logical, but a free creation. Each experience is thus a free act, in its final unity a 'self-created' actuality, enriching the sum of actualities by one new member.

Here is the ultimate meaning of creation – in the freedom or self-determination of any experience as a new 'one', arising out of a previous many, in terms of which it cannot, by any causal relationship, be fully described. Bergson and Peirce, I think independently, first came close to the point here. Whitehead, however, puts it even more plainly.

Once it is seen that each experience is a new unitary entity, deterministic arguments lose their cogency. For instance, the argument that action must be determined by character or by the strongest motive. A character or motive received from the past cannot be more than *one* of the factors entering into the experience; it cannot dictate the unity of itself with the other factors. Besides, if 'motive' means a purpose or plan of action, a goal set up in advance, it has to be something relatively vague, an outline, not a description of the new experience in its full unitary quality, but rather of some important aspect or aspects of the experience. The total unique feeling of the experience is still to be decided. And if the motive or character is *not* received from the past, it must be a *creation* of the present.

Experiential synthesis is the solution of the problem of 'the one and the many'. Experience puts together its data; these remain several, but the experience in and by which they are put together is one. Each synthesis is a single reality, not reducible to interrelated parts. It is a 'whole of parts', yet it is more than that phrase clearly states: the safest language is to call it a synthesis, or an inclusive reality. But the including reality is as much a unitary entity as is any one of the included items. Concrete unity in this view is always a unification, an integration, and what is unified is always a many. Unity and plurality thus complement, and do not exclude, one another.

'Creative' means, as in Bergson's 'Creative Evolution', unpredictable, incompletely determined in advance by causal conditions and laws. Accordingly, it means *additions to the definiteness of reality*. Every effect is in some degree, however slight, an 'emergent whole'. Emergence is no special case, but the general principle of process, although it may have privileged instances in which the extent of novelty (not determined by the conditions) is unusually pronounced. As Bergson and Peirce insist, prediction is limited, not alone by ignorance, but by the very meaning of the future as a sphere of decisions yet unmade, issues not yet settled even by the totality of causes already operating. Reality is predictable just in so far as it is not creative, but rather mechanical, automatic, compulsive, habit-ridden. Much of life is thus uncreative and hence predictable. Science has enough to do if it seeks to trace out the mechanisms which underlie and limit creativity. The creative as such is perhaps outside the sphere of science; yet the denial of the creative (such as we find in the works of some psychologists, for instance) is also, and much more surely, outside its proper sphere. If anything is unscientific, it is the denial of aspects of existence because they seem inconvenient for our methods.

Of course you might argue that, though the experience is not entirely derivable causally, the physical behaviour is so. You would then be in some danger of claiming a higher degree of predictability than most physicists think is attainable, even in some inorganic systems. You would also be asserting that experience is without influence upon behaviour; for if experience does influence behaviour and is itself not entirely determined causally, then one of the conditions of behaviour escapes complete causal derivability and so does behaviour itself.

The most respectable deterministic argument is methodological, the contention that science should not set limits in advance to its success in the search for causal explanations. But a methodological rule is not *ipso facto* convertible into an established or even a probable truth about the universe. That we should, perhaps, as scientists, avoid setting limits in advance to our finding of causal derivations affords no evidence that such limits are lacking in the nature of things. This is an independent question. And the evidence is the other way. There must, as we have seen, be limits to causal derivability. Moreover, what we should, as scientists, avoid doing may be the very thing that, as philosophers, or as human beings, we ought to do. Science is specialization, abstraction; philosophy and religion exist to restore the total perspective, taking all legitimate interests of man into account. Among these interests, or supreme over them, is the interest in creating. We are not merely inquirers predicting, we are also agents deciding, the future. And decision has to be made step by step. We cannot get everything decided, then sit back and merely predict. We should be dead, since to live is to decide, and decide anew, each moment. Think of the psychological or sociological predicter, calmly foreseeing his own actions, the future decisions of statesmen, the future compositions of musicians, the poems of poets, the future discoveries of his own science of psychology or some other science, the jokes his friends will make with him during the coming day!

People have looked for freedom in action, and of course freedom must somehow show up in action. But the first stage of free action is the way in which one interprets or experiences the world. Only you or I can determine our own way of feeling and thinking our environment. The utmost slave has some freedom here which none can wholly suppress in him while he is alive. No matter how others coerce or persuade him, he finally must make his own unique and only relatively or partially predictable response to the stimuli others bring to bear upon him. It is vain to talk about psychological prediction as an absolute; for even after an experience has taken place, not all the words in all languages could precisely describe that experience. And what cannot be said even afterwards certainly cannot be said in advance. A man grows angry; suppose we have predicted this. There are as many forms and qualities of angry experience as there are cases, and only more or less rough and crude descriptions are possible of the various respects in which they may differ. However, the mere indescribability of an experience is not the whole story.

Let me restate the basic argument: the stimuli moulding an experience are many: the five or more senses are operating, memory is relating us, at least unconsciously, to thousands of incidents of the past: but all this multiplicity of influences is to produce a single unitary experience, yours or mine right now, let us say. The effect is one; the causes, however, are many, literally hundreds of thousands, billions even, considering the cells in our brains, for example. This vast multitude of factors must flow together to produce a single new entity, the experience of the moment. The many stimuli are given, and certainly they tell us much about the response. But it is a logical impossibility that they should tell us all. An emergent synthesis is needed, to decide just how each item is to blend in a single complex sensory-emotional-intellectual whole, the experience. Any 'motive' determining this whole is either but an item going into the synthesis, or else is the synthesis, and you are arguing in a circle. To experience must be a free act, or nothing intelligible.

Why is this not more generally realized? In part, because we have our minds chiefly upon the more important and exceptional modes of creativity, and so we overlook the humbler ones which are always there, like the man in Molière who did not realize that he had been talking 'prose' all his life. Freedom is always there, but the unusual kinds and degrees of freedom are not always there. It is important to distinguish between the higher and lower forms of freedom; yet we shall never understand life and the world until we see that the zero of freedom can only be the zero of experiencing, and even of reality. (For, apart from experience, the idea of reality is empty, as some though not all philosophers admit.) Accordingly, Whitehead, Varisco, and others have proposed that we generalize, and take the free act of experiencing as the universal principle of reality. Not that human experience is the principle of reality, far from it. But human experience is only one form; there are the other vertebrate animals and their modes of experiencing; the lower animals and theirs – and where shall we stop? From man to molecules and atoms we have a series of modes of organization; at no point can one say, below this there could be no experience. If atoms respond to stimuli (and they do), how else could they show that they sense or feel? And if you say, they have no sense organs, the reply is: neither do one-celled animals, yet they seem to perceive their environments.

For the sake of the argument at least, then, let us imagine the universe as a vast system of experiencing individuals on innumerable levels. Each such individual is in some measure free; for experiencing is a partly free act. Thus creativity, emergent novelty, is universal. In this way we perhaps understand why the physicists have had to reformulate the laws of nature as statistical, rather than absolute uniformities.

If life is thus creative, why are there uncreative aspects which make scientific and also commonsense predictions of the future possible? The need for these is plain: to live is indeed to decide, and decide anew each moment; yet to live is also to foresee, to deal with the future to some extent as though it were already settled fact. How is this possible? We must here introduce the 'sharing' of creativity. The most obvious aspect of this is in memory. In memory one takes account of one's own previous decisions as relevant to the present decision. One participates or shares in past experiences, with their creative decisions. One also remembers past perceptions of how others thought and felt, and what they decided. Or one perceives now what they in the approximate present think, feel, and decide. One takes all this into account in one's own present decision. Thus the freedom of present creativity is not absolute, or in a vacuum. It accepts limits. But these limits are set by other acts of freedom, those that are known from memory or perception. Freedom is thus sharply limited, but by freedom itself, as embodied in other acts, either of oneself or one's acquaintances, enemies, friends, fellow animals, fellow creatures.

Why should one take free acts of the past into account? Why not ignore them? Because the very meaning of freedom is the transition from the experienced antecedent many to the new unit experience of that many, the many being the previous acts of freedom. We experience, in a free unique synthesis, the various experiences already actualized which we remember, or perceive in others. We cannot simply experience our present free experience – of what? There must be some content. In memory and social experience, and (some of us believe) in all experience, we find this content furnished by other experiences, each with its own freedom, belonging to other times or other individuals. Experience must have stimuli; there must be objects of experience, data which are already there, ready to be experienced. (Even in dreams, it is so.) Yet in this philosophy there is nothing in the world but creative experience. What, then, are the objects which are there to be experienced? Simply, previous cases of experience! Some of these are one's own earlier experiences as one now remembers them. The rest are of other types. For instance, the cells of one's body are, as various writers have suggested, constantly furnishing their little experiences or feelings which, being pooled in our more comprehensive experience, constitute what we call our sensations. And the cells, in their fashion, respond to or experience our experiences, as is shown by the influence which our thoughts and feelings have upon our bodily changes. Again, when two of us talk, each response of one becomes a stimulus to the other. Always there is a degree of freedom; and the inclusive limit upon the present act of freedom is the sum of past acts to which it is a reaction. Experience as emergent synthesis feeds on its own previous products, and on nothing else whatever! This is the 'ultimacy' of creativity.

Sharing of creativity is the social character of experience, its aspect of sympathy, participation, identification with others. Moreover, even one's own past self is, strictly speaking, 'another' – as hundreds of thousands of Buddhists have, for over a score of centuries, been trying to tell the world. I hold that in this they have simply been accurate. One can regard one's past self with love, but also with antipathy, much as one can the selves of other persons. Sheer identity or sheer non-identity cannot be the correct account of this matter. Our Western philosophies have, with rare exceptions, been excessively individualistic, but also insufficiently pluralistic. They have taken a perilous first step toward the mystic monism, the night of mere abstract identity in which 'all cows are black'.

It may seem that the entire content of a creative act cannot come from other cases of creativity. For what of the sensory material coming into our experiences? Let us grant that the stone we see is not a creative agent; also that our sense organs themselves are not literally such agents. However, atoms, molecules, and still more nerve cells, seem to exhibit signs of spontaneous activity not to be found in whole rocks or eye-balls. With reason many scientists hold that we can set no limits to the pervasiveness either of spontaneity or of feeling in nature. That there are statistical laws with very great exactitude and wide scope can be reconciled with this – as is widely admitted. This gives us a tremendous new speculative possibility, a great alternative to the Newtonian 'world-machine', and to the dualism of free mind and blindly obedient matter.

To exploit this new possibility we must overcome the prejudice that minds, or experiences, are 'inextended'. James, Peirce, Whitehead, and many others (and indeed modern physics itself, with its view of space as merely a pattern of causal inheritance among events, which may perfectly well be experiences) have shown that the denial of extension to experience is unfounded. With the abandonment of the definition of the psychical as inextended and with the admission of universal creativity, dualism loses its necessity. And only necessity will ever induce science or philosophy, with their drive toward conceptual unification, to accept an ultimate dualism. Yet the sole remaining alternative to psychical monism is a materialistic one whose implicit dualism is never successfully disguised. Experiences are facts; the only question is, what else is fact? If nothing else, then, and only then, is dualism avoided.

We have said that the limitation of freedom by past free acts is what makes a certain measure of prediction possible. The full explication of this would require us to consider not only human and subhuman types of freedom but also Supreme Freedom, the divine choice of certain patterns of order or laws for this world, this divine choice being taken into account – not consciously, as a rule, but nevertheless effectively – by all other forms of freedom. Freedom is limited only by acts of freedom already performed; but divine acts of cosmic relevance and influence must be included, to account for cosmic order. This brings us back to the theological problem of creation which was mentioned at the beginning of the chapter.

Let us consider again the traditional view of this matter. God was said to 'create' a world, something quite distinct from himself. The world was creature, God creator; the one wholly uncreative, the other wholly uncreated. This doctrine is neat and definitive, but there are reasons for thinking that the truth must be less simple (See Chapter XI).

First, the act of creating was thought of as voluntary, a decision from which the creator might have refrained. Suppose he had refrained: the world would then not have existed; however, something else would also not have existed, the decision itself. There would instead have been the decision not to create, or to create some world other than ours. This shows us that a free agent must create something *in himself*, even if he decides not to create anything else; for the decision, if free, is itself a creation. The world resulted, we are told, from a free *fiat*, 'Let there be a world!' But this *fiat*, like the world, need not have been. Like the world, then, it exists contingently, and is brought into being by the creator, but within himself. In short, *freedom is self-creation*, whatever else it may be. The will which freely determines another, or freely refrains from doing so, in any case determines itself. But this means that it is untrue that the creator is in no sense or aspect created; rather he is, in some aspect, a creature, a product – at least of his own making. This is an old view, found in Egypt, India, and Central America.

Second, let us consider the view that the creature is *merely* creature, in no way creator. Take man: we are told that he is made; he does not make himself. Yet we also say, in good English, that a person 'makes' a resolution or decision; hence, since an adult person is, in substantial degree, composed of the sum of his past decisions, if he has made these, has he not to that extent made himself? And if it be denied that a man has made his decisions, why call them his? Are they God's decisions, and not the man's? Or are they both? Can exactly the same decision be that of two agents? This difficulty is childishly simple; but I am persuaded that it is genuine. I find no clarification in the classical discussions of the problem, such as that by Thomas Aquinas. Of course, it may be held that these divine mysteries are too high for us. However, as Berdyaev shrewdly hints, the mystery seems all too plainly man made. It is human beings who invented such neat little phrases as 'creator and creature' or 'creatio ex nihilo'. Nor is the doctrine we are attacking, in its bare simplicity and starkness, to be found in the Bible. Rather, it is a stylized version of biblical thought, a version invented by philosophical theology. The invention need not be taken as sacred, whatever be thought of the Bible. The stylization may have squeezed out some truth, and introduced some error.

It is often said that since God, or nature and society, 'made' my original character and environment, he or they thereby determined what my decisions would be. But the word 'character' is merely a label for the pervasive quality of a person's past actions. Hence to explain actions by character is word-juggling. You may indeed substitute 'inherited genes' for the word 'character'. However, if actions do strictly follow either from the genes and the surrounding cosmic situation, or from a timeless divine decree, in what sense is a man now creative at all? And if he is not creative, how does he know what he means when he attributes creativity to God?

You may say that creative or free action is simply voluntary action, doing as one wishes. But is this all that is meant when

God is said to be free? For, please observe, when it is said that God is free to create or not to create this world, it is thereby denied that in *his* case actions follow necessarily from character. So theological determinism attributed to deity the supreme or perfect form of causally transcendent freedom, but to man the total absence of freedom in this sense! Thus the difference was not to be between the infinite and the finite, or perfect and imperfect, but between the infinite and zero. How, I ask, starting from zero, is there a path to the concept of the supreme case? One must start from something, not nothing, to derive the idea of the maximum or the unsurpassable.

The logical view of the situation is rather that God, being both self-creative and creative of others, produces creatures which likewise, though in radically inferior ways, are self-determining, and also productive of effects beyond themselves. In this fashion the theological view, with its inconsistencies removed, becomes a philosophy of universal creativity. We must not, however, stop with God and man, as self-creative creators; we must go on to conceive the lower animals, and even atoms, as in some slight or trivial way self-determining and creative of others. For if supreme creativity is the divine nature, and an inferior creativity is man's nature, then the lower animals must be still lower levels of creativity. The effect must in some way express the nature of its cause. How can an infinitely creative being produce an *absolutely* non-creative being? That which is absolutely devoid of what God supremely possesses – what can it be but the zero of actual existence?

A third difficulty with the supposedly absolute contrast between creative God and created world is the following. A free agent determines not only himself, in some aspect, but also all those who know him. If I 'make' the decision to perform such and such an act, and you are aware of my decision, then I will in effect have decided that you are to be the knower of my decision. Had I not made it, you certainly could not have known me as making it: and if you are a sufficiently close observer of me, I will by making the decision have established at least the probability that you should acquire knowledge of it.

This consideration applies also to our relation to God; indeed, it applies to that relation more strictly and absolutely than else-where. For no matter how well and closely you may have observed me, you might somehow fail to note my decision. But God cannot fail to know that I decide such and such – granted that I do so decide. This 'inability' not to know a thing if there is such a thing is his infallibility. Accordingly, all we have to do to determine something in God is to determine something in ourselves, as known to God, and if we cannot do this, we have no freedom whatever. Either we determine the divine knowing, in some degree, or we determine nothing at all. Jules Lequier, a hundred years ago, argued this out very carefully; he has not been refuted. He has, however, been widely ignored.

According to the old view, as set forth by most theologians and philosophers, God influences all things, nothing influences God. For him there are no 'stimuli'; hence when he influences or stimulates the world, it is in a wholly different way from the ordinary way. For normally, a stimulus or cause is but a previous effect, or response to some still earlier stimulus; yet God, it was thought, does not respond. He just – creates, 'out of nothing'. I think this was a mischievously unclear way of talking. We know creativity only as a responding to prior stimuli, and if we refuse to allow an analogy between such ordinary creative action and the divine 'creating' of the cosmos, we are using a word whose meaning we cannot provide. Our new philosophical doctrine is that even God's creativity is his higher form of emergent experiential synthesis, or response to stimuli. He influences us supremely because he is supremely open to our influence. He responds delicately to all things, as we respond more or less delicately to changes in our nerve cells. Of course, his delicacy is infinitely greater. He contributes to our lives in superior fashion because, in equally superior fashion, he receives contributions from us. Like the sensitive parent or ruler, he enjoys observing our feelings and thoughts, and responds to these with a perfection of appreciation to which no parent or ruler can attain. Because only God can appreciate us, or our neighbours, in our or their full worth, we unconsciously respond to this appreciation as we do to no other. And so the order of the world is possible, in spite of the assumption that only freedom exists to limit freedom.

Consider now some advantages of this way of viewing God. First, unlike the notion of divine creation as a purely one-way action proceeding from God, our view does not threaten to deny the freedom or creativity of the creatures. Of course a worshipful God must have the supreme, cosmic, or perfect form of creative power. But if to create is essentially to experience, and if this is to form an emergent synthesis of data coming from previous experiences, which must, in their way, also have been free, to say that in God is the perfect or infinite form of creative response is still to imply that he has the freedom of others to respond to.

Does such a view 'limit' the power of God? This way of putting the question prejudices the answer and is to be rejected. We must first ask, what is it to exert power? On our view it is to respond to the responses of others in such a way that the new response becomes in its turn a new stimulus. In this philosophy the word 'power' has no other meaning which could be used to describe God. So we do not have to limit God's power to make room for the freedom of the creatures (or to explain evil); we only have to take care that when we speak of divine or perfect 'power' we have a meaning for the word. This meaning will take care of creaturely freedom automatically. No special 'limits' are required.

So far we have argued that creative becoming is a reality, at least in human experiences, and that it is not obviously impossible that it should be universally real, present in all things from atoms to deity, and constitutive of reality as such. There is, however, a tradition that becoming is a secondary mode of reality, inferior to and less real than being. Our view affirms the contrary, that 'becoming is reality itself' (Bergson), and being only an aspect of this reality. How is this inversion of the great tradition to be justified?

One argument is this: whereas 'becoming' can be taken as inclusive without suppressing the contrast between itself and being, 'being' taken as inclusive would destroy this contrast. For no matter how much is uncreated, if the least thing is created, a totality results which embraces the uncreated and the created. *Creation is always of the total reality*, never of a part merely. Grant me x as eternal, and let me create y, and I will have created xy. For since x exists whether or not I create y, in causing y to be, I also cause the total reality, including x and y, to be. You cannot deny that, had y not been created, this totality would not have been, and you cannot deny that my creating Y results in the totality in question. So how can you deny that I have created this totality? True, I have not created everything that it contains. But it is the very meaning of becoming as creative synthesis that it puts together antecedent factors in a new unitary reality. To put together is not to create what is put together, but it is to create the new inclusive togetherness or synthesis itself as a single entity.

Does not the whole history of thought support the view that partisans of the primacy of being must either turn becoming into an 'illusion' (whatever that means in this case) or else must leave it 'outside' Being, in which case the total reality, 'What becomes and what does not', is left undescribed, and so the doctrine is unfinished. It cannot be finished without contradiction. On the contrary, what becomes can very well be a synthesis whose data do not (at least in this case of becoming) become, and they need not all ever have become. For an act of synthesis does not create its own concrete data; this has been done by previous acts. Moreover, 'synthesis as such', the universal, cannot be created, for in this creation there would be no data to synthesize. Becoming or creativity itself is necessary and eternal because it has nothing more general or ultimate above it. The contingent is that for which there is an alternative, and this always implies some more general conception embracing the alternatives. But *creativity embraces all alternatives, and is indeed alternativeness itself; therefore, although particular becomings or instances of creation are contingent, that something or other becomes or is created is necessary.*

The 'Philosophy of Process' is not the result of an arbitrary preference for becoming, but of the logical insight that, given a variable V and a constant C, the togetherness of the two, VC, must be a variable. Variability is the ultimate conception. (If you say, there is no variability but only permanence, no becoming but only being, you destroy the contrast upon which both concepts depend.) To derive constancy as a special case or aspect, we have only to remark that even to speak of V as one variable throughout its variations is to refer to an aspect which is fixed throughout. To create the new we not only do not have to have *exclusively* new items, but we must not have. For things wholly without anything similar or in common could not even be compared. However, the point often overlooked here is that the common element is contained in the diverse realities as a 'common denominator', an abstraction, while the concrete whole is the diverse, not the common. Being, as identical, is in the becoming of the new totality, not *vice versa*. From successive events, we can abstract what is common; but each event is more than any such common denominator of itself and its predecessors.

Becoming is not a special mode of reality, rather it is its overall character. However, our thesis is not merely the primacy of becoming, but its creative-synthetic nature. Let us suppose that there are two modes of becoming, the non-creative and the creative. Then what is the togetherness of the two? It is the creative which furnishes the unity of itself with its 'other', if such other there be. An unpredictable event and a predictable one must together form an unpredictable whole, an emergent synthesis.

Let us take a given act of synthesis, S, following upon other preceding acts, A, B. . . . In the act C, A, and B are not created, for they had already been created previously. Hence, in *this* act A and B are not created, do not become; rather they enjoy the status of having become. But in the becoming of C as successor-to-B, this relationship to (and including) B does become. Succession, as Bergson with fine genius perceived, is essentially cumulative. First B without reference to C, then C as successor-of-B. Relations between events must be somewhere, and where if not either in earlier events as predecessors, or in later events as successors? If (1) predecessor-of-B is an intrinsic property of A, then the character of A includes B, and the later event is there before it happens. If (2) successor-of-A is an intrinsic property of B, then the character of B includes A, and A is there after it happens. (1) is counter-intuitive: that an event is *before* it becomes is paradox, but that it is after having become is only to careless thinking a paradox. The products of creation cannot be until they are created, but having been created they are bound henceforth to be. Creation is synthesis.

But perhaps you suppose a negative process of de-creation, balancing that of creation? This leads to the most violent paradox of all. For if what becomes subsequently undergoes destruction, is turned into nothing, then the truth about it must be no more and no less than the truth about nothing. But the truth about my past headaches is not the truth about nothing. To avoid this absurdity you must posit something between nothing and the full reality of the headaches. What is this intermediate reality? Note that everything true about the headaches must be represented in it. Thus the event which has become unreal is a complete duplicate, character for character, of the real event as it was when present. So my present experience, which is destined to become 'unreal', is also destined to survive sufficiently to make still true everything that is now true of it. If the experience is now intense in just a certain degree and manner, it must always thereafter be true that there was this degree and manner. Thus the characters of the experience all survive, only with the label 'has been', or 'no longer'. Nothing positive truly assertible of the present can be obliterated by this translation into the has been. In spite of Mead's arguments in *The Philosophy of the Present*, I hold that the status 'has been' is not a subtraction from an event's characters. (Whitehead's unfortunate metaphor of 'perishing' has misled many here.) Any subtraction would have to be a transaction about which nothing could truly be said.

This consideration strongly supports the synthetic view of process. That past events are real enables there to be a *de facto* totality of genuinely successive events; that 'future events' are not real means that each event can constitute itself as a new synthesis, a new unified totality. 'The many *become* one and are increased by one', a new inclusive unity is born; and this unity forms an item in a new many. Truth about particular events is retrospective; truth about the future (see Chapter VII) is not about particular events but about tendencies, probabilities, and abstract characters bound to be embodied in some particulars or other. (See my essay, 'The Meaning of "Is going to be" ', *Mind*, Vol. 74 (1965), pp. 46–58)[1]

---

[1] Cf. S. M. Cahn, *Fate, Logic and Time* (New Haven and London: Yale University Press, 1967). Cahn's disagreement with me (pp. 60–4) is not metaphysical, for we agree that descriptions of future events cannot be timelessly true. His contention that my view conflicts with the law of contradiction depends upon assuming that 'X will occur' and 'X will not occur' are contradictories, whereas I take them to be contraries. We agree that some form of 'excluded middle' must be given up. For me this applies, not to truth values of propositions but to predicates and their negatives.

For a philosophy of becoming, basic terms like 'reality', 'truth', 'what there is', 'the universe', 'what is going on', really mean reality as of now, the truth now, what there is now, the universe now, what is going on now (as conditioned by what has already gone on) – or else they have no unambiguous meaning. If the basic terms are held not to be thus demonstrative, 'token-reflexive' or context-dependent, they force us to the 'illusion' concept, or pseudo-concept, of becoming, which 'explains' it by calling it bad names. If, as Bosanquet, Royce, Thomas, and Leibniz never doubted, 'there is' a total reality, once for all, not only inclusive of all that has happened but of 'future events' in their full detail, then events do not happen, but simply are. This neo-Parmenidean doctrine involves severe paradoxes. One must hope that it can be avoided, even though relativity physics seems to many to require it.

It follows from the foregoing that if God is purely immutable, he is merely an abstraction from process. This is reason enough for avoiding the doctrine. God must not have any external 'and' connecting him with the natural process; rather he must literally and absolutely embrace his own togetherness with it. *If* this were (but probably it is not) the meaning of the Vedantist doctrine of 'non-duality' we should have to accept it. God is in some fashion anything but the 'wholly other'; he is not on one side, with inferior things on the other, there is no mere alongside God, or mere 'beneath God'; he is 'the place' of all things, and all things are, in the most utterly literal sense, 'in' him. God is even his own togetherness-with-evil, and in that sense is qualified by evil. It is his internal *relatum*. To employ an analogy, a man who has a wicked acquaintance is not indeed thereby made wicked, but he is made somewhat unfortunate, he *suffers* the relationship of being connected with something partly evil. To attribute to God immunity in every sense to misfortune is merely to degrade God to the status of an abstraction from the total actuality. It also serves, most evilly, to reinforce our own tendency to deny our solidarity with the weal and woe of others, by making deity the model of such aloofness. Intrinsic togetherness

---

Between 'definitely rainy tomorrow' and 'definitely not rainy tomorrow' there can be a third case, 'indefinite with respect to rain tomorrow'. As the interval between the present and the future date dwindles, the indefiniteness also dwindles and finally reaches zero.

with things both good and evil is not a defect, but is the perfection of concreteness. The highest *de facto* good can only be realized as a creative synthesis, uniquely complete, of all so far actualized process.[2]

How can one tell whether or not the foregoing thoughts (in a sense they are meant to be but one thought) are true? Or at least, close to the truth? And if true what importance do they have? With these two questions the rest of this book is concerned.

[2] For a short introduction to the creationist philosophy see *The Creative Advance* by E. H. Peters (St Louis: The Bethany Press, 1966). Also *Philosophers of Process*, ed. D. Browning (New York: Random House, 1965.)

II

WHAT METAPHYSICS IS

METAPHYSICS may be described as the study which evaluates *a priori* statements about existence. *A priori* is here used in a somewhat Popperian sense of contradicting no conceivable observation. Unlike Popper – or Kant – I do not restrict the observations to those which human beings might perform. However, human beings must be able to conceive the observations. I hold that we can in principle conceive – though not imagine – experiences radically different from any we could possibly have. I also think Popper goes too far in denying induction, or verification, of general statements. At least he understresses the importance of 'corroboration' as yielding positive probabilities within certain limits. If what is to be established is a law claiming absolute quantitative precision and validity throughout all time, I fully agree that we cannot know any such law even with probability. But for most human purposes neither absolute precision nor eternal validity is required or even relevant. This being understood, I agree with those who say that Popper's denial of verification is too drastic. But I agree entirely with his claim that it is observational falsifiability which alone distinguishes empirical from metaphysical or *a priori* statements. This is a precious contribution to philosophical wisdom.

The reason Popper is right here is so obvious it seems almost silly. Yet how many have missed it! If there are truths which are non-empirical, non-contingent, holding *a priori*, any experience must be compatible with, and in so far corroborate, them. Thus agreement with experience could not possibly be the distinctive mark of *contingent* truths, but only of truth as such, whether contingent or necessary. *All* truths will agree with experience, hence the difference between contingent and necessary truths can show itself only in this, that the former could while the latter could not *conflict* with *conceivable* experiences. Popper's famous argument that a single instance can refute a law but none can prove it seems additional, and really unnecessary, ground for rejecting verifiability as mark of empirical truth. Such a mark it could not be for the simplest reason of modal logic.

Although a metaphysical mistake must be an absurdity fitting no conceivable experience, and a metaphysical truth must fit any conceivable experience, an *allegedly* metaphysical statement may really be empirical, in which case conceivable experiences will include some that would be incompatible with the statement. The notion of substance that it is an identical entity containing successive accidental properties is an absurdity, a misleading way of describing an individual enduring through change. The successive states are not 'in' the identical entity but rather (as I shall argue in Chapter IX) it is in them. But another issue connected with the idea of substance seems to be empirical. This is whether or not all happenings are states of at least potentially enduring individuals. Physicists deny this of elementary particles. Perhaps in some possible world systems there would be no events not belonging to genetically identical individuals, and in others there would be such events. If that is the metaphysical truth, the physicists' claim is compatible with but does not establish it. If the metaphysical principle is said to be that there cannot be unowned events, the physicists' claim seems to refute the principle. But those who fail to detect the arbitrariness of the reduction of events to mere adjectives will probably find it possible to reject the physicists' interpretation of their experiments, as Mortimer Adler does, deriving at least apparent support from Heisenberg.[1] And of course the falsity of the assertion that in no possible world state will there be unowned events does not entail the contrary assertion that in every world state there will be such events. The distinction between empirical and metaphysical may not always be easy to draw. But I contend that there is such a distinction.

Though verifiability has failed as criterion of empirical meaning, as Hempel has been finding out through the years, it can, if sufficiently liberalized to include non-human and super-

[1] M. J. Adler, *The Conditions of Philosophy* (New York: Atheneum, 1965), ch. 12.

human experiences, furnish a criterion of general meaning. By allowing even conceivable divine experiences to count we do not take away all cutting edge from the criterion. For instance, if we could not observe the actualization of the alleged possibility, 'there might have been nothing', no more could God observe it. It is not the kind of thing that could be observed. Also, if we could not observe the 'non-existence of God', neither obviously could God observe it. Not every verbally possible statement is made observationally verifiable by even the most generous notion of 'observation'. I believe that what is thus excluded is the genuinely nonsensical or contradictory, and only that.

'If no experience could count against it, it says nothing' – this slogan by which some seem to have hypnotized themselves into insensibility to metaphysical issues, but of which (or anything like it) Popper has never been guilty, is nothing but the declaration, 'There can be no *a priori* or necessary truth'. For of course no experience could count against such a truth. But any experience could, sufficiently wisely reflected upon, count for it. The universal requirement of significance is positive, not negative.

At best, or most generously interpreted, the slogan is ambiguous. Of course a necessary statement says nothing contingent, nothing distinctive of one experience or experienced world rather than any other. But so far from its being evident that conceivable data of experience have nothing in common, it is rather evident that they have in common at least two things: they are all instances of something rather than nothing, and they are all conceivable data of experience. And this may be enough to show the falsity of some philosophical doctrines. For example, if we know that we experience this or that, we must experience experiences themselves. Hence, no experience could count against the existence of experiences whose data are experiences. This is an important point. Santayana, at least, appeared to deny that experiencing could itself be experienced. How he could be in a position to say this he did not, so far as I know, explain.

In sum: verifiability as criterion of empirical meaning is modal nonsense, falsifiability as criterion of meaning in general merely begs the question against metaphysical truth; however, verifiability (liberally enough construed) is valid as criterion of meaning in general; and falsifiability is valid as criterion of empirical meaning. Of the four possibilities, two are right and two are wrong; the popular pair has been the two wrong ones! This in my opinion is a fair enough sample of how far from true it is that the possibilities for a reasonable approach to metaphysics have been fully explored in the past twenty-five centuries. Metaphysics has a future as well as a past.

The *a priori* truths that metaphysics seeks to clarify are highly abstract, such as, what it is in general to be or exist ('being *qua* being'), or still better, process *qua* process – what it is to become. Apart from some extreme forms of Platonism, there is perhaps broad agreement among philosophers – ancient and contemporary – that abstract entities are not real simply in themselves, apart from all concrete embodiment — if nothing else, embodiment in some concrete process of thinking. If so, the basic form of reality is concrete reality. But then, slightly paradoxically, the most fundamental abstraction is concreteness as such. Metaphysics is the study of the abstraction 'concreteness'. Mistakes in metaphysics can all be viewed as cases of 'the fallacy of misplaced concreteness', the confusion between concreteness as such and less basic abstractions whose instances are themselves abstract.

Concrete means determinate. Humanity, man in the abstract, is within certain limits indefinite as to height, weight, psychic disposition, etc. But a certain man at a certain moment is definite in these respects. Definiteness is the positive, hence basic idea. Negation is meaningless apart from something to negate. So abstract reality is somehow derivative. There is reason to charge both Greek and ancient Hindu and Buddhist philosophy with a tendency to invert the proper relations of abstract and concrete, to proceed as if the way to grasp reality is to equate it with indefiniteness. Spinoza gave the motto of this tendency: 'all determination is negation'. What he overlooked was that the alternative, indeterminateness, is also a negation and that the proper conclusion is that (as Hegelians and Marxists assert but also Plato) an element of negation is inescapable. The problem is to locate it correctly. The abstract is negative in one way, the concrete, in another. But the abstract, I hold, is the more completely negative.

Thus man in the abstract is not definitely either sober or intoxicated; but this man now is either definitely sober and not intoxicated, or not sober but intoxicated. One must choose between partial and complete privation. The direction towards the abstract or indefinite is the direction towards total privation, not towards fullness or richness of quality. In saying this one seems to defy deep intuitions which have been prominent in all the religions. To justify this defiance, if it can be justified, is no easy task. The reader must give this book, and perhaps others, a chance to make the case if he wishes to be in a position to judge the strength of that case.

If concreteness is definiteness, then, while an instance of concreteness will be something wholly definite, an instance of less basic abstractions will not be so. Take the abstraction being. Then *this* being, say this man, is an instance. Is this man wholly definite? At a given moment, yes, and in his history up to that moment, yes; but until the man is dead his future is, for our knowledge and for the metaphysics expounded in this book, partly indefinite. Indeed, if it makes sense to say that this man could (say from the time he was born) have had a somewhat different career – and I hold that it does make sense – then merely as this man, or as John Jones, he is a partly indefinite entity. Careers are definite, not men. Men are not the same as their careers (in spite of Leibniz). A self-identical individuality is an abstraction, not an instance of full concreteness. The unit of concrete reality is the state or singular event. This point is to be clarified gradually (see Chapter IX).

Are metaphysical judgments analytic? Assuming suitable meaning postulates, they can be made that.[2] If it be objected that scientific hypotheses, too, become analytic with suitable meaning postulates, the reply is that only observation prevents science, so taken, from describing an empty universe, whereas it is the task of metaphysics to find meaning postulates which describe the *necessarily non-empty* universe, or the common aspects of all possible states of affairs. Its meanings must be so general that we are in effect using them even when we think we are not. Nor do they exclude any conceivable observations. Also, a single meaning postulate suffices for metaphysics, the explication of the idea of God. It was Anselm, more than anyone else, who discovered the logical status of metaphysical ideas.

[2] See R. M. Martin, *The Notion of Analytic Truth* (Philadelphia: University of Pennsylvania Press, 1959), pp. 87ff.

Instead of postulating the meaning of 'God', we may instead take 'concrete entity', concreteness simply as such. Since the abstract presupposes a concrete from which it is abstracted, the general abstraction, 'concreteness as such', could not be unexemplified. Hence analytic judgments made possible by meaning postulates explicating 'concreteness' are necessarily applicable, no matter what the state of affairs may be. Whitehead's metaphysics, for instance, is just the attempted explication of what it is to be concrete (hence also of what it is to be abstract, in so far as the abstract-concrete contrast is inherent in concreteness as such). (In the foregoing I am indebted to one of my most lucid and gifted former students, Bowman Clarke.)

To bring out various aspects of the subject, I propose the following definitions of metaphysics.

(*a*) The unrestrictive or completely general theory of concreteness;

(*b*) The theory of experience as such;

(*c*) The clarification of strictly universal conceptions;

(*d*) The search for unconditionally necessary or eternal truths about existence;

(*e*) The theory of objective modality;

(*f*) The theory of possible world-states, or the *a priori* approach to cosmology;

(*g*) The general theory of creativity;

(*h*) The search for the common principle of structure and quality;

(*i*) Ultimate or *a priori* axiology (theory of value in general);

(*j*) The inquiry into the conceivability and existential status of infinity, perfection (unsurpassability), eternal and necessary existence;

(*k*) The rational or secular approach to theology.

Diverse as these formulae may seem at first glance, I believe that they all imply the same thing and differ only in emphasis and focus of explicitness. 'Unrestrictive' says the same as 'negates no positive or extra-linguistic possibility', and this is the same as 'unconditionally necessary' (*d*). 'Completely general' (*a*) or 'strictly universal' (*c*) imply, 'applicable both to what is and to what could be', and this coincides with what has no al-

ternative and is simply necessary (*d*). It also coincides with
what is eternal (*d, j*). The necessary must be known, if at all,
a priori (*f, i*), and must be valid of all possible world states (*f*).
What is inherent in experience as such (*b*) cannot be denied
except verbally, and must be necessary and knowable *a priori*
(*d, f, i, j*). 'Inherent in experience as such' means exactly what
it says; 'inherent in *human* experience as such' would mean
something else, and those who can see no great difference are
probably not fitted for metaphysical inquiry. The most general
factor in creativity (*g*) will be expressed in any possible creation;
as the very principle of alternativeness it will have no objective
or ontological alternative, but only a linguistic one, and thus be
necessary.

'Theory of concreteness' may be compared to the Aristotelian
'being *qua* being'. Collingwood bases his rejection of metaphysics, or his reduction of it to the making and historical study
of 'absolute presuppositions', partly upon the argument that
'being', purely in general, can have no distinctive characteristics, and hence there is nothing significant to be said about it.
But the theory of concreteness is not the bare theory of being, of
what an 'entity' is just as an entity. Rather it is primarily the
theory of what a concrete entity is, as concrete rather than
abstract. From this it appears that pure nominalism is metaphysically wrong, or at least anti-metaphysical; for it destroys
the distinction upon which metaphysics as such rests. Collingwood's argument is cogent enough if 'completely general' must
mean 'applies alike to the concrete and the abstract', or without
regard to any such distinction. What it should mean is, 'applies
in some way to the concrete as such, and in some presumably
different way to the abstract'. A purely general theory of
concreteness will include a theory of abstractness, but there will
be a real distinction between the two. (Actually, even an
Aristotelian is not without resources for defending himself
against Collingwood. Nevertheless, I believe we need a much
sharper sense of the meaning of 'concrete' than the Greeks or
the Schoolmen achieved. The 'fallacy of misplaced concreteness'
is pervasive in the history of philosophy.)

There is another counter-argument to Collingwood: it is idle
to speak of being, or concreteness either, unless we can relate
such a term to experience and knowledge. To generalize the

object of thought or experience is to generalize thought or experience itself. And again, please note that '*human* experience' is restrictive, rather than a harmless redundancy. The unrestrictive notion of being or reality cannot be separated from the unrestrictive notion of experience. Nor – as Plato saw – can this generic notion of experience be separated from the purely general notion of value, the form of the Good. (Note definition *i*.) Thus at least one thing is true of any entity whatever, that it can be thought, experienced, and valued. (Or, as Peirce put it, any concept is a potential contributor to the *summum bonum*, and how it can do so is its meaning.) In spite of Collingwood, this is worth saying and is true, rather than a mere presupposition.

'Being' suggests a contrast to becoming, yet, according to Collingwood's argument, the generic notion of being would ignore this contrast. Whitehead has shown that it need not be so. His formula is: any entity, abstract or concrete, has this in common with every other that it constitutes a 'potential for every becoming'. Past cases of becoming, and any eternal aspects of reality, are alike in this, that subsequent cases of becoming – and to the eternal all things are subsequent – will take them into account, be influenced by, make some use of, them. Here we have, for the first time in intellectual history so far as I know, a definition of 'being' in terms of 'becoming'. Hitherto, apart from Bergson, the effort had almost always been to define becoming in terms of being. This could only result in a fallacy of misplaced concreteness. Becoming is the richer, more concrete conception and includes within itself all needed contrasts with mere being. In each particular instance of becoming, what has previously become does not *then and there* become; yet it does constitute a causal factor in the new, and in all subsequent, instances of becoming. This cumulativeness of becoming is causality, the efficacy of the past in the present. And any eternal entity constitutes a factor in every becoming whatsoever. It is actual happenings, for instance our acts of thinking now, which relate themselves (consciously or not) to the eternal, as well as to past happenings. To try to put such relations into the eternal is either to eternalize everything, and therefore in no distinctive sense anything, or to dissolve the eternal into the flux, whereupon again the distinctive meaning of both terms is lost. It is the unique relatedness or relativity of becoming which makes it the inclusive or concrete form of reality. All else is abstraction.

If the reader asks, what does 'concrete' mean, he has just been given an indication, at least, of the answer. The concrete is the inclusive form of reality, from which the abstract is an abstracted aspect or constituent. Again, the concrete is the definite, for to abstract from details or aspects is, in so far, to conceive the indefinite. The number 'two' is abstract because it is indefinite or non-committal as between two apples, two persons, two ideas, two entities. (Extensional logic seems sometimes to obscure more than it clarifies such problems.)

Plato rightly regarded the Form of Good as more ultimate than 'being' taken in abstraction from value. Any such abstraction would conflict with (*b*), for valuation enters into every possible experience, and hence value enters into every possible object of experience or thought. As theory of concreteness, metaphysics can abstract neither from value nor from experience or thought. It abstracts from *this* concrete thing, this value, this thought or experience, also from this structure or quality, but not from concreteness, value, thought, experience, structure or quality in their pure generality. Materialism either has no theory of concreteness, or it tries to construct one while making some of the abstractions just mentioned. But this is impossible. Materialism is a covert dualism, and dualism is simply the refusal or failure to achieve a general theory of concreteness.

That metaphysics is theory of concreteness is implied by Whitehead's description 'the critic of abstractions'. The abstractions are criticized, not, as in science, because they are inaccurate to the facts, but because other *equally general* or even more general abstractions are left out of account, and thus the general meaning of 'concreteness' is not brought out. In all human knowing there must be abstraction, disregarding of details, but it is one thing to disregard details and another to disregard aspects quite as universal as those taken into account. Physics abstracts from mind, and even more obviously from value, and from quality as contrasted to structure. Yet any entity, even in merely being mentioned, is in some minimal way being related to experience and assigned a value; also structures, that is relations of relations, presuppose entities distinguished in some other way than merely by their relations. How else if not by their qualities? What physics abstracts from is therefore no detail, even in the broadest sense of 'detail', but a matter of principle.

The point about structure as the concern of science is not just that it is general, but that it is precisely or mathematically expressible (even though not without subtle qualifications which are commonly forgotten, but which Plato long ago saw). Also structure is intersubjectively observable in a sense or degree in which quality and value are not. Accordingly, to abstract from quality and value in science is reasonable; but not because we thus transcend details. Mere generality is not the goal of science, which is, rather, definite, or publicly and accurately manageable generality. Value as such, quality as such, like experience as such, are as far from mere details as any scientist can get; but their intersubjective manageability is difficult or problematic.

'Concreteness' is that abstraction in which *only* details are set aside, and even unmanageable generalities are given their due in whatever way possible. (Note especially formulae *b*, *g*, and *i*.) No study, unless metaphysics, is responsible for *this* abstraction. To deny metaphysics on principle is to guarantee that there will be no careful, disciplined theory of concreteness. The difficulties which cause science to set this notion aside form no absolute obstacle to such a theory, for in metaphysics we are seeking, not prediction or specific definiteness, but only generic understanding. We are looking, not for particular facts, but for the principle of factuality itself, the general status and value of facts as such, any facts.

How the secular approach to theology (*k*) leads in principle to all the metaphysical problems and suggests their solution I have tried to show in my *The Logic of Perfection*, Part Two; also in *Anselm's Discovery*.

In (*d*) it is assumed that, as Aristotle held, 'unconditionally necessary' and 'eternal' are equivalent. I hold that the common doctrine (held, e.g., by Quine) of the 'timelessness' of factual or contingent truths is metaphysical, and precisely in the bad sense. This is one of the most glaring illustrations of the charge that 'positivists' do not escape metaphysical commitments. Reichenbach and Felix Kaufmann almost alone, among anti-metaphysicians, have avoided this trap.

Concerning (*e*). Aristotle suggested, in somewhat uncertain outlines, a theory of objective modality, but failed to see or adhere to some of the implications of this theory. Nothing much was done about this until Peirce proposed his view of time as 'a species of objective modality' with explicit reference to Aristotle. That time is the 'schema' (Kant) of our basic conceptions was already almost seen by Aristotle, who, however, failed to realize that it is time or becoming which explains eternity or mere being, not *vice versa*. Eternity is a function of time, not the other way. The current view that modal concepts are merely linguistic or logical, rather than ontological, arises from not seeing that the structure of time or becoming is inherent in concreteness (and in factual truth) as such, and hence is *a priori*, and that this structure is modal and cannot be grasped in merely extensional terms. That 'only propositions can be necessary' is a mistake, if the creative process (one aspect of which is time) is the concrete from which alone any abstractions can be abstracted, and if alternative propositions are contingent only because and in so far as this process as such is free to realize what either alternative asserts. What is objectively necessary absolutely is that the creative process must produce and continue to produce creatures, and thereby itself continue to be, as creative. There can be no alternative to alternativeness itself. Deterministic philosophies fail to understand this; for they rule out alternativeness, at least as an inner-worldly principle, and leave at most a mysterious contingency of the world as a whole, to which conceivable alternatives are perhaps admitted, but no principle by which any such alternative could have been realized. Determinism attempts to abstract from the creative aspect of experience, as materialism attempts to abstract from experience itself. Neither can offer an intelligible theory of concreteness. Here Lequier, Bergson, Peirce, Varisco, Montague, Whitehead, Wenzl, and many others are at one. But this neo-classical tradition is largely unknown to most philosophers today.

The reader will note that, as I use terms, 'empirical metaphysics' is an absurdity. 'Empirical cosmology', perhaps – but then scientists are probably the best people to attempt this. And without an *a priori* element it is doubtful if much can be accomplished. Einstein has said that we might empirically show the world to be finite but could not thus show it to be infinite. This, I suspect, is correct. Infinity, whether of the actual past or of actual space, is not an empirical concept. It must then be a metaphysical one. (I also suspect that the world is necessarily finite in space, though not in time.)

Similarly with the qualitative infinity, or perfection (unsurpassability in some value sense) which defines deity. In spite of Leibniz, no one knows what a 'best possible world' would look like, nor if he did could he know that our world had this supposed character. Nor can inference from a perhaps partly botched product yield a flawless cause of that product. By no factual argument, therefore, can we reach divine perfection in any religiously significant sense. But on my view, nothing metaphysical, nothing in any strict sense necessary, infinite, eternal, universal, ultimate, absolute, unsurpassable, could be known empirically.

It might be thought that empirical evidence could at least *disprove* the existence of perfection. On the contrary, Anselm showed that any being whose existence would be contingent, that is, with a possible alternative which facts might have shown to obtain, must for that very reason lack perfection in any strict sense, 'even if it exists'. Thus to try to conceive a factual disproof of theism is already to change the subject. Only an idol, a fetish, could be subject to factual disproof. The divine existence is a non-empirical topic, and must be handled as such (see Chapters XII, XIV). Or else mishandled, as so often occurs, both in theistic and non-theistic circles.

The illusion of an empirical test for the existence of perfection arises partly because we are used to looking to observed facts to tell us what exists, and partly because of subtle confusions embodied in the conventional ideas of omnipotence and omniscience, that is, of unsurpassable power and unsurpassable wisdom. A perfectly created and perfectly managed universe – in whatever sense this is conceivable – cannot mean a predestined or absolutely controlled universe. Individuals (not alone human individuals) must in some degree be self-managed, agents acting to some extent on their own, or they are not individuals, concrete units of reality. This is inherent in the concept of concreteness. A definition of deity which violates this concept is illicit, regardless of facts. The very meaning of 'fact' involves creativity, as ground of the contingency of fact as such. I agree with Kant: empirical procedures to justify or falsify theism are one and all fraudulent – with all due respect to Mill, James, Brightman, Hick, and many others who have tried and are trying so valiantly to show the contrary.

But surely, you may be saying, concepts derive somehow from experience. Yes, but there are two classes of concepts, and two modes of derivation from experience. One set, the ordinary concepts, derive from special kinds of experience, and get their essential meaning from this specialization. The other set, the metaphysical concepts, derive from *any* experience in which reflection occurs, and they will be illustrated in any experience, even unreflective (if only *for* a reflective experience which is aware of the unreflective one). Such universal conceptions used to be called 'innate ideas', by which was meant something rather like what I have just described, though John Locke was perhaps not entirely to blame for misunderstanding this.

'No experience, no ideas.' Who has ever denied that? (At most, classical theists perhaps denied it of God, who apparently, in their view, did not experience, but just knew.) The metaphysical ideas, however, are unique in applying to *any* experience, human, sub-human, super-human; hence if someone does not have them, it is not because he lacks some particular sensory or perceptual experience to reflect upon, but because he does not reflect sufficiently, or in a sufficiently general way, upon those experiences which he has. As Leibniz cleverly put it, everything in the intellect comes from the senses – except the intellect itself! The intellect's self-understanding, that is the innate, *a priori*, or metaphysical. If Locke is supposed to have refuted innate ideas in this sense, it is because many other accidental and irrelevant factors have been allowed to confuse the record.

Locke was particularly, and rightly, concerned about the supposed certainty of the innate ideas. But it was accidental and irrelevant if the rationalists identified '*a priori*' with 'certain'. That any experience, *to sufficient reflection*, illustrates the metaphysical conceptions is no guarantee that a given individual at a given time has so reflected as to be 'clear and distinct' or certain about his formulation of the conceptions. Formulation, verbalization, is an art, and a fallible one whose success is a matter of more or less. Animals and infants have no such art. Who knows but that we are all partly infantile in this matter? Whitehead's reference, in this connection, to our 'ape-like consciousness' is a literary exaggeration, no doubt, but otherwise it is seriously intended and appropriate. Mistakes are possible in mathematics and formal logic; is not metaphysics just that part of *a priori* knowledge in which clarity and certainty are least readily attained? Intellectual history suggests that this is so. And there is no reason, apparent to me, why lack of clarity or confusion must always be due to insufficient awareness of relevant facts. It may be due to insufficient, or biassed, reflection. Accordingly, '*a priori*', or 'innate', is one thing, and 'certainly known' is quite another. If what a man most wants is certainty he might better turn his attention to arithmetic, elementary logic, or even some parts of natural science, than to metaphysics.

It is arguable that strictly speaking there is but *one* metaphysical, innate or strictly universal and necessary idea or principle, *concreteness* (containing internally its own contrast to abstractness), so that to speak of innate ideas in the plural is really to slur over the distinction between our formulations of metaphysical truth and the truth itself, or the necessary nonrestrictive aspect of reality. The former, the ideas in the plural, are our contingent ways of trying to become conscious of the non-contingent ground of all contingency.

Naturally, to show the equivalence of the various characterizations of metaphysics in detail would be to work out an entire system. Here I wish rather to indicate some relationships of metaphysics to other studies. In *logic* one speaks of entities on the first logical level, values of the variables for 'individuals', but one does not propose a general theory of what it is which assigns an entity to this level. One may say that one has in mind individual things existing in the spatio-temporal world order, or sense data, or sometimes, even individual numbers. But obviously numbers are abstract, compared to persons or physical things; moreover, events (in the most concrete sense, total unit-becomings) may also be taken as individuals, and then persons or physical things are more or less abstract by comparison, unless they are (wrongly, I hold) taken to be mere actual sequences of events. Metaphysics does what the logician would do if he really gave serious thought to the *a priori* or strictly universal traits of his first-level entities. In addition the logician assumes but does not investigate a concept of knowing or experiencing; this, in its purely generic sense, metaphysics does investigate.

That metaphysics deals with quality as well as structure (*h*) distinguishes it from *mathematics*, which deals with structure only.[3] Also mathematics, like logic, does not discuss the experience of structure, but only the structure experienced; thus it says nothing, except in an informal, semi-official way, about the value aspect which no mathematical experience, let alone non-mathematical experience, can lack. Nor is the mathematician interested in sub-human experience, whose possibility nevertheless comes somehow under the general concept of experience. He may perhaps discuss super-human (divine) experience, but casually or at most semi-officially. Yet the pure concept of experience must either entail the logical impossibility or entail the logical possibility of divine (in some sense unsurpassable, maximal) experience, and until we know what the entailment is we do not have a clear concept of experience as such.

That metaphysics seeks for necessary principles distinguishes it from physics and scientific cosmology. For, if these attempt to claim necessity for their principles, they are simply doing metaphysics. And no mere physical experiment or observation can justify the claim. Only an intellectual experiment can establish necessity. Whether and how it can do so is exactly the metaphysical question. It is not to be settled casually. But in recent decades that is how it has generally been disposed of.

To the eleven characterizations of metaphysics already given, I should like to add one more:

(*l*) The attempt to make non-exclusive or purely positive statements (see Chapter VIII).

Consider the sentence, 'there are men'. It seems purely positive. But in fact it has negative implications which are not merely verbal. Consider the forests which would still be standing

---

[3] P. Bernays writes: 'What contrasts phenomenologically with the qualitative is . . . the structural,' and, 'mathematics . . . can be regarded as the theoretical phenomenology of structures.' From 'Comments on Ludwig Wittgenstein's Remarks on the Foundations of Mathematics', *Ratio* 2 (1959–60). Reprinted in P. Benacerraf and H. Putnam (eds.), *Philosophy of Mathematics* (Prentice-Hall, Englewood Cliffs, N.J.: 1964).

had men not cut, burned, or bulldozed them down; the animal species which would still persist had men not exterminated them. True, men might have existed in less destructive ways, but this is a matter of degree; some destructiveness was inherent in the very existence of our species. Ordinary existence is perforce partly competitive, and only partly co-operative or symbiotic. It is this competitive 'existence' which cannot be necessary, for it cuts off extra-linguistic possibilities, and this is the very definition of contingency. No *a priori* science could tell us which extra-linguistic possibilities are cut off, and hence none could tell us what, in the ordinary sense, 'exists'.

But take such a statement as, 'There is something concrete'. What extra-linguistic possibility does it cut off? Not that there is something abstract. Indeed, unless extreme 'Platonism' or extreme anti-nominalism is correct, there can be something abstract only as an aspect of something concrete. So the sole possibility which could be said to be annulled by the statement is, 'There is nothing, whether concrete or abstract'. And what is this but mere verbiage? Certainly such a 'state' of reality must, at best, be absolutely unknowable. I hold that what the statement 'there is something concrete' excludes is purely linguistic, not an objective possibility at all. This is one mark of a metaphysical statement, that its denial is verbal only, signifying nothing beyond language.

Consider unqualified determinism, the doctrine that, in the actual world at least, there is an *absolute* order according to which the successor or outcome of any particular state of things is uniquely specified and alone causally possible, given that state. Is this statement partly exclusive, or is it wholly positive? It seems at first glance to be the pure affirmation of causal order, and so entirely positive. But this is deceptive. For in the absolutizing of the aspect of order, the aspect of creativity is equally absolutely *denied*. And creativity is positive. It does not mean merely that what happens is *not* fully specified by the causal conditions and laws; it means that there is *more* definiteness in reality after a causal situation has produced its effect than before. This increase or *growth in richness of determinations* is not an absence of something, it is a positive presence. True, there was first, if you like, an absence; but subsequently and forever after there will be the succession, absence-to-presence, and thus the richer conception has the last word. Growth is inherent in the very meaning of becoming, and a being is only a potential for becoming.

Or consider the atheistic denial that there is any unsurpassable or divine being, or the seemingly positive assertion that any being could be surpassed by another. The statement seems either negative or positive according to how it is stated. But the negativity is essential, while the positive character is no more than verbal. For only a surpassable being can in its mere existence compete with, or exclude, anything in other beings; the unsurpassable is unsurpassably able to harmonize its own existence with that of others, and consequently denying its existence opens up no positive possibility whatsoever, any more than 'there is nothing concrete' does so.

Leibniz was even more right than he knew in saying that philosophers err in what they deny, not in what they assert. But he himself often denied when he thought he asserted. His demand for a 'sufficient reason' for particular or concrete things reduced creativity, even in God, to zero (i.e., to God's enacting the conclusion of the syllogism, 'I do what is best, this is best, therefore I do this'). His assertion that an individual always possesses all its adventures reduced becoming to a sheer illusion. His acceptance of classical theism, or the view that all possible value is actualized in God, entailed the implicit renunciation of his own correct doctrine of genuine competition among possibles, for it rendered this doctrine irrelevant or unintelligible from the divine standpoint, that is, the standpoint of truth. But Leibniz's assertion that every individual (as distinct from aggregates of individuals) must have something like experience or perception was truly in accord with his doctrine of positivity. 'Every individual (not identical with an aggregate of individuals) has experience' denies nothing but what is itself a mere denial, viz., 'some individuals are absolutely insentient and mindless'.

Of course aggregates of individuals need not themselves be sentient individuals, and the possibility of forming such insentient aggregates is an *a priori* aspect of the idea of sentient individuality. Leibniz saw, as no man had before him, and not many have after him, that there is no other way, in any possible world, of giving positive meaning to the negative of 'sentient'.

An entity cannot show itself to be singular rather than a mere aggregate save by *acting* as a singular. But this is also the only way it can show that it is sentient, though perhaps not on the level of conscious thought. If we ask an atom, do you feel?, having no language, it can only answer just as it does, in effect, answer – by responding to stimuli (changes in its environment), by withdrawing in some situations, advancing in others, in some cases reorganizing itself internally, dropping constituents or assimilating them, acting in an 'excited' or in a 'satisfied' fashion. Any evidence there logically could be for very low-level sentience there actually seems to be. And in what possible world could it be otherwise? How in any world could one know *either* that a seemingly inert mass like a rock was inert also in its imperceptible parts or individual constituents, *or* that it had no such constituents? I hold that in any world, one *either* would not know what the individuals were *or* would know them as genuinely active – and so, by the behavioural criterion sentient – agents whose activities collectively produced the sensible effect of an inert mass. Agency and singular concrete reality are one; until one encounters the former, one does not know the latter. 'Insentient', in behavioural terms, taken absolutely, has the same force as 'individuals unidentified'.

What we need to do is to follow Leibniz's prescription not only where he followed it, but also where he did not. Metaphysical truth is *purely positive* truth; all else is partly negative, or, if absurd and a mere confusion, wholly so (see Chapter VIII).

When another great rationalist, Spinoza, said that *all* things follow from the essence of God, which also entails its own existence, he was really saying that 'metaphysical' has no distinctive meaning. Leibniz is by implication in the same difficulty. But these men fell into this trap not because they were rationalists, if that means believers in the possibility of *a priori* or non-exclusive and purely positive knowledge. No logical bridge leads from 'there is *a priori* or necessary truth about reality' to 'all truth about reality is *a priori* or necessary'. Quite the contrary, to regard all truth or knowledge as metaphysical is to fail to take the idea of the metaphysical seriously; for it deprives this idea of any distinctive meaning. Exaggeration is often in effect denial.

If Hegel was wiser than the previous rationalists in the matter presently being discussed, he hid his wisdom under elaborate dazzling systematic ambiguity such as only high genius could have conceived, but which can hardly serve the needs of our day or the future.

The way to discredit non-exclusive or necessary truth is the very way its sponsors adopted when they unduly extended its scope, so that contradictorily it became exclusive or contingent after all. Nothing is more necessary to the future of 'rationalism' in the good sense than the avoidance of this extravagance, which deflates rationalism's claims by over-inflating them until they burst. Metaphysical or non-restrictive truth is very little, rather than very much; but that little is precious nonetheless, provided it be seen in its purity and not adulterated by restrictive elements.

One might say that the seventeenth-century men were not so much rationalists or metaphysicians as intellectual imperialists. Like other ambitious men they wanted to take over any not too strongly contested territory. And as the excuse for political or military imperialists has been that if one's own country had not been the aggressor against some defenceless area another country would have been, so the excuse for the older rationalists was that empirical science had not yet learned to claim its own. Today the danger is in the opposite direction. Now it is metaphysical territory which is too weakly held, and it is empirical scientists or their admirers who want to take over even that extremely colourless or most abstract knowledge, the knowledge of non-restrictive truth. This is merely the old mistake, but now made by men proceeding in the opposite direction. Empire is always temporary and insecure. Just as it did not really exalt metaphysics to offer to let it swallow up science, so it does not exalt the empirical method to offer to let it adjudicate for possible worlds, necessities, or the Unsurpassable. Confusion weakens everything, strengthens nothing.

Another classical example of blurring the distinction between the genuinely *a priori* and the empirical is Kant's attempt to make Euclidean geometry (in a qualified fashion) *a priori*, on the ground that human cognitive powers require it. But they require at most the approximate validity of this geometry, and in this approximate form the requirement is shown by respectable empirical evidence to be met by the contingent structure of the universe. The idea that an absolutely precise requirement (with conceivable alternatives) could be justified by so vague a ground as man's self-awareness of the forms of his own intuition is logically incongruous. Absolute precision requires a more definite ground than that.

I recall these classical cases to remind the reader that the collapse of certain false claims to *a priori* necessity is no proof that all such claims must be false. Exaggerated reactions to exaggerated pretensions will not get rid of exaggeration itself.

A word about how 'God' is intended in definition (*k*). I am deeply convinced that classical metaphysics mistranslated the essential religious issue by misdefining 'God'. It confused the divine fullness with an abstraction called 'the absolute' or the 'unmoved mover', or 'most real being'. None of these, I am persuaded, is genuinely worshipful, though they can be subjects of intellectual amazement, wonder, or awe. I agree with one main conviction of current philosophizing, that people have been so eager to answer questions that they have failed to give proper heed to the way words are being used, and perhaps misused, in formulating these questions. 'Is there a greatest or most real being?' First of all does the notion of a 'greatest being', taken without qualification, make sense, any more than that of 'largest possible number'? I myself think the answer should be, No, neither 'greatness' nor 'reality' is without qualification logically capable of a maximum. Is there a strictly immutable yet living being? I think the answer is, No, life in any sense, no matter how exalted, implies some form of real change or becoming – indeed some form of real growth. I think the history of natural theology from Aristotle, Philo, and Augustine to Hume and Kant has brought out rather clearly that *if* God must be defined in terms of these traditional paradoxes, then theism has no rational content. But I am equally persuaded that this way of defining God is mistaken anyway, on both purely religious and philosophical grounds. This mistake is one of the penalties we have had to pay for putting too much trust in the first form of rational metaphysical thought, the Greek, which great as its achievements were was at best a one-sided first approximation, and at worst a mélange of calamitous errors.

There are several reasons why a metaphysician cannot sensibly proceed very far without considering how he is to handle the theistic question. First, the logic of the idea of God itself (see Chapters XI–XIII) shows that the whole content of metaphysics must be contained in the theory of deity. Comte was not mistaken in this: metaphysics is no more and no less than natural theology (supposing the latter is possible at all). For (*a*) the existence of God cannot be construed as contingent, an accidental exemplification of metaphysical principles, but must be admitted, if at all, as necessary, as inherent in these principles having any truth at all: moreover (*b*), the metaphysical or necessary features of the reality with which God deals (whether by creating it, knowing it, or what not) can only be the same as the intrinsic or implied correlates of whatever is necessary in God's being. That is, what God *must* create or *must* know is necessary, and that alone; anything he merely *can* create or know is contingent, and so a subject for science or faith, not for rational metaphysics. The adequate metaphysical theory of deity is either nonsense or it is simply metaphysical theory – period. I reject the old distinction between general and special metaphysics, unless this last means empirical cosmology – note definition (*f*). The only concession to make here is that the theistic meaning of metaphysical concepts may be left implicit, unformulated. But to that extent the concepts will be left vague or ambiguous, and the system will be too indeterminate to give much purchase to rational criticism.

Second, the history of metaphysics is so entangled in various ways of trying to adjudicate religious questions that nothing much is left if one tries to abstract a religiously neutral residue from this history. This is what one should expect from the logic of the case and it is what we find.

Third, I see in the application of metaphysical categories to religion their chief use and one test of their adequacy. If a metaphysician can make sense out of this topic so much the better, but if not why do we need his system? Science and common sense take care of factual (contingent) questions; art, or personal or group faith, can handle the rest, if there is any residuum. But only the metaphysician can clarify what it means intellectually to ask about God. I hold that Greek metaphysics, and I include even Kant as a kind of belated Greek, has failed this test. It has muddled almost as much as it has clarified the topic it chiefly sought to illuminate. Not that we owe it no thanks for this failure. If we see better on the same topic it is because we have these majestic examples of how *not* to define God. And such learning by mistakes seems the destiny of all non-divine consciousness. Moreover, the Greek way of defining God is not so much wrong as one-sided. Terms like absolute, infinite, independent, uncaused, do apply to God – but only on condition that the correlative terms, relative, finite, dependent, caused, also apply. Contradiction of course results if – but only if – no qualification such as 'in some respect' is attached to the attributions. The classical error was one of over-trust in extremely simple ways of characterizing God. It was a kind of learned simple-mindedness.

If the religious issue is as central in metaphysics as it seems to be, to attempt first to settle everything else and only then to ask about 'God' is to be in danger of begging the chief metaphysical questions. Hume and Kant did just that, in my opinion. Un-wittingly assuming anti-theistic postulates, they not surprisingly inferred the impossibility of a rational theism. But the reasoning can be reversed: since theism at the least deserves a hearing on its merits, the experiment should be made of provisionally rejecting every postulate which shows itself hostile to theism. And this includes the axiom, 'the distinguishable is separable' or independent, for though God (and this *is* inherent in the religious idea) exists no matter what other individuals may or may not exist, and thus is indeed separable from them, God is also thought of as the power upon whom all else depends, and thus the 'creatures', though distinguishable from him, are certainly not separable from, independent of, his existence. Several other assumptions of Hume, and some of Kant or Bradley, must likewise be 'put in brackets' while we consider what metaphysical system if any would harmonize with religious requirements. No other procedure is rational inquiry in this sphere, but rather is dogmatic rejection posing as judicial examination.

Such is my apology for intruding the theistic aspect into the definition of metaphysics. 'Neo-classical metaphysics', when its ideas are adequately explicated, is neo-classical natural theology, and *vice versa*. In three several books I have tried to show, at least in outline, how from the mere idea of God a whole metaphysical system follows; one may also proceed in the opposite direction, and show how from general secular considerations one may arrive at the idea of God and a judgment as to its validity. But the two ways of proceeding differ only relatively and as a matter of emphasis. In thinking metaphysically at all one is already more or less close to an explicit thinking about God, and in thinking at all clearly about God one is already somewhat conscious of metaphysical principles. *A priori* knowledge, valid 'for all possible worlds', must coincide in content with the most abstract aspects of omniscience. It is what is common to all that God *could* create or know, and of course knows that he could create or know. Scholz has pointed out how the symbolic logician is in a certain (very abstract) sense seeing things as God sees them. *A fortiori* the metaphysician is doing this – *if* he succeeds.

A metaphysician can be evaluated:

1. for his originality (if it has been said before we may not need his saying it);

2. his clarity (everyone knows vaguely those first principles which 'only exquisite care' – C. I. Lewis – can make explicit);

3. his coherence and integration (ultimate ideas are not mutually irrelevant, as whales to forest trees);

4. his comprehensiveness and balance (almost anyone may have partial, one-sided glimpses of metaphysical truth);

5. his ability to grasp diverse possible or historical perspectives on problems (why should we trust his choice of a view if he does not know what views have been or can be held?);

6. his ability to defend his view against others without making the task easy by presenting competing doctrines in less than their strongest form and without committing fallacies;

7. his readability (metaphysics is difficult enough without the additional obstacle of bad or dull writing).

In my opinion Peirce and Whitehead had all these traits in rather high degree, Peirce being weakest perhaps in (3) and Whitehead in (6) – not that he often argued fallaciously or misrepresented other views, but that he is somewhat sparing in argument. N. Hartmann (as metaphysician) was far below the two just mentioned, especially in (1), (5), and (6). Alexander rates well under criteria (1–3 and 7). In Paul Weiss I see a very high degree of (1), (4), and (7), but some lack in (2), (3), and (6). (His ultimates are mutually relevant but not clearly integrated and effectively defended against rival doctrines in their strength.) In G. Bergmann I see chiefly (2) and (3); in Donald Williams (2) and (7), with some strength in (6). Blanshard excels in (2) and (7) and is weakest in (1) and (4). In A. Bahm I find chiefly (4). Stephen Pepper is mildly impressive in all respects, John Findlay still more so, with some weakness in (2) and (6). (If he took Hegel, Husserl, and Plotinus with still more reservations than he does, he would be an even better metaphysician than he is.)

At any rate, it is by some such criteria that I should like this book to be judged.

III

PRESENT PROSPECTS FOR METAPHYSICS

THAT classical metaphysics, say from Aristotle and Plotinus to Hegel, Schopenhauer, Bradley, and Royce, was something less than a success is rather widely conceded. However, it might be thought that its failure is no worse than the fate which overtakes scientific views. Classical physics, too, has been set aside. Yet this is chiefly with respect to the very small and the very large in nature. In application to things of middling magnitudes Newton's principles are still largely valid, at least as first approximations. But what can one do today with Aristotelianism, Cartesianism, Spinozism, Leibnizianism, or Hegelianism? Not a great deal, many of us would say. What then was wrong? Why have these systems lost relevance to so great an extent? Here opinions differ considerably.

There are two main possibilities. Either classical metaphysics failed because it was metaphysics or there is a more special reason. On the first view, a metaphysician is one who attempts the impossible or absurd: perhaps he wants answers to unanswerable questions, or non-factual answers to factual questions (or *vice versa*); or he wants to describe the ineffable and say the unsayable or to give a linguistic proposal the value of a statement about existence. Or again perhaps he is engaged in explaining away the paradoxes engendered by some outrageous overstatement, such as 'nothing changes', or 'all is but mere appearance to my consciousness', or 'only atoms exist', or 'nature is but our (or God's) ideas', or 'other minds (or the past or future) cannot be known'.

Let us grant that metaphysicians have at times discussed questions too ill-defined to have definite answers, or dealt with empirical questions in unempirical ways; also that they have at times strained language to the breaking point and beyond, or have confused linguistic proposals with existential affirmations or negations; and finally, that some of them have presented foolishly one-sided or extreme doctrines – still, do these vagaries constitute all that metaphysics can be, if it is not to dissolve into the sciences, or into the study of language?

I believe that metaphysics has a proper task, which is not that of the special sciences, a task in which, in the near future, a certain measure of success can be attained. Indeed, I think that Peirce's prophecy, 'Early in the twentieth century metaphysics will become a science', has already had some degree of fulfilment – though one must here also take into account Whitehead's prediction in conversation, 'metaphysics will never be a popular science'. In my opinion, however, classical metaphysics suffered from certain handicaps which are not inherent in its task and which we are now for the first time in a favourable position to overcome.

Philosophy early acquired a bias from which it has been painfully struggling to free itself, a bias favouring one pole of certain ultimate contraries at the expense of the other pole, thus *being* at the expense of becoming, *identity* at the expense of diversity, the *absolute* or non-relative at the expense of the relative, the inextended or non-physical at the expense of the physical, *origins* or *causes* at the expense of outcomes or effects. This bias is found both in Ancient Greece and in the Orient. It appears to have several roots rather than one. In Greece, at least, it is due partly to the discovery of pure mathematics, and the one-sided enthusiasm for very abstract ideas which this discovery not unnaturally produced. In both Greece and India it arises from a certain despair of the values of concrete living which early civilization produced, especially in the Indian climate. Everywhere and always man's future is uncertain, and in view of death and the fragility of human institutions, no clear limit can easily be set to the scope of this uncertainty and its importance for our values. The simplest remedy is to attack the idea of change itself; if the 'true reality' is immune to change, we have but to identify ourselves in thought with this reality, and all danger and fear are felt to be, in principle, transcended. A similar argument favours identity over diversity. As the Upanishad has it, where there is no Other, there is nothing to fear.

The element of escapism just sketched joins the exaltation of mathematics. The relations of numbers are serenely indifferent to the chances of human life: they are fixed, independent, identical, immaterial. Thus in Augustine's discussion of God as the eternal Truth, mathematical ideas play a strikingly prominent role. The attitude is very Greek; but what is its relation to the Gospels, the God of which seems to respond rather to persons as a person than to abstract ideas as a pure knower or *nous*? The bland identification of God with the absolute or the infinite today appears to many of us as a species of idolatry.

But the roots of the classical bias are indeed complex. One aspect of this complexity is the following. The universality of death puts man, as it seems, before a dilemma. Either he lives on individually beyond death, or he becomes identical with a worthless corpse. The second view seems to make a mockery of all our intuitions of importance; the first is one of the most fertile sources of bad metaphysics. It has, for instance, been shown that Berkeley's one-sided idealism has as its principal motivation the hope of justifying the belief in personal immortality. Descartes's interest in the idea of the 'thinking substance' is explicitly connected by him with the same motif, which is found also in Kant's discussion of the soul. One could easily multiply these examples many times over. I hold that in all these cases the influence of the interest in individual immortality has been destructive of clear analysis. The notion of an 'immortal soul' or 'spiritual substance' has clarified no theoretical problem, as both Locke and Kant admitted. What they did not fully see is the extent to which it has muddled and confused many problems. If nevertheless the belief is required for ethical or religious reasons, then so much the worse for our prospect of a clear-headed metaphysics. But is it required? I do not believe that the immortality which is implied by our essential values has anything to do with that notion of soul-substance which runs through Western philosophy from Plato to modern Scholasticism.

Substance is a 'being' to which adventures happen, or experiences occur; to make it the primary conception is to assume the priority of being. The alternative, one version of which was taken long ago by the Buddhists but by almost no one else, is to view events or states (e.g., 'I now') as the concrete realities, and construe enduring things, substances, persons, as ways in which events are qualified, and related to other events. Unfortunately, the Buddhists failed to do full justice to the relatedness of events. They were not entirely free from the anti-relativistic bias. A metaphysics of becoming and relativity is the modern philosophical task. It was certainly not accomplished in former ages.

The reader may be wondering how metaphysics may be defined, if it concerns itself with becoming and relativity. Is not this the concern of the empirical sciences? I reply: they concern themselves with things or events which become and are relative, but not with becoming and relativity as such. Of all the kinds of entities which might become, or stand in relation, what kinds do become and in what particular sorts of relations do they stand? These are the scientific questions. But what is it to become or to be relative? This is a very different query. Metaphysics seeks, I suggest, the essential nature of becoming which does not itself become and cannot pass away; or, it seeks the universal principle of relativity whose validity is absolute. 'Nothing is absolute but relativity' – this saying, which I heard as a student, and which meant nothing much to me at the time, I have come to see as, properly construed, the secret of secrets, just as the man who uttered it claimed that it was (though I shall never know just what this meant to him).

It will perhaps be granted that it is the abstract, as seen in mathematics, which is exempt from relativity and becoming. Upon what does arithmetic depend? Upon nothing in the particular features of the actual world. Any abstraction is similarly independent of the concrete in proportion to its degree of abstractness. Very well, 'relativity' is as abstract a term as one is likely to find, and just as much so as 'absoluteness!' 'Becoming' is also exceedingly abstract. And its independence of circumstances is similarly great. No matter what in particular may happen, happening itself is and presumably will be a reality. That human beings can exist is relative to certain conditions of temperature, etc., but that something relative can exist, to what is that in turn relative? To the Absolute, some will say. Let us grant that relativity as such is correlative to absoluteness as such, the two concepts expressing the same contrast from opposite ends. We shall see later (Chapters VI, XI) how this contrast is illustrated even in the ordinary phenomena. But we shall still maintain that relativity as such is that which *could not not be*, its existence having no special conditions. Relativity is the absolute principle! Some may feel this proposition to be contradictory. If so, what do they make of Russell's similar statement: concreteness as such is a highly abstract term? And what else is it? Universals need not be, indeed usually are not, instances of themselves. Concreteness is not concrete, relativity is not relative. Indeed, it is as absolute as absoluteness. In a way it is *more* absolute. If there is such a thing as 'the absolute', it is some ultimate or supreme kind of relativity. And similarly, according to what I call 'neo-classical metaphysics', if there is an eternal Being, it is some ultimate form of becoming.

Was this the doctrine of classical metaphysicians? If so, they certainly chose remarkably indirect and confused ways of expressing themselves!

Instead of the contraries previously considered, let us take the pair, necessary-contingent. Classical metaphysics depreciated the contingent. Spinoza is an extreme case. But as late as Hegel, 'necessary' is a word of laudation, and 'contingent', of denigration. Metaphysics seeks to know what it is that is necessary, or 'could not be otherwise than it is'. But perhaps what is necessary is precisely and solely that a certain ultimate form of contingency should have instances. Perhaps even the 'necessary being' is not one 'without accidents', but one which is bound to have some appropriate accidents or other. It is no accident that there should be accidents; rather, there are bound to be accidents, just as it is predictable that unpredictable events will never cease to occur. In the same way, the divine being whose existence is not contingent may escape contingency only because, and only in the sense that, not only are accidents bound to occur, but divine accidents are bound to be among them. It is a defensible view that God is the one being to whom accidents are always bound to happen. Whereas, to the rest of us, nothing accidental occurred before we were born, nor will occur after we die, nor had we never been born would any accident ever have occurred to us, 'divine accidents', it may be held, are bound always to be. They form a class which could not ever have been or ever be empty.

I hope the reader begins to see that this new metaphysics does have a logic. Many difficulties of the older metaphysical systems are transformed by this logic into at least more manageable proportions. For instance, in those systems there was often the contradiction of a God held to be without accidental properties, although having knowledge of contingent truth. Thus he knows that a certain world exists which might not have existed; but surely had it not existed, he would not have known it to exist; hence he has knowledge which he might not have had. And still, none of his properties or qualities was admitted to be contingent! This is a typical antinomy of classical metaphysics. In the new metaphysics, where divine accidents are definitely admitted, there is no such antinomy. Yet, it can be held, there is also no need to admit divine ignorance or divine error. God, neo-classically conceived, knows whatever there is to know, just as it is.

Another customary antinomy was that the supreme reality, taken to be absolute, must be either all-inclusive or not all-inclusive. The supposition of inclusiveness involves a choice between the contradiction that constituents which could have been otherwise contribute to a totality which could *not* have been otherwise and the contrasting absurdity that neither the totality nor the constituents could have been otherwise, and thus that everything is absolute – wherewith both relativity and absoluteness lose all distinctive meaning. The supposition that the supreme reality is not all-inclusive implies that it is but a constituent of the totality, and so not the supreme reality after all. In the new metaphysics, the supreme reality is held to be supremely relative. It therefore can be all-inclusive, not only of all relative things, but also of 'the absolute', which is indeed but an abstract aspect of relative reality, its relativity as such or in principle (see Chapter VI, XI).

Another advantage enjoyed by metaphysics in our time is that the concept of mere matter, which haunted not only Greek and medieval but also Indian thought, has been shown, far more clearly than ever before, by the development from Leibniz to Bergson, Peirce, and Whitehead, to be superfluous. It was always a term for intellectual embarrassment, as anyone who has read the history of the concept must, I should think, know.

At this point current science is an asset which Aristotle and Descartes lacked. The division of nature into inanimate, vegetable, and animal is plausible enough in a primitive state of knowledge; for to the unaided senses that is how things appear to us. But the microscope and the even more powerful magnifying power of mathematical manipulation have shown us that these divisions are superficial. All life is either unicellular or multicellular, and a cell is a living individual which in a certain measure determines its own activities in response to stimuli from without. The division between vegetable and animal has no deep significance at this unicellular level. The great contrast between plants and animals, which makes the latter alone seem to have such psychical traits as sensation, feeling, or memory, is due to the fact that the multicellular plants (which alone are readily perceptible to our senses) are but colonies of cells, compared to the integration which nervous tissue gives to the multicellular animals. The *visible* plant individuals therefore seem not to have animal 'souls' (a term which here need only mean individual experiences or feelings), but this does not constitute any evidence, however weak, to show that the invisible plant individuals of which they are composed have none. A crowd of visible animals is generally not a sentient individual either. But single-celled animals give behavioural signs of individual sentience. So, I suggest, do single-celled plants.

Aristotle's expression 'vegetable soul' was his compromise term to cover at once his sound intuition that growth implies an internal principle of self-determination analogous to animal self-control, and his observation that nevertheless visible plants do not respond as individuals to external stimuli. He was wrong, first, in referring the principle of growth to the entire plant. It is cells which multiply and constantly form and reform themselves, and the growth of the visible plant is but our collective way of seeing these individually invisible actions. Aristotle was wrong, second, in referring his *denial* of individual sensitive response both to the entire visible plant and (tacitly and by omission) to its constituents as well. The absence of any (to us) perceptible behavioural signs of sensation tells nothing as to the absence of imperceptible behaviour appropriate to sensation.

As for inanimate nature, the apparent inertness of a stone, or of water, tells nothing as to the inactivity of its minute constituents. For the general situation is this: all concrete things (and the new metaphysics holds that something of the sort would be true in any really conceivable world) must react – if not as wholes then in their constituents – to their environments, they respond to what in effect are stimuli, and their responses become in turn stimuli to others. In our actual world, however, there is a vast difference between animals, plants, and the minerals in the extent to which individual agents of response are perceptible to the unaided senses of such higher animals as ourselves. Only when multicellular *animals* are observed is individuality of behaviour clearly discerned; in plants, individuality of action is hidden from us, though there is a semblance or illusion of active individuality which caused Aristotle to speak of 'soul'; while below the plants, dynamic individuality is not directly apparent to the senses at all. Either one supposes that the proposition, 'reality consists of active individuals', is true only of animal reality, or at most animal and vegetable reality, or else one must admit that direct perception fails to reveal the constituents of which natural things are composed. The Greek atomists and, much more clearly, Leibniz drew the correct conclusions: perception gives a largely blurred or indistinct outline of the acting physical things. The lack of individual self-activity which these outlines suggest is to be discounted; indirect means of knowledge are alone adequate at this point. Materialism or dualism (they come to much the same) rest on the failure to think through the relation of the category of individuality to the limitations of human perception.

The moral of the foregoing for metaphysical method is this: we must beware of allowing our theory of the categories (i.e., our metaphysics) to be determined by supposed 'facts' whose factuality itself depends upon presupposed decisions as to the categories. Aristotle did not *know* that nature consists, or could possibly consist, of the animata and the inanimata, in the absolute sense which alone is relevant to the controversy concerning mind as such and matter. He knew, to be sure, that *in our perceptions* individual agency is distinctly apparent only when we observe animals, or (in much vaguer, more problematic form) when we observe plants. However, before trying to turn this fact about our perceptions into a fact about nature at large, one must decide whether direct perception is to be expected always to reveal things as they are. But this, too, is a metaphysical question. For ultimately, one comes to this: only deity could have perceptions from which the characters of things experienced could simply be read off; and this would be one way and not a bad way, to define deity. (Here, too, is a source of poor metaphysics: men like to play at being God.) Thus it is a metaphysical mistake to decide the perceptual question as Aristotle did. Where individuality is as clearly perceived as it is when the perceived is a vertebrate animal, its presence is to be taken as probably factual, especially since we know our own individuality intuitively in memory, including immediate memory. But where we fail to perceive individuality of action this negative fact, this failure, must not be turned into a positive affirmation, a success, the insight that no such individuality is present in that part of nature. Rather, to avoid an unintelligible dualism, we should discount the apparent absence of individuality and look for indirect evidence of its presence. Science has turned up a great deal of such evidence.

In sum, scientific progress does not change the essential metaphysical evidence, but only alters its ready availability, its obviousness. Aristotle's metaphysics of mind and matter is at best mediocre, simply as metaphysics, no matter what science one does or does not know. However, it is a lot easier to avoid bad metaphysics if there is no bad science to furnish misleading suggestions as to the 'facts' which have to be accepted. 'Inanimateness' in the absolute sense never was or could be a fact; but it *seemed* to be so, by a natural illusion of commonsense and primitive science.

It is, I believe, similar with determinism. Newtonian and even Greek science seemed to favour determinism, partly for the reason, pointed out by Clerk Maxwell, that the statistical laws which are, as many of us now believe, the genuine stabilities of nature, were not yet accessible in application to the fine-structure of the world. Beginning with Maxwell's and Peirce's reflections upon the law of gases, and then the discoveries of Gibbs, Boltzmann, Darwin, Mendel, and finally Heisenberg, science has made it easier and easier to see, what metaphysically was always accessible to sufficiently resolute inquiry, that the absolutizing of law and regularity is self-defeating, and like many other modes of unlimited exaggeration finally destroys the meanings which it seeks to preserve or magnify. Here, too, science tells us no truth about the ultimate categories which we might not, if sufficiently intelligent, think out, even without science, from the inherent logic of the categories themselves. But perhaps we human beings could not be so intelligent as all that! At any rate, less intelligence is needed when science ceases to appear to be on the wrong metaphysical side.

It might seem that if relativity is the absolute principle, determination of events by causes must also be absolute, as expressing the way in which phenomena are relative to their antecedent conditions. But this is just what it fails to express! For if to be effect is to be dependent upon, relative to, a cause, to be cause is to be an independent or, in that context and in so far, a non-relative or absolute factor. The intuitive meaning of cause-effect implies one-way dependence or relativity, or – the same thing– one-way independence or absoluteness. This asymmetry is contradicted by the deterministic concept which has for so long been accepted as a harmless definition: 'necessary and sufficient condition'. The first adjective makes the effect imply the cause, and the second makes the cause imply the effect. Thus either (or neither) is relative to the other. Long, long ago in Asia, Nagarjuna showed the absurdities which result (see Chapter X). And since causal conditioning is thus turned into bi-conditioning or equivalence, it is surprising how few have noted, in this connection, as Meyerson did, that equivalence is a special and indeed degenerate form of implication. Determinism, taken without qualification, deprives causal relativity of any contrasting aspect of independence or absoluteness, and makes temporal relations for all practical purposes 'internal' in both directions. This is the one-sided monistic extreme to which Hume's pluralism of universal external relations is the opposite extreme. That Hume held both doctrines only shows on what a verbal level his thought, in some aspects, remained. At least one of the two, absolute causal determination, universal externality or independence, must be unreal. Neo-classical metaphysics holds that neither is real; but only indeterministic yet intrinsic causality, whereby events are relative to their predecessors but not to their successors. That a certain measure of prediction is thereby made possible I have shown elsewhere.[1]

The reader may still be wondering how relativity can be the absolute principle, if events are *not* relative to their successors.

[1] 'Causal Necessities: an Alternative to Hume', *The Philosophical Review* **63** (1954), pp. 479–99.

The answer is as follows: negative predicates are parasitic upon positive ones; non-relativity, therefore, upon relativity. When it becomes true that event *B* is actual, and is relative to previous event *A* (although *A* is *not* relative to *B*), this truth is made so entirely by the existence of the relativity of *B* to *A*. For 'not relative to *B*' has no definite referent until *B* occurs as successor to *A*. All one can say in advance, and all that ever qualifies *A* in itself, is that *A* is not relative to *any* later event. And this involves only negation, relativity, any, and later. And note that the relativity of events to their predecessors fully suffices to give each event its place in the time series. If *B* follows (and thus is relative to) *A*, and *C* follows *B*, no element of order is added by saying that *B* precedes *C* and *A* precedes *B*. The information is already complete with the statement of the backwards relatedness. Thus one-way relativity (positive in one direction, negative in the other) covers the whole story. Relativity as directional or non-symmetrical is the absolute principle, because it includes the idea of its own negative, absoluteness. Similarly, becoming includes being; contingency, necessity (which is merely the universal abstract constituent of the contingent); the complex, the simple (see Chapter VI).

The double advantage of our time, that we have finally seen the need and possibility of giving becoming and relativity their rights, and that many apparent facts of science supporting dualism, and hence destructive of metaphysical coherence, have turned out to be pseudo-facts or artifacts of primitive knowledge, does not quite mean that 'we now have it made'. There are also some new difficulties. Contemporary science is extremely difficult to grasp with any accuracy, and it is hard to know how much grasp we need to have. Certainly someone ought to correlate metaphysics and physics. For instance, if even the supreme reality is a kind of becoming, then it seems there must be a sort of divine time (even Barth says something like this), and the correlation of this with worldly time, as construed by relativity physics, is a neglected and apparently extremely formidable task.[2] Perhaps this is rather a problem in cosmology

[2] See John T. Wilcox, 'A Question from Physics for Certain Theists', *Journal of Religion* **61**, 1961, pp. 293–300. Several writers discuss the metaphysical bearings of relativity physics in the *Journal of Philosophy*, **46** (1969), no. 11, pp. 307–55. The discussion by Paul Fitzgerald is especially relevant.

than pure metaphysics, cosmology being the application of metaphysical principles to what science reveals as the structure of our 'cosmic epoch'. Yet unless either physicists or meta-physicians have erred, there must be an at least *possible* way of harmonizing what the physicists say is true of our epoch and what metaphysicians say is true of all possible epochs (since it forms the content of ideas of such generality that there is nothing we can think which is not a specialization of this content).

Another difficulty is the technical proliferation of formal logic. To master it is half a life-work. Can metaphysicians afford to know but little of this development? And what, for instance, is one to make of the contention of most logicians that truth is in no way time-bound, in contrast to the neo-classical doctrine that the reality which makes statements true is protean, and partly new each time we refer to it? I believe that the logicians' contention is subject to a qualification which they fail to make explicit. To call factual truths timeless is at best like calling a whole a part of itself, a convenient convention, not an insight into the proper or non-degenerate meaning of 'factual truth'. Logicians are beginning to look into this question.[3] Still another difficulty is that although science has destroyed the common-sensical and classical basis of the mind-matter division by removing the supposed evidence for inert matter, it has also tended to give new encouragement to materialistic or dualistic tendencies through the behaviouristic trend in the social and humanistic sciences. A 'methodological materialism' (better, 'physicalism') is in the saddle. What is its relation to the speculative psychicalism which alone can escape dualism without denial of any given aspects of reality? Here, too, is an interesting and difficult problem.[4]

A hopeful aspect of the present situation is the reconsideration being given to the most famous of all metaphysical arguments, Anselm's proof for God's existence. It has been made clear that neither critics nor defenders during eight centuries succeeded in laying bare either the real weaknesses or the real strength of Anselm's discovery. So far, I think, Malcolm, Findlay, Purtill,

[3] See A. N. Prior, *Past, Present and Future* (Oxford: Oxford University Press 1967), ch. 7.

[4] I shall have something to say about this problem in the book on bird song, *Born to Sing*, which I hope to publish in a year or two.

Hartshorne, and still others, agree. God's existence could not be one fact among others, if fact means contingent truth. Either God is the God of all possible worlds, not just of this one, or he is not even genuinely conceivable, an impossibility rather than an unrealized possibility. Since the idea of God contains implicitly the entire content of metaphysics, as I have argued in various places, the new perspective upon Anselm alone should suffice to open a new era in metaphysics.

Probably the most important function of metaphysics is to help in whatever way it can to enlighten and encourage man in his agonizing political and religious predicaments. Traditional religion is being reappraised; there are metaphysical aspects of religious problems. Some of these were hinted at above. The communist world understands (someone has said) the importance of political unity; the advanced democracies understand the importance of political freedom; how shall we achieve an understanding of both? It might help us if we realized more clearly and at all levels, including the ultimate or metaphysical level, that freedom can never be either absolute or wholly absent, that risk and uncertainty are inherent in existence as essentially creative becoming, with its always partly open future; but that if freedom is to have promise of producing harmony, limits must always be set to the scope of freedom. Yet ultimately it is freedom itself which sets these limits, divine freedom setting the cosmical limits, and the free decisions of minorities or majorities setting the local political limits for human beings. Sufficient order is a *sine qua non*, and technology has made the scale of the necessary order world-wide, in some minimal respects at least.

These problems, and all problems, are special cases of the ultimate or metaphysical problems of dependence and independence, or asymmetrical, positive-negative relativity between forms of more or less creative experiencing. In one sense, a metaphysics of relativity and creativity is very old, rather than a modern invention. To be relative is to take other things into account, to allow them to make a difference to oneself, in some sense to care about them. What else, then, can the ancient saying, *deus est caritas*, imply if not the supremacy of relativity? Yet nearly two thousand years have been partly wasted in the effort to make this deepest truth connote its opposite, the supremacy of absoluteness, i.e., of indifference to others. And so we have the shameful situation of communists preaching devotion to a super-individual goal, while Christians generally fail to reach any clear alternative to an ethics of enlightened self-interest. (Buddhism in some respects did better at this point.) It is the Christians, and the heirs of the Christian ethics, who ought logically to find this alternative. It is time philosophers gave them some assistance. A metaphysics of love, that is, of socially structured, and thus relative, creative experience is what we need, whether in ethics, religion, or politics – and indeed, in all our basic concerns.

IV

ABSTRACTION: THE QUESTION OF
NOMINALISM

THE philosopher, as Whitehead says, is the 'critic of abstractions'. He starts, not with the purely concrete, for which
abstractions are to be found, but with such more or less suitable
abstractions as are already available, and seeks to improve
them, having in mind experiences of the concrete. In so far,
philosophy is like science. (Science is not a movement from
observation innocent of ideas to ideas fitting the observations.
Non-scientists observe all their waking lives; but the accompanying ideas are usually too crude, trivial, or merely personal to give
the observations general cognitive significance.) Philosophy
differs from science by the scope of the abstractions with which
it deals. The scope is so great that negative instances of the
ideas not only will not in fact be found but such finding is
unthinkable. Thus if the abstraction is *being* or *reality*, the sheer
absence of reality cannot conceivably be experienced (not even
in dreams). Thus there are at least two levels of abstractness, the
specific, ordinary, empirical level characterized by the possibility of negative instances, and the non-specific or generic,
extraordinary, metaphysical level which admits only positive
instances. Whatever instances anything, say oxygen, instances
being – also (at least indirectly) becoming, according to the
metaphysics I accept – but the converse does not hold. Instances
of being need not be instances of oxygen. The line between
science and philosophy is determined by this distinction between
two sorts of abstraction.

It is to be noted that the requirement of possible negative
instances for specific or empirical ideas is not simply that such
instances can with some plausibility be said to be conceivable.
Rather – and here Popper is everlastingly and exactly correct

where so many have been in error or ambiguity – it must be conceivable that negative instances should be *experienced*. Otherwise the requirement is deprived of its cutting edge. For then it will be said that, for instance, the entire absence of being, the being of nothing at all, is conceivable. What is overlooked here is that once the connection with conceivable experience is broken, we lose control over the meaning of our words. 'There might be nothing' cannot, by any conceivable experience, be given a clear and consistent meaning, and I hold that this is the same as, 'It has no such meaning'. The being of sheer non-being would be both something and not something, being and not being, just as the experience of nothing would be the same as no experience.

But what is to be understood by the distinction, presupposed so far, between 'abstract' and 'concrete'? This is the age-old question of 'universals', the nominalist-realist battleground. The issue is far from simple. It takes many by no means equivalent forms. Can there be universals entirely apart from thought? Can there be anything whatever entirely apart from thought? No theist and no idealist (if indeed any genuine empiricist), no matter how broadly one defines these positions, can be happy with an affirmative answer. But it does not follow that a theist, idealist, or empiricist must be a 'conceptualist' in the trivializing sense according to which without *human* thought reality must be devoid of universal aspects. Universals as objectively real may be something like 'divine concepts'. And perhaps the other animals, or even all living things, have some primitive analogues to thought.

Again, the question, 'Are there objective universals, identical in various spatio-temporally distinct instances?', is not the same as the question, 'Are there *eternal* universals, absolutely independent of time, relevant to all conceivable stages of cosmic process?'. Whitehead's talk of 'eternal objects', rather than of 'universals', dangerously obscures this distinction. Time-independence may have relative as well as absolute forms. There may be emergent as well as eternal universals. Whitehead in fact admits this, but does not adequately take it into account. 'Lover of Shakespeare' is a universal, since it can have an indefinite number of instances. But it could not have had instances prior to the existence of Shakespeare. Every actuality, says

Whitehead, is a potential for subsequent objectification. Such a potential is or produces a universal, since innumerable actualities, e.g., actuality *a*, can instantiate 'objectifying actuality *b*'. Whitehead sees this clearly. But he assumes without argument that there are not some less obvious cases of emergent universal, perhaps a particular colour, say the precise shade and hue of blue in a certain iris flower, or in a certain experience of the flower. He attributes eternity to such a quality. I cannot believe in this extreme form of 'Platonism', setting aside the question of what Plato believed.

My view here is the Peircean one, obscure and difficult as it may be, that all specific qualities, i.e., those of which there can be negative instances in experience, are emergent, and that only the metaphysical universals are eternal, something like Peirce's Firstness, Secondness, Thirdness. I do not believe that a determinate colour is something haunting reality from all eternity, as it were, begging for instantiation, nor that God primordially envisages a complete set of such qualities. At this point I am no Whiteheadian. And it seems clear that a substantial part of the opposition to Whitehead's system loses its ground if the system is purified of this assumption. The nominalistic argument has never been more forcefully put than in this century, and one finds nothing like adequate refutation of it in Whitehead, so far as specific rather than metaphysical universals are concerned.

The explanation of similarity through partial identity has to justify itself against a rival view which has been shown to be far less vulnerable to criticism than Whitehead seems to assume, the view that similarity is as ultimate as identity. After all, universals are also more or less similar. And whereas similarity has degrees, identity, simply as such, does not. Hence the explanation of the former by the latter seems dubious or viciously circular. Identity is the zero of diversity, and it is always the positive which explains the negative, not the other way. That difference is positive is also shown by the way in which depth and variety of contrasts contribute to aesthetic value. This is unintelligible if difference is a mere privation of sameness. Rather, similarity is a privation or low degree of contrast.

In their emphasis upon the ultimacy of similarity and

contrast, nominalists seem to be in the right. But identity must also be taken as ultimate. The very idea of knowledge implies this. For if A and B can both know the same object O – and if not, of what use is the claim to know? – then there can be an identical element in the two instances of knowledge. Mere similarity of numerically distinct factors will not do here. For we need to talk about the same world of individuals or events, and this world must in some of its parts be common to us. Again, when one repeatedly remembers a past experience or sequence of experiences, the identical experiences must be elements in the remembering experiences. Memory of E is not memory of something like E (this would lead to a really vicious regress) but of E itself. Whitehead's theory of 'prehension' is a theory of literal identity, the same entities entering over and over again into subsequent entities. I accept this. But it is concrete entities which are here the identical elements. Two men do not need to have precisely the same abstract or universal quality of blue given to them in order to have cognitive communion. Close similarity is here sufficient.

In order to speak of close or remote similarity, however, must one not have identity, not only of concrete objects but also of at least *some* abstract ones? Similarity (or contrast) itself as an abstraction must, it seems, be an identical object for cognitive communion. And I hold that in any case the necessary aspect of deity is an abstract entity identically given to all. (It is not given with the same conscious distinctness to all. But clear and distinct ideas are an ideal, so far as human beings are concerned. Givenness is far indeed from a guarantee that the ideal has been realized.)

I have so far left out what may to some seem the chief point. Whether or not 'blue' is one entity for you and me, or for me in diverse circumstances, the word blue is just that word whenever it is used as colour label. True, each writing or pronouncing of the word is only more or less similar from occasion to occasion. But we are not normally interested in these differences. There is an ignoring of them by habit and convention. We take each 'token' (Peirce) as standing for the 'type'. Thus, though universality as humanly significant is language-dependent to a degree difficult to estimate, a merely linguistic account of universals begs the question. And the non-speaking animals seem in some fashion to react to instances of a universal as just that. A fox wanting to eat rabbit will grab the particular one that turns out to be catchable as just what he wants. So it would be a mistake to take language as the absolute basis of universality. The sense of the virtual identity of a word in its many 'tokens' cannot itself, without vicious regress, be made dependent upon talk about the tokens and their type.

There is one sense in which I have to hold that nominalism is simply wrong and realism right. This is the sense which Peirce gives to these terms. It is a generalization of the usual meaning. The realist affirms the objective reality of the universal, this is the usual definition. But for Peirce what the realist really affirms is the objective reality of the *distinction* between universal and particular. But then nominalism is not necessarily the denial of real universality; it may be the denial of real particularity. This is why Peirce could call Hegel a nominalist. I find this proposal extremely clarifying. The basic issue is the ontological status of logical polarities, e.g., universal-particular. But then the related contrasts actual-possible, or possible-necessary, or contingent-necessary must be similarly treated. The 'nitty-gritty' of the issue concerns the status of modality. Those who say that only propositions are necessary or contingent are the hard-core (or hopeless) nominalists. Here my view is as anti-nominalistic as possible. I take the contrasts universal-particular and possible-actual to be coincident. No possibility is literally particular, no universal is literally actual. Mr Micawber is not genuinely particular, but only seems so, thanks to Dickens's genius. And Platonic forms, though perhaps real, are so as unparticularized possibilities only.

One more step. Modal distinctions are ultimately coincident with temporal ones. The actual is the past, the possible is the future. A future actuality which is causally necessary, given the actual past, is a contradiction in terms. Here Peirce, Bergson, and Whitehead are at one. For them as for me determinism, taken without qualification, is categorial confusion or contradiction. It is a paradigm 'category mistake'; for it identifies the causally possible and the causally necessary, and this is modal absurdity.

To those who say that possibility, as distinct alike from actuality and necessity, is not experienced, one can reply that

futurity is experienced, and that futurity is irreducibly possibility. It is an aspect of events as such that they will and must
have suitable successors, but the nature of the successors is to
some extent left open by the requirement of 'suitability'. What
subsequently happens will not be the only sort of successors
which *could* have occurred, i.e., which would have fitted the
causal conditions. The necessity of successors is more or less
abstract or – the same thing – indeterminate. No concrete
happening is ever necessary, given the antecedent world state.
The remote future is much less necessary than the near future.
Also the past had its future, hence its open possibilities. To
account for the widest reaches of possibility is the same as to
survey time as a whole.

On the above view, our ability to understand universality or
possibility, as well as particularity or actuality, is the same as
our ability to grasp temporal distinctions. The distinction
between temporal and eternal is itself a temporal distinction,
that between dependence upon a particular situation in time
and absolute independence of situation. Eternity is a negative
aspect of temporality, not temporality a negative aspect of
eternity. Time is the positive idea, as Kant was prevented by
his dogmatic phenomenalism from seeing, but Peirce and
Bergson independently discovered. Time, as Kant said, but
more radically so than he thought, is the schema of all our
conceptions. Relax the absolute phenomenalism to a reasonably
relative form, and this becomes the doctrine I defend, provided
one also relaxes the absoluteness of Kant's determinism.

If temporal distinctions are modal distinctions, and if temporal order is independent of our thought and language, then
so are the modal aspects of reality. And these are in part universal, not exclusively particular, aspects.

Whitehead's view that actuality owes its definiteness to
specific universals, 'forms of definiteness', available from all
eternity seems to me, as I have said, arbitrary. The ultimate
principle is experiencing as partly free or self-creative, and this
principle, being ultimate, accounts for definiteness without help
from any other principle. The only definiteness a particular
instance of creative experience presupposes is that of previous
experiences, including divine experiences, it may be. However,
these are not 'primordial' but 'consequent' – even though

primordially God has had such experiences. This implies an actual infinity of past states. Finitism at this point I take to be incorrect. This is, I admit, not an easy assumption to justify.

Consider an artist deciding what colour to use in a certain part of a picture. Must he consult a store of eternal universals? Why not rather ask himself, shall it be like the blue of that sky, or the red that I used here in this other picture, or a mixture of this paint with that paint in whatever proportion seems to give good results? Why must eternal objects come into it? 'Resemblance' and 'quality' may be presupposed, and it seems unintelligible that they could be absolute emergents; but the blue, the red, why may these not emerge for the first time in some individual's experience, and originally in the whole of reality? After an experience has taken place we can always ask how it differs from, or resembles, previous experiences. We do not need to select some eternal point of reference – apart from those of metaphysical scope – in such comparisons.

Whitehead once argued, repeating Aristotle: a man cannot even be unmusical unless there is musicality for him to lack. But before there were any musical animals, what existed was perhaps neither musical nor unmusical but something simply unrelated to musicality. The argument would prove too much if it proved anything; for then before Shakespeare, one could argue, everyone was 'unlike or like Shakespeare' and this tautological property includes Shakespeare as irreducible element. And then there could be no emergent novelty at all. So the argument is a dangerous or improper one for process philosophy to employ. I take it to be a sophistry. The property in question is only tautological in a Pickwickian sense. The law of excluded middle is here misapplied. Relations to later actualities as particulars are only in the mind of the retrospective observer. And between eternal universals and absolute particulars there seems room for emergent universals other than those which obviously involve particulars, such as 'different from Shakespeare'.

An important point to observe is that the common assertion, the red of this flower (for example) is 'the same' as the red of that flower, taken as an empirical statement, only means that we are not aware of a difference. This is demonstrable by the well-known fact (rightly stressed by Koerner) that sameness in this observational sense is non-transitive. Since absolute qualitative sameness has no empirical meaning, it becomes a fair metaphysical question whether we should assume that it can occur. I argue for the negative view and hold with Stout that the precise qualities of particulars are themselves particular and unrepeatable. Only abstract, more or less generalized traits are repeatable. I am here differing from Santayana as well as Whitehead. Something very like this blue can occur over and over, but not precisely *this* blue. Particular qualities in their absolute definiteness are irreducibly relational and historical. The illusion to the contrary comes from forgetting that inability to detect a difference is not the same as ability to detect absolute similarity. If we were divine, it would be otherwise. But I assume that God knows all non-abstract or wholly determinate qualities of particulars to be unrepeatable.

Particularity is determinateness, universality (as W. E. Johnson suggested) is determinability. Only the past alone is fully determinate, the future is to be determined within the limits of causal possibility. These limits are just the determinateness of the past as capable of being superseded by some kinds of successors but not by other logically conceivable kinds. I fully agree with what Bergson seems to mean, but somewhat deplore his way of saying it, when he says that possibility is 'more' than actuality, not less. He means that the possibility of a certain concrete entity, the possibility taken as *identified* by this relation to the entity, as precisely *its* possibility, presupposes the entity as actual, and is the subsequent attribution to the previous situation of this completely determinate 'possibility'. Thus the determinateness of actuality is taken twice over, once in the present and once in the past. Bergson rightly regards this duplication as purely verbal. But why talk as though there were only this absurd sense of possibility? As Bergson surely knew, there is a reasonable sense. To take his example, before one cuts an apple in two, although there is not a possibility as determinate as either half which later results from such a cut, there is clearly the possibility of 'somehow halving the apple'. Actualizing a possibility is providing a determinate for a less definite antecedent determinable. Actuality is thus truly more than antecedent possibility, given a proper understanding of the latter.

Bergson is right in rejecting the reasoning: the particular half apple which results cannot have been impossible and therefore it must have been possible. One needs here to distinguish 'it is false that such and such was impossible' from 'it is true that such and such was possible'. Here again the law of excluded middle lacks valid application. If there was no such and such, there was neither a possible nor an impossible such and such. To reiterate, possibilities are determinables not determinates. The apple can be halved *somehow*, but to suppose that the determinate *how* that subsequently results is included in the somehow is just to deny the distinction, determinable-determinate, and to make the philosophy of being as opposed to the philosophy of process a mere consequence of a logical truism. Given a determinate how we can relate it to the somehow, but given only the somehow we cannot relate it to a determinate how. Determinables are not classes of determinates, but aspects of creativity relevant to such classes, so far as the latter are given.

The advance possibilities for a painting are only relatively definite. The pigments may already exist; the human senses are largely fixed. Thus the painter knows roughly what he can do. But that he can do just *this* which he subsequently does, not even deity can know until it is done. The 'this' of an actuality simply has no advance status, modal or otherwise. Creativity does not map the details of its future actions, even as possible. This, as Berdyaev says, is the non-Platonic meaning of real creativity, that it is not content with actualizing 'images' which are antecedently, or eternally, in being, but rather produces 'new images', sheer additions to the 'forms of definiteness', to use Whitehead's term for an idea that he seems at times to deny (unless I have misunderstood him).

My position with respect to eternal objects is simply that the necessary or eternal aspect of deity is the only eternal object. I should like to say that this eternal entity is not a multitude but, in the language of classical theism, is 'simple'. (Not that God is simple, but that this aspect of him is so.) However, I also see reason to say that the infinity of whole numbers must be included in the necessary aspect of deity, since like Kant I am not able to conceive a first state of process. It seems that God must eternally have been and be aware of an infinite number of already actualized entities. The problems which this suggests are baffling enough. But at any rate I see no good ground at all for supposing that, besides numbers or similarly abstract entities, including metaphysical categories, every quality of sensation or feeling that occurs in experience must have its eternal duplicate. Feeling as such, quality as such, yes, but not red, sweet, as determinate qualities identical with those we enjoy in experience. Feeling is a determinable of infinite range, not a vast sum of determinates. As Peirce held, possible qualities of feeling form a continuum without definite parts.[1]

It should be clear that the distinction abstract-concrete, like other basic logical distinctions, is also to be taken as ontological. Animals in their limited, primitive way abstract, i.e., sense universal aspects of things, and God in his eminent way does so. Not only relative to *our* type of understanding are there abstract as well as concrete aspects of reality, but relative to any form of knowledge or understanding, and in simple truth. This follows from the primacy of becoming or process, for the past-future distinction dissolves in hopeless paradox (as McTaggart showed) if all events throughout time are supposed to be on the same plane of concreteness. And if God did not grasp the difference between concrete actuality and abstract potentiality, he would be ignorant of that which we know to be as fundamental as any distinction whatever. Though God does not need universals to infer the past by discursive reasoning, as we do, because his memory and perception are adequate to reality, he still must see how actualities are determinates under antecedent determinables.

The foregoing account is defective to the extent that it fails to mention the relation between purpose and the abstract or universal. A purpose is a determinable, for which any realization of the purpose is a determinate. A complete nominalist can have no proper idea of purpose. A person who gets what he wanted cannot have wanted precisely what he got, but only something less completely defined. There can be no such thing as a final cause coincident in character with its fulfilment. Some views of providence, of course, overlook this truth, and hence talk nonsense. Neither man nor God can intend the concrete course of events, for 'intention' in the purposive sense contradicts such coincidence of aim and achievement. It would make the achievement merely the intention over again, and this is as much

---

[1] Charles Hartshorne and Paul Weiss (eds.), *The Collected Papers of Charles Sanders Peirce* (Harvard University Press, 1931–5), Vol. VI, ch. 7.

empty verbiage as the duplication of actual and possible spoken of above. If there are purposes influencing events, they are efficacious universals; but no universal can determine events in detail. For this reason alone the formula for determinism, 'the strongest motive determines the outcome', is mistaken. No motive can fully define its actual realization. Suppose the motive is to insult someone. There is not just one possible way to do this, even in a given situation, but always a range of possible ways. (Of course, too, the strongest motive is such either independently of how we attend to the factors given to us in the situation or not independently. If the latter, then determinism does not follow. If one assumes the former, the determinism issue has been begged.)

I trust the foregoing discussion has shown that while neo-classical metaphysics cannot in every sense be nominalistic, it may very well accept a good deal from some versions of nominalism. It can be hospitable to the idea that similarity is as ultimate as identity, and also to the idea that except for extremely general and abstract universals, qualities can be non-particular without being eternal, and that perhaps there are no eternal aspects of reality other than those included in what God necessarily-eternally is. And this non-contingent aspect of God must involve only universals of metaphysical scope, and not those which need not be embodied in every experience.

The nominalism that cannot be accepted is that which takes determinable aspects of reality to be merely our ignorance of the determinate aspects, and similarly futurity and possibility to be mere appearances relative to our mode of knowing. On the contrary, what can be, beyond what is, forms an irreducible aspect of what is. *Reality is protean, not for our ignorance merely, but in itself or for the most ideal form of knowledge you please.* (It is time to react against agnostics or atheists who blandly tell us that 'for omniscience there would be no question of what could or can be, but only of what is'. This is not the best meaning of 'omniscience', and the better meaning has been in the literature – in obscure places – for centuries if not millennia.) There are real universals in the sense that there are real possibilities, real determinables, and the idea of a fully particularized or determinate whole of reality, complete once for all, is confusion or contradiction.

An old query is, 'Which is prior, actuality or possibility?'
Actuality is prior in the sense that every case of futurity involves
a case of pastness, i.e., of actuality. What is possible next is
simply what is compatible with what has happened up to now.
Possibility without actual antecedents is merely the abstraction
from every definite stage of process, and its only truth is that
by going back far enough into the past one could (with sufficient
knowledge) come to a stage at which whatever definite specificity you wish to point to was not yet in being, and was in its
specificity neither possible nor impossible, though some less
definite possibility was established by what had happened up
till then. Anything genuinely thinkable and specific, even a
specific law of nature, was not always excluded by the actual
course of events. Thus all possibility is grounded in actual
process. This is a somewhat non-aristotelian version of the
Aristotelian doctrine of the priority of actuality.

The famous controversy over universals in the Middle Ages
produced the moderate realism of Thomas Aquinas. Given the
assumption of an immutable deity, a better solution could
scarcely be wished for. Process philosophy, however, with its
admission of emergence as well as eternal fixity in God, has
additional resources. The most abstract universal aspects of
things are embraced in the most abstract and hence most
independent aspect of deity – the eternal ideal and eternal
possibility for creative actualization. All more specific universals
emerge in the creative process involving both divine and non-
divine purposes, concepts, anticipations, or other forms of the
experience of what could be or (in less definite outlines) must be,
the sense of alternatives with common denominators of necessity
spanning the mutually exclusive options.

V

SOME PRINCIPLES OF METHOD

O UR age is method-conscious. So were my Harvard teachers fifty years ago. Throughout this period I have felt forced by the anti-metaphysical or non-rationalistic philosophies conspicuous in my environment to reflect upon questions of philosophical procedure.

It must first be understood that the method in question is that to be used in metaphysics. Since metaphysical statements are not observationally falsifiable, the question arises, how can we know when we make a mistake? We are often told that there are or may be internally consistent but mutually inconsistent metaphysical systems. Here I shall speak for myself: I am not sure that my own system is clear and consistent, and I am reasonably sure that every system I have been able to find that is plainly incompatible with mine is either unclear or inconsistent or both. Were there really two internally trouble-free but mutually incompatible systems, they must be alternative (empirically testable) specializations of a more general system which alone is metaphysical. Metaphysical statements are not opposed to anything except wrong ways of talking. Metaphysical error is exclusively a matter of confusion, inconsistency, or lack of definite meaning, rather than of factual mistakes.

To take some historical examples, I do not believe that Plato or anyone else has ever known definitely and consistently what he, or the spokesman in his dialogue, meant by a being (not a mere abstract aspect of a being or beings) so 'perfect' that it could in no respect change either for the better or for the worse. One can say such things, but not genuinely think them, as is shown by the attempt to 'draw out' the meaning into its implications. Either there are no definite implications, or they are inconsistent. Again, neither Aristotle nor anyone else has ever had a definite and consistent idea of a 'life' consisting exclusively of the 'thinking of thinking'. Neither Aquinas nor anyone else has ever had an idea of a 'pure actuality', a being (not merely abstract) which actualizes no antecedent potentialities for its own further development, or again of a being both in all respects independent, yet also cognizant, of the contingent world. Neither Descartes nor anyone else has really known what could be meant by 'inextended mental substance'. Neither Spinoza nor anyone else has had a definite consistent idea of non-contingent 'modifications' of substance. Neither Leibniz nor anyone else has succeeded in positively grasping without contradiction the import of 'best possible world' or of the 'principle of sufficient reason'. Neither Hume nor anyone else (including Ayer, Russell, and Von Wright) has been clear and consistent in believing that 'what is distinguishable is separable'. Neither Kant nor anyone else has been able to make good sense of the concept of appearances in which both the thing appearing and that to which it appears remain wholly inaccessible, or hidden.

The history of metaphysics is indeed in considerable part a story of failures to use words significantly and coherently. But then so is the history of science a story of factual errors (often mixed with metaphysical confusions); and the role of factual errors in science is analogous to that of lapses from significance in metaphysics. In both cases we learn by trial and mistake; the signs of mistakes being easier to read aright than the positive signs of being on the right track. To cite metaphysical absurdities (or factual errors in science) as representative, with no balancing attention to the elements of good sense (or factual discovery) is propaganda, not argument.

Plato *did* make sense (in vague, somewhat ambiguous fashion) when he said in effect that knowing is essentially valuing (the good is the supreme form), or that the soul is self-moved. Aristotle did have (an approximation to) a coherent idea when he said that the universal is real in, not apart from, concrete individuals. Aristotle, Philo, and Anselm did talk sense in holding that the eternal must also be necessarily existent. Spinoza did have an insight when he held that the world cannot be merely extrinsic to the divine actuality. Leibniz was very clear-headed in arguing that, on the most concrete level, (which he mislocated in substance) actualities can have no inessential qualifications (his principle of '*in esse*'). Hume was quite right in contending that sense perception cannot clearly exhibit causality operating in our physical environment and that a strict 'necessity' running from causal conditions to ensuing events is even unintelligible. Finally, Kant was right in holding that all our conceptions require temporal succession for their application.

Methodological discussions are rather dreary without examples. Also it is a moot question how far one can distinguish methodological from substantive issues. Hence, if the following appears to the reader more like an outline of my metaphysical beliefs than like a listing of rules which everyone ought to follow whatever his beliefs, he may be at least partly correct.

1. *Language*

It is agreed today that philosophical puzzles have large syntactical and semantic components. The remedy proposed by some is to set aside as at best problematic all traditional technical terms of philosophy, and go back to ordinary language, as used in the ordinary way, in order to recover the sanity embodied in that language. Within limits I accept this. But the limits are important.

(*a*) Ordinary modes of speaking, for ordinary purposes, are to be accepted as making sense, and as an important source of philosophical insight – provided it be borne in mind that philosophical purposes may differ from ordinary ones. They differ especially in the degree of generality sought, and this implies an unusual concern with extreme cases, such as things radically smaller or larger than, or in some other way radically different from, man and the things man commonly deals with. Science has had to enrich language to describe cell division, the nuclei of atoms, astronomical distances, universal gravitation, and other things that transcend ordinary human discourse. Philosophy, or at least metaphysics, is trying to reach a generality in some ways infinitely beyond that of physics or biology, for it seeks to survey the possible as such, in its most unrestricted or *a priori* sense. (The universal characters of the possible are the necessary, what will be in any possible case.)

Metaphysics asks questions not ordinarily put, such as, could any conceivable experience have as datum something in no way

constituted by experiencing of any kind, however remote from
the human form? Or – essentially the same question – if such
ideas as feeling, memory, desire, are generalized to the utmost,
will they not be somehow applicable not only to any experience but to any possible object of experience? Still again, does
the idea of mere 'dead', 'insentient' matter refer to anything
which could be experienced? Is the 'something' which cannot
but be experienced just experience itself and as such, or is
experience, even in its utmost generality, only a species of
experienceable and thinkable reality? Are the varieties of thinkable experiences and aspects of experiences less than the varieties
of thinkable realities and aspects of realities? Gravitation was
generalized by Newton for the entire visible cosmos. How far
can 'mind' be generalized? This is no ordinary question. Could
ordinary modes of speech, just as they stand, be expected to
answer it? Is it a merely scientific question? Not if it is a
question concerning conceptual possibility. Could there conceivably be divine mind, atomic mind? Could any conceivable
experience show the total absence of feeling in some part of
nature?

(*b*) Since ordinary language is not used to deal with the
most general questions, while philosophers for many centuries
have been trying to deal with them, it is wise to pay some
attention to the technical terminologies produced in this effort.
To take the clarity of these terminologies for granted is unjustified, in view of the endless disputes and mutual accusations
of misunderstanding characterizing the history of philosophy.
Yet, as suggestions to be looked into for what they may be
worth, they deserve more respect than some are giving them (see
below, IV).

(*c*) Philosophy, by virtue of its extreme generality, must (as
already remarked) take extreme cases more carefully and
explicitly into account than most discourse needs to do. Thus,
for example, the distinction between general (or abstract) and
particular (or concrete) aspects of things is recognized in ordinary speech; but the two extremes of the most and the least
particular or concrete (or the most and the least general or
abstract) ideas are not normally taken as definite topics of
discussion. Rather, one speaks of relatively general terms like
'human nature', and relatively particular terms like 'this man',

but not of such extremely general terms as 'concreteness', or such extremely particular ones as 'this man's first experience in the split second after coming out of deep or dreamless sleep early this morning'.

Common sense tends to think of a particular animal or physical thing as the extreme contrary of the abstract or general. But, as the Buddhists, Whitehead, and a few others have clearly seen, while most philosophers have been trapped in mere common sense, a particular person or thing, enduring and changing through time, is really a kind of low-level universal, compared to the momentary states or events in which alone the individual is fully concrete or actual. This is the greatest element of confusion in traditional 'substance' doctrines, and in this matter Locke, Aristotle, and Strawson seem not significantly different. None seems entirely clear about the greater concreteness of the event language (when used carefully for this very purpose) compared to the thing or person language. Not that ordinary speech is for its own needs unclear in this respect, but that ordinary speech has the advantage of context to a greater extent than technical discourse. It is the context which tells us whether by 'I', 'he', or 'John Smith' one means the person as identical entity from birth to death, or the person as concretely new at the moment of the utterance, or something between these extremes. 'I have just thought of something that never occurred to me before' distinguishes as well as identifies the referent of the two pronouns. The actual (concrete) thinker of the new thought is not the actual thinker of the contrasting thoughts of earlier times. A new thinking means a new thinker, if one is talking about the most particular or concrete subject. A thinker is concretized in his actual thoughts. But of course, from a more abstract point of view, it is the same thinker all the way back. I believe with Whitehead that philosophers generally have been unclear or inconsistent about this. The supposition that the indivisible units of concrete reality are single substances rather than single states or events has produced endless confusion, including ethical confusion, as the Buddhists saw so clearly. Self-interest theories of motivation are one result.

If the extreme of concreteness tends to be missed by ordinary speech, so does the extreme of abstractness. What is the *generic* meaning of concreteness as such, or what can be said *universally* about the most concrete levels of reality? The philosophical 'categories' are the attempt to answer this question. Only hints can be gleaned from the plain man or ordinary language as to what these are.

(d) Another pair of extreme cases not adequately illuminated by ordinary speech habits are the extremes of least and maximal value or worth. Here, too, it is the relatively rather than maximally superior and inferior with which we normally deal. The ideas of strictly unsurpassable value, or strictly minimal (or zero) value or worthlessness, are taken only in more or less loose or careless fashion by non-philosophical speech and writing. Are the lower animals simply worthless, or is it only inanimate objects for which we find no significant use of which this can be said? Indeed, is anything, strictly speaking, worthless, or even, valuable only as instrument? Or is being as such in some minimal fashion implicative of value? At the opposite pole, is God to be conceived as in every aspect maximal in value, hence incapable of increase, or is this an absurd idea? In what fashion, if any, is maximal value or 'eminence' conceivable?

(e) Analysis shows that there is one idea in which the extremes of greatest generality or abstractness, also greatest particularity or concreteness and unsurpassable value are all found together, namely in the idea of God as eminent individual who, though individual, is also somehow completely universal (ubiquitous, influential everywhere) and concretized in states whose range of possibilities is in some strict sense as wide as the possibilities for contrasting states of things in general. In so far as this is true, the relative unclarity of common sense concerning the extremes in question is bound, if philosophers are not critical in their adoption of common sense, to ruin the philosophy of religion. In my opinion, neither the abstractness nor the concreteness of God has been properly understood in philosophy. The millennium-old dispute over the ontological argument, a dispute which is still going on, and in which, so far as I can see, almost everyone has made serious mistakes, no matter whether he was defending or attacking Anselm's proposal, offers a good example. Indeed, the whole question of the status of existential statements as contingent or necessary can never be cleared up so long as the difference between *relatively* abstract (or concrete) and *fully* abstract (or concrete) is not carefully attended to, and so long as the *existence* of individuals is not sharply distinguished from the *actuality* of states or events. Four levels of reality, not the two of 'essence' and 'existence', are necessary if we are to reach clarity in metaphysics (see Chapter XII).

II. *Experience*

The roots of all abstract ideas are to be sought in concrete experiencing of various kinds. Thus there is a phenomenological aspect of philosophizing.

(*a*) Memory, perception, and imagination are three obvious aspects of concrete experiencing. A philosopher needs to make a careful examination of all three, in their essential or generic aspects. Hume made virtually no examination of memory, which may be one reason why his theory of perception and imagination is so inadequate. For in some ways memory is a better key to the nature of experience than perception, not only because, by the time we have used a datum of perception, it will already have been taken over by memory, but for the additional reasons: (a^1) in memory there is less mystery concerning what we are trying to know than there is in perception; also (a^{11}) the temporal structure of memory is more obvious.

(a^1) What we remember is our own past human experiences, more or less closely similar to the experience doing the remembering. Indeed, we remember remembering. By contrast, in the perceiving of a stone, say, the entire difference between human awareness and 'inanimate' matter, which has puzzled philosophers and scientists for thousands of years, has somehow to be assimilated.

(a^{11}) In memory we realize clearly that we are at least *trying* to know the past, while in perception it is rather natural to think that it is the present we have to do with. Yet science tells us, what a sufficiently subtle philosophy could have inferred, that the events perceived, at least if outside our bodies, are in the past quite as truly as what we remember. Thus the temporal structure of memory is initially clearer than that of perception. So in two ways memory is the clearer case, and should be studied first.

(*b*) From usual definitions of the aesthetic attitude it follows that it is in this attitude rather than in making ethical decisions or solving practical or cognitive problems that we are most attentive to experience in its concreteness. In listening to music, for instance, at least under ideal conditions, it is the whole of what we hear that we enjoy. Similarly, in adequate concentration upon a painting, it is the whole of what we see that is relevant. By contrast, in practical affairs, only certain features of the seen or heard count. Cognitive pursuits tend to be even more selective, even farther from the concrete in their interests. In spite of this, innumerable philosophers have discussed the content of perception almost exclusively as it appears to the pragmatic or cognitive stance, but not as it is present in and for aesthetic experience. Husserl, in my opinion, definitely made this mistake. On this point, as I told him, my *Wesensschau* contradicted his. (He looked startled, and said, 'Perhaps you have something'.) Traditional distinctions between 'secondary' and 'tertiary' qualities express the same attitude – as though mere sensations, emotionally neutral counters in the cognition game, were there first. On the contrary, the world is felt first and only then, perhaps, known. All qualities directly given in experience are aesthetic or emotional, and in this upside-down sense tertiary (see Chapter XV).

Berkeley in some passages, especially in the *Commonplace Book*, also Croce, Bosanquet, Bradley, Whitehead, in some passages Peirce, have been aware that it is aesthetic categories that are most relevant to the concrete as actually given. The use by the last four writers of the term *feeling* to cover all the qualitative aspects of experience is indicative of this awareness. But most philosophers have, as Whitehead says, been victims, even while denying it, of a 'faculty psychology' according to which we neutrally cognize the world, and any valuation or feeling is arbitrary addition to the primary data given to cognition. But cognition is only a way of using the felt qualities of things, taking them merely as signs of identities and differences which are structural rather than qualitative. There is no independent faculty of cognition which includes a neutral way of sensing qualities such as blue or sweet. The given world is the enjoyed and suffered world. Cognitive neutrality is a product of neutralization, a sophisticated achievement of which feeling is the presupposed substratum. Just the opposite is held in standard accounts: the substratum is taken to include the sensory qualities as in themselves devoid of feeling tone or aesthetic character, and any feeling tones or characters are held to be added, hence 'tertiary'. This I hold to be bad phenomenology. It also has no firm support from experimental psychology, as I have argued in my book on sensation. And it could, I think, be shown that ordinary language also, on the whole, supports my position.

(*c*) Imagination includes dreaming. It is no minor defect that Ryle's account of mind virtually ignores dreams and gives an implausible account of images; or that Malcolm's account of dreaming is so unconvincing; or that Descartes's sceptical argument (I might be dreaming, hence the physical world might be entirely unreal) is based on a view of what dreams are that is contradicted by any careful study of dreams. As Bergson says, sensory stimulation is clearly present in dreams, so that it will not do to disparage waking perceptions on the ground that in dreams, at least, the mind creates its own content and hence, since there is no absolute difference between dreaming and waking experience, all content, even of the latter, may be our own creation. Malcolm's answer to the sceptic is that dreaming is entirely different from waking experience, hence the non-objectivity of dreams does not imply that of waking experience. But why not answer the sceptic by pointing out that his initial premise asserting the complete non-objectivity of dreams is arbitrary, if not absurd? There is no hard factual proof that the sensory content of dreams is ever merely mental, rather than physiological – as when we dream (as I have done) of scratching an itchy place and waken to find a fresh mosquito bite in that very place.

Our bodies are as truly parts of the physical world as sticks and stones. Every experience, there is reason to think, is in its way and degree revelatory of the public physical world. To admit the absolute subjectivity of dreams and then seek to avoid solipsism by positing an equally absolute dichotomy between dreams and waking life (in sharp conflict, as Malcolm admits, with ordinary language, which tends to describe dreams as resembling other experiences) is to deal ingeniously with difficulties of our own invention, not with the necessities of the actual phenomena. Accept the evidence that dreams, too, are more or less objective and there will be no need to posit a language-defying total incomparability between dreaming and waking. If even dreams have some objectivity, much more do normal waking experiences.

Even on a common-sense level it seems obvious enough that dreams, very often at least, exhibit aspects of the actual physical world. We dream of being cold and waking find that we are cold; we dream about a noise and waking hear that very noise (e.g., a passing plane); we dream about being in an excited sexual state and waking find that we are in that state. Malcolm says that in such cases (which could be multiplied indefinitely) we are not really asleep and so are not really dreaming. He forgets to consider that he may have defined dreams as a null class. I see no good reason to suppose that what he defines as a dream ever occurs, or even could possibly occur. I hold with Bergson that in dreams there is always sensory content exhibiting an actual feature of the bodily state. The denial that this is so is not new with Malcolm. It is central in Descartes and many others. The error pervades philosophy, Eastern and Western. The suspicion that life may be only a dream, or a series of mere mental states without objective reference, is based on a verbal definition of 'mere dream' or mental state that, for all anyone has shown, is vacuous.

All experience can, and I hold should, be taken as response to physical realities actually given in the experience. The physical realities may be within the body more than outside it, but what of that? The supposition that what is inside the human skin is therefore non-physical (inextended) is one of the unconscious absurdities that sophisticated people easily fall into. (Recall Kant's ambiguous 'outside us in space'.) Spinoza was right on one point: to have a human experience is at least, whatever else it may be, to experience a real physical human body. This is true of dreaming and waking, perceiving and imagining, and of any concrete human experience whatever. Unless this is seen, little in epistemology can be understood correctly.

It may be said that I have been appealing to empirical facts, not *a priori* necessities, as metaphysics claims to do. But note that it is Descartes and Malcolm who take as empirical fact (or else as arbitrary definition) that dreams do not exhibit the physical world. I point out that there is no such fact. And I go further: there could not be such a fact in any possible world. It is a logical blunder to suppose that the concept of experience can be divested of the relativity, the relatedness to another, inherent in the notion. No experience could simply generate its own content. That the dreamer when awake may be unable to tell just what of the real physical world was given in his dream proves nothing, for reasons we are about to see.

(*d*) In studying memory, perception, or imagination one needs to distinguish between: (1) What is observably present in the experience; (2) what is not observably present; and (3) what is observably absent. The conversion of (2) into (3) is justified only if it is known that the factor in question must, if present at all, be so in perceptible degree or magnitude. Assuming that we directly experience physical reality at all, and that physicists and physiologists are not telling fairy tales in their account of that reality, a very great deal must be given in experience that we cannot observe as given. The supposition that our power of 'introspection' is absolute, so that, unless we can consciously detect a factor in an experience it does not contain the factor, is one of the many forms of the supposition that man is as God would be – equipped with infallibility. To fail to observe, or even to be unable to observe, a presence, even in our own experience, is one thing, to observe its absence is quite another. To identify the two is to make a hopeless riddle both of physics and of psychology. Above all, it is bad metaphysics. Complete power of self-knowledge, like other ideal functions, is appropriate with respect to God, not man.

Neglect of the foregoing consideration is a principal cause of the notions criticized above in II*a*, *b*, *c*. Descartes could not have known that his dreams were merely or absolutely subjective. Nor could anyone have known that the secondary qualities are absolutely distinct from qualities of feeling, or entirely value-neutral. Similarly with the view that perception gives us the absolutely simultaneous state of the environment, that there is no time lapse between perceiving and perceived. Such absolutes are not to be lightly affirmed.

(*e*) We need also to distinguish verbal judgments based on memory, perception, or introspection from the memory, perception, or introspection (really short-run memory used in a special way?) themselves. Mistakes of memory, about which we hear so much, are usually not carefully distinguished from mistakes of memory judgments. The mere process of verbal-ization, being a human and hence fallible operation, introduces possibilities of error that involve more than memory. The same is true of verbalized perceptual judgments.

(*f*) Still another needful precaution is to distinguish between those cases of perception and memory which involve the shortest chains of mediation between experience and thing experienced and those involving long and therefore complicated chains. Thus feeling pain on the one hand and seeing a far-off stellar explosion on the other; or remembering after less than a second that one has begun the sentence one is now completing, in con-trast to recalling what one experienced a year ago, or even yesterday. The rational way to proceed is to try to be clear first about the simpler case, the pain or the short-run memory, and then consider the opposite extremes. For all else must lie between. This rule implies that bodily experience, not vision of environmental objects, should be our initial sample of percep-tion, and that remote environmental objects should be decisive rather than those close by.

Neglect of (II*d, e, f, g*) has, I believe, led to extraordinary errors concerning the three basic forms of experience mentioned above. So far from furnishing the remedy, Husserl's '*epoche*' (if I understand him at all well, which I may not) introduced an additional error, the error that the physical world is a merely phenomenal affair, or that the strictly given consists only of qualities and structures of actual and possible experiences of beings such as ourselves. I hold that the given in perception consists of events real in the same sense as our experiences, but temporally prior to and in principle independent of these.

(*g*) Meaning, belief, and action. We experience ourselves as active agents, decision makers. Ideas are significant only if they can or could be believed, and there is no adequate test of the genuineness of belief other than this; can (and in suitable circumstances would) the belief be acted upon or in some sense lived by? On this point I agree with Peirce, James, Dewey, and (I rather think) Wittgenstein. Beliefs can be livable without being true, but if they are in no sense livable then they cannot be true, for they have no definite meaning. Example (from William James): absolute pessimism and absolute optimism are both incapable of being lived by. That all evil is good in disguise or all good, evil in disguise, implies that no action can be better than another. But to live is to exercise preference, and thus to imply that some results of action are good compared to others, and hence that any pessimism or optimism must be subject to qualification. There are many less obvious applications of this 'pragmatic' criterion of significance. It could also be called the existentialist criterion.

(*h*) The social structure of life and existence. That the social structure of life is basic is obvious in various ways. Language is nothing if not social. Man's intelligence is a social product through and through. In all religions love is taken as either the highest or nearly the highest value. Primitive man felt that the cosmos was essentially a vast society of which human nature is only one special part. Non-social conceptions are products of sophisticated abstraction, not of direct, primitive experience. All such abstractions must justify themselves, especially if they claim to give the concrete nature of experience or reality. Solipsism is wrong not merely because the not-self is known, but because other selves (using the word broadly so that it covers far more than just other vertebrate animals) are known. Social transcendence is undeniable, non-social transcendence is problematic. The *Umwelt* is certainly in part at least *Mitwelt*, no matter what else it may or may not be.

Experience of other human selves is only one, and not the most direct and constant, form of sociality. For one thing, it is demonstrable from suitable definitions that God could not exist unless experienced by every subject at all times. Also the idea that our bodily experiences have as data only a mass of insentient physical stuff is an attempt to get knowledge out of sheer ignorance (in violation of II*d*). Consciously detected data are a narrow sub-class of data, by any reasonable theory of experience. It is arguable that all experience of concrete and singular entities is experience of other, mostly subhuman subjects. But this cannot be established (or rationally refuted either) so long as mere common sense is taken as legislative even in questions in which it is essentially uninterested and does not attempt to discuss with any care. For some forty years I have been aware that many of my contemporaries take for granted that a psychicalistic theory of matter is false or absurd. They neglect to tell us plainly and cogently how they know this. Hence I am unimpressed by their assurance (note VI*b* below).

III. *Formal logic*

Formal logic, including finite arithmetic, is the one mode of analysing reasoning that can claim maximal clarity and rigour. Whatever help philosophers can get from its results they ought to take advantage of. It is true and important that there is room for dispute as to how far we have the formal logic we need. The ideal of extensionality has, I believe, sharply limited results so far. Still, some rather simple, though neglected, truths of formal logic as it now stands seem to me quite relevant to traditional philosophical problems.

(*a*) Formal logic has made it clear that thought turns upon relations, and that the relation of subject or predicate, or of a member of a class to a class, or of a class to another class, are far from being the only fundamental relations in which subjects enter. Rather the relation of a subject to other subjects, Rabc ... is the essential or general principle, of which 'S is P' is the special case in which the other subjects S^1, S^{11} ... are vacuous. But then, if relations are predicates, since relation to S includes S, subjects include other subjects. A man does not simply have the predicates: knowing, loving, hating, and so forth; he has the predicates: knowing X, Y ..., loving X but hating Y, and so on. Either what is in the man is mere knowing, loving, hating, with the object of these states simply outside them, not constitutive of them or of the man at all, or what is in the man is knowing, loving, hating just the objects he does know, love, hate. Is not the latter the right view? But then there is some truth in the concept of internal relations. Russell has, in almost unbelievable fashion, missed this all his long life. He will not allow knowing, as in a subject, to specify its object. Rather, it gives a description which may happen to fit one and only one existing thing. But in thinking this theory one imagines oneself in a different position than the theory provides for. On Russell's view the knower strictly has only himself, not a real world of existing things. The subject as of now is the only given reality (and even this givenness is paradoxical), a logically self-sufficient entity, not intrinsically related to any other existing thing.

On the other hand, formal logic makes very clear indeed that there must be some external relations. To say that *all* other subjects are constitutive of a given subject is to say that each subject is somehow the total universe and that all relations are analogous to the biconditional in propositional logic. But this conditional is obviously a special case of conditioning, not the universal one. Its very definition makes this clear. And if all relations are constitutive at both ends, i.e., symmetrically, reality is like a vast tautology. What logician can take this seriously? So of course Russell rejected 'absolute idealism', the thesis of universal internality. But he cannot claim that this and his own view exhaust the possibilities. They both assume symmetry, ignoring the one-way case, analogous to 'p entails q but not vice versa' (see Chapter X).

There are five formally possible views in this matter:

1. Every (dyadic) relation is *internal* to *both* terms;
2. Every relation is *external* to *both* terms;
3. Some relations are *internal* to *both* terms, the rest *external* to *both*;
4. Every relation is *internal* to *one* term, *external* to the *other*;
5. Some relations are internal to one term, external to the other; some internal to both terms; the rest external to both.

Since the first three doctrines are the purely symmetrical possibilities, and the fourth rules out symmetry, of course (5) is correct. Those who take one of the other views are bound in effect to illustrate (5) in spite of themselves.

Thus Russell, although adhering to (2) as alternative to (1), makes concessions to (4) and hence (5); but he does this only where no great care is needed to see the need for these concessions. Thus 'parts', he grants, are constitutive of 'wholes'. But he does not inquire whether there may not be more subtle yet pervasive instances of oneway internality, for example in the way past events enter into memory. Rather he leaps to the conclusion that, apart from obvious, part-whole relations, mutual externality is the rule; and he does this with no more hesitation than the monists show in asserting universal internality. Yet if events in nature are mutually independent, nature is analogous to a chaos of mutually independent propositions. If, on the contrary, the realities are mutually interdependent, nature is analogous to a vast tautology. Since (3) means that part of nature is mere chaos, and other parts are mere tautology, and (4) arbitrarily rules out symmetry, (5) is the reasonable initial guess.

(*b*) In spite of the lack of agreement about the status of modal logic, some things are clear enough, and they include relevant and helpful points, for instance that $N(p\&q) \equiv Np\&Nq$. This shows that the necessary cannot include the contingent, and that the total truth, assuming there are both contingent and necessary truths, must be contingent. It is easy to show some metaphysical bearings of this.

I am convinced that both Hegel and Heidegger are partly mistaken in their attitude towards what Hegel calls 'understanding', in contrast to reason or 'thought', and that Bergson was partly mistaken in defining metaphysics as the science which 'dispenses with symbols' or concepts. I too would like to 'listen to Being' or 'intuit' reality, but I think logical clarity can help in this very enterprise. Here I am close to Whitehead and Peirce.

Using formal logic will not enable one to dispense with intuition. Logicians appeal to it, too. But formal logic will help to clarify the task that intuition is being asked to perform. We shall see an example of this later (Chapter X) in connection with Bergson. Logical intuition is not to be despised, as it seems to be by Heidegger. For Heidegger's belief that Being or Reality is to be approached through an understanding of temporality, there are good reasons of a kind which logicians can, I incline to think, appreciate if they are properly presented. Becoming includes Being, as the contingent includes the necessary. Modal logic (as Prior and others have been trying to show) is the logic of temporality. Eternity or the necessary is only an abstract aspect of temporality. This does not, however, mean that God is only an aspect of man, or anything like that. The question of God, as Heidegger once suggested, is the question of 'infinite temporality', or better of eminent temporality. For this, too, the logic of carefully defined concepts gives support. We need better intuitions and better logic of concepts.

(*c*) A basic procedure in all thinking is to *exhaust possible solutions* to a problem and arrive at the best or truest by elimination of those that are unsatisfactory. 'This view is true because the others considered are false' is invalid if some possibilities have been overlooked. To be sure that one has exhausted possibilities, one must formalize the concepts. Or at least one must be so clear about them that formalization would be an easy matter. Very often what one needs are the three ideas of quantification: all, some, and none. For example, it is fallacious to say that either God is finite or he is not finite. The real disjunction is, God is in all aspects finite, in no aspect finite, or in some aspects finite and in others not. If it is denied that God has aspects, then of course the disjunction is reduced to the first two cases. But this needs to be argued for, not assumed unwittingly. If a severely extensional logic cannot recognize aspects, then so much the worse for thus limiting logic. There can be a logic of aspects.

There are people, e.g., Blanshard, who hold that all existential truths are necessary and others who hold that all are contingent. But neither party can justify itself merely by attacking the other. Both must also show reason for excluding 'some are and some are not'. To be sure, one would expect a reasonable principle for the division. Truths do not just happen to be necessary rather than contingent, or *vice versa*, as some people happen to get hit by lightning. But all the same there may for good reasons be two modally contrasting kinds of existential truth. The implausibility of Blanshard's position has no logical force of itself to justify the popularity of the contrary extreme.

The resources of formal logic to prove exhaustiveness are important philosophically for two reasons. Not only have philosophers habitually sought to justify their positions by refuting others; but we have every reason from intellectual history and the nature of man to think that this method must be followed. The idea that one can somehow hit on the manifest truth and simply forget about alternatives as mere curiosities receives little support from experience. As Popper has so well shown, in empirical inquiry at least, falsification is the most crucial operation. I hold that this is true in non-empirical inquiry also. But unless possible solutions can be exhausted, there is no reason why elimination should bring us to our goal. What we need is to put our views into finite sets of possible doctrines. I call these sets 'position matrices'. Only if they can be formalized can their exhaustiveness be proved. Anyone who says 'all' must show why 'some' or 'none' would not be better.

And he who says 'all or none' must justify the omission of 'some'. And so with other comparably abstract conceptions that form a complete set.

IV. *History of philosophy*

For suggestions from which to derive significant position matrices, and also for help in finding reasons favouring the elimination (ideally at least) of all but one of the possibilities, we should consult the history of philosophy (recall I*b*).

(*a*) The great philosophers of the past are not to be dismissed as casually as many are now doing. True, their convictions are not binding upon us. Human fallibility is a valid axiom, and it applies to contemporary philosophical fashions, which I cannot believe are as definitive as some imagine. However, we do have advantages over our ancestors. We have at least one opportunity they lacked: we can start where they left off. But we may or may not use this opportunity. When Malcolm (a writer I admire) wrote his book *Dreaming*, he made no use whatever of the most careful study of the subject ever made by a philosopher. True I hardly know how he could have used it except by not writing any such book as the one he did write.

(*b*) The customary way of looking at the history of philosophy is inadequate for the purpose just explained. With a few exceptions (Wolfson, Lovejoy), what writers give us is a history of important figures, not of important ideas. Minor points by great philosophers are dealt with, often with loving care, but major points by minor philosophers are missed. One reason for this is that the historians have not sufficiently considered beforehand what the important ideas might be. In doing general history good common sense, shrewdness, and broad culture enable the historian to know what the important possibilities for human action are, but in doing history of philosophy more than this is required. One must have in mind some carefully worked-out system of possible positions on various problems in order to decide what in intellectual history is most worth knowing. Here position matrices, made exhaustive by formal logical means, are valuable. With such schemes in mind the historian can ask himself, who has held position (1) out of a set of, say, three possible positions arising from a given matrix, and who has held positions (2) or (3)? It may then turn out that all the major philosophers missed one position, while some minor philosophers did not. This has in my view actually happened.

Thus before Whitehead no major philosopher had held a view of God very close to his view, but a number of minor ones (nearly all, perhaps, unknown to Whitehead) had done so, including one of my Harvard teachers, and myself as an immature participant in philosophical debate. For several centuries the view had been slowly gaining adherents, but these are missing from histories of philosophy. This is one of several reasons why the philosophical world was poorly prepared to evaluate Whitehead with some sense of the issues that concerned him. Again, Whitehead's view, according to which momentary realities, or unit-events, are the concrete entities rather than enduring substances or individual things and persons, seems to those accustomed to seeing the history of philosophy as only the history of Western philosophy an abrupt break with metaphysical traditions (setting aside Hume and his disciples as sceptics rather than metaphysicians). And some have thought such a view showed the dominance of relativity physics in Whitehead's thinking. But in fact countless Buddhists had for two thousand years taken a partly similar view, and some of them at least were constructive metaphysicians, very different from Hume. Moreover, the Buddhist interest in the positive ethico-religious value of the 'no soul, no substance' doctrine is very vividly present in Whitehead, with or without Buddhist influence upon him. Thus Whitehead's physics can hardly be *the* reason for his position. Moreover, the charge that Whitehead is undermining ordinary speech, or vainly attempting to discredit such speech, is less relevant than it may to some appear, since neither Whitehead nor the Buddhists have had any quarrel with ordinary practical uses of pronouns or proper names. In Whitehead, at least, it is explicitly made a criterion of sound philosophizing that a good meaning is found for these uses in their normal contexts. But there are purposes and contexts other than the ordinary ones for which the ordinary idioms are insufficient. And these extraordinary purposes and contexts are no new invention by Whitehead, but pervade the intellectual history of much of mankind for two millennia.

Buddhists are scarcely minor philosophers, though they have

generally been taken as such in the West. Buddhism is *the* international alternative to the religious traditions of Judaic origin. We can no longer ignore it. That we have done so is another reason why Whitehead's challenge found a partly unprepared public. Apart from this, an event language is the only clear alternative to a substance language (in spite of all the attempts to find a third possibility), and hence it cannot be an unimportant idea, no matter who has or has not defended it.

V.   *The principle of least paradox*

Every philosophical position strikes some intelligent persons as paradoxical. Hence no position can be argued for merely on the ground that other positions present paradoxes. One must decide which paradoxes are the really fatal ones, in comparison with those of contending positions. To effect this comparison one must make use of position matrices.

A philosopher once argued that the 'natural' view of memory must be false, since it led to the paradox that the past can be present, which is contradictory. But the other fellow's paradox tends to seem a contradiction while one's own seems only a difficulty. Is there no contradiction in the idea that the entire content of memory is merely present rather than past? I think myself that the natural view here gives the very definition of memory, and that there cannot be a contradiction in supposing that past events can be and are directly present in or to present experience. In spite of the author mentioned, and also Russell, 'presented now' is not the same as 'happening now' (supposing the presented is an event). The seeming contradiction derives from ambiguity. But 'memory has nothing past as its datum' says to my understanding that in memory nothing is remembered. And this is indeed a contradiction!

When one compares all the implications of the natural view of memory, properly and carefully qualified, with those of the unqualified denial that events can be literally given in, present to, later events, I find the least paradox on the side of the former. But the philosopher referred to (he is now dead) didn't even see the possibility of anyone deliberately taking this view. Yet Peirce, Bergson, Whitehead, and other extremely intelligent persons had taken it, not in the least because they overlooked the apparent contradiction in 'the past event is present', or in 'what no longer exists is a constituent of what now exists'. Rather they see ambiguity in taking 'present' to mean exclusively 'happening now', when their theory only requires 'is a constituent of what is happening now' (as the object is a constituent of the subject intuiting it); also ambiguity in 'no longer exists' as synonym for 'past'. Past events do not exist, or are not present, *in the same sense* as they once did or were, but they may yet be, in a genuine sense, still real and still present. The new event cannot be in the old, but the old can be in the new. A novel whole can contain parts which are not novel. Novelty is inclusive, for the combination of old and new is always new, not old. (This is an anticipatory example of VI below.) Becoming is the creation of novel wholes with non-novel elements. Bergson, Montague, and Whitehead are among the few who have seen this. Hence their 'cumulative' theory of process, or of process as 'creative synthesis'.

VI. *The principle of inclusive contrast*

Ideas express contrasts. Even so general an idea as 'reality' requires that some meaning be assigned to 'unreality'. For instance, we can say that while every act of intending or thinking is, so far as it occurs, itself a reality, the act may or may not succeed in its purpose of referring to something independent of itself. If it succeeds, then both the act and the intended object are realities; otherwise only the act is real, the object unreal – i.e., nothing is successfully designated.

(*a*) An idea either simply coincides with 'reality' or it applies to some but not all conceivable things. Thus to say, 'every possible entity is also necessary', is to destroy the contrast between possible, actual, and necessary as distinctive aspects of reality. This is to my mind a fatal objection to Spinoza's most basic doctrine. But I believe that it also casts reasonable suspicion upon unqualified or classical determinism. 'Real' or causal possibility ought not to coincide with causal necessity. Yet the assumption of this coincidence is the essential feature of classical determinism.

(*b*) Though some metaphysical generalizations merely explicate 'reality' as such, strict metaphysical generality can stop short of literally 'everything'. It is enough if a concept applies with complete and *a priori* universality within one logical level:

thus 'everything *concrete*', or 'everything *abstract*', or even 'everything on the highest level of abstractness'. For reality is distinguishable categorially or *a priori* into concrete and abstract, and there is at least one further distinction that is also *a priori* (see Chapter XII). Then there is the distinction, in its pure generality likewise non-empirical, between *singular* and *aggregate*, the full importance of which dawned for the first time in intellectual history upon the mind of Leibniz, but which many even today do not appreciate.

(*c*) Though basic or *a priori* concepts express dualities, such as concrete-abstract, relative-absolute, dependent-independent, subject-object, it is the error of dualism to take the relation between the contrasting poles as a mere conjunction or 'and'. 'The concrete and the abstract' need not be a third entity, but may be the concrete as containing the abstract (the 'ontological' or 'Aristotelian' principle – Whitehead). Similarly, the total situation of 'the dependent and the independent' is itself dependent, as can easily be proved, and in spite of a rather common contrary belief. Thus the ultimacy of dualities does not validate dualism. There can be an all-inclusive form of reality, within which every contrast falls. After all, a whole contrasts with its parts, yet 'the whole and its parts' is no more than the whole. This consideration seems often overlooked. The general rule I call the *principle of inclusive contrast*.

VII. *The principle of generality*

Since in metaphysics we are seeking ultimate or *a priori* generality, beyond all contingent special cases, every concept considered as even possibly metaphysical should be freed of limitations which do not seem inherent in its meaning. For example, 'experience' is of course not metaphysical if taken as equivalent to 'human experience'. The only chance of arriving at metaphysical ultimacy from this concept is if it can be seen that the special characters imposed by 'human' are very special indeed. Even 'animal experience' could only be an empirical, not an *a priori* idea. We must ask if there are not dimensions or variables within our experience whose range of possible values in principle infinitely exceed the range of these values found in our, or even in animal, experience. For example, memory or recollection with us stretches back many years, but not for millions of years. Also we are not capable of experiencing events occupying a few milliseconds, and remembering events previous by milliseconds. But the mere idea of memory seems quite neutral to such limitations. In such ways, and there are many, we can divest experience of its contingent specificities.

Take another example: the idea of intuition in Kant's sense of that aspect of experience in which we encounter the concrete and particular (Kant says, the individual) rather than the abstract or universal. We encounter the concrete in memory and perception. Remembering is as distinct from mere thinking as perception is. It is in principle just as direct. Evidence of mediation, whether by bodily process or by conceptual interpretation is as strong in the case of perception as of memory. Both give us particulars. What, then, is the concept of intuition which expresses what the two forms have in common? If there is none, then our metaphysical search is balked at an essential point. A unitary principle for both might be that the experiencing is simultaneous with the experienced, as perception is thought by many to be (though hardly with support from science), or it might be that both are experiences of something past, even though in the most direct case barely so. Thus perception would be assimilated to memory rather than *vice versa*. Non-metaphysical writers are often content to stop short of any sharp posing of this question, which merely shows that they are not much interested in one kind of intellectual work. Once the question is sharply put, the answer seems almost irresistible: direct experience is of the nearest past, not of the absolutely simultaneous.

It may seem that if memory and perception both give us the past, one of them should be superfluous. How are they to be distinguished? Quite simply: memory gives us past events of our own human experiencing; perception gives past events of our bodily members and environment. The difference is in what is given, not in the temporal structure of the givenness. Perception is 'impersonal memory', what is ordinarily called memory is the personal form. Obviously both are needed. Common to the two is what Whitehead calls 'prehension', intuition of the antecedently real. This is a specimen of what I mean by metaphysical discovery. It is no mere matter of human psychology. There are good reasons for holding that only what is already real could be given to any experience in any world. Intuition of the past seems a paradox to some, but if they had really tried to conceive how something strictly simultaneous with the experience could be given they might see where the real paradox would be.

Is it an accident that three of the greatest metaphysicians who have dealt with the question of the possible ultimacy of experience as infinitely less specific than human experience (Leibniz, Peirce, and Whitehead) were all great mathematicians? It is mathematicians, as Peirce himself pointed out, who tend to seek generality beyond generality. Again, is it accidental that it was Whitehead (not quite anticipated by Bergson or Peirce) who first discerned the common principle of memory and perception, intuition of antecedent events? People with merely literary training often have little sense for this kind of thing. G. E. Moore is an example.

A final illustration of the principle of generality. Kant inherited two concepts: substance and causality. The one, he said, gives persistence through change, the other, objective temporal order. Bergson (also initially a mathematician) began a process of fusing the two ideas which Whitehead completed. What persists from the past into the present is the past itself. This, in one aspect, is memory, in another, perception – generalizing both quite beyond the merely human forms. It is also causality, which is indeed essential to temporal order. All of these are but aspects of intuitive inheritance or prehension, the relation of relations. Substantiality is a special, concentrated, and orderly form of 'route' of inheritance. To have thought all this out so clearly seems to me a feat comparable to Einstein's. (Like Einstein, Whitehead also made some grandiose mistakes.) Generalized epistemic relations constitute the spatio-temporal causal order of changing things and persons. And there is no need for a mysterious Aristotelian 'matter', knowable 'only by analogy', as that which the present receives from the past. Events of experiencing themselves are the indestructible stuff out of which new events are produced. The rest is verbiage rather than genuine analogy.

VIII.   *The principle of balanced definiteness*

There are people who are struck by some one partial aspect

of a subject and can see no other. They are the 'unbalanced' or 'one-sided' people. There are also those whose thinking is hopelessly vague, unclear, or ambiguous. The ideal of reasonableness is to *combine balance with definiteness:* to see sharply, and all around a subject – as Lincoln put it, to 'bound it on the North, the East, the South, and the West'. The temptations to imbalance and to lazy indefiniteness are such that only an agonizing struggle for balanced definiteness can suffice. This struggle is what I conceive philosophy, at its best, to be.

In some vague or imperfect fashion everyone, and the 'ordinary language' used by men generally, must be in touch with philosophic truths. For these are the truths which, being by their generality implicitly relevant to every concrete context, cannot be and are not wholly dispensed with by anyone. But it does not follow that everyone is explicitly conscious of them. In addition, any bright person will have flashes of definite but incomplete or one-sided insight into such truths. The vague whole truth and the sharp half-truth about philosophic fundamentals – for these we scarcely need professional or full-time philosophers. It is the sharp vision of the whole truth we ask of the philosophic profession.

Obviously by 'whole truth' we mean nothing in the least like all factual and scientific knowledge, welded into a perfect system. We merely mean the whole truth about certain very basic and therefore extremely abstract principles pervasive of knowledge and reality. These principles not only do not sum up *all* factual knowledge, they do not (if 'fact' is used in a strict sense) contain *any* such knowledge at all; even though until they are applied factually they have only limited interest and value.

Vague totality and sharp one-sidedness, these are easy enough in philosophic matters. The very animals have the first. Thus every animal avoids the extremes of determinism and the opposite view that the future is in no degree predictable; for it acts as if it took it for granted that the future is partly settled and foreseeable, and partly in process of being presently decided. It so acts because there is no other way to act. The belief in a wholly determinate future is not translateable into action, and neither is belief in a wholly indeterminate one. It is language (subtly misused) which makes either 'absolute order' or 'absolute chaos' a problem. Action can only consist, not in simple foreseeing, but in step by step deciding, of the future, with each step in its concreteness left open until the previous step has been taken, and even then not simply predicted but created, settled by *fiat*; however, action can never wholly ignore the past and suppose that what can be or is being made to happen is unconnected with what has happened. Every animal views the future in the light of the past, but without ever simply deducing it from the past. The future, for all life, is what the past implies *plus* step by step decisions, none of which is concretely given until it has actually been taken. This is an example of the sanity inherent in life as such. If avoidance of the absurd philosophic extremes were all that we required, we would only need to be viable organisms, uncontaminated by theory. Take again the contrast of optimism and pessimism. No subhuman speechless animal is a mere optimist or a mere pessimist. It expects both good and evil, and acts accordingly. Only *thinking* animals get into one-sided views, such as that all apparent evil is really but good in disguise, or all apparent good but evil in disguise (Schopenhauer).

From the foregoing, sufficiently reflected upon, it seems to follow that metaphysical mistakes are due to man's rationality. More specifically, they are due to his symbolic power, primarily speech. Here contemporary philosophers might well agree, if they can agree upon anything: metaphysical blunders are due to the misuse of words. In this the 'linguistic' school is quite right. Factual blunders can be made without words, as when ducks come to wooden decoys. But ducks cannot be enticed into a metaphysical trap, such as 'all becoming is an illusion', or 'all permanence is an illusion'. Sub-linguistic life seems safe from such perversities. Obviously super-linguistic or divine life, if there can be such a thing, must also be safe from them. Thus it is the middle ground of language which generates metaphysical error, below and above which there can only be metaphysical truth, on the one hand expressed in mere action and feeling, on the other in super-linguistic consciousness.

Animals do not confront the problem, 'Can I know other minds?'. They just proceed to interpret their fellow animals as best they can, sensitive to the possibility of making mistakes, which they gradually learn to avoid where mistakes bring unpleasant consequences. Thus they have, in effect, the metaphysical truth that there is fallible knowledge of other minds. And 'one to whom all hearts are open' also confronts no problem of other mind; he just experiences or perceives the feelings and thoughts of all, not as his own but as theirs. So he must enjoy the metaphysical truth that there is infallible knowledge of other mind, and also the truth that there is fallible knowledge; for he perceives the mistakes of the others in their mutual interpretations and realizes that they cannot wholly avoid these.

Language is our means of transcending the merely pragmatic or emotional sanity of the other animals and achieving a status between it and the fully conscious divine sanity. The price of this ascent is metaphysical blundering. Language is not foolproof, and its metaphysical use is not necessarily the safest. Verbal formulations in metaphysics are simplest when they state half-truths. For example, 'God is infinite, creatures are finite'. No way of distinguishing them could be simpler than that. Such simplicity cannot but be initially pleasing. And one can conceal the essential crudity of the procedure by multiplying virtually synonymous formulations as though they added something. Thus: God is immutable, man is mutable; God is creator, man is creature. He is self-sufficient or self-existent, man is dependent, derivative. As Thomas Aquinas showed, once for all, these merely say the same thing in different ways. What Thomas did not show, but merely assumed, was that this 'same thing', in its unqualified simplicity, is correct. When he has proved the 'unmoved mover', he remarks, 'and this all men call God'. But do they? Should they? Is this really what men have worshipped? Or is it a theory, too simple and crude to be right, *about* the one who is worshipped? I am deeply confident it is the latter.

Again, what is simpler than 'all things change' (or 'only what always exists really exists') or 'all is one' (or 'there are many things')? To take such a half-truth (or less-than-half-truth) and expound it brilliantly is relatively easy, if one is born with an agile mind and happens to turn one's wits in a philosophic direction. Two men of recent times illustrate this on a high level. F. H. Bradley's career exhibits a very clever man exploiting the element of truth in metaphysical monism (and the devil take the truth in metaphysical pluralism); Russell is a very clever man exploiting the element of truth in metaphysical pluralism (and the devil take the truth in metaphysical monism). Neither was in the full sense responsive to the philosopher's ultimate calling, which is to transcend such warring exaggerations. James said, rightly I think, that Bradley was 'perverse'. But he himself was too close for comfort to the contrary perverseness.

Another example. Ryle's treatment of mind is, in spite of a few 'cagey' qualifications, essentially a very agile exploitation of the element of truth in behaviourism. There is no real attempt to see the other side of this ancient controversy. An equally extreme bias in the opposite direction is hard to find in recent writings. But E. S. Brightman, or going farther back, Bishop Berkeley, might do. And Husserl, in some at least of his writings, is a fair example, to which there is some reason to suspect Ryle was in part reacting.

The treacherous attraction of ultra-simplicity in the attempted verbalization of sanity is particularly dangerous because a sophisticated man can find plenty of use for his capacity to think in subtle and complex fashion without in essentials renouncing the ultra-simplicity of his basic position. Half-truths treated as truths yield stunning paradoxes and arouse vigorous opposition (coming especially from those wedded to contrary half-truths), and in the resulting controversies there is plenty of scope for people who are not *merely* simple-minded, even though all the time they *are* simple-minded in some of their basic commitments. As Descartes shrewdly said, brilliant men rather like to espouse absurd views, because they can display their brilliance in seeking to cover up the initial absurdities.

A tell-tale sign of the extremist is his fondness for the contrary extreme as his opponent or target of criticism. Thus Russell, the extreme external relations man, attacks Bradley and Hegel, who have little (or no) use for anything but internal relations. And Bradley or Blanshard, partisans of internal relations (so far as they admit relations at all), like nothing better than to refute Hume, James, or Russell. Neither side has much zest for the examination of the moderate position, such as that of Peirce, Dewitt Parker, Whitehead, or Hartshorne, who have recognized both types of relatedness in systematic interweaving. This neglect is not accidental. The preference for neatness, simplicity, trenchancy, which leads a man to adopt an extreme position also causes him to sympathize with and respect the same preference, turned in the opposite direction, in his opponent. (It is somewhat similar in politics: the extreme right and left like to belabour each other, and sensible positions are felt to be unimpressive by both.) The result of these tendencies is that the balanced truth is chronically unpopular and neglected. The future of speculative philosophy depends in no small measure, I suggest, upon the possibility of philosophers acquiring the self-knowledge and the self-control to overcome this defect. And note that not only do the extremes within metaphysics conspire, as it were, to turn attention away from the balanced truth to themselves, but extreme anti-metaphysicians join in the conspiracy. Simplicity, trenchancy – whether gained by having 'no' metaphysics, or by having, within metaphysics, the One but not the many, or the many but not the One, or necessity but not contingency or *vice versa* – these are all cut to a similar pattern, and what is ignored is only the truth, which is not quite so simple as all that.

(It is impossible not to wonder if, with all their faults, my own writings have not escaped critical examination as much as they have partly for the reason that the extremists have been so busy with each other. I have never, in the simple, unbalanced sense, been an absolutist or relativist, a rationalist or empiricist, a believer, atheist or agnostic, a monist or pluralist, a partisan of being or becoming, of universals or particulars. If this meant that I had merely affirmed the one 'and' the other in each case, this would justify ignoring me as a mere eclectic. But this also I have not done.)

The above considerations of method may not be the only ones by which I have been more or less consciously guided in my metaphysical thinking, but they perhaps suffice to show that if my work has been somewhat apart from what is mainly occurring in philosophy today, this is not an expression of any unadulterated methodological *naïveté* or unawareness of what others have been doing. Perhaps my greatest mistakes have been (1) in not stressing more than I have the extent of my agreement with 'ordinary language' partisans and (2) in not cultivating formal logic, including intuitionist logic, more than I have. At these points I might offer the old injunction, do as I say, not as I do.

The present age is deeply sceptical about the possibility of philosophical agreement – apart perhaps from the linguistic analysts who sometimes seem remarkably confident that they are about to reach universally acceptable insights. It may well be probable that no such principles as the above will be at all widely accepted, or that so far as accepted they will be applied in extremely diverse ways. I do not profess to know how far philosophers can arrive at the same truths, and I admit that so long as they do not, no one can be sure how far he has arrived at truth. Insecurity in this matter seems to be our human portion. However, I am not modest enough to take it for granted that I could be right only when agreeing with all, or even with a majority, of scholars. Metaphysical insight may be partly good luck of birth and training. I am willing to give reasons for my views and to consider the counter-reasons of others. As Popper so well says, this willingness is the indispensable requirement of rationality. What eventually comes out of rational human inquiry is for the last generation of men, if there is such, to discover.

VI

A LOGIC OF ULTIMATE CONTRASTS

THE conceptual structure of the neo-classical philosophy can be partly indicated by a rather simple yet comprehensive table. The aim is less to demonstrate than to explicate, and I shall not conceal certain puzzles that trouble me. The point is to show the interconnections between concepts and in so far to exhibit the philosophy as a system.

In every experience, if it is sufficiently reflective, certain abstract contrasts may be noted as somehow relevant, e.g., complex-simple, effect-cause. These contrasts are the ultimate or metaphysical contrarieties. A basic doctrine of this book is that the two poles of each contrast stand or fall together; neither is simply to be denied or explained away, or called 'unreal'. For if either pole is real the contrast itself, including both poles, is so. The unique contrast, real-unreal, may seem to violate this rule. But in the first place this contrast need not be taken as relevant to every reflective experience. Divine experience would consider the unreal either as the really possible ($9a$) or as the mistaken but themselves really occurrent fancies of lesser modes of experience. In the second place, even we can see that acts of fancying or mistakenly believing are real occurrences, so that the unreal is also a form of reality.

Though polarities are ultimate, it does not follow that the two poles are in every sense on an equal status. As mere abstract concepts they are indeed correlatives, each requiring the other for its own meaning. But if not the concepts but their examples or instances are considered, on one side are the dependent, inclusive entities, on the other the independent, included ones. One side forms, in the given context, the total reality, the other consists of mere though independent constituents or aspects. Thus the admission of ultimate dualities is one doctrine, dualism is quite another. The concept expressing the total reality is the entire truth, not because the correlative contrary concept can be dismissed or negated, but because the referents of the latter are included in those of the former, while the converse inclusion does not obtain. Thus a basic asymmetry is involved (Chapter X). Here is the essential difference between my philosophy and that of Weiss.

Taking into account the threefold distinction: concept X, contrary concept Y, and Z, the inclusive member in the given set of examples, we see that our dualities are enclosed in triadicities. Thus we meet Peirce's requirement: think in trichotomies not mere dichotomies, the latter being crude and misleading by themselves. To contrast, say, concreteness and abstractness, the two concepts or universals, is blind unless one bears in mind that concreteness is itself an extreme abstraction (to adapt a precious remark of Russell's) and that an instance of concreteness is by no means the concept over again, but something incomparably richer. As Plato and even Aristotle never quite saw, concrete actualities are the whole of what is (*pace* Weiss). There is also a deep truth in Peirce's contention that triads are incomparably more adequate than dyads and in a sense than tetrads, as intellectual instruments. Weiss's fourfold system, dualistically interpreted with respect to each pair, seems a brilliant illustration, as such a stroke of genius, of how *not* to build a metaphysical system. It is a regression from Aristotle, Bergson, Peirce, James, Dewey, and Whitehead, none of whom is finally or in intention a dualist even with respect to a single pair of basic concepts.

METAPHYSICAL CONTRARIES

r terms (Peirce's Seconds, Thirds)	*a* terms (Peirce's Firsts)
1*r* relative, dependent, internally related	1*a* absolute, independent, externally related
2*r* experience, subject	2*a* things experienced, objects
3*r* whole, inclusive	3*a* constituents, included
4*r* effect, conditioned	4*a* cause, condition (*sine qua non*)

5r later, successor	5a earlier, predecessor
6r becoming, nascent, being created	6a in being, already created
7r temporal, succeeding some, preceding others	7a non temporal as i. primordial, preceding every ii. everlasting, succeeding every
8r concrete, definite, particular	8a abstract, indefinite, universal
9r actual	9a potential
10r contingent	10a necessary
11r a portion, P, of process as past	11a earlier futuristic outline of P
12r finite	12a infinite
13r discrete	13a continuous
14r complex, with constituents	14a simple, without (or with fewer) constituents
15r singular, member ('mind')	15a composite, group, mass ('matter')
16r singular event, so and so now, individual state or actuality	16a so and so through change, individual being or existent
17r individual	17a specific character
18r specific character	18a generic character
19r generic character	19a metaphysical category
20r God now, divine state or actuality	20a God as primordial and everlasting, divine essence and existence
21r God now	21a God and the world as they just have been

Rules of Interpretation:

I. Proportionality: as an *r*-item in a specified context is to its *a*-correlate (say, 1r to 1a), so (*mutatis mutandis*) is any other *r*-item to its *a*-correlate (say, 2r to 2a). Thus (No. 2) an experience depends upon the things experienced, a subject upon things given to it, but these are independent of it.

II. Two-way, yet asymmetrical necessity: an *r*-item necessitates (10a) its particular contextual *a*-correlates; an *a*-item necessitates only that a class of suitable *r*-correlates be non-empty, the particular members of the class being (10*r*) contingent (others might have existed in their place). (In the case – 19*a* – of metaphysical categories, the class of suitable *r*-correlates is the widest class of particular actualities, in the case of generic or specific characters the *r*-correlate may be merely that the idea of the character is imagined in some actual experience.)

Applications. Rule I tells us that experiences or subjects depend upon their objects (Nos. 1, 2), though these do not depend upon them; however, by rule II we know that a thing experienced could not have been or remained entirely unexperienced by some suitable subject or other. Thus to be is to be experienced, but if S experiences O, O could have existed without being experienced by S. Berkeley's proposition is either correct, ambiguous, or erroneous, according to how we take it.

Using both rules (and Nos. 4, 1, 10) we see that a given effect depends upon conditions that did not depend upon and did not necessitate it; but yet the conditions did necessitate that some effect in the 'suitable class' should become actual (9*r*). How narrow or wide the suitable class is defines the question at issue in intelligent discussions of 'determinism', discussions that seek to explicate rather than explain away the asymmetry characterizing our intuition of causality, and therefore avoid taking with entire literalness the symmetrical or bi-conditional necessity implied by 'necessary and sufficient condition'. If fully concrete or definite effects are in question (8*r*) there are no such conditions. The phrase is only a first approximation to an explication of the causal principle.

Since an *r*-item always expresses the total reality being considered (3*r*), the scope of the *a*-items is to be determined by the scope assigned their *r*-correlates. This is especially important in certain cases. For instance, 5*a* and 9*a* together say that the possibility of a certain actuality is earlier than that actuality. What is possible for today is determined by what happened yesterday. In this sense possibility precedes actuality. True enough, what is actual today determines the possibilities for tomorrow; in this sense the actual precedes the possible. But the possibility we are talking about must, by the principle of scope mentioned above, be determined by considering a given actuality, say something that happened this morning, and asking about *its* possibility. And this will be found in its antecedent causes, i.e., earlier events (4*a*, 5*a*). Similarly, a cause or condition is a *sine qua non* (4*a*), necessary (10*a*) for a given later event, which (in its full actuality or concreteness) is contingent rather than necessary, given the condition (even all the antecedent conditions). Again 'independent' (1*a*) does not mean, independent of everything but only of the dependent factor taken as instance of 1*r*; nor does 'dependent' entail dependence upon everything, but only upon whatever the *r*-case in question does depend upon. Thus an event may depend upon antecedent events but be independent of subsequent ones. Indeed this follows from Nos. 1, 5, and 10.

Dependence simply means the impossibility of existing without the thing depended upon – i.e., *sine qua non possible*. From this we see the perversity of using the term 'absolute' to mean the all-inclusive reality. A thing cannot exist lacking any of its constituents (even though something very similar might exist lacking some of these), hence nothing is quite so dependent or relative as the inclusive or total reality. That the all-inclusive cannot depend upon something 'outside itself', something it does not include, is mere tautology; it will still depend upon all there is, and will be the most completely relative of all things.

Although, given a definite pair of *r* and *a* items, the first will be contingent granted the second, and the second necessary granted the first, yet there is always (Rule II) a generic necessity running in the other direction. Thus an independent factor must have been or become constituent in *some* whole or other, things experienced (2*a*) or objects must have had or have this status for *some* experience or subject, universals (8*a*) must be embodied, or at least entertained as ideas, in *some* concrete actualities (8*r*, 9*r*), causes must produce some suitable effects. The necessity of an *a*-correlate is particular and definite, given an *r*-item, but that of the *r*-correlate, given an *a*-item, is generic or indefinite. This is a basic asymmetry. From an *a*-item to its *r*-correlate is a creative step, one that must come *somehow*, but not in any fully predetermined manner; while that from an *r*-item to its *a*-correlate or correlates is a mere matter of analysis, of finding what is already there. Prospective freedom, which cannot be simply unexercised and is always within limits, and retrospective necessity form the directionality of creativity as at once preservative and enriching of reality, adding to, never diminishing, its determinateness.

Using Rule I we see that wholes ($3r$), metaphysically regarded, are not 'organic' (see Chapter VIII), since their constituents are independent of them. The constituents may be themselves wholes dependent upon *their* constituents. 'Absolute', i.e., non-relative, of course means 'in the specified context', not necessarily in every context. The context is the particular whole, or class of wholes taken as instance of $3r$. The limitation of the rules to a context is a principle of relativity, and thus an example of $1r$. Like most metaphysical categories, this one is so general that it even applies in some appropriate fashion to categories themselves.

Since 'absolute' is merely the negative of relative, it is clear that the basic principle of the entire table is relativity. The idolatry of absoluteness which disfigures the history of metaphysics needs to be unmasked and if possible done away with. The real absolute is relativity itself, since its limitations are provided by its own reflexivity, or self-applicability, together with negation. And negation is a subordinate principle in the sense that finally we must affirm the conjunction of true positive and true negative propositions to state the whole truth. (Denying a conjunction leaves the truth of the elementary propositions indeterminate.)

Proportionality and Nos. 2, 4, 5 tell us that experiences follow (rather than being simultaneous with) their given objects and are their effects; also (No. 3) that they include the objects, which yet ($1a$) are not dependent upon them. Thus idealists who held that objects are 'in' the mind and realists who held that objects are 'independent of' (particular) subjects are both in so far entirely right. Both erred grievously, however, in equating 'included in' with 'depends upon', an equation that obtains only if all wholes are taken as organic. Since it is a certain brand of idealism rather than its critics who have held this doctrine, one can only marvel that the realists should have shared the belief (unwittingly, it seems), in this special application.

A curiously similar confusion occurred in the Aristotelian tradition. States of an individual were taken as accidental predicates 'in', and *therefore* dependent upon, the individual for their existence.

But this 'therefore' presupposes that a constituent depends upon its whole. Quite the contrary. Constituents may have to be in *some* whole, but the particular whole is accidental or contingent. It is true that a man's state depends upon the prior existence of the same individual man, but not because the state is in the man; rather, because, as ordinary language, with profound justice has it, the man is 'in a state'. A whole depends upon its constituents, and one's past individuality is a constituent of one's present wholeness. States are *more* than identical individualities and contain them, not *vice versa*. But for that very reason they presuppose and depend upon them (apart from events not ordered into any individual sequence, such as microphysics seems to deal with).

From 3*r*, *a* and 5*r*, *a* we deduce that process is cumulative, as Bergson said, the later including the earlier. From 1*r*, *a* and 4*r*, *a* we see that causal dependence, taken strictly, runs backward only (a cause can be 'necessary', but it cannot be 'sufficient' to guarantee what concretely happens later). This does not mean that nothing can be predicted, but only that prediction is in principle abstract and incomplete and causal determinacy likewise. That details of the future are hidden from us is not solely a result of our being, as animal knowers, limited in perceptual and reasoning capacities, but expresses a metaphysical principle. That we do not fully know the past, on the contrary, is merely our human-animal limitation.

There is, it must be admitted, an element of idealization in the relations symbolized by the second and third rows. Ordinary subjects, at least, do not without qualification include the things they experience; but then they do not without qualification experience them. In memory I experience my past, but how inadequately, with what loss of vivid detail, accessible to introspection! One might argue, in spite of 14*r*, *a*, that the world we experience is much more complex than our experience of it. But again, we experience, yet do not experience, this world. If there is an ineradicable paradox in this philosophy here it may be. But the defence is that divine experiences can fulfil the principle in question in that they can adequately experience and hence adequately include their objects, and that even our experiences include in proportion as they adequately experience what they experience.

It is to be understood that by experienced objects is not meant intentional objects. Thus if I think of 'my future', my given object is not any concrete event later than the present. Givenness, in this philosophy, is one thing, intentionality or symbolic reference is another. That we lack *absolute* power to distinguish these introspectively is not surprising. Such power would be divine. But we can with relative success make the distinction. Even in illusions and dreams just prior bodily states are felt, states which must be there and be genuinely given. Intentionality adds more or less correct or incorrect beliefs about the external environment and the future, these additions being more or less at our risk.

The common objection to a 'causal theory' of perception that if experiences are effects then the real objects are unknown causes hidden behind the effects, is a confusion. The given things are not effects upon the experience, as a kind of stuff moulded by hidden influences; instead, the given things are the real things, and the effect is simply the experience itself, as experience of those very things. To infer that, not the things but the effects which they cause are the data is to assume that an experience has itself as object, i.e., that the subject-object relation is an identity. The causal theory is not responsible for this blunder. Givenness is a genuine relation, and it requires two terms. So does the causal relation. The experience of O is conditioned by O as antecedently there. And O itself is thus given. The experience as effect *intuits its own causes*, it does not have, as datum, itself the effect of those causes. How could this confusion ever have arisen? Is Kant free from it? I think not.

Since in memory we have as datum not just one previous experience but (a) an entire sequence of experiences, each experience in the past having its own memories, and since also (b) these past experiences included perceptions, in each of which its own causes were given, it is not merely the causes of present experience which are now given, but the causes of those causes indefinitely far back. We have a genuine sample of cause-effect relations. All we have to do to know the approximate state of the contemporary world and its probable future is to extrapolate the lines of causality already accessible to us.

By contrast, if the data of experience were simultaneous we should have a cross-section of process but no insight into its derivations and hence into its destiny. Symmetrical relations, such as those of simultaneity, are never the key to directional order (Chapter X), which is what we need to know. The strictly simultaneous is the last thing we have to worry about, for by the time we could think about it it must already have become past. We deal with the future by interpreting the past, the absolutely present being for our knowledge the same as the nearest part of the future.

All theories of the mind-body relation, such as parallelism, which take this relation to be one of simultaneity, are uneconomical of principles, since they cannot use the temporal cause-effect relation we employ in all other explanations of dependence. Thus we get the mysteries of the two-aspect view, or the identity theory, or epiphenomenalism, or what not. Whitehead's proposal here is that we take human experiences causally to 'inherit' directly from some bodily processes, and these to inherit directly from our experiences, inheriting in each case implying temporal 'following', rather than sheer 'accompanying'. Thus the general principle of causality is all we need. And since individual genetic identity (16a) is explicable as a distinctive special case of the way in which concrete actualities are caused by, follow, and include others, sharing abstract factors in common, the concept of 'substance' is shown to be no absolute addition. Causality, substance, memory, perception, temporal succession, modality, are all but modulations of one principle of creative synthetic experiencing, feeding entirely upon its own prior products. This I regard as the most powerful metaphysical generalization ever accomplished. It has many men of genius back of it, including Bergson, perhaps Alexander, the Buddhists, and many others. But Whitehead is its greatest single creator.

A striking lesson of the table is the unreliability of certain traditional value judgments. Thus the following terms have been taken as honorific: absolute, cause, earlier (first cause), non-temporal or eternal, universal, necessary, infinite, simple. All have been used to designate deity, in contrast with inferior beings. But if the table is not utterly misleading, this value judgment entailed the exaltation of objects rather than subjects, the abstract rather than the concrete, and the possible rather than the actual. It also implied that progress from earlier to later, or causes to effects, is a descent from better to worse, from more to less, which makes pessimism a metaphysical axiom. On the contrary, on my principle the dependent is more and better than the merely independent, effects than mere causes, results than conditions, the complex than the simple.

Note that the *a*-items are more or less plainly negative or privative: not relative, not temporal, not definite, merely possible, not finite, not complex. In other cases the privative character is less obvious but readily detected: mere constituent, cause abstracting from what it produces, the earlier abstracting from what followed, what has been created already or up to a certain time only, the common element in every possibility abstracting from the differences (the necessary), the undifferentiated continuum, with no actual but only possible divisions.

It is notorious that negation presupposes something to negate. Hence, unless one is indeed bemused by the 'negative theology', one would not expect absoluteness or infinity to explain relativity or finitude, but the contrary. And certainly it is the idea of whole that gives meaning to that of constituent. Even to say that items taken together constitute a whole is to forget that 'together' is just another way to say, 'forming a whole'. Nor is it really true that the idea of number is generated by the notion of unit. On the contrary, only the idea of number in the sense of 'several' gives meaning to 'one' or 'zero' in the numerical senses. Hence the Greeks did not speak of either one or zero as 'numbers'. And they are indeed very special cases, and derivative ones. To be aware of one thing we must contrast it with at least one other, so that there is always the idea of a whole, however little stressed it may be.

Obviously it is subjectivity that gives meaning to objectivity, not *vice versa*. Intersubjectivity, and the notion of other subjects independent of the subject in question, are the only identifiable positive meanings for objectivity. The object is either merely an object, a constituent in subjects, an abstraction, or it is an antecedently real subject, or set of subjects. The endless controversies over phenomenalism and realism arise from the belief that there is some further meaning for objectivity. All over the world for thousands of years men have seen through this illusion, but have failed to make fully clear the compatibility of its avoidance with the full admission of independently real objects of our experiences. There is no contradiction at all, if one is careful to make the proper distinction between particular and generic necessity as posited by Rule II.

That subjects are later (2*r*, 5*r*) and objects earlier (2*a*, 5*a*) will surprise many. It enshrines the doctrine that, both in memory and in perception, the given entities are antecedent events. As Bergson said, perhaps as the first, it is the past which is actual, there to be experienced. The present is nascent, it is coming into being, rather than in being, and there is no definite entity to prehend. Peirce hints at this. Whitehead, so far as I know, is the first thinker in all the world to take the position with full explicitness that experiencing is *never* simultaneous with its concrete objects but always subsequent. Perception may then be called 'impersonal memory', intuition not of our own past experiences, but of past events in and around the body. The scientific facts and the metaphysical requirements fit effortlessly together, if we take this view. That we seem to perceive what is happening absolutely 'now' is a harmless exaggeration of the truth that the time-lapse for near events is negligible and that the causal stability of much of the world guarantees that what has just been happening is close to what is still happening.

Moreover, if there is an illusion of simultaneity in perceiving, there is a nicely parallel illusion in remembering. For what is 'introspection' if not very short-run memory utilized to tell us what we are *approximately* now thinking and feeling? That we are always a trifle behind ourselves in this is not only harmless but the only way to note our mental processes without interfering with them. We do not inspect our mental processes simultaneously with their occurrence. This is nonsense. But through immediate memory we can keep noticing what they have just been.

Nos. 3, 6, and 7 tell us that becoming includes being, whether in the form of the uncreated or primordial (7*ai*), or in the form of what has already become. This is the revolution first announced clearly by Bergson. Anything which does not now become is an abstraction (8*a*) from what does now become. Process, as including its own past and abstract aspects, is the reality itself (*la réalité même*). Or as Whitehead puts it: What an actuality is cannot be abstracted from how it becomes; also 'to be is to be a potential (9*a*) for every (subsequent) becoming' or every subsequent actuality (9*r*). Any subject which follows a temporal actuality will include it as object (not necessarily accessible to introspection) and will also include any non-temporal factor.

Nos. 5–14 tell us that an actuality (or the concrete or definite) becomes, is temporal, contingent, finite, discrete, and complex (or – No. 3 – a whole with independent constituents). Recalling 2*r*, we see that it is subjects which are actual, and objects which are 'potentials' (9*a*) for subsequent experiencing. What actual subjects may ever experience them they are indifferent to; but they must (Rule II) be experienced by some suitable subjects, where suitable means, 'able to experience them'. The historical idealisms and realisms are almost equally far from meeting the requirements of our table, as I hope is obvious.

The table does not directly say so, but since, as we all know, experiences can temporally follow experiences they can depend (5*r*, 7*r*) upon the prior experiences causally, and have them as objects. Thus being an experience does not conflict with being an object (for other subjects). Objectivity is not a different kind of stuff from subjectivity, but a relation into which subjectivity, by virtue of further subjectivity, can pass. Subjectivity, which (8*r*) is the concrete form of relativity, is thus the inclusive principle. Objectivity in all senses, including the scientific sense of intersubjective validity, is a function of multiple subjectivity. It refers to one of the following: (a) subjects prior to and independent of the subject under consideration, (b) potential or future subjects, (c) elements shared among subjects, i.e., common constituents (3*a*), objects (2*a*), or abstractions (8*a*) from subjective actualities.

The 'subject which can never become object' haunting some thinkers must, it seems, be either the everchanging class of 'latest subjects' that have not yet been objectified though they are about to be so, or it is subjectivity in general and as such, which is indeed an object, though a very abstract one. True, 'latest subjects' includes deity as eminent instance, and this is no obvious object, even subsequently. Here is mystery enough, perhaps.

Objectivity as a special kind of stuff is the result of a very natural illusion, the key to the removal of which is No. 15. But we must first deal with a puzzle which this pair presents.

No. 15, with No. 3, seems to say that a member of a group contains the group; but not *vice versa*. Are not members constituents, as in No. 3? Also is not the group more complex than any single member (No. 14)? But the question is, what makes a group a whole, a single entity? If members are enduring individuals (Nos. 5, 16*a*, 17*r*), they interact, unless spatially remote relative to their duration, and therefore groups (so far as composed of individuals) tend to be organic wholes rather than metaphysical ones (composed of states). This means that each member, in his own way, sums up the group, and so the complexity of the group tends to reappear in its members. However, the group must be considered either as subject or as object, for there is no third possibility in this system. As object, as something given and so far as it is given to someone, the group possesses the full complexity of the members only when God is the subject. Otherwise there will be partiality, abstraction, failure to fully experience and include the members. As object for God the group will indeed exceed the members distributively in complexity. But hold – not quite. For God is the supreme member. And the subject in principle exceeds the object in complexity, so far as the subject adequately experiences the object. Thus the group, even as including God, taken as object is simpler than God as the not yet objectified singular subject objectifying the group. And the group can only be taken as object, for no mere group is a subject. Groups do not literally experience; saying that they do is mere shorthand for saying that the members do. I hope that this reconciles Nos. 3, 14, 15.

The importance of distinguishing singulars and groups is chiefly in two contexts. One is the context of valuation. Groups are real and important only because their members are. All the happiness and intrinsic value in the cosmos is in singulars, for they alone enjoy and suffer and find or fail to find satisfaction. One would be as important as billions, if no one objectified the billions in a single experience. The other context is that in which the duality 'mind-matter' is under consideration. This duality is not, as such, metaphysically ultimate. Subjects must have objects, but these can be other subjects. *Mere* objects, or merely 'physical' things, are unnecessary, save in two senses: abstract aspects of subjects and groups of subjects whose members are not distinctly given or attended to and which therefore do not appear as groups but as 'masses' of stuff. The fact that one can speak of a mass of wax, say, but also of 'the masses', meaning groups or classes of people taken indiscriminately or 'in the lump', is an ordinary language indication pointing to the greatest of Leibnizian discoveries, the real difference between 'mind' and 'matter'. It is not an absolute difference in kind of singulars, but (a) a relative difference in kind (between high and low forms) of experiencing singulars, this difference falling within mind in the broadest sense, plus (b) a difference in kind, not between singular and singular but between singular and inadequately apprehended group, the latter being irreducibly object rather than subject, and irreducibly abstract, since what makes it a single entity is its being objectified by subjects which in principle are richer in determinations than any of their objects, singular or compound.

Materialism, dualism, and some forms of idealism take as an absolute difference of level (sentient vs. insentient) what is a merely relative difference of level (inferior vs. superior forms of experiencing) with a resulting difficulty of distinguishing singulars from groups. This latter distinction is metaphysical or categorial, the other is empirical and a matter of degree. The social dimension of experience, that it always deals with other experiences, or of mind that it deals with 'other mind', fulfils the metaphysical requirement that subjects must have objects, with no necessary help from 'matter'.

True enough, human subjects could not deal with one another as they do without something like flesh, sticks, stones, metals, gases and liquids. But what is required is not that these consist of mere inert, insentient matter: but rather that any sentience composing them, anything like impulse or will, must be on such a primitive level that human impulse and will can approximately control them (and foresee their behaviour) as we in fact control and foresee flesh, sticks, stones, and the rest. And the Leibnizian distinction between active singulars and seemingly inactive composites whose active singulars escape our sensory detection, taken in conjunction with modern physics and biology, is showing ever more clearly that the concept of mere insentient matter plays no role in explaining the world. We can indeed abstract from whatever sentience may be there, but the denial that it is there adds nothing to the explanatory power of our science. On the other hand, admitting that some sort of sentience must be there explains a number of things, including the sense in which physics is an abstract science. If there is anything a philosopher should wish to be clear about it is what scientific abstraction omits.

No future discovery can change the essential situation just discussed. Inertness cannot explain the processes of nature, and it was inertness in the apparent singulars of the macroscopic environment which gave what justification there was for materialism and dualism. The Platonic and Aristotelian definitions of soul imply this.

True, one must explain 'extension', spatiality. But spatial order is the order of coexistence (Leibniz, Merleau-Ponty, not to mention relativity physics), or, in other words, symmetrical existential relations. And existential relations are causal. To exist is to act upon other existing things. If minds can influence minds they can have causal relations to them and can constitute a spatio-temporal order. And if they can become objects for other minds they can influence them. If they could not become objects we should not be talking about them. And in memory past experience, past subjectivity, is given. In a pain I share the suffering of some bodily members of mine. Leibniz's discovery, made in vain for most people, is that extension and matter are not metaphysical ultimates, save in the sense that subjects may be present in such multitudes of similars that to vastly higher types of subjects the active singulars in the masses are imperceptible, being too trivial to notice one by one. A 'mere body' is a composite object for a subject unable or unwilling to discriminate its individual members.

There are, in fact, two meanings of 'extension' in its spatial aspect. Given many entities, perceived *en masse* rather than individually, each entity of course in a slightly different place, the mass of entities will appear as extended, and indeed will be extended. This is the only way in which we can physically perceive singular entities. (An animal body, it is true, *discloses* a singular entity, but it *is* a collective one, a society of cells.) This is one meaning of 'extended'. The other meaning cannot be exhibited to physical perception, but only to self-awareness, analogically applied to other creatures. Even a true singular, e.g., my present self or experience, is extended. It is not confined to a point, it is not ubiquitous, nor is it nowhere. There only remains that it is in a region, that is extended, but as one, not as many. Since no such unity is datum of sight, hearing, or touch, we can have no sensory image of this mode of extension. But we are aware of our experiences as by no means punctiform, but rather with internal heres and theres and elsewheres, with betweens and next to's, and so forth. How could it be otherwise, since we directly respond to bodily processes whose parts are in different places, and since our experience directly controls or influences these bodily processes? A thing is where it acts and is acted upon!

How is an electron or even an atom extended? Physicists agree that no sensory image will do here. Does it follow that these entities are nowhere, or ubiquitous, or punctiform? Spatial extension has more forms than the obvious ones we see or touch. How is light extended? The mystery of extended singular human minds is merely one high-level, and very special, case of the general mystery of how singulars, none of which is directly perceivable by vision or touch, are extended. But unless they are, aggregates cannot be extended either. (Here I depart somewhat from Leibniz.) Each singular enjoys-suffers and influences the world in a certain perspective. The 'origin' of this perspective is not a point but a volume.

There is an analogous problem for time, as we shall see in Chapter IX. A temporally singular event is not instantaneous, but has a finite time length, yet this does not mean that it has temporal parts succeeding one another, any more than the voluminous origin of my perspective on the world means that I am an aggregate of momentary selves or experiences.

It is meaningless to ask what a singular is 'in itself', if this is taken to mean, 'supposing it were alone in existence'. It would then have no character whatever, extension or any other. To be is to be in relation; to be a subject or experience is to have other subjects as objects, forming a world system of such subjects. This system is the space-time world. The mere term 'matter' adds nothing but six letters to a problem exactly as mysterious or intelligible without that term. Only entities intrinsically relative to other like entities can constitute a spatio-temporal or temporo-spatial system. And experiences are indeed intrinsically relative to other experiences, as we learn in memory, and less obviously in perception, as when we feel a bodily pain or pleasure. Two great geometricians, Peirce and Whitehead, agree that this is all we need to explain spatiality.

The reader may have noted that, although temporal relations of before and after are covered by the table, as well as relations of the temporal to the non-temporal, relations of contemporaries, i.e., spatial relations, are not directly accounted for. It is apparently chiefly these relations which Weiss has in mind in his doctrine of 'Existence' as irreducible to Actuality, Possibility, or Deity. I have some feeling for his problem, though I find his solution merely verbal, except so far as it seems to involve a doctrine of complete interdependence between contemporaries, each influencing and being influenced by all the others. Relativity physics is brushed aside here as in some sense incorrect. I once held this doctrine of absolute simultaneous interaction myself. I cannot now believe it. But there does seem to be a puzzle. Contemporaries apparently form a whole which is actual or concrete, and yet this whole is not a subject, contrary to 2r. True, the whole will eventually be in a subject, but not until a long time has passed, unless one conceives deity as somehow escaping relativity principles. (As ubiquitous, God must somehow be a, in principle, unique case.) However, I should deny interaction between God, as in a certain state, and any other individual in a strictly simultaneous state. On the most concrete level, that of states, there is action, not interaction. And if there could be mutual interaction of actualities, this would mean that this 'mode of being' took care of the problem, and there would be no need of Existence to solve it. The question of mutual relatedness will be dealt with in Chapter X. What I am sure of is that the concept of mere matter is no help at this point.

Aristotle appealed to matter partly to account for possibility as well as determinate form. But the notion that the psychical is on one side only of the contrast 'actual-possible' is so arbitrary that it seems a miracle it could ever have been believed. Possibility is experienced as the dimension of futurity. It is mind that looks to the future, that freely creates ever new values because any sum of actual values could always be increased (Chapter XVI). The concept – or word – 'matter' throws not one scintilla of light on why experience can reach no final maximum of beauty, but always faces a future. It is mind's ideal of beauty which implies this.

Nor does 'matter' help to explain (Plato and Plotinus show this) why even definite or limited ideals cannot be fully realized. What a flood of light is shed on Plato's notion of the hampering 'necessity', or better, 'hindrance', 'constraint', which impedes the demiurge in its effort to conform the world, or the contents of the 'receptacle', to the ideal, if we reflect that 'self-moving soul' is really, if intelligible at all, Whitehead's or Bergson's cosmic 'creativity', which necessarily, for the value of contrast and richness, exists in pluralized form and on various levels. For then the recalcitrance of the 'material' any world-architect must be moulding (it makes no difference if the material is said to be created or merely found) is just the familiar difficulty of eliciting harmony among a plurality of creatures each having its own freedom which is never fully determined by anything antecedent, including its own past nature.

Social order cannot but have elements of anarchy in it. And social order is *the* order, the principle of all good as well as of all evil. Such order cannot be entirely imposed by any designer, however exalted. The difficulty is logical. And the concept of matter adds nothing, bare nothing, to the problem. If each atom must at every moment have something like will or free synthesis of its own origination, then of course no perfect order can result. Multiple, many-level freedom is all the 'stuff' a demiurge, or any creator you wish to conceive, can use in forming a world.

Plato's handicap was not that he had never heard of *creatio ex nihilo* (which leaves the freedom problem unchanged), but that he lacked a clear idea of what 'self-moving', self-determining implies, and that he did not succeed in imagining how what seems mere matter could consist of multitudinous 'souls' of extremely subhuman kinds. He did have a glimmering that it was the multiplicity of souls that made absolute order impossible. But he entirely lacked the insight that no definite order whatever could be an absolute good forever, the one right everlasting aesthetic pattern for a cosmos. Rather, the basic ideal has a dimension of inexhaustible infinity. The Christians (except for Leibniz) realized that no pattern for the world could be exclusively right, but somehow persuaded themselves that God, in total independence of the world, could in himself actualize a maximum of value. But this, too, was an unjustified assumption. God's ideal for himself is infinite, but actuality is in principle somehow finite.

Whereas Aristotle and others thought that later events inherit some sort of stuff from earlier events, Bergson, Peirce, and Whitehead hold that what is inherited is simply the earlier events themselves. As the earnest poet has it: 'Our todays and yesterdays are the blocks with which we build.'

Strange that Longfellow saw the point so long before the philosophers did! The constraint of the past upon the present is simply that an experience cannot generate its own data, but must find them in what has already occurred. The experience is free to make its own 'decision' as to how to accommodate, utilize, or enjoy the data, the previous happenings, but accommodate them it must. If neural activity is a causal condition of human or vertebrate experience, this simply means that just-antecedent neural happenings are among the indispensable data of this type of experience. That introspection cannot discover much about these happenings is of a piece with the general feebleness of man's introspective and inspective powers. (Much of Wittgenstein consists in exploiting and perhaps over-exploiting this very feebleness.) There is vastly more given in our experience than we can discover there by mere inspection. Antecedent bodily activities are one part of this 'more'. Nos. 3, 5, tell us that the primary wholes (by which all wholes can be explained) are formed out of temporally prior and (therefore) independent (1a) constituents, and Nos. 2, 16, imply that these wholes are singular experient-events (note that 'singular' does not contradict 'complex' or imply mere simplicity – 14a) whose prior and independent constituents are their objects. Thus an actuality is a subjective synthesis, a single experiencing, of objective factors (which may consist of other instances of subjective synthesis).

Is there any other equally definite, equally economical theory of concreteness or actuality to compete with this? That 'actual' process is past process (9r, 11r), rather than strictly present process (6r), will trouble or offend some readers, I fear. But I hold with Bergson that actuality is pastness, since presentness is a becoming actual rather than a being actual. Whitehead calls all past events 'actual entities', or 'actual occasions', and this in spite of his saying that actualities 'perish', a metaphor which has sadly misled many (unless something else has sadly misled me). They 'perish yet live for evermore' is the final word of *Process and Reality*, and to this I adhere, whether or not Whitehead did. The perishing, taken anything like literally, is an illusion occasioned by the hiddenness of deity from us. But, as Whitehead at least sometimes explicates the term, it has nothing to do with an internal change from vital actuality to a corpse or skeleton, but is merely the fact that the definite actual subject is now *also* object for further subjects. No longer is it the latest verge of actuality, since there is now a richer reality, including the once latest one. This has nothing to do, at least in my theory, with an inner shrinkage or impoverishment. Peirce's 'the past is the sum of accomplished facts' is not to be taken to refer to a mere propositional outline of the once concrete. This would imply that some facts, having been accomplished, had been dropped out. For our knowledge yes, but not for the cosmos or for deity.

Bradley and McTaggart argue against the reality of becoming by subtly assuming their conclusion, in neglecting the indeterminacy of the future as such, or in failing to see that a stage of process (No. 11) does not consist of definite events until it is all in the past, so that the survey of definite events definitely related is entirely retrospective. In effect, they are imagining all events as though all were in the past. But, as Peirce insisted, they could not possibly all be in the past. 'Reality' means 'as of now', and the 'now' acquires new reference each moment. Events can be surveyed only from within some event or sequence of events. *Sub specie aeternitatis* only eternal abstractions could be contemplated.

Since r-terms are inclusive and express the overall truth, the entire table tells us that we can find the absolute only in the relative, objects (or anything other than subjects) only in subjects, causes only in effects (any knowledge of a cause is already an effect of it), earlier events only in later, being only in becoming, the eternal only in the temporal, the abstract only in the concrete, the potential only in the actual, the necessary only in the contingent, the future as such only in the past (every past has faced a future), the infinite only in the finite, the simple only in the complex, the individual only in the state, the specific only in the individual, the generic only in the specific, the metaphysical only in the generic, God in his necessary, eternal essence only in God in his contingent, temporal states. (It was Heidegger who once said that not timelessness but infinite temporality distinguishes God.) If one wants to understand an *a*-term one should locate it in its *r*-correlate. There are not subjects *and* objects but only objects in subjects, not causes and effects but only causes in effects, not earlier and later but earlier in later, not necessary things and contingent things but necessary constituents of contingent wholes (though the class of such wholes could not be empty), not God and the world but the world in God (No. 21).

The old dictum that the supreme understanding was of cause as implying its effect is erroneous. It was a naïve preformationism. Understanding of the actual or concrete is retrospective, not prospective. (Our business with the future is more than understanding, it is deciding, creating.) He who adequately knows an effect thereby knows its causes, but the converse is not true. Similarly, it is false that he who knows the universal, the form, knows all that is worth knowing. The concrete is the richest, the most worth knowing. History is the cognitive paradigm, not mathematics, which is chiefly a tool for investigating historical sequences in man and nature. The abstractions of metaphysics are not chiefly ends in themselves, but means to wisdom and goodness in the enjoyment and creation of the concrete.

All through intellectual and religious history there has been a bias towards *a*-terms and a notion that *r*-terms are opprobrious. But staring at the essence of 'rational animality', or even at a set of psychological laws, is a poor substitute for knowing actual human beings. Yet the latter are incomparably more relative, changeable, dependent, finite, conditioned, contingent, and discontinuous. Abstractions are objects, not subjects; but in comparison to concrete entities they have most of the characters often supposed to define deity. Such definitions turn God into a mere object or abstraction. Of course God is no mere object, since the moment we objectify him he in turn objectifies us as doing so. Yet of course God is object, for anything mentionable is so. But only the dead or the abstract are mere objects. And for the same reason only the dead or the abstract can be (henceforth) absolute, immune to further influence. Like everyone, God is both subject and object, but he alone (through his states) is universal subject, inheriting everything as object; and he alone is universal object, object for every subject. The divine Father or creator is alone universal father or creative power, the divine lover alone is universal lover, sensitive to influence not by some only but by all; the divine beloved is alone universally beloved.

'Universal' is an *a*-term, and it is true that the 'defining characteristic' of deity, what makes God God and no one else, must be extremely abstract and thus absolute; but no abstraction whatever is anything except thanks to something concrete. And the concrete is precisely the most completely particularized, the contrary of universal, and the contrary of absolute. It takes the entire table to describe God, not just the absolute column alone. This is what I call the principle of dual transcendence (Chapter XI). It is the only logical way to combine a negative with a positive theology.

If there is anything abstract and independent in every comparison, Peirce's 'absolute first', it must be 20*a*, the mere eternal essence of deity. (This includes 19*a* as 'eternal object' for God.) And if there is anything concrete in every comparison, it must be 20–21*r*, the concrete divine state. But this, too, will be abstract, less rich in definite determinations, by comparison with subsequent divine states. Relatively, positive and negative, instances of the first including those of the second, is the absolute (i.e., the non-relative) principle. For twenty-five centuries philosophers seemed to have missed this as if by magic. One could say also that absoluteness, positive and negative, was the absolute principle, but here the inclusive form is really a double negative, the not-not-relative; and so this formulation is upside down.

The key to the idea of independent constituent is the idea of dependent whole, to the idea of necessity that of contingency or indeterminate-determinable possibility, to that of the abstract that of the concrete, to the infinite the finite, to the simple the complex. It is comic to watch Plotinus, say, trying to prove the opposite. Without unity, simplicity, he says we cannot understand the multiple, the complex. Apart from unity there is no plurality and no beauty, goodness, value, or reality. How true! And apart from plurality, contrast, complexity, there is also no unity, beauty, goodness, value, or reality. Moreover, while it is obvious that although the complex can without the slightest inconsistency contain the simple, the converse inclusion is glaringly impossible. Similarly, 'the contingent truth that p is necessary and q contingently true' is allowable in anyone's modal logic, but 'the necessary truth that p is necessary and q contingently true' is allowed in no such logic. For all these centuries metaphysicians have been defying elementary logical truisms. Why? This is quite a question. There is no need to defy these truisms in order to have a metaphysics at least as intelligible as any produced in this strange fashion.

Concerning 7a ii: it may seem impossible that what is successor to every (event) should be included (3a) in what is predecessor to some (7r). However, there is an ambiguity in the definition of 'everlasting'. An actual event cannot literally succeed every (other) event: for there can be no last event, creativity being inexhaustibly fertile. Only something less concrete than an event, an individual being, can be everlasting and only by endlessly having new states each of which, of course, inherits from the world antecedent to that state. If one accepts personal immortality, then some beings would be everlasting but not primordial. In Asia the belief has often been held that individual creatures are primordial but not everlasting; for they may be 'absorbed' into the One which is timeless. In this book the view is favoured that only the primordial being can be everlasting. However, every event is everlasting 'by proxy' as it were, in that it is bound to be inherited as antecedent condition or datum by every subsequent event, and hence also any everlasting being that there may be. This is Whitehead's 'objective immortality', which seems a significant counter to the negativity of death only if we assume an everlasting being able ever afterwards fully to appreciate our lives (Chapter XIV).

Things more abstract than events or individuals may be primordial and everlasting by proxy in being always found embodied in inherited events. Whitehead's eternal objects are such; in my view only the most abstract universals, the metaphysical principles themselves, are eternal in this sense. They precede *every* event, but not *all* events, because every event has predecessors and any event must instance the metaphysical universals. This is a sort of version of Plato's doctrine that forms are known by reminiscence. Memory is an ingredient in thought as such. But this is an unplatonic platonism.

The implication of 9*r*, *a*, together with 3*r*, *a*, that actuality includes possibility, has often been denied. Is not the actual world but one among possible worlds? Is not the possible more complex (14*r*) than the actual? By no means. As process philosophers (in this, including Weiss) agree, the possible is always less definite than the actual. There is no such thing as a possible particular (cf. 8*r* and 8*a*). Not even God can fully define a world without creating it. Possibilities are irreducibly non-particular. It is determinate particulars which have a horizon of futurity and indeterminacy. The definite can include the indefinite as the richer can include the poorer, but not conversely. The definite past in outlines implies its own successors, but when these are definite or actual, there will be in them that which their mere possibility failed to embrace, namely determinates corresponding to the antecedent determinables or universals. The fulfilment of a plan, which is always an outline only, implies the plan, but the latter, being more meagre in definiteness, cannot imply the fulfilment. That Weiss admits all this yet makes possibility co-ordinate with actuality I can only view as an almost tragic mistake.

That continuity (12*a*) belongs with the abstract, indefinite, possible, infinite, not with the concrete, definite, actual, finite, is the truth missed by Bergson, Peirce, and Dewey, but seen by James and Whitehead (anticipated by Buddhists and some Islamic thinkers). It seems to be the real bearing of the Zeno paradoxes. A continuum either has no parts, or indefinite or infinite but merely possible parts; definite multiple actuality must be discrete, and, at least for any finite portion of space-time, finite in its actual constituents. Peirce saw that possibilities form continua, thus all possible hues, shades, and tints of red. But it seems obvious that an actual array of colours does not present all of these: there are always gaps. Similarly, between any shape and any other there is a continuum of possible intermediate shapes; but in an actual part of nature only discrete, finitely different shapes occur. It could not be otherwise. Actuality as such implies arbitrary breaking of a continuum, as Peirce himself in some contexts pointed out. Quantum mechanics was in principle metaphysically inevitable (apart from special features). Peirce should have anticipated the basic idea. He ardently desired to be prophetic of the future of microphysics, but largely failed in this. His bias towards continuity, which made him blur the distinction between discrete actuality and continuous possibility in favour of a belief in actually continuous becoming and motion, was responsible. It led him to his extraordinary doctrine that a human experience has neither finite nor zero but infinitesimal duration so that in a single second, say, we have an infinite number of successive experiences, each drawing inferences from the previous, and thus we are always infinitely far from identifying a definite experience with definite direct unmediated data. Bergson does no better. He replies to Zeno by citing a finite movement as a single not further analysable unit, but fails to refer to unit experiences, with finite temporal spread, yet without internal actual succession, which is the basic point.

James, with his strange flair for (often) reaching the right conclusion though 'only God knows how he got there' (C. I. Lewis), decided that experience comes in finite 'drops'. Whether this led Whitehead to his own doctrine of quanta of becoming I do not know. Doubtless quantum mechanics helped. But the Buddhists seem to have reached about the same conclusion, as did James independently of physics and Buddhism.

A paradox, though I hope not a contradiction, obtains with respect to 2o*r*, taking relativity physics into account. What can be meant by 'God now'? Is this a cosmic simultaneity? Any process philosopher who is serious about the relations of metaphysics and physics must deal with this question.

Because God is universal or ubiquitous, not exclusively localized, and because according to relativity physics there is no cosmic now, it seems that, unless – as Howard Stein (in a letter) puts it – physics fails to give us 'the deep truth about time', we should express 2o*r* as 'God here-now'. That is, Stein suggests, God as perceiving us now is a divine state or event; God as perceiving a state of some inhabitant of another planet is another divine event. The two events will be embraced in later divine events in which God perceives remote descendants both of us and of our far-off contemporaries. All terms and relations thus become divinely known, and are immortalized beyond possibility of corruption. But the analogy between divine states and states of localized individuals is by this assumption rendered much more complex and difficult to conceive than if one could dismiss relativity considerations. It is a little like the mysteries of the trinity, only incomparably more complex.

Is the foregoing an empirical issue? I doubt it. For relativity, like the quantum principle, is a categorical question on the highest level of abstractness. And it could not, so far as I can see, be observationally falsified. Einstein's formulae could be falsified; but the degree of relativity is one thing, the question of relativity or no relativity is another. Zero relativity would mean that velocities of messages were infinite or at least had no upper limit. And how could this be known?

There is a teleological fitness in relativity as such. For it means that creatures in one part of space are without responsibility for what happens in other, far-off parts. By the time we can know what is happening light years away it is too late to send advice as to what should be done there, still more, to try to go there and do something about it ourselves. The velocity of light and radio waves is fast enough; because of it we have to be concerned about events in China or India. But to have immediate communications with, hence possible responsibilities in, other galaxies would be too much! I strongly suspect that there should not, and indeed could not be absolute simultaneity, at least not such as would be detectable by localized observers.

If *God here now* is not the same concrete unit of reality as God somewhere else 'now', then the simple analogy with human consciousness as a single linear succession of states collapses. I have mixed feelings about this. It seems, on the one hand, that the idea of God as an individual though cosmic being is thus compromised; but, on the other hand, I wonder if this is not rather what we might expect when an analogy is extended to include deity. Maybe it is not divine individuality that is threatened, but only the assumption that this individuality should be simple and easy for us to grasp. However, there is the haunting question, can physics, judging reality from the stand-point of localized observers, give us the deep truth about time as it would appear to a non-localized observer?

Repeatedly, interpreters of relativity physics (d'Abro, Putnam) have asserted that this theory rules out any contrast between determinate past and indeterminate future. Repeatedly, other interpreters (Stein, Capek) deny this. I find myself sadly handicapped in trying to think about this question. But the concept of creativity is for me more convincing than any argument which assumes that physics, by one disputed interpretation, can give us the final truth about the relations of being and becoming, or settle the Parmenidean question.

Taking Stein's view of God complicates and perhaps fatally weakens one of the chief merits of a theistic philosophy, that it can explain the outlines of the world-order, the laws of nature, as divine decrees. 'The rule of one is best', but Stein's view seems a kind of oligarchy, since God here now and God there now are not in a single linear or 'personally ordered' sequence. How do these gods make the same decision? It may be absurd, but I wonder if the 'big bang' theory of cosmic development could be relevant here. The relativity problem arises because of the spatial expanse of the world process; but the laws of nature may have been decided at a moment in the cosmic process when there was no such expanse. This is a possibly wild suggestion.

No. 12 is rather puzzling, to me at least. That actuality is finite in space I readily believe. It is certainly finite in some respects; for to say otherwise would be to say that everything thinkable was also actual, and this is absurd. But the serious question concerns the past of the creative process. Is there an actually infinite regress of past stages – if nowhere else, then at least in the divine becoming? If not, how can a first stage be either avoided or made intelligible, if every experience must have antecedent objects (Nos. 1, 6)? So Kant's first antinomy, his most potent argument, stares us in the face. All I can see to do is to reject his disproof of the possibility of an actual infinity. But then, am I not compromising item 1? This question I cannot at present answer to my own complete satisfaction.

G. E. Moore argued that while there is no need to conceive actuality as spatially infinite, there is need to conceive the past

as an actual infinity of realized events.[1] For a first event seems
to be unintelligible. Finitists hold that an actual infinity is also
unintelligible. Counting to infinity is an incompletable process.
Of course this is true if the process has a beginning. But that is
the question at issue. Must it have a beginning? And must it be
a question of counting? Suppose God is in every new state of
himself aware of an infinity of prior states, but that the additional
set of items he then receives from the world is always finite.
Such an addition does not change the numerical order of the
totality. This is still just infinity. But it does add new qualities,
and thus aesthetically enriches the whole. (Russell once told me
that he found this logically admissible.) And note that God
never has had, and never will have, to make an infinite addition
to his own life, but always only a finite addition. Moreover, the
infinity of prior states is not a mere infinity of mutually independent items; for the just preceding state will have included all
earlier ones in its own unity. So in a sense God is combining
finites, not an infinite and a finite. The numerical infinity of the
previous multiplicity is entirely embraced in the aesthetic
unity of an experience. The numerical aspect is a mere aspect
of this unity. At least some of the paradoxes which bother
finitists are removed by this view. There is no 'hotel with an
infinite number of rooms, all occupied, into which new occu-
pants can nevertheless without difficulty be introduced'. There
is no infinity of coexisting objects, but only of successively
realized events. Nor can anything be inserted into a past event
that is not already there.

The foregoing depends upon taking spatial plurality as finite.
I strongly incline to this form of finitism. I think we should
assume that the number of stars is finite. And of course I am
rejecting Kant's phenomenalism, for which his first antinomy is,
in my opinion, the strongest argument.

It should be apparent that it is the continuous (13*a*) that is
simple and the discontinuous that is complex. Continuity is a
single idea; but the sum of discrete items in the world is as far
from that as possible. Similarly, infinity in the absolute sense
is simpler and is less than the finite, not more; for definiteness is
required for actuality, or value in a more than minimal sense.
The finite or actual includes the infinite as an idea or potentiality.

---

[1] *Some Main Problems of Philosophy* (New York: Collier, 1962).

a terms, we have seen, are negative or privative by comparison with *r* terms. For example the data of an experience are what is left when one sets aside everything which a particular *experience* of *x*, *y*, *z*, . . . adds to mere *x*, *y*, *z*. A man is now what he is always *plus* what is peculiar to his present reality. Always the *r* terms affirm more than their correlates. If traditional philosophies understood this, they failed to express their insight.

It is clear that negative or privative properties of constituents or aspects need not apply in the same sense to wholes containing them. Thus a house can be large though some part of it is not; it can be valuable though some part is not. Positive properties accrue from parts to wholes. A whole can be more than its constituents, but it cannot be less. Since, as modal logic shows, the contingent contains the necessary, but not *vice versa*, it is plain that whatever terms belong with contingency are the inclusive characters of reality, and whatever terms belong with necessity are non-inclusive or privative. But then the exaltation of 'the absolute' or 'the infinite' or the necessary is simply a preference for something which in principle is less than the relative or the finite or the contingent. In worshipping the independent, people really worshipped the abstract, and preferred the less to the more valuable. I venture to regard this as a species of idolatry.

That an effect (7, 9) is more concrete, rich in definiteness, than a cause would hardly have occurred to one in the main European tradition, which was afflicted with 'etiolatry' (worship of causes). That causation is creation, enrichment of reality as a whole, was the last thing clearly envisaged. Origins, the philosophy of creativity holds, are inferior to what comes out of them, and the *de facto* supreme reality must be the *de facto* supreme effect, which must include its cause or causes. Nothing, just in itself, is cause of anything in particular, but effects just in themselves are caused by whatever did cause them. This is the secret of memory and perception. Only from the standpoint of the effect is the causal relation definite at both ends. God merely as cause of all would not only not know all, he would know indeterminate possibilities for worlds, nothing more. As causes we never know just what we are causing; as effects we always at least subconsciously know what caused us.

From No. 20 one sees that God must be successor of every becoming as well as its predecessor. As the former, he is influenced by and knows each event; as the latter, he is its supreme causal condition.

Nothing of this could be seen while etiolatry held minds under its spell. Nor could the greater concreteness of becoming be seen while 'ontolatry' or being-worship prevailed. Alas, that Heidegger used 'Being' for the basic principle, thus verbally negating his own insight into the primacy of process!

The philosophies hopelessly incompatible with the table are those which take every whole to be 'organic' so that parts depend upon just the wholes they are in; or which take wholly independent terms to be actual and concrete; or things experienced to depend upon the particular experiences had of them; or effects and causes mutually to imply each other, or to be equally concrete and rich in actuality (or effects as such to be inferior to causes as such); or the simple to be in principle superior to the complex; or becoming to be merely an aspect, or inferior kind, of being.

In Paul Weiss's uniquely complicated system[2] a table of concepts must, I suppose, be in four columns to cover his four modes of being, and there seems no simple formula illuminating their relationships, unless it is that there is interaction between each and every other. But thus symmetry would be enthroned as ultimate. Rather, experiences are inclusive, and divine experiences, all inclusive. Everything else is abstraction. In this way we avoid any mere dualism of particulars and universals or mind and matter or God and world. We avoid even Whitehead's eternal objects and actual entities. For the 'pure potentials' are not definite entities, they form a continuum (13a) which is without definite parts (8a). Only impure, non-eternal, relatively independent potentials can exist in definite plurality. As Peirce put it, possibilities as such 'have no identity'.

According to Stephen Pepper, a metaphysics is the exploitation of a 'root metaphor'.[3] Neo-classicism takes a momentary experience as the model or paradigm of concrete reality. But is this just a metaphor? Except in and through experiences there

---

[2] *Modes of Being* (Carbondale: Southern Illinois University Press, 1958).
[3] *World Hypotheses: a Study in Evidence* (Berkeley: University of California Press, 1942). Also *Concept and Quality* (La Salle, Ill.: Open Court, 1969).

are no metaphors! What resembles no aspect of experience is 'nothing, nothing, bare nothing'.

The basic decisions are not as to metaphors, but as to logical structure. What depends upon what, what includes what, what is necessary to or contingent upon what? Is symmetry or asymmetry basic in explanation? These are the crucial questions. That experience must somehow be central seems obvious, since the only possible answer to the question, 'What illustrations of meaning do you have?', seems to be, 'Experience, in this or that aspect or datum'. In this sense, as Bergson said, 'every philosophy that understands itself' is in a broad sense idealistic, some form of psychicalism.

According to Richard McKeon, metaphysical systems may explain things in terms of: (1) the all-inclusive whole; (2) least parts: (3) the problems of man (who is neither all-inclusive nor a least part); (4) operations.[4] In terms of diverse methods, and other factors, many sub-divisions of these are suggested. It seems to me, however, that one must use man as the model in any case, and work from there towards larger wholes and lesser parts. However, there is at least one ambiguity about 'all-inclusive whole': does it mean all that ever has been or will be in the future (assuming that the future is no less definite than the past), or is every cosmic whole merely the summation of what *has* happened, so that the next moment there will be a new whole, not fully determinate in advance? The first view implies (as the 'absolute idealists' insisted) that all wholes are organic and all relations internal to all their terms. The second view implies that there are both internal and external relations. Again, I think logical issues such as the one just mentioned should not be decided by some vague hunch like 'the whole explains its parts' or the like.

An adequate philosophy should clarify the question of whole and parts, provide a proper setting for human problems, and use operations in some broad sense to help explicate concepts. Both Pepper and McKeon seem to set somewhat artificial boundaries to speculation. One must, they suggest, think either in one of four speculative compartments or in one of four styles

[4] McKeon's scheme is not readily learned from his published statements. But see *Thought, Action and Passion* (Chicago: The University of Chicago Press, 1954).

(Pepper: organicism, mechanism, formism, contextualism; McKeon: holoscopic, meroscopic, pragmatic, operational) or be a weak eclectic. Moreover, it is implied that the choice cannot be rationally demonstrated, but is personal and rather arbitrary. This is historically plausible, except that the great philosophers have always thought that they had rational arguments against one another. I think one must avoid both extremes of dismissing this as pure illusion and supposing that the refutations were as definitive as they were intended to be. When all hope of reasonable refutation dies, philosophy is not in very good health.

VII

WITTGENSTEIN AND TILLICH:
REFLECTIONS ON METAPHYSICS
AND LANGUAGE

WITTGENSTEIN once said, 'theology is grammar'. Speaking equally broadly, one might also say, 'metaphysics is grammar'. One would hardly say, 'physics is grammar' or 'biology is grammar' – still less, 'history is grammar'. One could, perhaps, say, 'arithmetic is grammar'. What is the reason for this difference?

In the 'grammatical' subjects the question is, how do we talk sense rather than nonsense, or how can we be clear and consistent, rather than confused or inconsistent? In the nongrammatical subjects, while of course we want to talk clearly and consistently, this is merely preliminary. The main thing is to choose between those clear and consistent ways of speaking which best fit the actual course of history, including natural or cosmic history, and those which fit this course less well, if at all. In arithmetic we relate numbers (that is, certain abstractions) not to cosmic history but to other numbers; in physics we relate certain numbers to observed facts. What do we do in metaphysics and natural theology? Do we relate ideas to observed facts, or only to other ideas? I hold that we do the latter. In so far I am perhaps in agreement with Wittgenstein. But there are many sources of misunderstanding as to what the indicated common ground commits one to.

That theology is grammatical is one way of putting the point of Anselm's proof for God. What he discovered (and my defence of the view that it was a discovery, not a mere blunder, has not, I think, been refuted) is that atheism is bad grammar.[1]

[1] See my *Logic of Perfection*; also *Anselm's Discovery* (La Salle, Ill.: Open Court 1962, 1965).

It is a confused or self-inconsistent way of talking. If 'God' is the term for the referent of the attitude of worship, then a unique mode of existence, excluding even the conceivability of non-existence, is part of the import of that term. Hence 'there is in fact no worshipful being' either lacks clarity, or it affirms a contradiction. To speak of 'fact', in the normal usage which implies contingency (the conceivability of an alternative), in connection with the divine existence is logically inadmissible. And if 'fact' is meant in the sense in which one might say, 'it is a fact that 3 and 4 are 7', then it follows that either the non-existence of God is absurd, just as '3 and 4 are less than 7' is absurd, or the existence and the non-existence of the worshipful being are alike absurd. And this is one of Anselm's greatest mistakes: he failed to realize with sufficient distinctness that to prove the absurdity of atheism is not to establish the logical possibility of theism. Perhaps, as Carneades had argued, the very idea of deity is a confusion or inconsistency. 'There are no round-squares' no more states a fact, in the straightforward sense of 'fact', than 'there are round-squares'. To assert or deny a paradoxical statement is very different from asserting or denying a non-paradoxical one. Anselm discovered that theism is either a hopeless paradox or a necessary truth. What it could not be is a simple factual error. But the choice between hopeless paradox and necessary truth remains to be made.

As I use the term, 'metaphysics' stands for all questions whose answers are non-factual in the same sense as the theistic question. For example, I do not believe that 'materialism' is an empirical hypothesis, factually true or factually false. I believe it is either clear, consistent, and necessarily true, or not clear or consistent, and so not possibly true. The same holds of 'solipsism', 'idealism' (in a number of senses), 'phenomenalism', 'determinism', 'tychism', 'process philosophy', 'monism' (in various senses), and many other doctrines. If they make sense they are necessary truths. But do they make sense? Many of course do not.

There is a view, first expressed by Hobbes, that necessity is simply a matter of the language we adopt, or as Hobbes put it, the way we use names. No one defends Hobbes's notion that words are merely names for things, but otherwise his view of modality, that it expresses only our ways of talking or writing, has a large following. Necessary judgments are analytic, and an analytic judgment says nothing about reality, but only something about our concepts, in other words, about the meanings we assign certain terms. By changing our definitions or 'meaning postulates' we can make any general statement analytic or synthetic, as we please. Richard Martin argues that modal logic 'rests upon a mistake', since necessity is not properly part of the content of a proposition in the object-language, but is its classification as analytic within a given system, and hence belongs in the metalanguage.

It is important to realize that there is another theory of modality, which is apparently very old, in that it was more or less unsystematically and waveringly stated by Aristotle, but which has been reaffirmed in modern times by Lequier, Peirce, and others, including the present writer. This is the theory (a) that possibility and necessity are in the first place ontological (and only derivatively logical or linguistic) and (b) that they are ontological as *modi* of time or process. That is necessarily which is always; that happens of necessity which never fails to happen; that exists or happens contingently which exists or happens only at, during, or after, a particular or limited time. A Socinian theologian of the seventeenth century explicated God's eternity as follows: 'He is eternal because he cannot not exist.' Aristotle had said long before: 'with eternal things, to be possible and to be are the same'.

If modality is essentially temporal, then time, and hence modality, is not an intra-linguistic phenomenon! The contrast between the past as wholly fixed, no longer open to decision, and the future, as a mixture of the fixed or already settled and alternative possibilities really open for decision, is no more dependent upon language than anything you please. But, given this contrast of past and future, we can define the necessary as that which has *always* been part of the settled content of the future, and thus has never been and will never be an open possibility.

There is an ambiguity in the notion of the fixed or settled aspect of the future. Does it mean merely that some causal law stands in the way of any alternative? But what stands in the way of a change in the law? If alternative laws are conceivable, may they not sometime also be real? Only if becoming as such requires the specified feature is it impossible there should ever be an alternative. This is the key to real necessity. Contingent laws of nature must have had a genesis. They are not eternal.

One use of language which has puzzled philosophers since Aristotle is its use to predict future events. We say, 'what will be will be', and 'what will not be will not be'. If 'it will' is true, 'it will not' must, it is supposed, be false.

So the future is apparently determinate, after all. Also, after an event has occurred, we sometimes say that it 'was going to happen'. In this fashion we seem able to read the definiteness of events back into earlier and earlier stages of the 'advance of nature'. I once got Russell to admit that his own appeal to such considerations to prove the definiteness of the future was a begging of the question. For that question just is, do 'will' and 'will not' form an exhaustive dichotomy? They are incompatible; but then contraries are incompatible yet inexhaustive since both may be false. Thus 'all S is P' and 'no S is P', if in truth some and only some S is P. To negate 'will' is perhaps not the same as asserting 'will not', just as 'I *will* (i.e., have decided) to do it' may be negated without asserting 'I *will* (i.e., have decided) not to do it'. Suppose I have no definite volition in the matter? Here one finds 'will' and 'will not' behaving as contraries. These considerations are not irrelevant. For, according to the modal theory of time or temporal theory of modality, 'will happen' means that the present causal conditions definitely entail and as it were, decide for, the happening, 'will not' means that the conditions definitely entail the absence of or decide against the happening. Both statements may be false, since the future may not be definite or decided either way. Ordinary language has no trouble in expressing this by the phrase, it may or may not happen; or, it could happen and it could also fail to happen. Suppose this is the real situation, i.e., the truth just is the indeterminacy of the future in the specified respect, as of now. After all, 'future' is a relative status, no event being future to every other event, but only to some others. And no temporally defined moment of time remains for ever future only, but each eventually becomes past to other actual events. It then is no longer indeterminate. This is the only view compatible with the ultimacy of creativity.

Note that nothing said in the previous paragraph implies that statements about the future are 'neither true nor false'.

Rather 'will' is false if either 'will not' or 'may or may not' is true. We need here no third truth value, but we do need a third type of predicate for future moments of process besides 'definitely P' and 'definitely not P', namely 'indefinite with respect to P'. But this triad is just like the familiar one of 'you are commanded to do it', 'you are commanded not to do it' and 'you are given no command with respect to "it" '. By analogy, the world, as of now, causally (a) requires such and such a future occurrence, (b) excludes it, or (c) neither requires not excludes but permits it. Two truth values suffice in such cases. The truth of one of the three (a, b, or c) is the falsity of the other two.

Consider the consequence of this doctrine for the old problem of divine foresight. According to the classical view, God already (or, if you prefer, eternally) knows our future actions. And of course what he knows us as doing we will do. This puzzled many minds. But the error is the assumption that our actions are already (or, if you say 'eternally', that only makes it worse) in being for God to know. Thus time is spread out, 'spatialized', for God like the road upon which (to use the Thomistic analogy) travellers are proceeding, too far apart to see those ahead, but all alike visible to a spectator looking down from a great height. This is exactly what Bergson attacks as the 'spatialization of time'. The analogy is suspect. There is not (either now or eternally) a fixed totality of travellers for God to survey, but a new totality each moment.

A consequence of this view which troubles some is that it conflicts with the venerable dogma that 'truth is timeless'. It is wonderful to see many who are proud of their freedom from superstition accepting this baseless pronouncement. I say baseless; for no ground has ever been given, if we set aside arguments from classical theism, i.e., from the posited immutability and omniscience of deity. A number of writers have recently attempted to furnish other arguments, but so far as I can discover they merely beg the question in ingenious ways. One argument (Waismann) is that if we suppose that reality, and hence what is true of reality, is richer in definiteness each moment, we face the absurd question, when did it become true that a certain date and place, say, definitely involved rain? But in principle the question is not absurd at all. It became true (and ever thereafter continued to be true) at precisely the moment when the causal conditions first definitely required rainy weather and excluded non-rainy weather for that space-time locus. In the remote past rain was merely possible, or more or less probable or improbable, for the locus. But at some moment (presumably) before rain actually started, the probability of rain became infinite. Then for omniscience 'it will rain' was a known truth. The better our knowledge the closer we can come to judging, if not the precise moment when the probability of no rain dropped to zero, at least about when it became overwhelmingly improbable. Years before a suicide happened there was only a possibility or mild probability that the suicide would take place. But a few seconds before, it may have been impossible, considering the laws of nature, including human nature, that the man should not take his life. And at any rate we know that the truth of an occurrence comes into being with, or at some finite time before, the occurrence.

One objection must be granted: our doctrine introduces complications into logic, since for complete correctness every statement about contingent things must specify the stage of the world process at (and after) which the statement is affirmed to hold. To say, 'it happens at time t' is only a proposition schema, not a definite proposition. To become a proposition it must read, 'As of, and after' time t, a certain feature definitely belongs to time t'. Two dates, date of the affirmation and date of the event, are in principle required. I do not regard this complexity as evidence of incorrectness. Rather the contrary, I am confident that reality is at least *that* complicated, whatever it may be convenient for us to say. If today, Thursday, 'rain on Friday' is probable but not inevitable, then for ever after it will be true that Friday, as future to that Thursday, was 'probably rainy'. Suppose it rains tomorrow. Will this turn the probability into certainty? Yes, for Friday as no longer future but present or past; no, for Friday as future to Thursday. 'But what,' you may ask, 'about Friday's events not as future or past, but just in themselves?' I reply that there are and never will be any such events. And if you ask, 'What about the events as co-present with all others to the eternal?' I again reply, there are no such events. From the standpoint of eternity nothing not eternal can be seen. Events have being only in time. And there is no totality once for all of real events.

The Aristotelian view may be expressed in Kantian terms by saying that 'time is the schema' of all our basic conceptions, including the concepts of modality; however, contrary to Kant, time is ontological, and is no merely phenomenal affair, as it most certainly is no merely linguistic one. Kant's Newtonian determinism and view of physical geometry, and his traditional view of God as wholly timeless, stood in the way of his adopting any such theory of modality. But it is an alternative to the linguistic theory. If, as I suspect, logic itself is in process of invalidating the latter, should we not reconsider the Aristotelian alternative? (Note that medieval Aristotelianism was unable to take this side of Aristotle seriously; for one reason, because the standard medieval doctrine of God implied that all truth is timelessly there for omniscience. Only for ignorance – the doctrine ran – is the future irreducibly potential or indeterminate; for the wisdom that measures reality all events are equally definite.)

In another way, however, medieval thought about modality was sounder than most modern thought. It held that God could create any logically possible state of affairs, his power extending to all that is conceivable. In this way logical and real possibility ultimately coincide. There were two difficulties. One is that in a purely eternal deity there is no room for real alternatives, and hence none for real freedom. An eternal divine decision must be a necessary decision, by the Aristotelian principle. But then worlds excluded by such a decision are not really possible even for God, and the decision is no decision, just as Spinoza said it was not, but a sheer necessity. This difficulty can be overcome by admitting a temporal aspect of deity, as is done in this book. The other difficulty is that God's power to have any logically possible world as his creation was taken to mean that he could, by a simple fiat or choice, infallibly produce such a world. But then creaturely freedom is mere illusion and all evil is deliberately imposed upon the creatures by the divine will. This difficulty can only be removed by defining God's power to have any logically possible world not as his freedom to choose that world, but as his freedom to choose the basic laws of such a world and his capacity adequately to know and thus in the most absolute sense possess whatever world results from the laws plus the choices of the creatures so far as left open by the divine choice.

Knowing is one thing, choosing is another thing, and it will not do to try to obliterate the distinction, even in God. God can know the world whatever it may be; but no world could be determined merely by divine choice, since the very meaning of 'world' is a set of individuals to some extent determining what divine choice has left indeterminate though determinable. To be possible is to be possible content of divine knowledge, but not necessarily to be possible object of divine choice. God cannot choose a single creaturely act in its concreteness, for the simple reason that it would not then be a creaturely act. Thomism has a formula with which it tries to have it both ways, but I find only contradiction or no meaning at all in this procedure.

It is important to realize that the coincidence of eternal and necessary does not mean that 'necessary' is here used as mere synonym for 'always so'. On the contrary, what makes something to obtain always is simply the impossibility of its not obtaining. Not even God can perceptually or mentally run through the totality of events, for there is no such totality, complete once for all. Hence even God can know the eternal only by knowing something the non-being of which is meaningless or contradictory. For example, if any law of nature is eternal, then it can have no conceivable alternative. Since possibility and futurity are in principle one, what has never been future can never have been a mere possibility. Aristotle in his modal doctrine was profounder than he knew. He should have noted that the only evidence for eternity, since we cannot know all the past, let alone all the future, is the impossibility of an alternative. But then how could we know the eternity of the heavenly bodies or of earthly species? Obviously, alternatives are thinkable. Any metaphysician should be an evolutionist in some sense. Specific forms cannot be eternal or unalterable.

However all this may be, the assumption that only propositions can be necessary is plainly question-begging in a context in which the possibility of metaphysics is the issue. Metaphysics by definition takes necessity to be ontological as well as logical. (Recall Aristotle's: 'that which could not be otherwise than it is'.) So, in my view, does theism, belief in the divine existence.

What is the relation between metaphysics, thus conceived, and normal ways of using words? The commonest notion today seems to be that metaphysical assertions are one and all what Carneades took the idea of God to be, and what I grant many such assertions are – confused or inconsistent applications of words which in more normal applications make good sense. If this is correct, then worship is in principle nonsensical, and irreligion logically obligatory. Perhaps so, but I see no conclusive argument for this conclusion in contemporary discussion. If worship is in principle sensible, then there are metaphysical views which are also sensible, though their denials are not. If theism (properly defined) is good grammar it must be true, since its denial is in any case bad grammar; but then the possibility obtains of other metaphysical statements similarly making sense and being necessarily true. Moreover, from the idea of God, suitably clarified as the referent of worship, a whole metaphysical system can, by at least plausible arguments, be derived.

Let us suppose, for the purposes of this discussion, that there are necessary metaphysical truths, denials of which are all in some fashion absurd. Is language, with its basis in everyday communication, equipped to express such truths? Presumably any answer must be qualified. If there were no difficulty in expressing metaphysical necessities, would not more agreement have long ago been reached? If there were no possibility of expressing them, would the attempt have been persisted in so long by so many superior intellects?

One requirement for lucidity in metaphysics is that the contrast inherent in concepts should not be repudiated by giving one side of the contrast exclusive validity.

When Spinoza said or implied that not simply God but all things have their existence by necessity, his error was not factual but 'grammatical'. He destroyed the contrast necessary for the significance of his concept. When Quine says, or seems to say, that nothing is, strictly speaking, necessary, he commits a less obvious form of the same mistake. But when the negative theology says that no conceptions apply to God, it is, in a perhaps still subtler way, making a comparable mistake. For where there are no definite common aspects there are no definite contrasts either. For instance, if God in no sense has magnitude or parts, then he cannot be contrasted with creatures as quantitatively infinite rather than finite; and if he also has

no common qualities with creatures, then he cannot be contrasted with them as, in a definite sense, qualitatively infinite
either. If God is not cause or influence, he cannot contrast with
all other beings as cosmically rather than locally causative or
influential. If God is said to be supremely good, then at least he
is good. And if it be said that he is 'goodness itself', not one more
instance of goodness, then either this is bad grammar or some
qualification is required. For God is not a mere universal. In
addition 'goodness' has to have some common meaning in this
and other uses.

It is to be noted that this requirement of common meaning in
metaphysical contrast may be broken in many ways. To say,
'only God literally creates', is not to exalt God in any definite
way. For you might as well say, 'only God dubdubs'. What does
'create' mean if there are no other examples? To say (with
Tillich – and Peirce, in some passages), 'only creatures literally
exist', is again not to exalt God in any definite way – unless
another word, perhaps 'being', is introduced for God which does
apply to the creatures as well, and this will repeat the problem.
Although metaphysics tries to find ideas applying to all things,
it still need not violate the requirement of contrast.

At least two basic forms of contrast are not abolished by
metaphysical conceptions. One is that between God and any
other individual being; the other is that between logical types.
To take the latter first: what is *necessarily* true of any possible
individual need not be true of any possible event; yet both
truths are metaphysical rather than factual, i.e., they concern
what makes sense rather than merely what happens in the
actual world. Again, what must be true of every possible
abstract quality need not be true either of every individual or of
every event. Yet again it will be metaphysical. The generality
which metaphysics requires need not – indeed it must not – in
all cases transcend logical-type distinctions. It need only cover
all possible cases of each type.

True, we need a general idea of reality which applies to
individuals, as well as to events and abstract qualities; but then
there will be the contrast between real and fictitious entities,
whether individuals, events, or qualities. Whitehead's 'to be is
to be a potential for becoming' applies to any reality whatever;
but it leaves intact the contrast between merely supposed or

fancied and real potentials. If Peary did not really get to the North Pole, his getting there will influence no case of becoming, though his really claiming that he did will do so. And if 'being a fairy' has no definite and consistent meaning, as I suspect it has not, then this alleged quality is not a potential for any future becoming.

In addition to the most general or neutral idea of reality, spanning all logical types, we need metaphysical universals valid only within one type. Only if this is seen can certain historical doctrines be appropriately evaluated. That minority of philosophers (sometimes termed 'panpsychists', but I prefer 'psychicalists') who have said that sentience, or some minimal form of experiencing or mind, is universal have not really said that literally 'everything' feels or experiences. For no one ever thought that the colour blue is a subject with feelings, still less, if possible, that triangularity is such a subject. Abstractions do not feel or think, not even the abstraction 'feeling' or 'thinking'. These are objects of feeling or thought, not feelers or thinkers. Moreover, the proposition, 'every individual feels', does not entail that every group of individuals is a single subject with its own feelings. If each of two birds feels, there is not a third subject of feeling, the pair of birds. The 'group mind' is either metaphorical, in an extreme sense, or its applicability has definite limits. Thus psychicalism not only does not hold that everything feels, it doesn't even hold that everything concrete feels, if groups of individuals are regarded as concrete. I suggest, however, that groups, merely as such, are not fully concrete. Collections require collectors, sums summators. A pair of birds is perhaps an entity for each member of the pair – if they are mated, or neighbours, say – but it is not concretely the same entity in the two cases. The concrete reality of groups is in individuals, not *vice versa*. (A theist may argue that the definitive or fully concrete reality of all groups is in God's appreciation of the individuals composing them.) Groups fail to be subjects only because they are irreducibly objects for subjects; they are individuals only as particular collective termini for the perceptions and thoughts of individuals. If this point can be maintained, then we may say that psychicalism is the doctrine that everything concrete feels, with the understanding that nothing irreducibly collective is, as such, concrete.

It follows from the foregoing that a metaphysician must eschew extreme nominalism, he must admit that distinctions of logical type have counterparts in extra-linguistic reality. But this is in any case necessary for a viable metaphysics.

Is not a table a single concrete yet insentient thing? Of course the psychicalist must reject this example. He must say that while this table here before us is relatively concrete, compared, say, to the general idea of tables as such, it is still far from absolutely concrete. The senses are abstractive agencies, as Whitehead has sought to explain in his theory of perceptual 'transmutation'. There are cogent biological reasons why they must be so. However, it is not apparent that 'ordinary language' needs to recognize, in any obvious way, the pervasive abstractness of our pragmatic concepts of physical instrumentalities. Normally we simply *use* 'inanimate' physical things, and perceive them chiefly with an eye to their use; we do not ordinarily even ask what they are apart from our uses, or apart from the human species, or 'in themselves', or for God. These questions are somewhat abnormal, hence their answers will not lie on the surface of normal language.

Of course tables do not feel; but it does not follow that there is no feeling in them. There is feeling in a flock of birds or in a swarm of bees, but the flock or the swarm feels nothing. So there can be feeling in a swarm of molecules, though the swarm does not feel. The analogy is intelligible, and I fail to see any hopeless misuse of language in stating it.

Is the question one of fact? Yes, but only in its detailed or specific aspects. Thus it might be atoms not molecules, or *vice versa*, or both, which are the concrete singulars. And it is also a mere matter of fact that some visible objects in our world, such as vertebrate animals, are genuine singulars, whereas in large parts of nature the visible entities are exclusively collections, unified only as objects for our perceptions. Such un-individual parts of nature we term 'inanimate' – or 'vegetable'; for it seems likely that trees, for example, are essentially collectives, colonies of cells, without any unity comparable either to that of single cells or to that which a nervous system gives vertebrates.

By recognizing the logical-type distinctions involved (as no philosopher before Leibniz, so far as I know, ever did, and disgracefully few have done since Leibniz) we show that the apparent absurdity of generalizing physical conceptions to cover all possible (concrete) reality is apparent only.

Psychicalism, I hold, is implicit in theism. If supreme reality is supreme mind or experience, lesser forms of reality can only be lesser forms of mind or experience. To introduce mere matter is to destroy the intelligibility of the doctrine. Mere matter, as the zero of feeling and intrinsic value, is an absolute negation whose meaning is wholly parasitic on what it denies. Matter is no more the principle of reality than zero is of number. Primitive animism or hylozoism, though of course fanciful in all details, was yet sound in its broad principle. Also not without reason have materialists seldom been theists, while theists have generally felt antipathy for materialism. But dualism is merely an evasion of the issue. The very concept of mere matter as a possible form of reality has no place in a theistic metaphysics (really, in any metaphysics). The zero of mind is the zero of likeness to deity; but (assuming theism is good grammar) the creature can only be some sort of inferior resemblance to the supreme creative cause.

If all individuals (other than mere collectives) are sentient, then does not 'sentient individual' lose its distinctive meaning? It does indeed become truistic, a sort of redundancy. Yet redundancy is not always useless. Since there are many sorts of deceptive pseudo-individuals (individual only as objects, relative to certain subjects) which of course are not sentient, it is worth-while to insist that the task of finding genuinely or intrinsically individual entities is the same as that of finding genuinely sentient entities. And indeed the criteria are the same. That is individual which either acts or feels individually. Tables do neither; they are not sentient individuals, because they are not in themselves individual. They do not act on their own, so of course they do not feel on their own. Feeling as one and acting as one are but two sides of the same thing – i.e., existing as one.

Ordinary language is largely concerned with specifically human purposes and feelings, not purposes or feelings at large. This strong anthropomorphic bias is normal. Since metaphysics is the extreme form of trying to transcend it, the metaphysician is in a somewhat abnormal attitude.

The pure materialist absolutizes the normal bias in a strange way, while also negating it. He carries to the limit that neglect and seeming denial of the inner, qualitative feeling-side of reality which the collective selfishness of human beings has already accepted for most of nature and argues that we can achieve conceptual universality and objectivity only by getting rid of this aspect, even in our own human case. I sympathize with the attack on anthropomorphic subjectivism but hold that the way to overcome the latter is to see that we have no conceivable ground for limiting feeling to our kind of individual, say the vertebrates, or even to animals. The way out of collective selfishness is into completely generalized unselfishness, sympathy with the universal 'life of things', the 'ocean of feelings', which is reality in its concrete character.

We have said that there are two forms of contrast which fall within metaphysics, i.e., are *a priori* not empirical, one being contrasts of logical type and the other being the distinction between God and other things. We have now to see that this is really a unique form of logical-type distinction. As necessary in his existence God is *logically* different from other individuals. Here you may well ask: What common meaning can individual then have? My answer, not the traditional one by any means, is this: existing necessarily, God nevertheless, like any individual you please, exists by virtue of concrete states ('experiences') which themselves, in their concreteness, are contingent. Thus, on his concrete side, God is of the same logical type as other individuals. Where then is his necessity? In this: the class of his possible states could not be empty; whereas with other individuals there might not have been *any* such states.

To say that a class could not be empty is not at all to say that its particular members are necessary. 'You must come to a decision' does not say, there is a certain particular decision to which you must come. It only says, the class of your decisions for this matter cannot remain empty. God has no option between existing and not existing, but – and there is no inconsistency in this – he has options as to *how* he exists, in what particular states. (I am of course fully aware that this is a shocking departure from much of the tradition. I can only say that, for me, what is shocking is precisely this part of the tradition. It seems to me incompatible with the notion of worship.) Between 'possibly empty' and 'necessarily non-empty' classes there is a logical-type distinction – logical because modal, and a matter of meaning, not contingent fact.

Some will doubtless fear that putting God, even though only on one side of his nature, into the same logical type with creatures destroys the awe-inspiring gulf between him and us. I think this is a mistake, though a natural one. (1) The contingent side of God is the concrete side. The concrete embraces the abstract, not *vice versa*. Hence God *qua* contingent is more than God *qua* necessary, not less. (2) Whereas we as contingent are contingent all through, nothing unique to us being necessary, God's contingent states, on the contrary, contain his necessary eternal essence. (3) God's contingent actuality includes ours fully and adequately (omniscience), but not *vice versa*. Any value in us is therefore *ipso facto* in him; the converse does not hold. Thus he transcends any and all other concrete realities, and it is impossible they could surpass or rival him. If anyone feels no awe before the idea of one 'to whom all hearts are open', to whom all past cosmic history is a fully legible book, and by whom all that ever comes to be will be fully appreciated in every nuance of quality, then I can only suppose he does not genuinely contemplate the meaning of such expressions. But they are not only compatible with the contingency of God as concrete, they imply it, if I understand their meaning at all.

Note that one who treats 'mind' or 'feeling' as a limited affair can certainly not make sense out of 'God'. If the concept of mind, spirit, or awareness can stretch all the way up to deity (as knowing and valuing his creatures), it must have strictly infinite possibilities. What then could prevent it from covering also the gap (surely smaller) between man and atom? Logical-type differences alone can set limits to the applicability of 'X feels'. Moreover, even the logical-type difference between God and the mere creatures does not forbid the application of this formula to both sides of this supreme gap. For, as argued above, God must be allowed a contingent aspect by virtue of which he is, on that side, of one logical type with other individuals. And in fact, only *as* contingent does God feel. In his merely eternal and necessary aspect he is not an actual subject of thinking or feeling, but only an object, both of his own thinking – which in each actual case is contingent – and of creaturely thought.

I believe that it is reasonable enough to tie together suspicion of metaphysics as such and suspicion of theism as such. To this extent, Carneades (and Comte) saw the issue correctly. Metaphysics and natural theology share a common fate. But that Carneades (or Hume) correctly decided the issue – that is another matter!

If metaphysical statements are to be possible, certain assumptions about language must be avoided. One must *not* say that all existential propositions are contingent or factual, or that all positive generalizations are so – for instance, 'every event is influenced by, but partially transcends, antecedent events (its causal conditions)'. If this statement is metaphysically correct, both determinism and the admission of causally uninfluenced happenings fail to make sense. Creativity and causal limitations are metaphysical correlates.

Consider the endless attempts to show the compatibility of freedom and determinism. As Bridgman, Koerner, and others have shown, every attempt to take the causal principle absolutely leads to paradox, not simply because of freedom, but in many other ways. No one knows what it would be like for causal order to be absolute. Why try to harmonize freedom with a conception we do not possess? The real question is not, is causality limited or unlimited, but rather, what can we know about its limits?

The classic example of begging metaphysical questions unconsciously is Hume's *Dialogues*. He asserts as a dogma that non-existence is conceivable in all cases – from which it follows that theism is bad grammar! But then the empirical arguments of the *Dialogue* are irrelevant. Hume also asserts that if two entities are distinguishable they are mutually independent. In that case the creatures, being distinguishable from their creator, could exist without him. Again, bad grammar. Thirdly, Hume assumes that strict determinism makes sense. But the absolutizing of order destroys its contrast with disorder and implies the absurdity of theism as belief in supreme creativity.

Is it any wonder that Hume could arrive at no plausible metaphysical or theistic conclusion? His rules forbade a metaphysical outcome in any sensible form. Is it not permissible to derive some amusement from the way so many of our contemporaries re-enact Hume's performance – without seeing the joke? Or the way Mill and William James re-enacted it?

One of the ways in which critics of metaphysics beg the question about the possibility of a sane metaphysics is by selecting as examples of metaphysical doctrine egregiously bad ones, which can plausibly be interpreted as disguised commands not to use certain parts of normal language. Thus 'time is unreal' means, when claiming to talk seriously or profoundly, do not make temporal distinctions, talk about dates, or before and after! Or 'everything changes' means, do not talk about individuals or properties as identifiable through time. But sane metaphysics is rather the opposite of this. It tries to make sense out of change *and* permanence, time *and* eternity, unity *and* plurality, quality *and* structure, freedom *and* order, dependence *and* independence. Hume's dictum, no event is logically dependent upon any other, is no better and no worse than Blanshard's contention that every event implicates every other. The proper metaphysical question is, what rules govern relations, making them extrinsic or dispensable to some terms, and intrinsic or indispensable to others? The answer will not readily be found simply by asking how we ordinarily talk, though this may well carry us part of the way.

We do talk as though events depend upon what happens before, not upon what happens afterwards, as though dependence were asymmetrical. Hume (like Russell) never seriously considers this; he and his opponents Green or Bradley take symmetry for granted. On that basis events are either independent both ways, or dependent both ways. Similarly, Spinoza makes God necessitate the modes and the modes necessitate God, neither being independent of the other. (Or at least, he does not clearly say what else his view is.) Here, too, symmetry is assumed.

The theist has a clue to this problem in the *unique* necessity of the divine existence, which implies that while God could exist without this particular world, the latter could not exist without God. Indeed, 'without God' is ungrammatical. To ask, What could exist without God?, is like asking, What could exist if 3 and 4 were not 7? The question is no question. But 3 and 4 could and would be 7, even though this particular world did not exist. So could and would God exist as God without this world. Dependence is here asymmetrical fundamentally. The assumption of universal symmetry – whether of dependence or independence – is anti-theistic. It is also absurd on the face of it. (see Chapter IX).

Tillich and symbolic meanings

There has been much talk, by Tillich and others, about the special way in which words function in religion. No one doubts that some religious talk is symbolic, as when God is called the good shepherd. According to Tillich there is at most one literal statement about God, that he is being itself. He also gives a functional or pragmatic definition, relative to human attitudes: God is the object of 'ultimate concern'. Otherwise talk about God is held to be symbolic. It does not describe God, but somehow makes us aware of him, rather as poetry and art make us aware of things.

I think that Tillich's view is one-sided, and that both his literal and his functional definitions can be so interpreted that they agree, but also so that they imply a number of literal truths about God. As explication of 'ultimate concern', Tillich helpfully suggests that it means loving God with all one's mind and heart and soul and strength – in short, with all one's being. Now I find in this a quite literal and precise meaning. If God is what can genuinely and without illusion be loved with all one's capacities, then he must in some sense coincide with being or reality itself. For to acknowledge any item of reality is to express some interest in it, however slight, and this interest, too, must have God as its object. The whole mind must be turned to God. He must be the universal object of every interest or attachment whatever. We are not to love or be interested in our neighbour, or some creature, *and* God, or God *and* the creature; rather, we are to love the creature as somehow God. Interest is not to be divided between God and anything whatever, which implies that being or reality is also not divided between him and anything else. More clearly: the distinction between God and anything else must fall within God. If and only if he is somehow all being, all reality, actual or possible, can devotion to him be all devotion. Thus Tillich's two proposals for defining God are not only mutually consistent, but they are equivalent. The one makes deity the universal object of possible interest, the other of possible thought, and these of course can only coincide, since to think X is to be interested in X, and to be interested in X is to imply *X* as at least the possible object of thought. So far I hold that Tillich is absolutely right.

It has been objected to 'being itself' that there is no such thing, the verb 'to be' constituting only a bond between various subjects and their predicates. This objection is rather trivial, and indeed beside the point. One need not use the word 'being' at all to express what I hope Tillich wishes to say. 'Reality itself' will do even better, for one thing, because it avoids the contrast with becoming which 'being' suggests. 'Reality' contrasts only with 'unreality', 'mere appearance', or fiction.

To say that God is reality itself means, in my view, that any assertion whatever can, without loss, be translated into an assertion about God. Thus 'John runs' implies no more, and no less, than that *John running* somehow qualifies God. If this were not the case, the commandment to turn one's whole mind, heart, and soul to God could not be obeyed; for if I recognize the fact of John running, I have turned that much of my mind to John; yet I must not have turned even that much of my mind away from God. Hence John running must be an aspect of deity, no more and no less. I hope that Tillich would accept the foregoing explication, though I cannot be sure. He would perhaps want to say that 'John running' qualifies God only symbolically. My objection is simple: we cannot but be interested in the literal facts about our neighbours, and if these are neither more nor less than facts about God then I see no sense in denying that they are facts literally obtaining of God. We are to love our neighbour as he literally is, and yet to love God with that very aspect of our minds or hearts; and I conclude that the neighbour must in some appropriate and quite literal sense be a constituent of the divine life. Very literally we are 'in' God, and all our properties are divine possessions.

If God is literally being (reality) itself, then he literally has all the categorial features of reality, reality as conditioned and as unconditioned, as actual and as potential, as relative and as absolute, as concrete and as abstract. Should this be denied, I just do not know what, on that assumption, the meaning of the allegedly unique literal truth about God might be. Literal truths always have literal logical consequences. By denying these, one nullifies the supposed literalness.

Let us now look at some of Tillich's negations. He says that

God is not literally cause; for a cause in the ordinary sense is always also effect, and God as cause would be caught in the causal chain. Yes, true enough, and why not? God is *universal* cause, creative of everything whatever; but as reality itself, God is likewise universal effect, influenced by everything whatever. It is the universality, the coincidence with reality in its polar aspects, which makes God supreme, not his cuddling up to the category of cause and shrinking away from that of effect. Cause-effect belong together, and God is the sole *universal* cause-effect.

Instead of 'cause', Tillich prefers 'ground of being' or 'power of being'. I think that these, as he uses them, either say nothing definite, or else they imply precisely that favouritism of cause over effect, unconditioned over conditioned, which I regard as idolatrous, since it denies the coincidence of God with reality which Tillich rightly sees as definitive of the divine. Reality is just as truly effect as cause; and so is deity. True, God's existence is not caused, but only his actuality. This introduces another question: Does God 'exist'? Tillich says the word is unsuitable. But I say that it – like any categorial word – is suitable if and only if construed in the required uniquely universal sense. God has universal existence, not particular existence. He does not merely happen to exist, as one thing among others. He always, necessarily, essentially exists; and only he exists in this sense. I see no valid argument in Tillich against this. Indeed in effect it is his view.

If it be asked what 'universal', 'necessary', or 'essential' existence has in common with ordinary existence, the answer can be given fairly simply, and quite literally. For an individual to exist is always for it to be actualized in concrete states, none of which (unless the first one) is absolutely necessary for the existence of that individual. Since God has no beginning, one can drop the qualifying 'unless the first one' and say that, conceiving him by analogy with ordinary individuals, his existence must consist in his nature being actualized in states which do not follow necessarily from his individual essence. That, nevertheless, God 'exists necessarily' means that his individual nature is inevitably and invincibly actualized *somehow*, but just how, in what actual states, is a further and contingent truth about him.

Actuality, even divine, is always contingent; but it does not follow that all existence is contingent; for in the eminent or divine existence the contingency applies only to the particular actualities by which the divine essence is concretized, not to the truth that it is actualized by some actualities or other.

Consider Tillich's denial that God is *a* being. This is argued for by taking the disjunction, 'being itself or *a* being', as exclusive. But on what ground? Can being itself in no fashion constitute *a* being? Suppose the Berkeleyan formula, 'to be is to be perceived', is in some sense true with reference to God as the universal perceiver. Then the divine perceiver is *a* – or rather *the* – being.

But also: possible being is what God might perceive, actual being (including his own) is what he does perceive; thus his perceiving, with its content, is reality as such in a definite, literal sense.

Tillich's doctrine of the symbolic character of theological terms is in part a concession to that core of the Great Tradition, the 'negative theology'. At first blush, it seems a reasonable doctrine. Does not a modest estimate of our human capacity to understand God imply that our concepts cannot properly apply to him? So it is held to be quite safe to say, without qualification, that he is *not* finite, *not* relative, *not* possible or open to influence. I think, however, that the modesty is only apparent. We dare to forbid God to sustain relations, to accept the definiteness that comes through limits, to respond to the creatures and thus be influenced by them. He may, we concede, do these things 'symbolically', whatever that may mean, but we tell him in no uncertain terms that he must not literally do them! Is this modesty – or is it monstrous presumption? Have we this veto power upon divinity? Not to sustain relationships, not to respond sensitively to the existence of others is to be wooden, stupid, or an utterly empty abstraction. It is the abstract which has these negative characteristics, not the concrete. Whiteness does not relate itself to white things, for whiteness is whiteness, no matter which white things may happen to exist. Whiteness, compared to white things, is 'impossible'. Is God to be found merely in this direction, looking towards the less and less concrete?

When we say that God is not literally a shepherd, ruler, or

potter, but only symbolically these things, we are indeed following a safe and modest way. But why is this so? Because shepherd, ruler, potter, are quite specific sorts of things, definite items found here and there in existence. Hence the alternative to being a ruler or a shepherd must cover a vast miscellaneous infinity of possibilities, only a few of which are known to the human mind. To 'forbid' God to be literally a shepherd is to impose no restrictions on his freedom to be. Of course he cannot be simply identical with such a special item of reality. So we can say that in religion 'shepherd' symbolizes Something, or Someone, literally quite other than a shepherd and also than any specific localized thing in the world not a shepherd. Who can quarrel with this procedure?

It is, however, a very different affair when we treat utterly abstract terms like 'finite' or 'relative' in this same manner. There are not an infinity of miscellaneous possible positive forms of reality alternative to being relative; there is only being non-relative or absolute. If God is not literally finite and relative, then he is literally and exclusively infinite and absolute. For there is no third possibility: here the law of excluded middle must, I submit, apply. That which is 'not literally a shepherd' may yet have all sorts of resemblances to as well as differences from an actual shepherd; and so it may, symbolically, be called a shepherd. But that which is not literally 'in some degree and quality made what it is by contingent relations', i.e., relative, can only be something which is in no degree so constituted, i.e., it must be quite literally and entirely absolute. Where is there a place for anything symbolic here?

Tillich's examples of the symbolic taken from the arts confirm my point. It is the more or less concrete and specific which is expressed in artistic images for which there is no literal substitute. But the converse also holds: for the ultimate abstractions like relativity there is no symbolic substitute either. And the reason, we have seen, is that while 'not a shepherd' covers anything and everything, actual or possible, other than one very special sort of item in the universe, by contrast, 'not open to influence or limitation' is merely the equally abstract other pole of the categorial contrast, 'relative-absolute'. To compare this with poetry is quite illegitimate. It is totally non-poetic, because totally non-concrete.

'God is not a shepherd' leaves God entirely free to be some sort of super-shepherd. But 'super-relative' can only be construed as an eminent form of perfectly literal relativity. I believe in this eminent form, this uniquely divine relativity, but it, just as literally as ordinary relativity, implies 'in some way and degree constituted by contingent relations'. There is no symbolic way of being, in a certain aspect, contingent, having qualities one might not have had: either one might, or one might not, have been otherwise. *Tertium non datur.* Traditional theological theory had a headlong tendency, almost wholly ungovernable, and even today in many circles largely uncontrolled, to 'plump' for one side – the negative side – of the ultimate polar contraries, in application to God. But this indeed 'limits' God – for instance, if we deny him all definiteness, or all responsiveness to the contingent creatures. To be definitely this is to be definitely not that; 'all possible definiteness' is merely total indefiniteness and vacuity. And we think to honour God by offering him this vacuity as his sole portion! I have been protesting against this for twenty years (written in 1960). I hope to live to add another ten, and by sheer persistence, and also by resourcefully exploring the possible ways of approaching this matter, to wake up many of those theologians who in this regard are still sleeping (they are far fewer now, to be sure, than they used to be) so that they will honestly reflect upon this problem.

The modesty of the negative theology is highly suspect. It puts an infinite human veto upon the wealth of the divine life, cutting it off from all but the purely abstract. All abstractions, just so far as they are abstract, are infinite, absolute, or impassible. The God of the negative theology is not only 'a mathematician', he is exclusively some such thing – if indeed the topic of his preoccupation must not be even emptier than mere numbers and algebraic orders!

'Pure actuality' must either mean all possible actuality – and this is the same as all possible confusion, for possibilities have relations of incompossibility – or it has no relation to possibility at all. But then the term expresses no analogy to actuality as we know it, and one might as well say 'pure blub-blub'. As for infinity, what could be more 'absolutely infinite' than the totality of all that is logically possible? Is the divine actuality simply identical with this totality? Then the meaning of both 'actual' and 'possible' is lost. So it appears that we had better worship God, not 'the infinite'. I admit that Tillich tries to take such considerations into the reckoning, in some degree; but I I also feel fairly confident that his veneration for the traditional systems has warped his treatment, causing him to underestimate the significance of the problems we have been discussing.

There is a set of concepts often applied to God which are distinct both from very specific terms like 'shepherd' and very abstract terms like 'relative'. These are psychical terms like 'knowledge', 'will', 'love'. If these denote, as they tend to do, states or functions very like the human, then they are essentially in a class with shepherd, although not nearly so narrowly specific. But it is a central philosophical issue how far psychical terms can be broadened beyond the human application. Does a dog 'know' symbolically? Does a dog simply not know, or only know? The questions are not easy to answer. My own position is that there is a legitimate broadest possible meaning of psychical terms which is applicable to all individuals whatever, from atoms to deity. In this broadest meaning, these terms are almost categorial, like relativity. There is, however, a difference. For only individuals, not abstractions, can feel or think or remember, whereas both individuals and abstractions (other than those of uttermost generality) can have aspects of relativity, can depend in some way and degree upon contingent relations. As a result of this still wider applicability, or greater abstractness, of the strictly categorial notions, their meaning does not vary from one level to another in the scale of beings. To be 'constituted in some way by contingent relations' is simply and literally that, no more, no less, and no other. But to 'know', to 'feel', to 'remember' – here there are qualitative differences which are not easily covered by empty terms like 'way' or 'degree'.

Does God know, simply as a man knows? Of course not, only men do that. But dogs know in doggish fashion, and God knows in divine fashion. Tillich says that if we take this latter statement literally we become involved in 'absurd questions'. I should like very much to see a list of the questions, and I am willing to wager that their absurdity is relative, in part at least, to some element or other of the negative theology which Tillich – a bit uncritically, as I think – has taken over from the past.

Of course merely absolute, wholly non-relative, 'knowledge' is an absurdity. But the veto upon literal relatedness (a veto which must itself be literal or else merely misleading) is in my view unwitting blasphemy.

Is then 'know' merely symbolic, as applied to God? It is in such application not literal in the simple sense in which 'relative' can be. For relative is a more abstract term, hence less sensitive to differences in levels of reality. But yet it is arguable that neither is 'know' simply symbolic, as 'shepherd' certainly is. For this is the question: does our concept of 'know' come merely from intra-human experience, analogically extended to what is below and above the human, or does the concept come partly from religious experience, from some dim but direct awareness of deity? Brunner, I think, has suggested or implied that it is God who is unqualifiedly personal, and human beings are only imperfect, fragmentary pointers towards true personality.

It is indeed a curious thing to see how much need there is, not so much of a negative theology as of a 'negative anthropology'. We say we know – ah, but do we? We guess, on more or less reasonable grounds, but do we literally know? If 'know' means to have conclusive evidence, then when do we literally attain knowledge? And if it doesn't mean this, but only to have inconclusive evidence, then how vague the idea becomes! Theories of human knowledge vary as much as those of divine knowledge. I really believe that we know what 'knowledge' is partly by knowing God, and that though it is true that we form the idea of divine knowledge by analogical extension from our experience of human knowledge, this is not the whole truth, the other side of the matter being that we form our idea of human knowledge by exploiting the intuition (called by Descartes, 'innate idea', and as such not really disproved, except in a straw-man version, by Locke) which we have of God. To 'know' *ought* to mean, having conclusive evidence, such as God has, shutting off the very possibility of error; but to apply this idea to man we must tone it down drastically indeed.

My proposal is that we should distinguish in theology between (1) plainly symbolic terms like shepherd or ruler, (2) plainly literal terms like relative or absolute, and (3) 'problematic' terms, which may be literal if or in so far as we have religious intuition, like 'know' or 'love'. Man loves, but how far and how much? He either hates or is apathetic towards most of his surroundings. It is God who loves – without any distorting antipathies or blind spots of mere indifference. God loves the creatures – period. We love a few creatures some of the time, and seldom or never wholly without complicating feelings of vanity, envy, irritation, fear, and the like.

In view of the foregoing, I find myself more in sympathy with the old label 'analogical' in preference to 'symbolic' for the third or problematic class of theological concepts (those neither unambiguously literal nor unambiguously non-literal). There is in some sense analogy between divine and human knowledge; but to say this is not to answer the question: Which way is the analogy to be read? Are we merely using our awareness of man to point the way to the divine nature, or are we also using our awareness of God to furnish a criterion for the weaknesses of man? If both procedures can and do occur, then 'human knowledge' is no mere symbol for an otherwise inaccessible divine nature, since it may also be a derivative concept, produced by drastically restricting the idea arising from our intuition of deity. I believe with John Oman – and in line with the suggestion of Brunner above referred to – that man's awareness of God is no mere contingent extension of his awareness of himself, but is rather an indispensable element of that awareness. In this view, the divine-human contrast is the basic principle of all human thought, never wholly submerged, though it may often be driven rather deep into the dimly-lighted regions of experience.

I would go even further, and say that the lower animals, while they cannot think God, do feel him, and so even for them the divine-non-divine contrast is constitutive of all experience. Thus there is no simple inaccessibility of God, though it may well be that the higher levels of awareness of deity involve a divine decision of special self-revelation. God may 'reveal himself to whom he pleases', for all I know; but I do think I know that he cannot absolutely conceal himself from *any* creature, for the omnipresent can never be more than relatively inaccessible.

Some will say that in the foregoing account I have overlooked the infinite gulf between God and the creatures. But not so. Between the finite-infinite individual and the merely finite individuals there is a gap in natures which is literally infinite.

And between the divine cause-effect which influences and is influenced by *every* reality and ordinary cause-effects which, since they begin to be at a certain stage of the creative advance of existence, are exclusively causes of what comes after, and which also, since they must die at a later stage, will be exclusively effects of what came before, there is again a doubly infinite distinction. God both infinitely precedes and infinitely outlasts every other individual, so that all are influenced by, and also influence, his actuality.

Are not these issues too subtle for the traditional modes of analysis? To go on repeating the old decisions plus little more than the new word 'symbolic' or phrases like 'religious language' is not to shed much new light on the old issues. Our ancestors had their word, 'analogical', which is, if anything, clearer. The real trouble is less in the exaggeration of literalness than in the idolatry of infinity, being, cause, and absoluteness, accepted as substitutes for the divine unity of the contraries, finite-infinite, being-creativity, cause-effect, absolute-relational, being as such and *a* being. God is, in diverse aspects of his reality, on both sides of these polarities.

'Etiolatry', worship of cause, and 'ontolatry', worship of being (in contrast to becoming), or worship of 'the absolute' (in contrast to the all-loving and hence all-related God), have too long masqueraded as true worship. I believe that they are impostors. But Tillich himself has shown us the remedy. The twofold definition of deity which he proposes, suitably interpreted and followed out without deviation or contrary assumptions, leads us past the ancient confusions into the light of the supreme Light, so far as it is accessible to our intellects.

To sum up this discussion of symbols in theology: many theological terms are more or less symbolic; others may be now symbolic (here better termed analogical), now literal, depending upon the availability of religious intuition; but the most completely abstract general terms applicable to deity are quite literal. True, there is always a difference in principle between this and other applications. But the difference itself can be literally stated. Thus only of God is it true that his capacity to be this, or that instead – his range of contingent possible qualities – is absolutely infinite, so that the entire difference between some possible thing X and some other possible thing Y

must be embraced in the difference between the possibility of God as qualified by X and God as qualified by Y.

Thus the 'unlimitedness' of God is in his contingent potential aspects, not his actuality. And 'contingent' has here its usual meaning, 'could be this, or that instead'. The lack of limits is also literal.

The widespread belief that there is no genuine logic of metaphysical conceptions, no rules of the game of talking metaphysically, seems to me incorrect. The logic may not be easy to get clear about, and the rules have perhaps scarcely been set forth in print, much less generally heeded by those classed as metaphysicians. But there are those of us who think we know some such rules and are trying to state and obey them.

It should be clear that I am in hearty agreement with much current writing in treating metaphysical questions as meaning questions. Metaphysical truths are necessary, not factual. But when Wittgenstein says that necessary propositions 'say nothing' I want to add to 'nothing' the words 'factual or contingent'. Yet the propositions do say something true about God and any possible creatures, for instance that God exists and could not not exist, but that any creature could have failed to exist; also that God or creatures could have existed in different states, and in their creative freedom transcend causal conditioning and are never causally limited to a single course of action. Also that only collectives or abstractions are strictly insentient.

Since students of the logic of mathematics have not been able to agree upon the axioms of set theory, nor in spite of Quine to agree that such questions are ultimately factual, with what right can anyone rule out the possibility that metaphysical questions are neither factual nor trivially analytic, but in some subtle and difficult sense questions of meaning and consistency?

VIII

NON-RESTRICTIVE EXISTENTIAL STATEMENTS

ORDINARY factual statements are partially restrictive of existential possibilities: for, if they are affirmative, they also implicitly deny something; and if they are negative, they also implicitly affirm something. Thus, 'There are men in the room' denies that the room is filled solid from floor to ceiling with non-human bodies; and 'There are no men in the room' affirms that every substantial part of the room contains something (if only air, or a 'vacuum' furnishing free passage to radiant energy) other than a man. In addition to statements *partially* restrictive in this sense, there are two other kinds: the *completely restrictive*, and the *completely non-restrictive*.

A completely restrictive statement denies that any existential possibility is realized. If, for instance, we were to say, 'Nothing exists', this would exclude anything and everything from existing. (For 'nothing' is not the name of a kind of entity.) Such a statement could not conceivably be verified; since the verifying experience itself must exist; nor can anyone experience bare nothing. However, our completely restrictive statement can be falsified; we falsify it every moment. It is untrue that nothing exists. Here, then, we have a falsifiable, yet not conceivably verifiable, statement. Can such a statement be false in the merely factual or contingent sense? Is it not rather a statement which is bound to be false? If nothing were to exist, what would make this true? Bare nothing? And what would 'existence' mean, if it were wholly unexemplified? Would the idea or possibility of 'existence' still remain in some Platonic heaven of forms? I submit that the more plausible view is that a completely restrictive or wholly negative statement expresses an impossibility, not a conceivable but unrealized fact.

It is important to realize that the exclusion of 'nothing exists' as an absurdity carries with it certain consequences. One of these is that we must also exclude all statements professing to be free from positive implications. We must not admit 'There are no dodos' if this is alleged to denote a purely 'negative fact'. For if one purely negative fact is admitted, why could not all facts be purely negative? Then 'Nothing exists' would, it seems, be true. The non-existence of dodos means that where dodos might conceivably be, every suitable portion of space contains something which could not be there if a dodo were there. Observation, as Popper admirably says, is not basically of the form, 'Such and such is not the case', but rather, 'Such and such is the case'. 'His purse was empty' does not mean it had literally 'nothing' in it, but that it had only things other than money, such as air, or light waves by which one sees the sides or bottom of the purse unhindered by solid objects. Essentially, presences are observed, not absences. But of course presences always imply absences. The basic asymmetry is seen in this, however, that the absent things are indefinite or infinite, compared to those present. Definiteness cannot be gained by listing what is not to be observed. The positive is the key to the negative, not *vice versa*.

The principle of the partial positiveness of every fact is a fertile one. Consider one interesting application. There is a form of (scarcely genuine) scepticism: perhaps other human bodies, different from mine physically in slight details only, are utterly unlike mine in this, that there are no feelings, thoughts, or other forms of experiencing in them. This sheer absence of the psychical has no positive bearings. It tells me nothing as to how those mindless bodies will behave. In all relevant respects they behave as I do. But whereas with me such behaviour would imply experiences of such and such kinds, in them it implies nothing of the sort. Our principle that there can be no such thing as a mere absence rules out this form of scepticism. Unless something is in the other bodies which could not be there if they had experiences, they do have them. So the 'argument by analogy' can get a grip on the situation.

Apply the same principle to the general question, 'Is any portion of nature simply without any kind of experiences?' If something can be observed which logically could not coexist with experience, then the answer is affirmative. Descartes takes extension as excluding the psychical. But he cannot deny that a man feels and thinks and is also extended. So, if a human 'in-extended' psyche can be in an extended human body, it can, so far as mere extension is concerned, be in a mountain. It must be some special sort of extension which excludes the psychical as such. And what sort? I think the critics of psychicalism will never agree on any answer, and I think there is no positive answer which makes sense other than something like the follow-ing. A completely static body, inert as a whole and in its parts, cannot contain any feeling or thought, and a body and parts moving purely monotonously cannot do so either. Also a body lacking functional unity as a whole, or lacking definite differ-entiation from its environment (e.g., the Arctic Ocean) cannot plausibly be viewed as a single subject of experiencing. All of these specifications have positive implications as well as negative ones. But none of them apply to any portion of nature taken both as a whole and in its constituent elements. Inert rocks have active atoms, molecules, or particles. Homogeneous fluids have differentiated microscopic parts. So our principle, no merely negative facts, no mere absences, supports our psychicalism.

It also enables us to answer another form of scepticism (materialism, by the way, except as reaction against a narrow form of idealism, is a kind of scepticism, a doubt that most of nature contains anything analogous, even remotely, to what in us we call experience or feeling), the scepticism which runs: for all we know, process will come to an end, possibly this moment is the last. What positive bearing could this have? After this – nothing. A mere absence. This is an in principle wholly restrictive statement. Does it make sense?

Let us now consider the third class of statements, those com-pletely non-restrictive. For example, 'Something exists'. Since this is the pure contradictory of the wholly restrictive, 'Nothing exists', which we have found reason to regard as impossible, and since the contradictory of an impossible statement is necessary, we should expect 'Something exists' to be necessarily true, a statement valid *a priori*. And we see that it excludes nothing from existence, except bare 'nothing' itself. But the existence of bare nothing is no existence. Further, 'Something exists' is in no

conceivable circumstances falsifiable, since the falsifying experience would have to exist, and it would also have to be the
experience *of* something existing – at least if, as I should maintain, experience is essentially a relative term, requiring that to
which it is relative, or of which it is the experience. But though
'Something exists' is unfalsifiable, it is verified every moment.
Could the verifiable but in any conceivable world absolutely
unfalsifiable be false? I hold that the necessarily true must be
knowable as true and only as true, and that, conversely, whatever is in principle verifiable though not falsifiable is thereby
shown to be necessarily true. (We shall consider some apparent
exceptions later.) A necessary proposition, in Lewis's modal
logic, is one 'implied by any and every proposition'. It thus
forms an aspect of the meaning of any statement you please.
Clearly, 'Something exists' is included in the meaning of any
restrictive existential statement, such as , 'Elephants exist'. It
therefore entirely avoids conflict with existential possibilities.

Metaphysics, as I view it, studies non-restrictive existential
affirmations. It differs from mathematics, which also studies
non-restrictive statements, in that mathematical statements are
non-existential. As usually interpreted they affirm, not that
something with a certain character exists, but that, if it did, such
and such would also be the case. Thus they affirm relations
between conceivable states of affairs, without affirming any such
state to be actualized. Mathematics explores possibilities; metaphysics tries to express what *all* possibilities of existence have in
common, excluding blank non-existence as an impossibility. It
searches for the common elements of all positive existential
possibilities, some of which *must* be actualized – if not this, then
that; if not that, then still another – but at any rate something.
Metaphysics, in the old phrase, explores 'being *qua* being', or
reality *qua* reality, meaning by this, the strictly universal features
of existential possibility, those which cannot be unexemplified.

Metaphysics has been described as 'either platitude or paradox'. 'Something exists' is platitudinous enough; but, 'It is
necessary that something should exist' has been denied by leading philosophers, and is, to this extent, no mere platitude.
William James for one denied it, and he was not alone. Moreover, if the proposition, 'something exists' is necessary, then we
must give up the reigning dogma that a statement is rendered

contingent by the mere fact that it asserts existence. The consequences of this renunciation are far-reaching. We must substitute for the false principle, all existential statements are contingent, the significantly different one, *all partially restrictive statements are contingent*, that is, all those which, affirming or denying the existence of something, also by implication deny or affirm the existence of something else likewise conceivable. Only when this substitution has been made can we stop talking confused nonsense and arbitrary dogma concerning the question, Is metaphysics a possible mode of knowledge?

The real meaning of this last question is, Can anything more interesting than the bare 'something exists' be proved equally non-restrictive and existential, i.e., metaphysical? The answer, I believe, is this: the class of wholly non-restrictive existential statements contains 'something exists' together with all statements which are implied by this one; and some of these implied statements are decidedly interesting and important.

Seeing that a necessary or non-restrictive proposition is implied by any proposition, it certainly is implied by any necessary proposition, so that 'something exists' must embrace within its meaning all the metaphysical truths. But it need not contain them in an immediately obvious manner, somewhat as mathematical postulates have consequences which only a good mathematician may succeed in making clear. In this sense, metaphysics is not platitude though it is truistic, in that, in so far as you see the point, you see that its propositions could not but be true. However, the point may not be easy to see. The stubborn disagreements in metaphysics are due in part to mistaking what its task is, for example, to supposing that it seeks some queer kind of 'fact', that is, restrictive truth, which nevertheless is necessary or *a priori*, and so not really restrictive after all. This contradictory undertaking could scarcely lead to harmonious opinions. The disagreements are also due in part to the circumstance that man is able to gain certain satisfactions by exaggerating or otherwise misstating metaphysical truths so that they become paradoxes, e.g., by saying, 'change is unreal', or 'nothing is permanent'. These paradoxes are bound to generate disagreement; for either they provoke their own contraries, as is illustrated by the pair of paradoxes just mentioned about change and permanence, or else they lead to the rejection of metaphysics as a tissue of absurdities. Only a renewed search for non-paradoxical versions of unrestrictive existential truth offers hope of eventual agreement; but this search has been somewhat neglected in the last two decades, and has rarely been pursued with single-minded clarity, free from religious, irreligious, or other hampering pre-commitments.

Let us now look at a few candidates for the status of non-restrictive affirmations of existence. Consider the statement, 'Some experience occurs' (or, is had). This is easily verified, as Descartes pointed out – albeit somewhat ambiguously, as has often been shown. Certainly experience does occur. Is the statement conceivably falsifiable? Would any experience exhibit the total non-occurrence of experience? Clearly not. This strongly suggests, and I think proves, that it is a necessarily true, or *a priori* valid statement. Accordingly, to the unexciting truism, 'something exists', we may now add, 'there are experiences', as equally non-restrictive. And indeed, what existential possibility is cut off by the existence of experiences of some unspecified variety? Would it be the sort of world which obtained prior to the advent of animal life on the earth, or perhaps any other planet?

Of course the existence of *human*, or of vertebrate, experience would exclude the geological situation spoken of, but how does one show that the mere existence of experience, as such, would do so? One must then know that 'sub-animal experience' is a meaningless or self-contradictory expression; which would imply that panpsychists have been talking in self-contradiction. They have not thought so. And moreover, since anything, if it comes to be known, must exhibit its character in some experience, it is hard to see how experience can be limited to just certain characters. As Aristotle very profoundly said, 'the soul is in a manner all things'. Also, we have the question of divine experiences; must these have been absent in the geologic past, or in any other conceivable situation? I conclude that if the statement, 'There are experiences', is restrictive, there is no way to ascertain this. I think it is non-restrictive, and so necessary.

Non-restrictive propositions which nevertheless affirm existence are able to do this only because they employ concepts with the extreme range of possible meanings. 'Something', 'experience', have such extreme ranges of meaning. There is no determinate, finite limit to the possible cases of something or of experience. Any particular experience may perhaps have to be finite, in some sense, and so may any actual something. But even so, it would not follow that the ideas of something or of experience must have the same finitude. The mere notion of 'being limited' sets no particular limit, just as the mere notion of finite number allows for instances as large as you please. The notion of finite number has an infinite range. Similarly, the notion of limited attention span, or memory span, leaves entirely open what the magnitude of the span may be. (In addition, the notion of unlimited memory may not be self-contradictory.) Thus memory as such is a variable with an infinite (perhaps absolutely infinite) range of possible values. One might also speak of its infinite flexibility. Non-restrictive concepts are maximally flexible. They are variables admitting values of any magnitude whatever.

Let us now consider the notion of process, conceived as creative synthesis, a putting together of data or elements into an emergent unity. An experience is such a process. It synthesizes its data, the things experienced. Does the affirmation that such process occurs impose any limitation upon the realization of possibilities? It does not prevent there being a great deal of permanence; for in a synthesis the antecedent data are preserved, the act of synthesis being the holding together of the data in a new unity. There is also novelty, since the unity cannot be contained in the previous many to be synthesized, and the new whole is thus in some degree unpredictable or 'emergent'. However, the extent of the emergence, or the unpredictability, admits an infinity of degrees. Thus relative indeterminism (equivalent to relative determinism) has the complete flexibility characteristic of non-restrictive or metaphysically valid ideas. Absolute determinism, on the contrary, is the wholly special, and indeed impossible, limiting case of zero creativity in the synthesis constitutive of reality. 'Absolute order' coincides with 'absolute nothing', and is equally not the name of a possible state of affairs.

There is a sense in which order can be viewed as absolute, even though indeterminism be accepted. One thing is strictly predictable about an emergent synthesis: that it will express the data available for it. Retrospectively, causal connections are rigorous: the effect strictly entails its causal conditions, even though these entail only an approximate or statistical prediction of the effect. And this much even in the prediction is not approximate or statistical: the entire previous reality will be made permanent in subsequent becoming, which will entail it as cause. (The laws known to physics do not express this relation, being – I presume – too abstract to do so.) All possible permanence is thereby granted, compatible with there being any additional determinations, any real becoming or creation at all. And without such real becoming, there could be no real permanence either; for then the contrast between the terms, and therewith their meaning, must vanish. So we see that the metaphysics of 'creative process' is non-restrictive: it allows for all the permanent being you wish, and it also allows for novelty. But it can only be the novel which includes the permanent, not the permanent the novel, since a single new item in a total reality means a new totality. In general, the ultimate or all-explanatory pole of a contrast is that one whose instances can consistently include the instances of the other pole within themselves. Creative synthesis has this inclusive character.

The conclusion just reached is strengthened if we ask how, if at all, complete predictability could be falsified or verified. It is unverifiable by man, since omniscience would be required, as Clerk Maxwell pointed out. But is it verifiable, even supposing omniscience? According to classical theism, omniscience would not predict, but eternally know: this involves paradox; for how can what is not eternally actualized be eternally known? The datum of knowledge is essential to that knowledge, and hence an eternally known datum, being integral to the eternal, must be as eternal as the knowledge itself. So omniscience as classically conceived does not render determinism verifiable, but merely destroys the notion of process on which the problem turns. There is a neo-classical (and, I hold, better) theory of omniscience which does not have this result, but it also fails to make determinism verifiable, for it implies that even God faces a partially indeterminate or open future. I conclude that determinism is absolutely unverifiable, and therefore affirms no conceivable state of existence. Is it falsifiable? Yes, and in two ways. Omniscience would know the openness of the future, so far as it is open; and we can infer this openness from certain intuitive grounds, including our experience of the very meaning of 'future', in contrast to 'past', as that which is not yet settled, and which is, in some measure, awaiting our free decision to settle it. Furthermore, while indeterminism seems to exclude absolute causal order, this absoluteness, as we have seen, is really negative. It would reduce becoming to identity, and embrace all novelty in a pre-existence blueprint. But becoming as creative is the positive principle here, and sheer regularity its merely conceptual negative limit.

So far we have found that 'something exists', when considered more closely, expands into, 'experience occurs', and 'process as creative occurs'. We may combine these into the single statement, 'experience as creative process occurs'. This, remember, is held to be not merely true but necessary. Or, in other words, reality as such is creative experience, taken as a process which cannot not occur, though the particular forms in which it occurs are all contingent, since they partly exclude one another, or are partially restrictive. Experience in general, and merely as creative, excludes nothing positively conceivable.

Let us take another step. Suppose we say, 'All relations of concrete realities (i.e., processes) are extrinsic or non-constitutive relations'. How is this statement to be classified with respect to its degree of restrictiveness? It forbids concrete realities, that is, experiences, to have any objects, relation to which is essential to them. But an experience is always 'of' something, and this relation is essential. Thus the wholesale denial of internal relations is completely restrictive or impossible; for it denies an essential feature of experience as such, which we have seen to be inherent in the meaning of reality as such. But the wholesale denial of external relations is in the same case; for, if an experience is essentially relative to that of which it is the experience, and which it enjoys as its object, the thing which it has as object cannot be relative to it. To know X is not to make it; when, for example, I remember my past act I do not enact or alter it, though I may regret its unalterable reality. 'Experience of' implies one-way dependence, it requires *both* the relativity of subject to object and the non-relativity, or absoluteness, of object with respect to the particular subject which has it. I conclude that Bradley, with his universal denial of external relations, and Hume with his of internal relations, are alike in metaphysical error. The valid metaphysical or non-restrictive statement is that cases of internal relatedness universally occur, namely experiences as having particular objects, but that each such case is also one of external relatedness, namely an object as had by particular subjects. Realism was right all along about the dependence of the subject on its objects, and the independence of the objects. But this very epistemological realism or non-subjectivism is integral to a sound ontological subjectivism. Let us see why.

First, the relative includes that to which it is relative: experience-of-X includes X, otherwise it would be merely experience of . . . The relative includes the absolute, and subjects include objects. Obviously if X includes Y, it cannot exist without Y and thus is not independent of it. And if X does depend on Y, then it must include it in its own nature; for how could it be impossible that there be X without Y (the meaning of, 'X depends on Y'), if Y were simply external to X? Dependence, inclusion, relativity, are thus equivalent. And therefore the sum of relative things includes all things. Hence experience, the universal relative thing, is all-inclusive: reality, all told, is experience, mostly no doubt in non-human forms.

Second, though *every experience is relative to objects which are absolute in respect to it*, we should note that experiences can be experienced (in immediate memory, if in no other way), and accordingly an experience, which is relative to its objects, may itself become an object and so something absolute, though not in respect to the same relationship. Thus, if we verbally 'restrict' concrete realities to experient processes, we do not really restrict them. We allow them to be absolute as well as relative; and indeed, as we have seen, to have any conceivably knowable properties. The character of experience, merely as experience, is not a particular character, unless it be particular to be in some way knowable. The soul is very literally all things, if by 'soul' you mean experience in general, in all its aspects.

Experience has two at least verbally contrasting forms; these are, partially ignorant, unclear, uncertain, or 'fragmentary' experience, as opposed to wholly cognitive, clear, certain, and 'complete' experience. Let us simply say, fallible and infallible experience. Now the striking thing about this contrast is that neither contrary in any way restricts the other. That fallible experience occurs does not prevent infallible experience from occurring, and *vice versa*. These two forms are non-competitive. Only different *particular* fallible experiences, or different *particular* infallible experiences, are restrictive. If there is infallible experience of a certain apple now falling, there cannot be infallible experience of it now not falling; and if there be infallible experience having a certain fallible experience as object, then this latter experience does occur, and not something else instead. Also, my fallible experience that you are now over there excludes my having now even a fallible experience that I am over there. Exclusiveness is due to the particularity of the fallible or infallible experience, not to its fallibility or infallibility. Fallibility or infallibility are non-restrictive characters, and the affirmation that they both occur or exist is therefore metaphysically valid. So our truism, 'experiences occur', becomes: 'fallible experiences occur and also infallible experiences'. How indeed could this statement be falsified? Neither form of experience could falsify its own existence. Could fallible experience falsify the existence of the infallible? This would mean a disproof of any and every form of theism. Perhaps such a disproof might be achieved by pointing to the existence of evil? Yet not if it be correct that reality must be creative or self-determinative in every instance; for then omnipotence, conceived as the sheer monopoly of determining power in one agent, the possessor of infallible experience, is not a permissible way to construe infallibility. I do not believe that the existence of infallible experience is falsifiable by fallible experience; and it clearly is not by infallible experience itself. Is this existence verifiable? Infallible experience could verify itself; and if there is any force in the theistic proofs, or any validity to the claims of mystical experience, fallible experience also can verify the existence of the infallible. Thus the occurrence of infallible experience seems to be metaphysical, a verifiable but not conceivably falsifiable, hence non-restrictive or necessary truth.

The existence of fallible experience could not be falsified, unless by infallible experience. In that case, the infallible experience would have no object save cases of itself. Is this self-consistent? I doubt it. If this negative suspicion is correct, then fallible experience, which certainly is verifiable, both by itself and by infallible experience, is metaphysically existent. Both God and world are, then, necessary beings; but since subject includes object, the two are really but the one necessary being, God-as-experiencing-a-world – some world or other, no matter what. The metaphysically true is thus wholly embraced in the simple affirmation, 'Necessarily, divine experiences occur.' The only difficulty (which may be serious enough) is to be sure as to the meaning of 'divine' and of 'experiences' when so qualified.

The positivistic denial of meaning to this combination has not been refuted by anything we have so far said. I here offer this suggestion: if 'infallible experience' is meaningless, what can be conveyed by the contrasting term, 'fallible experience'? If we hold that all knowledge is essentially fallible, that it must fail to be adequate to reality, how do we give content to this 'reality' which can never be reached by any knowledge? Is not reality that which the perfect form of knowledge would or does know? *Which* can we start with, in trying to define the other, 'knowledge' or 'reality'? With Peirce, and all the idealists, if not all the metaphysicians, I submit that we must start with experience or knowledge, and in terms of it define 'reality'. But then we cannot declare our experience 'inadequate' to reality without implying the idea of an experience which is adequate. This Roycean argument, I believe, is sound, particularly as an argument against positivism. So, for this and other reasons, I reject positivism, and accept a certain version of theism as necessarily true. But it is not classical theism (see Chapters X–XVI).

There may appear to be some exceptions to the principle, upon which we have been relying, that exclusive verifiability means necessity, and exclusive falsifiability, impossibility. Take, 'I am living'. (I owe this and the following example to David Keyt.) Who could falsify this? If it were not true, the statement, with the meaning which it normally has, could not even be discussed. Still, the proposition is not in every sense unfalsifiable. For if 'I' is to mean a definite subject (other than God), then some other subject could know of its non-existence. And if 'I' is wholly indeterminate as to subject, then it is non-restrictive or necessary, since, as we have seen, experience is a metaphysical principle. Again consider, 'No one will ever live to be 500 years old'. Could this be known to be true? According to the theory of creative process, truth about the future depends upon the present phase of process as ground of the real possibilities for future creation. As Aristotle put it, 'the man will die' is true because there are in the man now the factors which make his death inevitable. But if, due to the aspects of chance in the world, springing from the multiple strands of freedom, the particular circumstances of the death are not inevitable, then the truth is merely that the man may die in this way, or that way, or some other way – in any case, in some way. To know a negative truth about the future is, then, to know that the present conditions render a certain outcome impossible for all the future; and perhaps only omniscience can distinguish between extremely low probability and real impossibility. Such factual absolutes transcend our grasp, and this is one of the indications that fallible experience is not self-sufficient but requires infallible experience as measure of its exact degree of fallibility.

Naturally, if we appeal to 'verifiable by omniscience' as a criterion, we must be able to show how, in terms of our own limited experience, this appeal can be given a meaning. We must somehow conceive the verification by fallible experience of the reality of infallible experience. As we have already seen, the theistic proofs and mystic experience are the two forms in which the requirement may be met. Only if no such experience and no such proofs are possible, is God unverifiable by non-divine subjects. I believe they are possible. But the extension of 'conceivably verifiable' to include divine verification does not render the verifiability criterion useless. Rather it alone gives it a use. For then we can avoid self-contradictory demands, such as that limited knowledge should survey all reality and detect an absolute absence (e.g., 'no possibility, however improbable, of living beyond 500 years'). But we can still insist that fallible knowledge should not be declared incompetent to discover a certain thing without a clear reason based on fallibility as such, and that omniscience should not be declared competent to discover something merely because it can be put into words which to casual inspection seem significant. We must rather show that, with due heed to the analogies and experiences upon which our concept of omniscience is based, the words in question do have a meaning as descriptive of conceivable objects of divine knowledge. I question if 'there is no world' or 'mere dead matter exists', or 'events are absolutely determined in advance by conditions and causal laws', come under this head. Even for God these are not, I hold, meaningful formulae.

We have defined metaphysics as the subject which tries to formulate non-restrictive or necessary existential truths. The following have been offered as examples:

Necessarily, something exists.

Necessarily, experience occurs.

Necessarily, creative synthesis occurs.

Necessarily, there are concrete actualities all of which are both externally and internally related, both absolute and relative.

Necessarily, divine or infallible experience, having fallible experiences among its objects, occurs.

It is suggested that the last formulation sums up the others.

IX

EVENTS, INDIVIDUALS AND PREDICATION:
A DEFENCE OF EVENT PLURALISM

A statement, capable of being true or false, correctly describes or characterizes something. Philosophies may differ in the class of entities which they suppose to be the basic descripta, those which all true characterizations correctly, and at least indirectly, describe. Aristotle codified one answer: what is described is the substance or enduring individual. However, since he also held that only the species, not the individual, is truly knowable, his answer was somewhat ambiguous; for it seems that the knowable truth is truth not about the individual but about the species or form, even though this is real only in individual cases.

There are difficulties with this view. (1) Why not say that the genus rather than the species is the truly knowable? Individuals are special cases of the species; are not species special cases of the genus? And, as no one can exhaust what is peculiar to this or that individual, so no one can exhaust what is peculiar to a species. As individuals are constantly changing and being replaced by others, so are species. Aristotle did not admit all this, but here he was mistaken. Species, like individuals, are inexhaustibly subtle and ultimately impermanent entities.

(2) The species is more determinate or definite than the genus, the individual than the species; but so is the event more determinate than the individual. It is indeed possible to use the word 'event' so that this is not so; thus a shift in the weather could be called an event, and the shift, as one is likely to identify it, is not as rich in determinations as an individual entity. But suppose by event we mean a minimal temporal unit, or cross section, so to speak, of some actual process, such as the process of experiencing in a certain human being. Thus, all my experience at this moment – the moment when I wrote 'moment'. This is more

definite than is Charles Hartshorne. For that might mean only, eldest son of F. C. Hartshorne and Marguerite Hartshorne, indifferently whether at age one hour, or 72 years, indifferently whether awake or asleep, and so forth.

There is here a dilemma. (*a*) One may, with Leibniz, hold that by *so and so* one means all that occurs in the specified individual between birth and death, or beyond if there is a beyond. In this case we do not know who anyone is until he is dead, if even then. This is plainly not the commonsense meaning of individual person. Identity is not normally defined in terms of the total definiteness of a person's life. If it were, it would be contradiction to say that a person could have acted and experienced otherwise than he has. Determinists may like this implication, but it is not what we normally mean by individuality. According to this normal view, it is sheer fact, not logical necessity, that 'I' have experienced or done this instead of that on such and such a date. There are other objections to Leibnizianism.

(*b*) One may hold, with Aristotle, that self-indentity involves essential as opposed to contingent determinations or 'accidents'. But then the accidental state in which one is at a given moment is more definite than that in which one is simply by being oneself, since the state includes both essential and contingent properties. Yet this is like the relation between individual and species, or species and genus: a species has what is essential to the genus *plus* something; an individual has the specific essence plus some arbitrary addition; but so, finally, we come to the momentary state ('event' in the concrete sense) which has the character of the genus, and that of the species, and individual identity plus arbitrary additions at each moment. This final dose of arbitrariness alone gives fully definite and concrete reality. If this is so, and for non-Leibnizian substantialists it must be so, then Aristotle should not have stopped either with the species or with the individual, but he should have gone on to the event-state, in his search for the determinate or concrete unit of reality which true statements correctly, and at least indirectly, describe.

I see no escape from this conclusion, provided it be agreed that Leibnizianism is unacceptable. The logic which drives us from genus to species to individual is the very logic which should drive us still further, to the event, or momentary state, of the individual process in question. If truth is finally about individual rather than species, or species rather than genus, is this not because the individual is more definite (richer in determinations) than species, and species than genus? We think of an abstract property, like animality, and we ask, What entities, more definite than just bare 'instances of animality', actually have this property? 'Animals', merely as such, are neither large nor small, neither aquatic, terrestrial, nor aerial, neither of one colour nor another. But North American crows are black, and this crow has in addition a broken wing, or is tame and has learned to say 'Hello'. But similarly, this crow just now has further characteristics, no less arbitrary with respect to its being this crow than is its special ability to say 'hello' with respect to its being *a* crow. The definiteness of truth (this is Leibniz's profound principle of *'in esse'*) is due precisely to the definiteness of individual as compared to species, or species as compared to genus (or some still more abstract qualification or classification). But is not the full definiteness of truth due to the definiteness of event, as compared even to individual?

To know all events in the history of an individual is to know all there is to know of that individual and is incomparably more than simply to know which individual it is. For the latter is, in principle, knowable at birth, but not the former. Again Leibniz denies the distinction, but anyone who follows him here implicitly accepts some of the most extreme paradoxes of the Monadology.

My conclusion is simply that the most analytically complete way of speaking is event-speaking, not thing- or substance-speaking. The latter is a simplification or shorthand, which is indispensable for much the same reasons that led Aristotle to say that really the species, rather than the individual, is known. If the human 'present' has as its maximal length about 1/10 of a second, then obviously we must normally think together in a few bundles the hundreds of thousands of events in each person's experience in a single day; and for many purposes the identity of the event-sequence to which these events belong, that they constitute the life of a certain person with a given proper name, is much more important than most of the peculiarities distinguishing one event in the sequence from another. Similarly, for many purposes of naturalists, it is more important that what one observes is a crow instead of a raven than that it is *this* crow rather than that. So we speak of 'the voice of the crow', 'the song of the skylark', though what we hear is this crow, this skylark. Similarly, we take all the events of a man's life as describable aspects of one entity, so and so. Yet really the determinate entities to be described are not this single entity itself from birth to death, any more than it is the species rather than its members which is the ultimately determinate entity which the naturalist is studying.

We say, the man 'is' sick. Yet his bare identity does not embrace the sickness (unless perhaps he has never been well). Predication is in this respect an ambiguous procedure. (*a*) It may refer an abstract or logically weak characterization, such as 'animality', to something less abstract, logically stronger, such as the class of 'birds'. Thus 'birds are animals'. In this case, what makes the statement true is that the more definite or less abstract entity includes 'animality' among its determinations. But (*b*) so and so 'is' sick not only has not this structure, it has precisely the opposite form. The identity of 'so and so' is less definite than his actual state of sickness and does not include it – quite the contrary. Here the 'subject' fails to perform its primary function of furnishing the definiteness of truth. Only 'so and so now' yields the required definiteness; but it does this, not by virtue of a date on a calendar, but by virtue of perceptual observation, and observation not just of so and so, but of a definite event-sequence (not implicated by X's being so and so plus the date), which we observe to occur. This sequence is an arbitrary addition to the conjunction of the individual and the date.

The old language of 'essence' and 'accident' among predicates is thus deeply misleading; for it conceals the reversal of meaning which 'predication' itself here undergoes. Just as one may say either that so and so is sick, or that sickness is in him, so one may say that crows are black or that the colour black 'is' in crows. Nevertheless the logical subject, in the sense of the more determinate, less abstract or less general entity, is not black but crows, and by the same logic, the least abstract entity in 'so and so is sick' is not so and so, nor yet sickness, but the actual event-sequence going on now and (somewhat arbitrarily) prolonging the event-sequence which from his birth has been identifiable as the life of so and so. Leibniz was right in demanding that truth be *in esse*; determinateness can be correctly ascribed only because there is something whose definiteness includes the predicates in question. But his error was in supposing that the self-identical individual was the most definite something. Rather it is the event, or event-sequence, and this is fully determinate only retrospectively.

So far in this section we have made the assumption that truth as a whole, the totality of truths, consists in the correct characterization, not of a single subject or descriptum, but of many subjects. In a broad sense, we have assumed a 'pluralistic' ontology. This is the normal commonsense view; it is also the view of most philosophers in our Western tradition. However, Parmenides, the Stoics, Spinoza, and, perhaps one should add, the German idealists, as well as their Anglo-American disciples, such as Bradley, have appeared to hold the monistic alternative. All statements describe (or misdescribe) but one subject: Substance, Reality, or 'the Absolute'. The main stream of the Hindu tradition may also be associated with this view. It is, indeed, a significant fact, in my opinion, that ancient India produced both the most radical of monisms and the most radical of pluralisms. On the one hand, the Hindu said that all things and all persons were in reality, or apart from the 'Maya' correlative with ignorance, simply *the* Person, Self, or unutterable spiritual mystery; on the other hand, the Buddhist said that even the unity through time of a physical thing, animal, or person covered an ultimate multiplicity of momentary states or 'flashes' of reality. Here, and not in Heraclitus, was the emergence of a radical philosophy of process. (For one thing, from the Greek we have some epigrams, from Buddha and his followers, a library. Our provincial Western neglect of this great tradition is out of keeping with the global responsibilities of our time.)

Is it merely accidental that radical monism and radical pluralism first achieved wide acceptance in the same part of the world and at nearly the same time? Perhaps not; for, suppose one attempts to combat mystical monism in behalf of the commonsense pluralism of things and persons. One will argue:

if one man says 'I' and another man uses the same word, they cannot mean the same self, since their thoughts, beliefs, actions, experiences, are by no means the same and will often be manifestly contradictory. If I believe p and you believe not-p, 'we' cannot constitute an identical believer. Why not, objects the monist, since, as you must admit, even the same man may at different times hold contradictory beliefs? Ah, replies the commonsensist, but the law of non-contradiction only says that the same thing cannot *at the same time* have contradictory predicates. Monist: Very well, but then why may I not amend the law in my favour so that it runs: the same thing may not, at the same time and in the same place, have contradictory predicates? Thus Brahma thinks both my thoughts and yours (so far as they are real), but he thinks my thoughts in that manifestation of himself which is 'here' and is me, and he thinks your thoughts in that manifestation which is there and is you. Contradictory predicates, you must agree, are all right so far as there is a distinction of 'respect', and why should not a temporal respect and a spatial respect be on the same footing?

One may, of course, object that this is just the difference between space and time, in that, while what is *here* must be one thing and what is *there* another, what is earlier and what is later can be the same thing. In short, spatial divisions are substantial, temporal divisions only adjectival. Indeed, space and time have sometimes been characterized by saying that whereas the first is the order of things whereby it is possible for different subjects to have identical predicates, time is the order whereby the same subject can have contradictory predicates. There are the following defects in this contention: (1) It requires us to renounce the Leibnizian 'Identity of Indiscernibles', for which there are respectable reasons. (2) If different leaves here and there in the same tree can be exactly alike at a given time, why could not two leaves from different seasons, perhaps in the 'same place', be so? Thus it seems that time could transcend the Leibnizian principle if space could. (3) The doctrine assumes a unity of the subject which is more or less independent of its quality, and this is at best a vague idea. How far independent? (4) One thing could have contradictory predicates by virtue not of temporal but of spatial diversity. The box is red and not-red, red on the sides but not on top. It could

even be red-topped and not red-topped, if one part of the top
was red and the rest not. (5) The decisive objection is that both
space and time are being characterized by the theory in merely
symmetrical terms, and this means, as we shall see later
(Chapter X), superficially. A thing can be red and not red either
at different times, or in different spatial parts; any one-way
order among the parts or the times seems, in so far, irrelevant.
Diversity of times, diversity of places, suffice for the law of
contradiction. So far, space and time are on the same footing.
Yet space and time are not the same.

The distinctive character of time consists, not in that what is
red at t may be not-red at t^1, but in this, that the earlier members
of an event-sequence contain only a more or less indefinite
specification of their successors, while the successors are
essentially successors of the very members they succeed.
Asymmetrical dependence, or (the same) asymmetrical independence, this is the temporal order. Space, on the other
hand, is the symmetrical aspect of dynamic relatedness, the
aspect of mutuality, whether mutuality of dependence or (and
here it is not the same) of independence. Space is how we have
'neighbours', time, how we have ancestors and descendants;
but whereas one may say that A and B are neighbours (one of
another), we cannot unambiguously say, C and D are descendants (or ancestors) one of another. The ancestral relation
discriminates between its terms, the neighbourhood relation
as such does not.

If one wants to reconcile contradictory predicates with the
unity of a single subject through time, it must be in terms of this
asymmetry. Otherwise one might as well be talking about space.
The 'same man' can be an innocent child and a sophisticated
adult, meaning, however, that whereas only the potentiality of
the sophistication was in the child, the prior actuality of the inno-
cence (the 'having been' innocent) *together with* the actual sophistication is in the adult. The directional order is lost if one insists
that just as the adult 'has been' innocent so the child 'will be'
sophisticated. The child may never even be an adult; but the
adult has been a child and just that child which he was. In my
presence two well-known scientists, one an astronomer, one an
atomic physicist, agreed upon this: the past but not the future is
in principle (apart from human limitations) knowable in detail.

I believe this is part of the very meaning of temporal versus spatial distinctions. If the child is only potentially, i.e., somewhat indefinitely, destined to become an adult, but the adult has perfectly definitely been such and such a child, then to call the child and the adult the identical concrete entity is erroneous. Identity is directionless, symmetrical. The adult is more determinate, and in this reasonable sense more concrete. The more can contain the less, the less cannot contain the more. Hence the subject which really 'has' the contradictory predicates is only the later, not the earlier one. The two belong in the same ordered sequence, but they are not one identical concrete reality. It is one thing to say that the same concrete entity is both in pain and not in pain (in pain in a tooth, say, but not in digestive organs) by virtue of spatial distinction of parts; and another and much more ambiguous thing to say that the same entity is both in pain and not in pain by virtue of a temporal distinction. For the spatial diversity of parts can be *possessed together* by the individual, but the temporal diversity is so possessed, if at all, only in the later phase. Hence the genuinely concrete or inclusive unity, the determinate subject, is a new creation each moment. Only in this way does time relate itself distinctively to the law of non-contradiction.

There is another difficulty with the view we are combating. If the temporal order is essentially that of combining incompatible predicates in identical subjects which endure throughout the succession of predicates, then all change should be 'accidental' rather than 'substantial', and substances should be incapable of creation or destruction. Leibniz accepted this implication, weakly adding that God by a miracle can either create or destroy substances. Some philosophers have been willing to be more consistent, and have declared all substances to be eternal. This view is so replete with difficulties that I refrain, at least here, from mentioning them. In any case, it is not a commonsense position; and a good part of the appeal of substance philosophy is its apparent agreement with common sense. On the other hand, if substantial change – i.e., creation – is admitted, this greatly weakens the idea that substance is a final term of analysis. For what is the difference between (1) saying that, while the first step in the formation of a child consists in the jump from no child to child, the subsequent steps consist merely in altering what has been produced, and (2) saying that, while the first step initiates (by producing its first member) an event sequence not previously represented in nature, the second step merely prolongs the sequence by producing its second member, and so on – what difference except that the second mode of speech is freer from ambiguity and misleading suggestions? If to arrive at the barest minimum of a child means 'creation', then getting from that practically mindless beginning to adult consciousness must *a fortiori* be a creative step, or innumerable such steps, many of them perhaps far greater than the first step. To have a conceptually clear theory, one should either give up creation or generalize it to cover all change, admitting that in many cases the aspect of novelty may be trivial enough. Thus we admit frankly the relativity of our ideas, instead of proclaiming pseudo-absolute distinctions as though they could be taken literally.

The Buddhists are in the stronger pluralistic position. For they can say that contradictory predicates simply do not apply to the same subject. Successive events are not mutually co-existent parts. The coexistence is at most retrospective, and requires a new subject each moment. If I change my beliefs – and in subtle ways they are ever-changing – this means that there are really successive believers, all belonging, to be sure, to the same personal sequence, and readily distinguished from any member of the sequence constituting a different human life history. Buddhism was the first, and for many centuries the only, great tradition which, in a consistent fashion, took *space-time*, rather than just space, as the principle of plurality. (Some philosophers of Islam had a partially similar doctrine.) A unit of concrete or determinate reality is not merely something here, in contrast to something there; it is something here-now, in contrast to something there-then; it is an event or experience, not a thing or person.

The objection that 'without an enduring subject of change there can be no change' is rather trifling, though often proposed as conclusive. (1) The Buddhist or radical pluralist can simply say that 'change' in a single 'thing' is shorthand for the *succession* of a number of contrasting events, where the sequence of events has some connectedness and continuity of character which lead us to verbalize it as the history of a single enduring 'individual'. (2) Moreover, the radical pluralist may point out the undeniable fact that nothing is commoner than to speak of change where even the substantialist does not suppose an enduring substance as subject of the change. Thus the 'weather changes', 'public opinion changes', 'the situation changes', the sunset glow on the clouds changes, the rainbow changes, a forest fire or storm changes – and who thinks of these as substances? It is thus vain to try to disprove event pluralism from the uses of the word change. What 'change' commits us to is only the *becoming of novelty*; it remains to decide whether this means new adjectival states of one and the same entity, or new adjectival aspects of new entities. If an identical entity can have new properties (on the face of it a severe paradox), then certainly a new entity can do so! For 'new property' here simply means, different from any properties previously embodied, whether in the 'thing' or in the event-sequence. If yesterday 'it' rained all day, and today 'it' is brilliantly clear, certainly 'it' or the weather has changed, or there has been a 'change in the weather', substance or no substance. Thus the talk about 'subjects of change' is merely question-begging, as argument for substantialism. Aristotle and many another have been confused at this point.

An old Hindu argument against event-pluralism ran: how could 'I' remember 'myself' doing such and such in the past if the self remembering and the self remembered were not the same? One remembers 'oneself', not another self, as doing, feeling, thinking, perceiving, such and such. This is a subtler objection than the previous one. Still, it too begs the question. For no Buddhist denies that my sequence of past experiences is distinct from yours or any other human being's; and why should not 'myself', as in the past, refer to the special continuity of character connecting the experiences in question with the remembering one? Moreover, to explain the possibility of memory through identity overshoots the mark, for if *I now* can remember the past 'I' because the two egos are identical, then why did not the past self foresee the present one? Identity is symmetrical and directionless, while memory is not. More than that, to 'explain' the relation of memory between later and earlier experience by connecting both to an identical subject merely adds two more relations to those requiring explanation;

for now, besides the relation of event or experience E^1 to event E, we have the relation of each to the ego. And we have really done nothing to solve the original problem, how E^1 can relate itself to E. For it is in E^1, in present experience, that the relation must obtain. It does not obtain in E, for E is (was) unaware of E^1. But if both E and E^1 are related to the identical ego, and this is how the later is related to the earlier, why does the relation run but the one way? Mere identity cannot be the explanation of an asymmetry!

You may say that what we have here is not 'mere', but 'genetic', identity. Very true, but the correct logical analysis of this concept is precisely the question at issue. I have yet to read a substantialist, old or new, who gave an account of this relation which was, at the same time, both clear and clearly distinct from the neo-Buddhistic account which I am recommending.

Much recent, and no doubt much old, controversy on the substance question suffers from a lack of clarity as to what is denied by the event-pluralist. It is not, if the latter is sensible, the propriety of ordinary uses of personal pronouns and nouns. Of course from birth to death I am I and not any other human person. I have never been and never will be Paul Weiss, or my second cousin Hugh, or anyone else but Charles Hartshorne. Nor have I ever been a tree or a lion. This means (for one thing), that the series of experiences of which I have intimate memory contains no members of the series of which you have (or a lion has) intimate memory; and for another thing, that the series of states which are referred to as the history of a certain human organism or body, called mine, contains no members belonging also to the series referred to as the history of someone else's body, or of a tree or a lion. Events have the relations which they have, whatever our language; and the event language need deny none of these. A lot of effort could be saved if people would stop supposing that, whereas substantialists sagely recognize the intimate relations of memory and persistence of character traits involved in certain event-sequences, event-pluralists, as such, must be more grudging in their recognition of these facts. Genetic 'identity', simply as fact, is not in dispute; only its analysis or logical structure.

Let us recall, too, that the real issue concerns the concrete or most *determinate* level of reality, in contrast to the more abstract or less determinate. Of course, in some sense I am always numerically the same person, but of course also in some sense I am different – even numerically different, since I am actual by virtue of a numerically different 'state' at each moment. It remains to learn which is the fully concrete reality, myself now, as partly new and different, or myself as always the same. Only Leibnizianism can clear-headedly affirm that the identical self is concrete. For if there is real novelty of qualities each moment, then it is the different self which includes the self that was there all along, not *vice versa*. The contrast between my present reality and my past reality includes this past reality, for 'contrast of *B* to *A*' includes *A*. But it is my present which contrasts itself with my past, not the other way; hence one cannot use the reverse argument, that the contrast between the old reality and the new includes the new. The old reality enjoyed or suffered no contrast with what came later; life is cumulative, and hence asymmetrical in its relatedness. Thus the self as numerically the same is an abstraction, the latest self as new is the total concrete reality containing the former.

The failure of substantialism to be really clear about this asymmetry is written large over its entire history. For example, Aristotle had quite a theory about the future as 'potential' in the present; but was he so explicit about the mode of reality of the past in the present? The present is actual, the future, potential. Is the past actual, potential, or a third modality? And medieval Aristotelianism, by making the divine perspective timeless, in principle attributed perfect symmetry to the temporal order. All events are co-present to deity. This means, in effect, that in the divine mind the order of the universe sinks to a lower level! For co-presence, like other mutual relationships, is, in so far, unordered. (See Chapter X.)

The greater concreteness of states, compared to things or persons, is expressed in the common mode of speech, '*x* is in a state of. . . .' Substance theory should say, the state is in the man; but ordinary speech is apparently wiser! Of course the state is in 'the man now', but this is only saying, the state is in itself. For the state of the man, or the man now, what is the difference? Aside from his present state of experience and body, the man now is nothing actual or determinate. But though the state is in the man now, it is by no means in the man as always the same, and as already existent at birth. To assert this would be the Leibnizian paradox. Rather the identical man is 'in' one new state after another.

Inherence here is comparable to that of genus 'in' species and species 'in' individual. Just so, the mere individual, the pure numerical unit of substance, is an abstract determination in something still more determinate or concrete.

Wilfrid Sellars tells us that no set of statements about events can be equivalent to statements about enduring individuals. With certain qualifications, he is right. Taking a purely extensional point of view, according to which a class or group is identified simply by its actual members, it would be the Leibnizian paradox to identify a man with the sequence of his states. (So much the worse, perhaps, for the hope that extensional logic will suffice for philosophy.) We must identify the event-sequence partly intensionally. Once a man is born, or perhaps exists as a developed foetus, the particular events which prolong his existence are in details arbitrary additions to the sequence. The unique gene structure in his cells is not such an addition, and the unconscious memories of his earliest moments will always form part of his individual nature. But innumerable details of his life will be further determinations, not part of the definiteness of his mere identity as that human being and no other. With this understanding, the event and event-sequence language seems able to state the whole truth.

It may be thought that we have merely substituted 'event sequence' for substance, without any further alterations, in which case the issue is purely verbal. But the 'merely' is unjustified. In the first place, we get rid of the suggestion that a single event is adjectival, an abstracted aspect of something more concrete. We also make explicit the profoundly important truth that genetic identity is a special strand of the causal order of the world, and rests on the same principle of inheritance from the past as causality in general does. The problems of substance and of causality are essentially the same problem. We also take into proper account the truth that a first event in a series might have been the last, and then there would have been no sequence, no enduring individual, except as an unfulfilled potentiality. Finally we do justice to the truth that the latest event sums up the entire reality of the sequence so far. (The full explication of this, however, requires consideration of divine events.)

It seems necessary to deal with Strawson's defence of the substance concept in explicit contrast to that of event in his book *Individuals*.[1] The only carefully elaborated argument against event pluralism I can find here seems less an argument than a question-begging manoeuvre. By choosing examples of event calculated to produce the result aimed at he shows that mere sequences of events would not suffice to constitute a world in which there could be inter-subjective or linguistic agreement concerning what is being talked about. Spatio-temporal orientation requires more than events. Yes, more than the sorts of events his discussion takes into account, such as 'flashes' or 'bangs'. A whole chapter is devoted to sounds, and it is shown that a merely 'auditory universe' would not make discourse possible. But sounds in the phenomenal sense here in question are not events in the concrete sense we have been discussing; nor are they events making up the actuality of 'individuals', i.e., forming highly integrated and well demarcated sequences. 'Births', 'deaths', 'battles', are also not concrete unit-events. Here the choice of examples derives from the conclusion, not the other way, so far as the conclusion concerns the validity of event-pluralism. Apparently, the main object of the author is not to refute this latter doctrine but to show, and for all I know he does show, (1) that such event sequences (he would not call them that) as constitute the actuality of human 'minds' can be identified only through association with sequences constituting human bodies, and (2) that unobservable particulars, theoretical constructs, such as the particles of physics, must be identified by 'reference to those grosser, observable bodies of which perhaps, like Locke, we think of them [the particles] as the minute, unobservable constituents'.[2] Now the physicists are quite clear that we do in fact detect invisibly small objects only in terms of their relations to observable objects, that the knowability of the micro-world presupposes that of the macro-world. But this, of course, is not an argument against event-pluralism,

---

[1] P. F. Strawson, *Individuals: An Essay in Descriptive Metaphysics* (New York: Doubleday & Company, 1959), p. 34.
[2] *Op. cit.*, p. 34.

nor is it intended to be. But what argument worthy of the name is given? I find none. Moreover, if we turn to what the physicists say about this problem, we find the following:

(a) The particles are precisely not 'identifiable' if this means that the 'same' particle can be conceived as moving about, or internally altering from one state to another. Strawson protects himself a bit by saying that at least groups of particles must be identifiable. But if this means, 'groups whose members may be supposed to remain objectively identical through change', then this is incorrect. Physical laws as now conceived entail that such identity is lacking. The category of substance does not strictly apply to events on the ultra-microscopic level. Schroedinger is particularly clear and explicit on this point.[3] The particle events sometimes arrange themselves so as to make the substance idea a convenient (but still not literally true) approximation, but sometimes so as to make it radically false. Thus, whether or not there are substances in nature, it seems a result of our best physical knowledge that there are events additional to any which constitute states of substances. Thus the universal category is event, not substance. If Strawson knows that this is the upshot of physical theorizing, might he not have just mentioned the fact?

(b) The physicists know as well as anyone that we have to identify enduring physical things of the macroscopic kind in order to deal with the unidentical particles. But they also (or at least some of them) see that the macroscopic identity is not, in any perceptual or pragmatic way, distinguishable from an identity of form in an unbroken or quasi-continuous event-sequence.[3] Here, as rather often, I have the feeling that the scientists are in some ways more philosophical than my fellow professionals. Schroedinger seems to show more, rather than less, sensitivity to the philosophical history of this problem than Strawson. Obviously one cannot demonstrate the invalidity of the event-philosophy by considering it only in extremely weak formulations. The physicists have learned in a hard school that it is the strongest, most intelligent version of an opposing theory one must refute. They would scarcely treat a fellow physicist as it is now fashionable in philosophy to treat Whitehead, namely

[3] Ernest Schroedinger, *Science and Humanism* (Cambridge: Cambridge University Press, 1951), pp. 17–21.

by the 'method of convenient ignorance', or the substitution of a doctrine which differs from his in precisely those ways which make refutation easy – and irrelevant.

What Strawson shows is that if events did not form some relatively unbroken sequences with recognizably identical spatial and qualitative structures persisting from one event to the next through more or less long periods of time, as in the case of mountains, trees, or people, we could not find our way about or communicate even with ourselves in language. This assertion no Buddhist, nor Whitehead, has so far as I know ever wished to deny, nor has had any doctrinal reason to deny. When Strawson says that things not processes fill space-time, I reply that on the contrary in my experience processes do fill space-time. Granted that Caesar is not the same as his history; this is indistinguishable, by all perceptual tests, from some such statement as the following: People knew who Caesar was long before they knew anything of his history after a certain early date; moreover, it makes sense to say that Caesar, the same man, could have had a largely different history. But this in turn is only to say that at each moment an individual event-sequence confronts alternative possibilities within the limits fixed by its 'defining characteristic' (in Whitehead's careful phrase). To insist that the recognizable sameness of form belongs to a thing or substance, not to an event-sequence defined (like the substance) by the formal sameness (and its unbroken continuance or 'inheritance' through space-time) is to play with words. For physics, all that matters, as Schroedinger lucidly points out, is the recognizable sameness of pattern in a sequence of happenings sufficiently unbroken for our perceptual and practical requirements. Happenings are discerned perceptually; persistence of quality and pattern is also observed, as are changes of quality and pattern, and persistence of past events in subsequent ones; but persistence of something additional, that is, thinghood or substance, who has observed that? Not I, at least, in more than forty years of philosophizing.

It is sometimes said that if substance is what has various qualities, the unitary subject of many predicates, then in *this* sense an event is a substance. It surely is, but this does not imply that the schema, identical subject with *changing* qualities, is equally correct. For here is just the issue: How does time or change affect identity? Mere universals cannot by snuggling up together form a concrete reality, granted. But still the search for the concrete subject must go not only beyond the species to the individual case, in the ordinary meaning of individual thing or person, but a step further, to the temporally as well as spatially individual case. This is the state or event.

Strawson points out that event, in the concrete sense which event-pluralism has in mind, is not a concept that we have in ordinary discourse. Thus, for instance, we do not ordinarily think of a 'happening' as having a spatial shape, as a tree or a man does. But since the man-now has a shape which varies at least imperceptibly with each new now, even though a fraction of a second later, and the man-now is the same as the set of mental and bodily events which presently prolongs his sequence, events can have shape. Is it of any decisive ontological significance that ordinary discourse deals with concrete events in somewhat wholesale fashion, or in terms of partial, abstract aspects of event sequences, such as a battle, a flash of lightning, someone's birth or death, or meeting a friend? Ordinary discourse furnishes notions from which the ontological event-concept can be constructed, and through which it can be explained. What more is necessary? That events happen 'to' something or someone, means in the event language simply that they usually fit into well-ordered unbroken sequences of the sort we term things or persons. However, the physicists now claim to have shown that in the micro-realm we cannot dispense with the idea of events which do *not* fit neatly into any such sequences. In Whitehead's terms these are events with a low degree of 'social order'. But the existence of conscious minds consists in high degrees of such order, nor could such minds exist (the reasons seem quite definite) save in organisms themselves highly ordered. These in turn impose certain requirements upon their environment of the sort Strawson is talking about (using the substance rather than the event language, but saying, if I am right, nothing additional).

That the concept of substance, taken seriously and literally, is an intellectual prison can be illustrated in numberless ways. Recently, for example, there was a discussion of individualism in which a sociologist, Leslie White, held that it was unscientific to talk about the individual 'in last analysis' making culture, rather than culture making individuals. He had strong arguments. However, his hearers, of course, had difficulty with his doctrine. For what is culture if not certain things which individuals do to themselves and other individuals? But all parties were assuming 'identity' through time as unproblematic. To add 'culture', as identical – though also changing – through time, to the individuals as also persistent changing identities is not sufficient. What is really 'in last analysis' there in social reality is neither culture nor individual people, but certain rather highly-ordered sequences of events characterized by the high level of symbolic functioning and creative freedom that is found on this planet only in those event-sequences which we call human beings. Each such event is intimately dependent upon and, except for a final and in many respects minute aspect of self-determination, causally determined by, events which have gone before, including especially events of a similar human kind, resulting in language habits, also in such event-sequences as buildings, tools, books, totems, flags, and so on and so on. 'The individual' is indeed a product, something made, and the concrete making is not *by* 'the individual' itself but by *de facto* members of individual sequences. Individuality is *not* the last, most concrete term of analysis. Here White is right. But neither is culture, though it may for some purposes be a more useful abstraction than 'individual'.

Our whole Western tradition is warped and confused by the concept of individual taken as ultimate. The results are ethical and not just theoretical. Nor is the issue irrelevant to the Cold War, as I have argued elsewhere. The ignoble side of our 'noble individualism' is very much with us, and is aided and abetted by metaphysical confusions about the relations of events to enduring things.

The individual who now acts creatively is not simply I, or you, but I now, or you now. I yesterday, you yesterday, did not enact and can never enact our today's actions; only today's selves can do that. And since there is a new agent each tenth of a second or so, the actual momentary freedom cannot be very large. At a given moment, we are *almost* entirely a product, not a producer. And what productive power we have would be totally vacuous without inheritance from past actions, our own and those of countless others.

Similarly transcendent of individual identity is any rational motivation. Even to want to be appreciated and loved is in part to value others for their own sakes. Would one wish to be praised by a robot? Also any future self, call it mine or not mine, which can benefit from my present act will be numerically a new and distinct unity of concrete reality. Hence self-interest has no privileged metaphysical basis whatever. No wonder, perhaps, that the event-philosophy is unpopular. Do we not prefer to cherish our ego-illusion? Only Buddhism, by specializing in combating this illusion through a whole way of living, could popularize its overcoming, and even then hardly in a whole society.

Alas, the metaphysical baselessness of selfishness does not mean that metaphysical truth makes saints of those who discern it. Ethical issues are more concrete than this. Absolute selfishness is nonsense; and it is worth realizing that this is so. But each person must still incline to take himself and his intimates more seriously than he takes human beings in general. Think of men continuing to advertise cigarettes, because one can always demand even more conclusive proof than is yet available that cigarettes are killing multitudes of men and women. Are these manufacturers merely selfish? They have families and employees they justifiably want to be able to provide for, investors to whom they want to yield a return, they have pride in their business success, they sympathize with people's wish to smoke. One can scarcely live without some such concrete motivations as these. We could choose many other examples, and sooner or later the writer or the reader would be hard hit. Such is man, a monstrously confused mixture of motives. How would it help if purely theoretical inquiries such as metaphysics would stop giving aid and comfort to the actual (but at worst relative) selfishness of people? Who knows? But it might help some.

This subject is too sad and tragic for prolonged scrutiny, so far as I am concerned. If there is no 'original sin' there is something not obviously less awful, and it was never more apparent than now.

An argument that Strawson might have used, but so far as I can find did not employ, is this: Whereas substances are rather definitely bounded units: this man, that man, this tree, that tree, etc., we do not so readily divide a process into definite event-units. 'There are six persons in the room' can be a definite fact; but how many human events occur in the room during the time in question? Is not any assignment of number arbitrary?

We here confront one of the subtlest problems which event pluralism has to face, that of the apparent continuity of process, its apparent lack of distinct units. Dewey, Bergson, Peirce, all three careful thinkers much interested in the analysis of experience as such (and to them Husserl and Heidegger could, so far as I know, be added), found no definite discreteness in the becoming of human experience. And no process directly exhibited in human experience seems to come in clearly discrete units. Here is a splendid example of a seemingly strong (empirical) case for a philosophical view, a case which is nevertheless inconclusive, and indeed can be opposed by perhaps a still stronger though non-empirical case. No better example of the difficulty of philosophical issues is needed.

Before we deal with the empirical objection, let us dispose of a poor argument for the lack of discrete events. Bergson says that mental states observably 'interpenetrate'. This is the sort of thing one learns to expect from anti-intellectualists, even great ones like Bergson. They repudiate concepts in principle, but use them – sometimes very badly – in practice. The symmetry which 'inter' conveys, if it conveys anything, is exactly what is out of place in Bergson's own theory of becoming as creation and preservation, one-way cumulative establishment of the details of reality. Thus the term either says nothing or what it says is wrong, on Bergson's own premises. Past states may penetrate into present ones, but never present ones into past.

Another slightly more subtle, but still poor, argument is that even the one-way penetration spoken of is incompatible with discreteness. Discreteness must mean mutually external units. But this amounts to the prejudice of symmetry raised to a dogma. There is no law of logic opposing the view that an event A could be taken into an event B as its past, and similarly B into C, and so on, without there being a continuum of actual events between the time of A and that of C. If 'continuity' is used loosely to mean any kind of intrinsic connectedness among events, of course becoming is continuous in that sense; but there is no logic in pretending to deduce the strict mathematical meaning of continuity, or anything much like it, from the far looser concept. Yet one meets apparently intelligent philosophers who solemnly go through this deduction.

The real difficulties are two: the apparently given continuity of process, and the question how we are to relate a real discreteness of becoming with the mathematical concept of time as continuous, a concept too important and useful to be dismissed as a mere mistake or illusion.

Let us take the mathematical point first. The present view of geometry rules out once for all a simple deduction of physical or actual from mathematical continuity. Mathematics shows what is possible, never what is actual. (One of Kant's antinomies fails to observe this distinction.) Indeed, it is a great deal too much to say that geometry proves even the possibility of an actuality continuous either in space or in time. For the continuity of points or instants implies nothing about even the possibility of a continuity of existing or actual things, unless one can make sense out of an existing or actual thing strictly correlative to a sheer point or instant. There is no mathematical need to assume that points are more than ideals of subdivision or than mere limiting concepts. Continuity is the system of all possible subdivisions; but it is a commonplace of modal theory that not all possibilities are compossible. Hence the sheer actualization of continuity is presumably *im*possible! Thus I hold that the mathematical argument really turns in favour of event pluralism. And when one considers the role which spatial discreteness has played in modern physics, one must be very suspicious indeed of the presumption that temporal discreteness is ruled out *a priori* by mathematics. With profound intellectual intuitiveness, physicists are increasingly searching for evidences of a basic discreteness of actuality both in space and in time.

The illicit inference from mathematics to physics or psychology is hard to banish. It keeps reasserting itself. People say, if there is a discrete series of events in a finite time, then each of these events, say E, occupies a lapse of time, and does this not imply sub-events within each single event? The answer is simply, 'not physically real sub-events, only possibilities'.

It was, perhaps, Royce who first pointed out that since the human 'specious present' has a logically arbitrary time length, there may well be in the universe much longer and much shorter specious presents than the human. As in all cases of physical magnitude, size is comparative, and there is no purely mathematical meaning to spatial or temporal quantity. To say that a unit of human experience occupies something like 1/10 of a second is to say how many successive units of this kind would occur while the earth rotates once, or how many events of a specified kind on the atomic level could occur during a single human experience, and so on and so on. It is not to say anything about real parts (sub-events) of the human experience itself.

Perhaps we have disposed of the confusion between mathematics and physics (or psychology). There remains the argument from givenness. If there are discrete events, why are they not experienced? If there are atoms and molecules in all matter, why are they not perceived? Must the temporal aspect of reality be more distinctly experienced than the spatial? The hard fact, very hard indeed for man to admit, seems to be that direct conscious human perception reveals only certain of the gross outlines, vague in every spatial and temporal way as to exact details, of the world, including particularly that often forgotten part of the world, a man's own nervous system. It is not that the objects of perception are 'unreal'. This locution is a 'red herring'. The point is rather that the objects are defined by perception only up to a point, beyond which perception is neutral, or indefinite. Perception is not wrong, but it is in large part non-committal. Yet, since the urge to interpret is overwhelming, the man often commits himself where 'his senses' do not. In principle this is, as Descartes said, the source of all perceptual error and illusion, even in dreams.

Is process given as continuous, or is it merely not given as discrete? There is all the difference, but the answer is often rendered with gay heedlessness. The answer which seems to meet all the essentials of the situation is that experience is merely vague as to any discreteness which may be there. This vagueness is misread as a revelation of actual continuity. Experience is at most quasi-continuous, or pseudo-continuous. To say more implies a fundamental error in theory of perception, of what it could possibly accomplish.

That we do not distinctly or consciously perceive atoms is not accidental. The utterly unmanageable complexity, calling for a radically superhuman intelligence to handle, which would thus be forced uselessly, and far worse than uselessly, upon our notice furnishes an altogether adequate evolutionary reason. Individual atoms are not biologically significant, hence not perceived. But likewise individual events, even on the human level, are also insignificant for ordinary purposes, hence they too are not clearly perceived. A unit event of human experience cannot occupy much more, rather less, than 1/10 of a second. But the important stages of thought or purpose which we normally need to distinguish and refer to as definite items succeed each other at a much slower rate.

Hence we do not normally think of our lives as consisting each day of tens of thousands of successive experiences, though in fact this is what they do consist of. But sheer continuity of experiencing would mean that 'tens of millions of daily experiences' would also make sense, and so would numbers astronomically vast. Obviously there is something wrong with the notion that continuity, in any strict sense, is given. Yet definite discreteness is also not given. The third possibility, which seems to fit the hard facts, is that a real discreteness is vaguely or approximately given. The spatial case is analogous. True enough, atoms are not even approximately given. But then the direct contact of experience with the physical world is in the nervous system, and here it is a question of cells, not just of atoms or molecules. Moreover, the number of least perceptible parts in the visual field is of a similar order of magnitude to that of the retinal cells. Thus, approximately and vaguely, cells are given, just as in retrospection the unit events of our own experiencings are approximately and vaguely given. We can almost introspect a single experience, most easily in special cases, such as in listening to music, or in 'flicker' experiments.

If the foregoing resolution of the difficulty concerning givenness is valid, event-pluralism emerges with some very strong claims to our confidence. It is the most consistent and clear of all the forms of pluralism. For (1) it has a common logic for all becoming, whereas commonsense pluralism, taken as ultimate, has to make an absolute distinction between substantial and adjectival change, though everything conspires to indicate the relativity of the distinction. Event-pluralism takes 'change' to mean becoming so far as exhibiting novelty in some respect. If an event is of the kind which can initiate a well-marked, quasi-continuous, and well-integrated sequence (perhaps with lively memory connections, certainly with clear-cut character inheritance from event to event), then the becoming of this event is 'substantial change'. Its successors in the sequence will be merely 'adjectival', if you want to label things so. None the less, in both cases, as in all becoming, there is the creation of a new unit of definite reality, not the insertion of new predicates in an old unit.

(2) Event-pluralism treats spatial and temporal multiplicity according to a common formula: real plurality in space or in time is taken to mean real countable units. This was a basic intuition in Leibniz's system, that if there are many things there are single things; groups must have members, collectives imply singulars. But – here Leibniz was careless or prejudiced – there are successive things as well as things coexisting (for Leibniz, only represented as) in space. It is important to realize here that in speaking of 'things' we are not talking about such abstract entities as 'aspects' or 'thoughts'. There are many aspects of things, and many thoughts in people's minds; this, however, need not imply strictly singular aspects or thoughts. For an abstraction is relative to an abstractive perspective, and is not wholly objective. Yet, if one is realistic at all, one must admit that, however we look at the world, it does contain many cells, many people, and that there must be definitely single cells and single people. Yet succession is as objective as spatial coexistence; it should then likewise involve a definite plurality, not relative to an arbitrary point of view. Only event-pluralism carries out the implications of this.

(3) Event-pluralism has a clear-cut version of the law of non-contradiction. It can simply say that no subject can have contradictory predicates – instead of having to treat a difference of spatial aspect in one way and of temporal aspect in another. And, after all, how can one believer believe contradictory assertions, even at different times? For to be one believer implies a unity of awareness which precisely ought to rule out clear and manifest contradictions. The distinction of times removes the difficulty only because it really means two concrete or definite unities of consciousness and not just one. But 'subject', in the strictest psychological sense, means one such unity.

(4) The charge that the temporal distinctness of events is arbitrary, or relative to the point of view, can be turned against substances fully as well as against events. When does a human individual life begin, with the fertilized egg, with the four-months or five-months-old foetus, with birth? When does it end, with absolute death, or with a coma from which consciousness will never be recovered? And if a human being is a conscious individual, does this individual, as such, actually exist in deep sleep? It is impossible, I submit, to give a strictly objective unique meaning to individual genetic identity. But a unit event is not similarly relative to arbitrary criteria. For a sufficiently penetrating perception, say the divine, it would simply be given in its discreteness. By contrast, not even God could make more than an arbitrary decision as to when 'John Jones' begins, or when he ceases to be. For there is no absolute meaning to the question. And during the division of one-celled animals, when does the one animal become two, and is there nothing in between? Or, with greatly advanced surgery and interchange of organs, when would one person become transformed into another? Such questions cannot have unique objective answers. With electrons and other particles, the machinery of substance thinking apparently breaks down altogether. The event language remains. It is the ultimate language, the final measure of things.

(5) An important advantage of event-pluralism is that it enables us to detect a subtle fallacy in arguments for 'organic wholes', taken as wholes which are implied by their parts, with the result – since of course parts are implied by their wholes – that every part must imply every other symmetrically, and a part and its whole must symmetrically imply each other. This is one source of Spinoza's or 'absolute idealism's' doctrine of universal necessity or interdependence. It exploits our intuition that in a living body the various organs could not be what they are, nor do what they do, without the other organs. What is overlooked is that it takes time for influence to pass from one organ to another, so that if, instead of heart, lungs, or brain, one takes the heart just now, the lungs or brain just now, it is no longer correct to speak of 'interdependence'. The one organ now depends not upon the other organs now but upon the other organs as they just have been. Thus in terms of events or states

one has dependence upon past, but independence of contemporary or subsequent, entities or parts. So we cut the nerve of a pernicious argument. But we do it, not in terms of substance but of 'actual entity', a reality which becomes rather than changes.

(6) Above all, and here I am heartily in agreement with Buddhists and Whitehead, but for reasons that in my life go back of any knowledge of either, event-pluralism cuts the nerve of even the subtlest form of argument for a self-interest theory of motivation. All interest in the future, so I have believed since before I was a philosophy major, is in a basic generalized sense altruistic, the concern of an actual reality for other and potential realities whose coming to be it is in a position to influence. It is a secondary question in what event-sequence these entities will fall. Buddhism discovered this long ago, Whitehead (presumably independently) rediscovered it, and some others in the West (none professional philosophers, so far as I know) have made the same point. We can love the other *as ourselves* because even the self as future is also another. The barrier to obeying the Great Commandment is then not metaphysical or absolute, but psychological and relative. On this ground alone I would not give up the event doctrine without the most rigorous proofs of its erroneousness.

The ethical argument for event-pluralism has, to be sure, been matched by ethical arguments against it. If, it is said, a person is a sequence of actualities, responsibility is lost. Why keep a promise if it was made by another actuality? Why does the incoming officer of an organization pay debts incurred by previous officers? Because they both represent the same ongoing society. Exactly, and each of my successive selves represents me as such a society. Whitehead uses the very word for an enduring individual. Each such self inherits purposes from its predecessors, and the more it can accept and execute these purposes, the richer and more harmonious will be its own content. But more than that. In my view a rational self, no matter how momentary, cannot be satisfied with less than a rational aim, and no aim short of some universal long-run good is fully rational. If it serves the general good that promises be kept (and of course, in general, it does), then any momentary self will make good on any promise it is in a position appropriately to make good on, unless there is a reason related to the general good why this rule should be broken. And this is the situation a rational person is in with or without event-pluralism. It is obvious that if rationality implies an interest in future consequences, and if the present self cannot benefit from any future good (since it is already all it ever can be), then a rational momentary self must in a generalized sense be unselfish. It must aim at a future good, although its own good is already complete. Aiming at this good which is not to be its own is indeed part of its own present good, but this is its only necessary share in the matter. If the present self must transcend its own good, why should it tie itself down to consideration only of future good for members of its own personal sequence? It is vastly more interesting to have less restricted objectives, and the inevitability of the cessation of one's own sequence in death implies that the quest for a rational aim in the present but *for* the future will look beyond the fortunes of any mortal animals (see Chapter XVI).

It is also urged that the feeling of remorse or repentance does not make sense, on the event analysis. Ah, but it does. First, a person in part *is* his past, since process is cumulative. If one could totally dismiss and disown one's past experiences, present experience would be limited to bodily sensations for its content. Moreover, the additions which even a year of adult life makes to the apperceptive mass of background memories are, after all, minor. Still further, personality traits persist with much stubbornness. So, if a man says, not I but that past self did the deed, hence I need feel no guilt, he forgets that the relevant question is whether his present self is qualitatively better than the past self, as well as distinguishable from it. Is he even now free from the habits or dispositions which once led to his misdeed? If not, he had better repent before he commits another bad act. True, there is the question of making restitution. Here again, if the rule that restitution will be made by John Jones for what past selves in the John Jones society have done is favourable to the general good (and it is), the event-pluralism has as much reason to follow this rule as anyone can have. One may make restitution for what a parent has done, a friend, a child. Negroes say, with some cogency, that white society should make restitution to them for past mistreatment by white society.

The mere idea of the identity of various substances is just not the key to matters of value. Suffering is suffering, whether one says an identical entity or not an identical entity endures it, and happiness is happiness. He who does not in principle respond negatively to suffering and positively to happiness, no matter in what entity it is, is deficient in rational sympathy. And that same sympathy will incline one to keep promises, make restitutions, and do whatever else will increase happiness and diminish frustration and agony. To act on suitable occasions from enlightened self-interest, interest in the future of one's own personal sequence, is merely one corollary from this. It has no absolute primacy or centrality. One's future happiness is important because it is happiness, and of the human kind, and subject to influence by present actions. So, for the same reason, is someone else's happiness important. It is the quality, degree, and level of the happiness that matters, not the thread of identity that does or does not connect it with a particular rational self.

There is a further point. If a person has really effectively repented, the old idea of forgiveness of sins becomes relevant. Remorse for adequately and effectively repented misdeeds is itself a misdeed, against oneself and deity. It is a new sin. One should be 'born anew', if possible, so that past guilt is simply not present guilt at all. One might very well go right on making restitution, for that is a helpful act which no one else may be in as good a position to perform. But remorse is not restitution, and remorse except as element in repentance, or in restoring broken social relations, is bad, as Spinoza said it was. I do not believe that punishment is ever rightfully an end in itself, even if it is self-punishment.

The ethical arguments against event-pluralism seem to me to be superficial, while the Buddhistic-Whiteheadian insight into the connection between self-interest theories of motivation and the metaphysics of not further analysable entities called substances or selves, I hold, goes very deep indeed into the ethical problem. To love oneself as identical with oneself and the other as not identical with oneself is not, whatever else it may be, to love the neighbour as oneself. Rather it is to put a metaphysical difference between the two loves. At this point (here I agree with Whiteman of S. Africa) Buddhism and a

Christianity or Judaism that understands itself are at one. The difference between self-love and love of others is not metaphysical, nor anything absolute, but a relative matter.

It is hard for me to argue this patiently since it is not a topic about which I have had any uncertainty since in 1918 I came to see that sympathy cannot be derived from self-interest, but is a direct interest of present life in other life, sometimes in the same personal series, sometimes not (this is secondary). The chief thing is whether or not one is able to form a vivid idea of the other life, and whether one can harmonize this idea with other factors in present experience. For here is the central confusion in the self-interest argument: true enough, my action is bound to express my feeling, my positive action, positive feeling, negative action, negative feeling; so, it is inferred, the unselfish enjoy their unselfishness, and hence in a subtle or wise way are selfish after all. This is utter confusion. Present action expresses present feeling, no one denies that. But future feeling, my own or anyone else's, moves me now only if it does move me – only if I happen to imagine, and care about it. And imagining is imagining, no matter whose future feelings are imagined. Here the supposed metaphysical difference between identity and non-identity shows itself to be irrelevant. My tomorrow's suffering or pleasure that I do not now think of has no more to do with my present action than anyone else's tomorrow's feelings. As soon as I saw this, and some related considerations, as a private in the US Army Medical Corps, I was through with even the subtlest forms of self-interest doctrine. The present self has its present interests, but what it is interested *in* is not these interests, but their objects, and so far as the interests are 'in' future results they cannot be in the pleasure now realized by having the interests. For that pleasure is not a possible future result.

The following are to be avoided: the confusion between the pleasure of anticipating pleasure and the pleasure anticipated; the obviously false dogma that one takes pleasure only in anticipating one's own pleasure; the *non sequitur* that since I am myself I must care about myself, in a sense in which, since I am not you, I cannot care about you (as though *X* being interested in *X* could really be a relation of sheer identity); finally, the arbitrary exaggeration of ordinary relative self-centredness into a metaphysical absolute. Beyond these mistakes, I see nothing in the notion, which has pervaded western philosophy from Plato to Aquinas, and from which Kant is not wholly free (Hume is in some ways superior here) that, as Hobbes put it, 'of every voluntary act the object is some good to the man himself', from which it was inferred that a rational ethics depends upon the possibility of showing that the good man is bound to be benefited in the long run by his own good acts. To mention only one objection, in the long run the man will be dead. This, too, seemed to me in 1918 obviously relevant. And I did not then and do not now accept the idea of heaven and hell as making it possible to rescue the self-interest argument from its obvious difficulty in view of mortality. This vicious misuse of speculation I cannot agree to condone. Mortality is to be faced by human reason, not explained away. And an obvious implication of mortality is that a rational aim must transcend one's own fortunes altogether, including them only incidentally as constituting one temporary portion of the 'good in the long run', which is the only truly rational aim. Kant's problem of the rational aim or *summum bonum* is a valid problem, but, alas, his solution makes most of the possible mistakes (see Chapter XIV). Only a philosophy of process in the form of an event-pluralism can entirely avoid these mistakes.

There are other ethical advantages of the doctrine. The twin statements that a person is numerically new in actuality each moment, a new concrete self, and that causality is strict or particular necessity, read backwards, but generic necessity (Chapter VI, Rule II) read forwards enable us to reconcile the elements of sense in the contentions: (*a*) acts must causally flow from (antecedent) character if a man is to be responsible for them, *and* (*b*) it must have been causally possible for the man in that situation with that past to have made a different decision.

(*a*) Each momentary actuality necessarily inherits causally from its past, and this inheritance necessitates that a certain class of possible successors to that past should not remain empty. That what happens falls within this class is not 'chance' at all. Moreover, there will be probability differences between various sub-classes of the possibilities then and there obtaining. A man's settled character is expressed in these probabilities, as well as in the boundaries of decisions of which, under such and such circumstances, he is capable. Each new act of the man alters the character and shifts the probabilities in question, perhaps for good, perhaps for ill, perhaps neutrally to good and ill. So of course the man has responsibility for his actions. Those who think that probability is not enough here are, as it were, living in the stone age. Probability really is the guide of life, as a sagacious English bishop said it was. And of course very high probabilities have virtually all the practical meaning of certainties.

(*b*) Each new concrete self faces the task, not merely of prolonging a chain of causal necessities (concretely there are no such chains in the forward reading), or of continuing to express an antecedent character which, with circumstances, uniquely determines concrete actions (there are no such characters), but of freely creating a slightly new character, and thus establishing a new set of causal possibilities and probabilities. We can excuse Kant for not thinking in probability terms, but today when every scientist does so it is harder to excuse what one continually encounters in philosophical discussions of freedom and determinism. The rage for the absolute, for sheer (rather than approximate or stochastic) order, confuses everything in this topic. But besides the longing for absolute causality, the similar desire for absolute genetic identity also causes trouble. 'Self-determination' thus is taken to mean that John Jones, along with circumstances, determines John Jones, from birth to death. But it is John Jones now that acts now, not John Jones as in infancy. And if John Jones now is to be self-determined, then the John Joneses of the past must not, with circumstances, entirely determine what John Jones now is or does. One's past self is subtly another, and even it must not be complete master of the new self. To take it to be that leads, as William James so well pointed out, to making the squalling infant (and circumstances) absolute master of the grown man, and then by the same absolute causal principle, one's ancestors and the world at large master of oneself at all times.

If character, as distinctive matrix of probabilities, is to have much meaning, it is of course requisite that the range of possibilities at each moment should be narrow. And we have every reason to suppose that it is so. But the great point is that many times a second we are creating something additional, however slight, in the mass of memories and bodily habits which makes up character, and that always this addition is incompletely specified in advance by the prior causal conditions. Just now one is *almost*, but not entirely, the slave of causal necessities; yet by persistently leaning towards the better side of the causally open actions, we can – who knows how far – improve our character. We *can* do this. But we can also not do it. The idea that we always have at least a small range of possibilities can help us to take seriously the difference between using our little freedom well and using it ill.

It is quite true that determinism does not justify folding our hands and saying 'there is no use trying', since if we keep on trying the determinist can always hold that this, too, was determined. But who fails to see that this *ex post facto* use of determinism is no practical use whatever? In principle, determinism in the absolute sense, like so many absolutes, is useless. It does no harm only if it does nothing. Relative determinism, thinking in terms of futuristic outlines of possibility and probability, with boundaries of necessity, is indeed useful. More, it is what we all, determinists or not, unconsciously or not, live by. Nothing else is or could be lived by. The rest, as Peirce said, is make-believe, mere talk.

The arguments of this chapter are not intended to show that the 'substance' or enduring individual concept is simply wrong. In the normal everyday uses it is a perfectly acceptable, indeed scarcely dispensable, way of putting what the event-language analyses into event-sequences or Whiteheadian 'societies'.

Only in science, philosophy, and theology do we need to look beyond this normal simplification of a fantastically complex reality. But in these subjects we do need to look beyond it, and, until this is more generally admitted, much avoidable confusion will continue to result from trying to force ordinary linguistic insight to yield what only extraordinary insight can provide. Convenient simplifications do not really simplify when pressed beyond their proper applications.

X

THE PREJUDICE IN FAVOUR OF SYMMETRY

THE logic of relations, or as Peirce still better expressed it, of 'relatives' or relative terms, has been with us for nearly a century; but it is clear to me that philosophers for the most part have yet to realize the importance of this logic for metaphysics or speculative philosophy. Any philosophy, except perhaps absolute mystical monism, needs a theory of relations, or of relative predicates: e.g., effect of, successor to, sign of, and the like. Carnap's terminology is clear: there are one-place, two-place, three-place, predicates, and so on, according to the number of subjects a predicate requires. Peirce makes the distinctions, in some ways much more profoundly, in his categories of Firstness, Secondness, and Thirdness, or Feeling-quality, Reaction, and Representation. The one-place predicates are absolute, the rest relative. With merely absolute predicates, mere Firsts or Qualities, there could be no causality, no temporal succession, no spatial order, and no knowledge – for knowledge is a way of being related to something, the thing known.

A supremely important but much neglected distinction is that between directed or one-way relations and directionless or symmetrical ones. Equality is directionless, x equal to y and y equal to x being the same fact. In contrast, x greater than y, y greater than x, are not only different, they are contradictory. In between, x at least as great as y, y at least as great as x, though compatible, are the same only in the special and 'degenerate' case in which the actual relation is one of equality. And this is a point I wish to stress: *symmetry is a special case*, not the general principle. To see the importance of this one must consider, besides relations of comparison, such as equality or greater than, relations of existential or dynamic connectedness, e.g., effect to cause, experience to things experienced, events to predecessors. In each case the basic idea is directional. The primary notion of cause is that of antecedent conditioning; the primary idea of experience is that it reveals and depends upon objects not dependent upon it. Similarly, if *x* succeeds *y*, the converse does not hold.

Suppose we know the words in a foreign language for some one-way or non-symmetrical relations, such as greater than, acting upon, temporally succeeding, knowing, cherishing. We then do not need to know the words for the corresponding symmetrical relations: equal, interacting, contemporary, mutually acquainted, friend, in order to express these relations – – provided we have words for negation and conjunction. Thus *x* and *y* are equal if *x* is not greater than *y* and *y* is not greater than *x*; they interact if *x* acts upon *y* and *y* acts upon *x*, contemporary if neither succeeds the other, mutually acquainted if each knows or experiences the other, friends if each knows and cherishes the other. But words for *equal* (or some other symmetrical relation) plus those for negation and conjunction, will not enable us to express *greater than* (or any other one-way relation).

It may seem that the idea of conjunction just mentioned is symmetrical. But although, taken as a dyadic operation of combining, conjunction is of course symmetrical or directionless, yet taken as a triadic relation between two propositions and the compound proposition produced by the operation, conjunction is less symmetrical than most propositional functions (such as *equivalence, either but not both*, etc.), and when negation is added to conjunction (as in *not both*, or *neither*) the highest degree of asymmetry or directionality is reached, and also the highest defining power since *not both, neither nor*, are (as Peirce was the first to see and Sheffer to publish) the only functions each of which, taken singly, can define all the others.

That the defining power of propositional functions varies inversely with their symmetry can be shown in various ways. Here is one (using a method suggested to me by Quine):

$$\begin{array}{ccc} (1) & (2) & (3) \\ (p \equiv p) \equiv (p \equiv p) & (p \& p) \equiv p \qquad (p/p) \equiv \sim p & (p \downarrow p) \equiv \sim p \end{array}$$

Equivalence (1) has low defining power since not even with

negation will it define the other functions. Used reflexively (to relate a proposition to itself) it yields only an idle symmetrical tautology. Conjunction (2) with negation will define all the functions. Used reflexively it yields a somewhat asymmetrical expression. The two 'Sheffer functions' (3), *not both* and *neither*, used reflexively yield doubly asymmetrical expressions giving information about the proposition and showing how negation (and, in more complicated ways, all the functions) can be defined.

All possible dyadic propositional functions (16 in number) can be arranged in order of decreasingly symmetrical truth tables. The two least symmetrical ones will be the Sheffer functions. Thus, compare the extreme cases:

		(A)					(B)				
1.	p	q	f	p	q	f	p	q	f	p	q	f
	T	T	T	T	T	F	T	T	F	T	T	F
	T	F	T	T	F	F	T	F	T	T	F	F
	F	T	T	F	T	F	F	T	T	F	T	F
	F	F	T	F	F	F	F	F	T	F	F	T

Symmetry is functional sameness or interchangeability of elements. In each truth table the first two columns merely exhaust the possible combinations of values for the two elementary propositions p, q. The symmetries in these columns are common to all 16 cases and so may be ignored in comparing them. Also common to all is the *partial* agreement-disagreement between the TF, FT in the second and third rows with the corresponding functional values given in the third column. If both the latter are T or both are F there is binary symmetry, if one is T and the other F there is dyadic asymmetry (as in material implication); but in any case there is triadic half-symmetry, whether TF T, TF F, FT T, or FT F. From the triadic point of view, therefore, the only differences in symmetry are as follows:

(*a*) Relations of agreement or disagreement between the first two and the third value in rows (1, 4), whether TT T, FF F, or TT F, FF T. In each of these two rows we either have complete agreement or complete disagreement between the p, q values on the one hand and the functional value on the other.

(*b*) Relations among the four functional or third-column values. Three degrees of decreasing symmetry occur here: (as in A) all four values the same, whether T or F: two T and two F; (as in B) three one value and the fourth the other.

Combining (*a*) and (*b*) we deduce that the least symmetrical cases are:

$$
\begin{array}{cc}
\text{TT F} & \text{TT F} \\
\text{T} & \text{F} \\
\text{T} & \text{F} \\
\text{FF T} & \text{FF T}
\end{array}
$$

In these tables alone there is no avoidable symmetry.

(A logician has worked out the conditions for full definability with many-valued logics. Each condition is the exclusion of some form of symmetry.)[1]

Material implication comes next in defining power and degree of symmetry. The first row, TT T, is its one avoidable symmetrical aspect.

Yet, in spite of its dyadic asymmetry, its triadic structure is more symmetrical than the dyadically symmetrical Sheffer functions, and this on our principle explains its lesser defining power. (For in extensional logic the truth table analysis is definitive.) Implication must be supplemented by negation. However, whether considered dyadically or triadically, it is less symmetrical than conjunction or disjunction, and it has a corresponding slight advantage over these in that it transforms into an all-defining Sheffer function more simply than they. We have only to write p→∼q.

[1] William Werneck, 'Complete sets of logical functions', *Transactions of the American Mathematical Society*, 51 (1942), pp. 117–32. I owe this reference to my colleague Norman Martin. Martin himself has shown that a definition of Sheffer functions adapted to three-valued logics requires, as two among four essential traits, the exclusion of 'Proper substitution' and 'co-substitution' among truth values. See 'The Sheffer Functions of 3-Valued Logic'. *Journal of Symbolic Logic* 19 (1954), pp. 45–59.

An apparent counter-example to the primacy of non-symmetrical relations is the de Laguna-Whitehead procedure in geometry of defining one-way relations, e.g. inclusion, in terms of a symmetrical relation of 'extensive connection'. A. N. Whitehead, *Process and Reality* (New York: The Macmillan Co., 1929), Part IV, ch. II. This relation is symmetrical, like equality and simultaneity, but unlike them is non-transitive. This, I take it, is an aspect of asymmetry. I leave to others further reflections on the significance of this seemingly recalcitrant example.

The next degree of symmetry and of defining power is found in conjunction and disjunction. Thus

```
      TT  T            TT  T
          F                T
          F                T
      FF  F            FF  F
```

Here are two degrees of avoidable symmetry (in the first and last rows). Defining power is as in implication, but requiring greater complication, as in -p & -q or -(p & q).

A still more symmetrical group of functions includes equivalence. Here there are three degrees of symmetry: the first row, and each of the two pairs of functional values in the third column.

```
      TT  T
          F
          F
      FF  T
```

Even with negation these functions will not define the remaining ones.

Higher degrees of symmetry and still weaker defining powers occur (see A in our first set of tables). Here either the first or last row is symmetrical, and any functional value interchanges with every other. This is a purely tautological function, saying that no matter what truth values p, q may have, their relation is the same. In other words, there is no distinctive relation dependent upon their truth values.

Since negation added to any of several functions gives them complete defining power, let us consider the degree of symmetry of this monary function. Quine (in personal correspondence) has objected to my calling it asymmetrical. But perhaps I was right after all. There are four monary functions, including negation, and it is the least symmetrical of the four.

(1) p	p	(2) p	p V ~p	(3) p	p & ~p	(4) p	~p
T	T	T	T	T	F	T	F
F	F	F	T	F	F	F	T

The asymmetry in the first column is common and so irrelevant. Relevant are the agreements or disagreements within the rows or in the second column. In the first three tables there are two such agreements, whether (1) in the two rows or (2, 3) in one row and the second column. In (4) there are no relevant agreements or repetitions at all. Thus, in spite of its visual (diagonal) symmetry, this is logically the least symmetrical of the four monary tables. Even if we count the really irrelevant diagonal repetitions, we still have only two such symmetries, whereas in (2, 3) there are one diagonal and the two horizontal or vertical symmetries, and in (1) the two columns, and the values in each row, interchange. Thus (4) has either no or two forms of symmetry, while the rest have either two or three, depending upon the criteria. So negation has all the asymmetry a monary function could have.

It is significant that implication, or 'false if and only if p is true and q is false', involves a partial symmetry in the repetition of false in its definition, in comparison with

'false if and only if both are true' – stroke (/)
'true if and only if both are false' – dagger (↑)

Thus we see that radical triadic asymmetry must include radical dyadic symmetry. It is this feature which enables the Sheffer functions to define negation. Substituting a second p for q we have $p/p \equiv -p$ ('not both p and p' is the same as 'not p'). The dyadic symmetry of the functions is thus essential to their superior defining power, the reason being that this dyadic symmetry is required to render the triadic asymmetry, i.e., the contrast in truth values, unambiguous (true that both are false, false that both are true, as compared to, false that p is true and q is false). This pattern, *symmetry within an overall asymmetry*, we meet again and again. I see in it a paradigm for metaphysics. What we are to look for in basic concepts is comprehensive asymmetry or directional order embracing a subordinate aspect of symmetry. Traditionally, neither the one aspect nor the other was systematically sought in its appropriate role, and in both cases the results were, we shall hold, unfortunate.

As examples of how symmetries are made possible by, and in a sense contained within, asymmetries, consider: brotherhood as an aspect of the one-way relation of inheritance; mutual independence of contemporary events as aspects of causal dependence; human equality as a common superiority to the non-rational animals and perhaps inferiority to deity. In each case the one-way or directed relation is the key.

For two thousand years, at least, philosophers have in certain crucial cases proceeded as though symmetry were basic, not one-way connectedness. I shall now give some examples of this. Bergson asked, are the moments of duration mutually external or do they 'interpenetrate'? The question implies symmetry for either answer. Yet Bergson believed in a basic asymmetry of time, a closed past and an open future. Unluckily he failed to notice that 'interpenetration' implies symmetry. He should have said, The past penetrates the present but not the present the past. Penetration is one thing, interpenetration is another. (Incidentally this example shows how an intuitionist, claiming to dismiss concepts, may in practice use them – but, alas, the wrong concepts.) When asked by Lovejoy to clarify his position, Bergson merely shifted from the concept of interpenetration to that of continuity or indivisibility.[3] But these, as he presents them, are also symmetrical ideas. Lovejoy, whose mental alertness was of a higher order than that of most historians of philosophy, noted that Bergson's intuitive view was of a one-way relationship of present to past, rather than of a symmetrical inclusion of past and future in the present.

David Hume, otherwise very different from Bergson, is equally or even more heedless of the distinction between one-way and symmetrical inclusion or dependence. 'What is distinguishable is separable' – this famous dictum blurs together a symmetrical relation of comparison with a non-symmetrical relation of existential independence. This is easily shown. Thus x and xy (that is, a whole containing x and some additional factor) are distinguishable, but while x may in some cases be separable from xy, xy can in no case be separated from x. In other words, given x, there is not necessarily xy, but given xy there is certainly x. Thus, symmetrical separability by no means follows from distinguishability.

On one assumption Hume is right. An x separable from xy, which here denotes x and something additional, must be simpler than xy. Hume assumes that the entities he will apply

[3] A. O. Lovejoy, *The Reason, the Understanding, and Time* (Baltimore: The Johns Hopkins Press, 1961) pp. 89–99, 185–202.

his maxim to are equally simple. Successive 'impressions' or events are not related, he implies, as x and xy. However, the phenomenon of memory suggests the contrary: that later experience refers back to and is complicated by earlier experience in a manner not matched by the forward reference of anticipation. At any rate, Hume's maxim is useless in metaphysics until the issue of equal complexity has been settled. So clear a head as Von Wright has overlooked this point, as has Ayer.

Let us now consider Bradley, seemingly at the opposite extreme from Hume. We shall again meet the assumption of symmetry, again not clearly stated as such. He asked, Are relations external to their terms, and answered, No. Are they internal to their terms? Here his answer is more complex: Yes, so far as relations are real at all, but 'ultimately' this alternative breaks down also. So relations are unreal. The formulation is symmetrical throughout. Not only that, the force of the arguments (as far as they have force) rests upon this symmetry. 'External relation' is taken to mean external to both terms, 'internal' likewise is to hold at both ends of the relation. In the symmetrically external case, relations have no home in things, and thus become additional things calling for relations to the others. In the symmetrically internal case, no term can really be distinguished from another; for each includes the other and, by the same logic, the entirety of reality. But suppose relations are external at one end and internal at the other. They then have a home in things – at the internal end – and the very contrast between the dependence or relativity of the internally-related term and the independence or absoluteness of the externally-related one makes the terms clearly distinguishable. So Bradley's dialectic against relations has begged the question by its assumption of symmetry.

The critics of Bradley, including Russell, R. B. Perry (one of my teachers), and G. E. Moore, fail to point out the neglect of the asymmetrical case. Russell does use asymmetrical relations to refute Bradley, but precisely not the asymmetry of internality-externality- or dependence-independence-itself. He thus fails to generalize his justified complaint that asymmetry has been neglected. And to Bradley's contention that (symmetrically) internal relations are the most real form, Russell opposes the opposite view that (symmetrically) external relations are basic. In the very language of the debate, or in the definitions employed, symmetry is assumed. Thus internal relations are said to be those 'grounded in the natures of their terms'. What, both terms, or only one? This issue is not focused by either side in the argument.

Moore only argues, and (in spite of Leibniz) rightly, that the usable concept of the genetically identical thing does not make the identity dependent upon all properties, relational or otherwise, of the thing. C. I. Lewis, in class, used (mistakenly I thought and think) to defend Leibniz at this point, and his objections to the extreme 'idealistic' theory (e.g., Royce's) of relations were only that universal internality is but a 'regulative ideal' which cannot be literally true, and that relations of objects to particular subjects are not important ones for the objects. I hold that the universal symmetrical theory of dependence is no ideal at all but a blunder, and that relations of objects to particular subjects are not simply unimportant, they are nothing, to the objects.

Let us go back eighteen centuries, to Nagarjuna the Mahayana Buddhist, a man at least comparable to Bradley or Hume in subtlety, and a man who, like them, wishes to show that there is no rationale for the idea of real connectedness.[4] An exhaustive division is proposed. Effects are one of the following: different from their causes, not different, both different and not different, neither different nor not different. Each of the four cases is then shown to be irrational. But all four are couched in symmetrical terms! Since intuitively the cause-effect relation has a direction, is not symmetrical, the analysis cannot be correct. Also, please note that while x and xy are different, the

---

[4] See T. R. V. Murti, *The Central Philosophy of Buddhism* (London: George Allen and Unwin, 1955), pp. 121–39, 168–72, 177, 196. It is interesting that Murti sees the necessity that relations should involve dependence at one end and independence at the other (p. 324). His proof of this is lucid and cogent. But his conclusion that the independent factor is the reality of both seems a *non sequitur* from his argument. Quite the contrary, it is the relative factor which contains both, as knowledge is relative to and contains its object, or a whole, its parts. See also A. K. Chatterjee, *The Yogācāra Idealism.* (Varanasi: Banaras Hindu University, 1962), pp. 10–14, 89ff.

For Nagarjuna see also K. Venkata Ramanan, *Nagarjuna's Philosophy* (Rutland, Vermont, and Tokyo: Charles E. Tuttle Company, 1966), pp. 157–66, 183f.

difference read one way is that of element from whole, read the other way that of whole from element. These are very different differences. The symmetrical formulation masks the essential directedness of the relations. What a cause produces is an occurrence – a human experience, for example – which utilizes the cause as datum in a creative synthesis, a novel experience remembering or perceiving its predecessors. Nagarjuna's arguments lose much of their plausibility where the concealed asymmetry is taken into account.

Nagarjuna has some arguments which may seem not to depend upon an assumed symmetry, such as the argument that if the cause has ceased to be it cannot act to produce the effect, yet as past and different from the effect it must have ceased to be. Here the 'objective immortality', or immanence of the past as datum in the present, is ignored. Asymmetry is hinted at but not made explicit.

It is to be said in Nagarjuna's favour that he does explicitly make the assumption of simplicity by which alone asymmetry can be ruled out. Some of his opponents may have accepted the assumption, but perhaps that was their mistake as well as Nagarjuna's. Plainly xy differs from x by being more, but x from xy by being less. These are non-symmetrical relations. The lack of symmetry is not taken into account in Nagarjuna's critique of the four possibilities. He argues that if the cause is not different from the effect, there is only one term, not two, and if it is different, why could not anything cause anything? And if the two are both different and not different, then they are not simple. Perhaps so, but an event which includes its causal antecedents differs from and also resembles them not just in any way, but in a partly determinate way. So of course it does not follow that anything could cause anything you please. If Nagarjuna means that absolute determinism is ruled out, he is right. Determinism is a metaphysical blunder, as many great philosophers of the last ten or twelve decades have realized. But science and common sense require no absolute determinism, only a qualified or relative one.

Nagarjuna perhaps comes closer to the real issue when he drops mere relations of comparison, such as likeness and difference, and considers the existential relations, dependent and independent. But, alas, independence seems to be viewed as necessarily symmetrical, and dependence or relativity is equated with 'interdependence', thus ruling out the one-way forms. Simply dependent things, simply independent things, neither make an intelligible world. But what of the third possibility, a world with both dependence and independence and with both symmetrical and non-symmetrical dependence and independence relations? The symmetrical cases will be derivative and inexplicable simply in their own terms. To say, for example, that two individuals, A and B, interact is to say that a state S of A influences a subsequent state S^1 of B, while a previous state S of B influences state S^1 of A. In this way the two individuals can retain their distinctness by virtue of successive states between which only one-way dependencies obtain. Symmetrical relations of independence are also to be explicated through one-way relations. Independent contemporaries are in the same universe at all only through their partly overlapping causal antecedents and their partly overlapping consequences.

That absolute simples must all be wholly, and hence mutually, independent is enough to rule out the idea of such simples. Wittgenstein apparently came to realize this after writing the *Tractatus*, though he never clearly formulated an alternative. Russell has failed to realize it.

Idealistic critics of the logical atomism of Hume and his followers have accepted the assumption of symmetry, but, seeing the absurdities of logical atomism, have advocated universal interdependence or monism. This is true of Royce, for all his pretended pluralism. Too bad, since he was in some ways a splendid thinker and writer.

One idealistic argument against any independence recalls Nagarjuna's by employing the idea of likeness or difference, that is to say, relations of comparison. Two items of reality must resemble or differ from one another, it is urged, in ways that are fully determined by their natures. In whatever way A resembles or differs from B, neither term could be what it is without this resemblance or difference. Thus if A is taller than B, then to change this relation is to change at least one of the terms. The relation is 'grounded in the natures of the terms'. It is curious that whereas Bradley and, with some qualification, Weiss argue for interdependence from relations of comparison, Hume and his innumerable followers (all anticipated by Ockham) argue for mutual independence from these same relations ('what is distinguishable is separable'). Both, I believe, are mistaken.

Suppose A has a certain height H and B a different and lesser one, H^1. There is then a difference in height, $H - H^1 = D$. Is D essential to A? It is essential to A that anything with height H^1 will be shorter than A by D. But why is it essential to A that there is something, namely B, with height H^1? This indeed is the very question at issue, the question, does A depend upon B? So the argument is circular. True enough, neither A nor B could have a definite height just in itself, apart from all other things; but things can have definite properties without being compared to everything whatever, no matter where and when in the spatio-temporal system. When we measure a man, we do not do this by comparing him to remote contemporaries (still less to remote) descendants), but to objects in our own portion of the world process, essentially to standards fixed in the past.

Russell once said to me: 'A philosopher can be an absolute monist or an absolute pluralist, and I see no rational ground for making the decision one way rather than the other.' But what rational ground is there for reducing the options to these two? This is the prior question, which Russell seems never to have permitted himself to consider with much, if any, care. Such a mental cramp in so great an intellect seems extraordinary, and rather tragic.

One may parody the prejudice of symmetry as follows: Suppose a carpenter were to insist that if hinges on one side of a door are good, hinges on both sides would be better. So he hangs a door by hinging it on both sides, and it then appears that the hinges cannot function, so that the door is not a door but a wall. 'We'll fix that,' says another carpenter, and removes all the hinges. So now the door is again not a door, but a board lying on the floor. This is how I see the famous controversy about internal and external relations. The first carpenter is Spinoza, Bradley, Royce, or Blanshard; the second carpenter is Hume, Russell, Von Wright, Ayer, or R. B. Perry.

I ought to admit that the assumption of the equal simplicity of earlier and later events has its plausibility. It seems that memory is extremely partial, and hence (as Lovejoy and Russell agree in urging against Bergson) cannot mean the literal inclusion of earlier in later experience. Some qualities or aspects at most are included. And, in so far as there is foresight, some qualities or aspects of later events are, by the same principle, it might be thought, ingredients in the present. Also, if foresight can err, so can memory. Thus it appears that in principle symmetry is the correct view. One could also argue that inclusion or dependence should be transitive, so that if memory is inclusion of earlier in later experience, we should remember experiences of the remote past as well as those of the recent past, which is not the case. Although these considerations are plausible, I believe they involve errors. Among these are the confusion between judgments based on memory and memory itself, also the assumption that the entire content of experience is open to conscious detection. But my main point now is that the mere denial of symmetrical inclusion or dependence does not entail the assertion of symmetrical independence and that many great philosophers have talked as though it did.

Since symmetrical relations are based upon one-way or directed ones, there is a presumption in favour of the intuitive claim that memory gives us the past in the present and that there is no comparable intuition of the future. Consider then perception. The general rule seems to be that the perceived entity does not perceive its perceiver. Even if two animals perceive each other, the state of A which B perceives will be temporally earlier than the state of A which perceives B as its perceiver. I say this in spite of the fact that philosophers in general seem to have taken the basic temporal relation of perceiver to perceived as one of simultaneity. Since this relation is symmetrical and the relation of perceiving is not (at least in general), the incongruity is manifest. The very idea of perception as a form of knowledge is that of a one-way dependence upon an independent reality. We perceive something because it is there, it is not there because we perceive it. In other words, the perceiving is an effect; and the perceived a causal condition of that effect. How can simultaneity be the temporal structure of such a one-way conditioning? From this point of view the factual scientific evidence that time elapses before we see states of affairs is not the essential reason for denying the temporal symmetry of the relation, but merely an illustration of what should be held *a priori*. Perception never should have been taken as simultaneous with its object.

But if perception has the one-way temporal structure appropriate to its epistemic function of exhibiting facts which are what they are independently of our perceptions, it seems doubly perverse to deny that memory also has past, not present, states for its data. It turns out that the paradigm of realistic awareness is rather memory than perception, since memory more obviously seems to be what perception after all also is: awareness of the past. The supposed oddity of memory, as claiming to have the past as its content, is no oddity at all. Perception's seeming confinement to the present is the oddity, the illusion indeed.

Suppose we did only experience things simultaneous with the experience. What would follow? Not even the idea of succession. From symmetrical relations asymmetries cannot be derived! But, on the other hand, given a stretch of the past, with the bits of causal regularity exhibited in that past, the contemporary world and the future world are more or less inferrible.

One of the reasons why I think highly of Peirce and Whitehead is that they take memory as the paradigm of realistic experiencing and interpret perception as similar in temporal structure, memory being experience of one's own previous experience, perception experience of the wider or impersonal past. Peirce is less clear than Whitehead on this, and even Whitehead's language is sometimes careless, but essentially they see what Hume, Russell, Bradley, miss. My own rejection of the symmetrical views came, however, partly from other influences, e.g., James, Bergson, and my teacher W. E. Hocking, who led me to see the future as open and the past as closed, and therefore retrospective relations as different in logical structure from prospective ones. It also seemed to me (in 1922–3) that merely external relations and merely internal ones were alike absurd for reasons that Bradley and Russell between them had made clear.

Many other applications of the primacy of directional relations can be given. Here is one. Time is the aspect of space-time in which asymmetry comes to a focus, space, the aspect of symmetry. By our rule, space is really a complication of time, not time of space. Causality is the key to all relations of events, and any single chain of cause-effects is 'time-like'. Space is a complication in temporal succession or inheritance. An entity could have one parent or source in time; but two parents require space, just as two coexisting offspring require it. Space is multiple lines of inheritance. But inheritance, in itself and as a one-way relation, is temporal. Space means two forms of symmetry: a negative form, mutual independence between events or short-lived individuals, and a positive form, mutual interaction between individuals enduring long enough to exchange influences. (Those that must endure very long for this are far apart, perhaps millions of light years, spatially.) Space, then, like symmetrical forms generally, is not the basic principle, but time. Čapek I take to be right about this.[5]

That symmetry is secondary in a certain technical sense does not imply its unimportance. It has its indispensable place. A world of action without interaction is doubtfully conceivable and would certainly be a poor thing at best. If there were speakers and listeners, no one would ever speak and listen to the same person. There would be no dialogue, no I and Thou.

The problem of extension, spatiality, is essentially that of symmetrical causal relations. According to relativity physics, there are no causal relations between brief contemporary events spatially separated from each other. However, sequences of events may interact, if spatially close or long-lasting enough. If they do interact, the coexistence is a real relation in both terms. In the former case, where there has not been time for any influence to pass from one term to the other, coexistence is not a relational property of either term but of some reality inclusive of both. Any event occurring sufficiently long after the two events to have both in its past will possess the relation in question. It will enjoy both as its data. They will be coexistent items of *its* past. Thus it is the future which reunites the separated realities of the present. In another way they are connected by their overlapping pasts. An observer on earth and another observer on a remote planet might both inherit light from the same past item. But this does not establish a real relational property of coexistence in the two observers. That A and B inherit from C does not imply that A inherits from B or B from A. It takes something subsequent alike to A and B to put them together in definite relationship.

[5] Milič Čapek, *Philosophical Impact of Contemporary Physics* (New York: Van Nostrand & Co.), 1961.

To some there seems an absurdity in this situation. I once thought that contemporaries, no matter how far apart and short-lived, must interact. Weiss takes this position, with some eloquence, in connection with his 'Third Mode of Being', which he calls Existence, but which seems rather 'Coexistence'.

That two events are in one space has its meaning from the overlapping of their pasts and futures. A thing coexists with whatever inherits from part of the same past and is destined to influence part of the same future.

Since deity is not, at least in the same sense, localized spatially, the theistic account must somehow alter or complete the foregoing picture. But just *how* I find myself unable to understand. What Weiss has to say about Existence I do not find helpful, for as he uses the word it seems a mere label for the problem. This could be said about the word God; but, I think, with less justice, since that word stands for an analogy (difficult no doubt) between the thinking animal and the cosmos conceived as animate. For Weiss's 'Existence' I find no analogy at all, unless it is the foregoing analogy over again.

It is to be noted that the difficulty about coexistence, that is to say, about spatial extension, has nothing to do with any difference between mind and mere matter. Materialism is no help whatever in solving it, or indeed in solving any other genuine problem. By genuine I mean, not entirely due to the exaggerations of one-sided forms of idealism. Materialists are valuable as critics of such absurdities as the notion of inextended spiritual substance, parallelism, or epiphenomenalism.

If the 'identity theory' of mind-body means only that the sensory qualities of experience apply to neural processes, as well as to our sensory experiences, and that the latter logically entail the former, I incline to accept it. But the subject-object duality is ultimate, in my view, and it involves a real and indeed temporal priority of the object in each case. In a human sensory experience the sensing is slightly subsequent to the occurrence in certain cells of certain subhuman feelings. Our sensation of red comes just after these cells have been themselves enjoying their subhuman counterpart of redness. Thus redness is present on two levels, but the higher level consists in a sort of pooling of a large number of individual cases on the lower level. In short the objective parts, the data, of the experience are identical with something physiological. But the experience as a whole is just itself, identical with nothing else.

Taking any event in the nervous system, its effect in human experience is immediately subsequent; taking any event in human experience, its effects in the nervous system are also immediately subsequent. Thus there is interaction. I believe that the only alternative to parallelism, epiphenomenalism, and mere identity is interactionism, with a temporal difference between cause and effect in either direction. This is not an absolute symmetry, in that the way in which cellular feelings participate in (and are influenced by) human feelings is very different indeed from the way human feelings participate in cellular ones. The superiority of the human over the subhuman is expressed in this difference. For one thing, a single cell makes only negligible difference to the human individual, while the single human individual makes a great difference to each cell. Here, as always, symmetry is a partial or abstract aspect of what in its concrete wholeness is an asymmetry. Yet in its partial role symmetry is as ultimate as asymmetry.

Was it not a gigantic if unintentional betrayal of religion when theologians denied interaction, hence dialogue in any (however analogical) sense, between creator and creatures? God must be effect as well as cause, patient as well as agent. The indispensable asymmetry between the eminent being and all others must be expressed less simple-mindedly than the sheer denial of interaction. Action upon God must be real yet different in principle from God's action upon the world (see Chapter XI). This view combines both a sublime symmetry and a sublime asymmetry, and thus does justice to both aspects of the religious relationship. The traditional theism had a falsely simple asymmetry, and no proper symmetry.

Symmetry is in a sense a lack of order. The equality of x and y puts them in no definite order, relative to one another. But the superiority of one to the other orders them. To exalt symmetry is to depreciate order. Those who absolutize the idea of human equality are advocating chaos. True, there may be inequalities running both ways between two individuals. My wife would not want to try to rival me in philosophy, and I could even less dream of rivalling her in music, to mention only one skill of many in which she excels. So we don't have even to raise the question of overall inequality. However, human individuals are not all strictly equal in any factual sense whatever. A baby is unequal to an adult, an imbecile to a normal person, a hopelessly spoiled child to a well-brought-up one. Moreover (as we shall see in Chapter XVI), it is the comparable inequalities of their individual members that justifies the assumption of approximate equality, at least innately, between certain groups of persons.

The notion that haunts formal logicians, as it haunted medieval theologians, that all truths are timeless, is a symmetrical view of truth. For in eternity things can only coexist, there can be no order of derivation. So all truths, including the most trivial items of worldly happening, clutter up eternity on a basis of equal freedom from generation and destruction. Logical precedence, where there is no possibility of a temporal one, is a mere rhetorical flourish; no one knows what it means. Only in process taken as creation of novelties can ideas of derivation and dependence have meaning. In eternity, things must be like neighbours in space, mutually interdependent. One-way dependence is the essence of time, and the basis of spatial order as well, since all that puts contemporaries into a common order is their partly common past and common future, their overlapping causes and effects. Mere eternity would be like space without time, a meaningless abstraction. I see no good reason to accept the timelessness of truth, apart at least from very abstract truths about things themselves eternal or timeless, such as those of arithmetic or formal logic, including the logic of symmetrical and one-way relations.

If one goes through philosophical writings, as I sometimes do, and puts 'Sym' in the margin wherever the assumption of symmetry, introduced without argument, manifests itself, it is remarkable how often this occurs.

Another example: Quite often when the view is proposed that the past is determinate but the future not, an objector with an air of confidence queries, 'Why play favourites between past and future, why not both as determinate – or indeterminate?' Why not hinge doors on both sides? Or neither side? In other words, the appeal to symmetry is not a sufficient argument. (I am aware that in physics it is often taken to be so. I have not, in my ignorance, been able, so far, to interpret this in terms of the views set forth in the present essay.) Asymmetry is basic in formal logic; with what right does one assume the reverse everywhere else?

It is notable that while the word 'symmetrical' seems positive, the more descriptive 'directionless' is negative. The concept 'non-symmetrical' is only the ambiguous case, as 'symmetry' is the zero case, of directionality. Thus inequality and equality are both in a genuine sense negative or privations, since the one is the withholding of information as to which is superior, and the other is the joint absence of superiority. But greater than, successor to, effect of, are essentially positive. To know that x and y are friends is not *ipso facto* to know which is the more friendly or kind of understanding towards the other. Mere symmetry is obtained only by abstraction. The concrete situation is always one of contrast, and the contrast of x with y is not the contrast of y with x, save in the limiting and scarcely realizable case in which x and y are in perfect balance. 'Interaction' conceals the difference between x's action upon y and y's action upon x. To know all the actions in the world is to know all the interactions, but the converse is not true. Look to the asymmetrical relations and the rest will tend to take care of themselves.

To begin an inquiry with symmetrical ideas is, as intellectual history shows, to run a great risk of overlooking the one-way cases. Directed relations are more likely to remind us of the symmetrical forms. Had people talked about dependence instead of internal relations, there would have been less confusion and it would more easily have been seen that dependence need not, though it can, run both ways. Cause-effect might intuitively have suggested asymmetry, but the sophisticated formula 'necessary and sufficient condition', like many another sophisticated formula (here I agree partly with ordinary language enthusiasts), has led to error, since it implies symmetry and thus begs an important question.

The word 'sufficient' is ambiguous. Sufficient to make what happens next really possible, or to make it actual? The causally implied 'effect' of a situation need not be so determinate as what concretely comes out of it. The orderliness of nature is not so absolute as all that. On the creationist doctrine, concrete actualities must determine themselves, their sufficient antecedent conditions merely establishing a range of real possibilities, what happens being a selection from and specification of these. This is the asymmetrical or indeterministic view of causality. The deterministic bias is one form of misplaced symmetry. Nicolai Hartmann throughout his career apparently never realized that his argument for determinism was a mere begging of the question, an argument from a definition his opponent would deliberately reject. He never saw that the assumption of symmetry was indeed an assumption, and a counter-intuitive one at that. Nor, so far as I can find out, did Kant see this. Causality is conditioning, not bi-conditioning. The adult must have been a child, the child may or may not become an adult.

Dualistic philosophies afford another illustration of misplaced symmetry. There are particulars and universals, or universals and particulars; there are souls and bodies, or bodies and souls; there is no order or direction in a mere 'and'. We face the question, what concept applies to the total reality formed by souls and bodies? Is the togetherness of soul and body material or psychical? Does the soul have a body or the body a soul? Since the basic idea of the psychical is that of experiencing or knowing, and since both soul and body must be known if there is a real problem, the key to the duality of body and mind is the relation of knowing or experiencing to the known or experienced. It is knowing which relates itself to the known, not *vice versa*. Our knowing Plato relates us to Plato, not Plato to us. It is we, not Plato, who thereby acquire a relative property. If formal logicians cannot see this, then they are allowing formalities to obscure what they might otherwise know. *The whole of knowing and known is the knowing, not the known.* Thus the asymmetry of mind and matter can only be understood through some form of psychicalism. The critics of idealism have shown nothing against this. They have spent, and I am tempted to say wasted, their ammunition attacking not the basic thesis of idealism that reality in general is mind in general but some logically independent and even contrary thesis, such as that all relations are internal. The proper basis of idealism is that the *one-way dependence of mind upon its objects is the key to all the asymmetries, and hence also all the symmetries, of reality.*

Is the togetherness of universals and particulars itself universal or particular? It can only be particular; for particularity is determinateness, and a whole cannot have fewer determinations than its constituents. Similarly the togetherness of actuality and possibility can only be in actuality. Indeed the possibility of the future is the same as the actuality of the past and present, in their character as destined to be included in some richer total reality. The potentiality of an event is just the actuality of its predecessors. Aristotle and the Greeks generally seemed to think that mind was somehow on the side of universality and actuality, not on that of particularity and potentiality. This is a double mistake. Particular and actual are essentially one, and so are universal and potential; but in addition, mind as concrete feeling is particular, while as purposive and abstractive it is universal and faces a determinable rather than determinate future. The malleable stuff which the future will inherit from the present may be called 'matter', but this is a mere word for the truth that the present is capable of being objectified in more than one way by subsequent experiences. The creative, temporal character of experiencing yields all the light upon modality as ontological that we are going to get. (In defining soul as 'self-moved', Plato seems to have had some inkling of this truth. Aristotle fiercely attacks the definition, with clever and, I believe, bad arguments.)

I give two final examples of the primacy of directional relationships. My colleague Professor Brogan has for many years defended the view that the asymmetrical relation 'better than' or 'preferable to' is the basic value idea, not the idea of good. Good is an extremely vague idea, since almost anything is good compared to something or other. The purpose of valuation is to establish an order of priorities. Good as an absolute would have to mean, 'Such that nothing could be better'. But it is not self-evident, if even true, that value in all its dimensions admits an absolute maximum. The history of theology is strewn with doctrines wrecked on this rock. Even Kant was unable to free himself from the idea that God must be an absolute maximum of value. But all that is necessary to exalt God above all beings, actual or possible, is to require that he be unsurpassable *by another*. Or, put positively, God is the *all-surpassing, self-surpassing being*. In this way the asymmetrical idea of superiority is made basic, as it ought to be.

One last and surprising example. Jonathan Edwards argued against theological indeterminists that to compromise the principle of causality in favour of human freedom is to give up the basis of an inference to the existence of God as cause of the world. But this is a formal fallacy, except on the assumption of symmetry. For to infer God (as creator) from the world is to reason from effect to cause, whereas the inference that the indeterminist rejects, or rather qualifies, is only the opposite passage from cause to effect. There is no contradiction in holding that effects require their precise causal conditions while the conditions do not require their precise outcomes, any more than there is contradiction in saying, *p* entails *q* but not *vice versa*. Moreover, if Edwards is indeed reasoning from an assumption of symmetry, then he is making the world, just as it is, a necessary consequence of the existence of God, and is in Spinoza's camp and a heretic indeed. The neglect of the directedness of the causal relation thus vitiates his argument.

A theistic philosophy cannot do either of the following: (1) It cannot explain relations away, as Bradley or Sankara do. For the creatures must really depend upon God for their existence. (2) It cannot admit symmetry in this relation of existential dependence, since God is not thought to depend upon any particular creatures for his very existence. Relations to God are intrinsic to a creature, constitutive of its very existence; but relations to the creatures are extrinsic to the mere existence of God (though not to his total actuality, including his contingent qualities). Therefore any doctrine, such as Hume's or Russell's, that all relations are external, and any doctrine such as Spinoza's, Royce's, Blanshard's, that all relations are internal to both or all their terms, contradict theism. These doctrines also contradict any realistic view of experience and knowledge, any view that knowledge is dependent upon a world which is found rather than made by particular acts of experiencing or knowing that world. One-way dependence is required both for theistic religion and for epistemology.

In this chapter I have argued that non-symmetrical concepts are logically primary, and symmetrical concepts derivative. Yet both are needed to make an intelligible philosophy. The two things to avoid are: taking symmetry as primary, and failing to do justice to symmetry in its proper subordinate role. Metaphysicians have tended to commit both of these mistakes in different aspects of their systems

XI

THE PRINCIPLE OF DUAL TRANSCENDENCE AND ITS BASIS IN ORDINARY LANGUAGE

IN philosophy and theology there has been much talk about 'transcendence'. The word has been used in many ways. The use I have in mind is to refer to a form of reality exalted in principle above all others. Sometimes, but not always, the reality thus exalted has been thought of as God. In Buddhism a transcendent reality is recognized, but it is not, at least explicitly or obviously, taken to be God. In much Hindu thought a deity – Isvara – transcending the world is admitted, but it is distinguished from the still higher, or more strictly 'real', impersonal absolute or Brahman. I favour a more theistic view. But the question I wish to discuss is the following: What is it that could exalt one kind of reality above all others? The question may be put in the converse form: What is it that could make every sort of thing except one inferior to that one? Although this question has been debated for over twenty centuries, remarkably little heed has been given to the logic of the words employed. Yet these words, I believe, have or can be given a good logic.

The transcendent is clearly intended as a radical exception, an utterly extraordinary form or level of reality. By comparison, everything else may be termed ordinary. Since ordinary things are those with which we are familiar, and to which most linguistic expressions refer, let us begin by considering wherein ordinariness might consist. There is a traditional view about this, reiterated with minor variations by countless writers in English, Sanskrit, Greek, Latin, and many other tongues. It runs as follows: ordinary things are limited or finite, in that other things are, or conceivably may be, greater or better; also ordinary things are relative, that is, dependent upon other things for their existence and qualities. To reach the concept of the transcendent, it was thought, we simply deny any and every limitation or form of dependence. We thus produce the idea of 'the absolute', or 'the infinite', or – to speak with Spinoza – the 'absolutely infinite', infinite in every respect.

There is at least one obvious objection to this. These expressions as they stand are pure negations. The transcendent is not limited, not dependent. What is it positively? If the meaning is merely negative, how does the transcendent differ from bare nothing? If you reply, 'at least it is or has being, and it is good, supremely good', the objector can then ask, 'But how do you know that being, and goodness or value, are compatible with the complete absence of limitation or dependence?' Perhaps to be is to be limited and to have intrinsic relatedness to or dependence upon other things. And perhaps value also requires limitation and relativity. Is not love the supreme value, and does not love cause us to be influenced by what happens to those we care about – to suffer with those who suffer, and rejoice with those who rejoice? Can the independent have love? If not, can it have supreme value?

On the other hand, it does not seem reasonable to suppose that everything whatever, actual or possible, must be limited and dependent. We would hardly talk about dependence were there no such thing as independence, or about finitude if everything whatever were finite. There is a case for the traditional assumption in philosophy of religion that the negations by which the transcendent has been defined do somehow apply. But then there must also be some positive aspects of the transcendent reality, and the problem becomes how these are to be construed. A merely 'negative' theology, like a purely positive one, is – here Hegel is right – an absurdity.

Descartes thought he had a positive meaning for transcendence in the concept of perfection. In this case it is ordinary things that are described negatively, all of them being in various senses imperfect. So perhaps perfection is the positive meaning of transcendence? Yet there are difficulties. The etymological meaning of perfect – 'finished', 'completed' – implies that the thing has been made or produced, and hence is dependent upon causes. However, Anselm, Aquinas, and Spinoza, among others, proposed a way out: the transcendent, they said, is the actuality of all possible qualities, just so far as these are affirmative and good. The Thomistic phrase for this is 'pure actuality', that is, a reality in which nothing positive is left merely potential. Thus the 'negative theology' is verbally turned into sheer affirmation. *Ens realissimum*, most real being, was one label for this idea. Such a being could not change, by the old Platonic argument that there is no room in it for improvement, and of course no possibility of decay. Nothing could act upon or influence it, since it has, once for all and eternally, all that it possibly could have, or all that is worth having.

From Aristotle to Kant, this idea played a central role. A similar conception haunted religion and philosophy in Asia. In spite of its prestige, the idea is quite vulnerable to criticism. It assumes that the affirmative elements in statements or ideas are entirely independent of the negative elements, so that when all negation or exclusion is abstracted from them, the positive meanings can still remain intact. This implies that there are no incompatible yet genuine value possibilities, and that potential value could be exhaustively actualized. Experience suggests the contrary view. In every choice some good possibilities are rejected, in every artistic creation possible forms of beauty are renounced. Spinoza remarked that 'all determination is negation'; but is not sheer indetermination the greatest negation of all? Definiteness, being this and therefore not that, or that but therefore not this, seems essential to all beauty, all value, and all actuality of which we have any conception. Perhaps a merely positive entity is as little distinguishable from nonentity as a merely negative one.

Consider the transcendent reality in relation to lesser things: either it derives value from them or it does not. If it thus derives value, it could not derive all possible value in this way, because the definiteness of things means their exclusion of some possibilities. Spinoza tried to avoid this by supposing that all possible things were actual. But this contention commends itself to few and involves difficulties of its own. If, however, the transcendent derives no value from other things, this is very odd. Either it knows the other things or it does not. If it does not, it lacks the value of knowledge, which seems positive and good. If it knows the things, the knowledge either has value or is valueless. If it has value – and how can knowledge be valueless?

– it cannot have all the value possible in this way, because the things known do not actualize all possibilities, and even the transcendent could not know to exist things which do not exist. In this sense knowledge is bound to be limited.

Another move to save the *ens realissimum* is to deny the reality of ordinary things. But this seems only a verbal solution. Events in the everyday world are admittedly not bare nothings, and to say that they are makes nonsense of language itself. We have knowledge of such events. If the transcendent lacks this knowledge, then there is something positive which it lacks.

If one claims that knowledge, beauty, definiteness, are really negative, and that the truly positive and truly good are entirely independent of such things, what meaning can be left even for the word good or the word positive? And if we contribute no value to the transcendent, why should we concern ourselves with it? All talk of serving a God thus described is absurd.

My conclusion is that the *ens realissimum* is a pseudo-conception. Yet how else can we give positive meaning to the idea of transcendence?

Let us, in the spirit of contemporary philosophy, consider how words like 'dependent' or 'independent' are ordinarily used. A man would be said to depend upon his parents, teachers, friends, enemies, for at least much of what he is; but does he depend in any way upon descendants born after his death? Or upon the hypothetical contemporary inhabitants of some remote planet? We would not normally suppose so. Nor does astronomy support the supposition.

I have now given away my secret. To turn from ordinary things to the transcendent cannot be to turn from dependence to independence, but only from selective or non-universal forms of dependence or independence to the universal forms of both. In ordinary cases dependence and independence occur together, but neither one in universal form. Thus, Plato's philosophizing was independent of that of Whitehead but not of that of Socrates. Or again the truths of arithmetic are, on the one hand, independent of those of natural science, while the latter, more concrete truths cannot be clearly expressed in total abstraction from numerical relationships. Moreover, the truths of arithmetic are not independent of one another. Dependence

and independence are thus equally ordinary, familiar phenomena. Where one is, there is also the other.

To reach transcendence we must negate not dependence but
limited scope, both of dependence and of independence. This
yields two contrary and seemingly rival forms of the extraordinary: universally positive or universally negative dependence. Tradition accepted the universally negative form but
ignored the positive one. It saw that independence with cosmic
scope is no ordinary property, but failed to see that dependence
with similar scope must be equally extraordinary. This over-
sight, as I take it to be, occurred in many parts of the world, and
through millennia rather than centuries. It was, however,
fortunate for a few of us that it occurred, since it left a vacuum
to be occupied by any intelligent persons who happened to
think of it and were not easily intimidated.

The belief that independence, despite its negative form, is
really positive and dependence negative or bad, is perhaps
natural, but upon careful consideration it proves indefensible.
Financial independence, for example, has no doubt its merits,
but then it is really a kind of dependence – upon banks, govern-
ments, industries, and so forth. The only strict forms of independence attributable to ordinary individuals are sheer
deficiencies or privations. Thus, Plato's total independence of
Whitehead is inseparable from Plato's total ignorance of Whitehead, and it was especially Whitehead's knowledge of Plato,
through his writings, or through people who had read Plato,
which caused the modern thinker to depend upon or be
influenced by the ancient one. Ignorance is negative if anything
is, and a list of the things of which a person is totally independent will include only things of which the person is totally
unaware. Indeed, someone else must make the list. It is impossible that our knowledge of a thing should in no way alter or
qualify us, for knowing is a qualification. Subjects depend for
their experiences upon their given objects, the world which is
there for them to experience. Yet subjects are not therefore
inferior to objects! The venerable dogma, 'agent is superior to
patient', is not derived from the study of knowledge. Indeed it is
not derived from any careful examination of ordinary cases. To
speak is to be agent, to listen is to be patient, and those who
want to show their superiority by speaking without listening are

not trustworthy authorities in theory of value. Man listens to, observes, patiently receives influences from, the other animals far more than they listen to or observe him, and this is his superiority, not theirs.

It is as true that a man is comprehensively influenced by the cells composing his body as that he comprehensively influences them, and this double comprehensiveness constitutes his superiority. For among themselves the cells chiefly and directly influence and are influenced by only a few neighbouring cells, while the man gives and receives influences, directly to and from millions, if not billions, of cells. A somewhat similar difference obtains between political rulers and citizens. It is a poor ruler who speaks but does not listen, and a good ruler listens to many.

There is an explanation for the traditional failure to consider the possibility of a transcendent form of dependence. Independence, in one sense, is a positive and good thing, and it might be supposed that if the transcendent is to be completely independent in this good sense it would be contradictory for it to be dependent in any sense. However, what is the good meaning of independence if not this: that one is able to maintain one's existence and essential character, one's 'integrity', no matter what others may do? To partake faithfully in dialogue, which is in principle the highest form of existence, as Buber rightly insists, one must accept influences coming from another, allow the other to determine part of the perceptual content of one's own experience. One must 'adjust' to the other in some degree and fashion. However, one's own very existence need not be, and ideally is not, thereby threatened, and one's basic principles or purposes, one's essential personal style or 'identity', may remain intact, no matter what the other says to us. Here is the clearly positive side of independence: ability to adapt without compromise in essentials. But this independence in essentials does not by any logical necessity limit the scope of the sources of influence in inessentials. Human beings, to be sure, are not strong, flexible, or resourceful enough to maintain their integrity in every possible context. But if we dare to conceive transcendence at all, why not have the courage of this bold enterprise and conceive an unlimited capacity to adapt, without loss of integrity, to everything whatever? There seems no contradiction in holding that in the transcendent being the essential core of identity is infallibly secure, while the peripheral content is responsive to every item of reality. No rule of logic forbids saying that a thing has a property and also its negative, provided the positive and the negative properties are referred to the thing in diverse aspects. The same reality may in one aspect be universally open to influence, and in another aspect universally closed to influence.

I have said that independence as compared to dependence is negative, but I have also just said that independence in a sense is positive. Here, too, a legitimate distinction removes the semblance of inconsistency. What is negative or a privation is that an individual should in his total or concrete reality be independent of other things. For such total independence entails ignorance. The positive or good form of independence can concern only a partial aspect of the individual, his essential integrity, including a connectedness of memory and purpose through successive experiences. This essential integrity and connectedness is an abstraction from the total reality of the individual. Only this abstract form of independence can be positive. Thus the positive value of arithmetical knowledge lies in its abstractness and consequent independence of the particular circumstances of its application. Arithmetical knowledge as such ought not to include knowledge of contingent circumstances. Its merit is that it abstracts from such things. But nothing so independent could be concrete, or knowledge of the concrete.

We may now improve upon our formulation of the mutual compatibility of the two forms of transcendence. They fail to conflict only because while one, universal independence, applies to an abstract aspect of the transcendent, the other applies, not just to a second abstract aspect, but to the total or concrete reality of the transcendent being. And by the old Aristotelian principle, the abstract or general is real in the concrete or particular, not separately. Hence transcendent or universal relativity includes all that is positive in transcendent absoluteness or independence. This relation is mirrored in modal logic, where the conjunction of a necessary with a contingent proposition yields a compound proposition which is contingent. 'Necessarily p and contingently q' must itself be contingent. Since it is the necessary which is independent or absolute, not the contingent, the overall character of the absolute and the relative is given by relativity or contingency, not by absoluteness or necessity.

Consider the traditional transcendent property of omniscience or cognitive infallibility. Whatever exists, the infallible (analogically speaking) knows this existence; yet not even the infallible can know the possible but non-existent as existent, for this would be error, not knowledge. The infallibile must, of course, be *capable* of knowing and certain to know the actuality of the possible should it be actual. To be infallible, then, is to be actually in cognitive relation to what actually exists, and potentially in relation to what could exist. The duality of actual and possible, or of concrete and abstract, cannot be suspended even with reference to the omniscient.

Infallibility is as such an extreme abstraction. One may show this as follows: From the assertion, there is an infallible knower, one cannot deduce that this knower knows your existence or mine, for example. For this deduction, one must add the premise that we are among the existing things. Thus God, simply as infallible, is not the concrete God who actually knows the concrete world. Infallibility belongs to the essential integrity of the transcendent, and is totally independent of circumstances. Nothing can produce or destroy infallibility; eternally and independently and necessarily it simply is. But, as with all abstractions, its importance is its presence in concrete form. And this concrete form is not eternal or necessary, except in the sense that there must always be some appropriate concrete realization of the abstract divine nature. The nature must be concretized somehow, but there is no must about the particular how. Transcendence entails both necessity and contingency, both independence and dependence, each in a unique or eminent form.

It is not difficult to show that finitude and infinity involve the same double duality as dependence and independence. There is an infinite aspect even of ordinary things. For instance, consider the question, how many different actions could a man have performed in his past life? His actual deeds will have been finite, but, supposing there is some causal indeterminacy, there is no finite number which can express all the possibilities among which a man has chosen. Possibilities transcend number; for they are too indefinite or continuous to be counted save by arbitrary division. But at the same time, a man's possibilities are always within limits. God's possibilities are beyond limits, in the sense that if a world could exist it could be content of his knowledge. What could exist could be divinely known to exist. In contrast, many things could exist that a man could not know to exist – for instance a world incompatible with the man's existence, or perhaps with any man's existence. In short, there is an ordinary and a transcendent infinity, with respect to potentiality.

A more difficult question is whether there is any sense in which God may be infinite in actuality. He cannot be so in all respects because this would mean having all possible worlds as actual, and they are not all mutually compatible. But in one respect it seems possible for there to be a transcendently infinite actuality, provided an infinite series of actual worlds, or world states, successive to one another, is conceivable. This brings us face to face with Kant's first antinomy about the infinity or finitude of the past. I incline to the infinite horn of the dilemma, though I confess myself puzzled in the matter. In any case, it seems unavoidable to define transcendence partly through a strict infinity, at least of potentiality.

Ordinary 'finitude' is poorly expressed by this word. Not merely is a man, for instance, limited in magnitude, duration, or value, but his magnitude, duration, value, is but a fragment of that of actuality as a whole. *Fragmentariness*, the status of being a portion of finite actuality, not the whole, is the ordinary or non-transcendent form. Even actuality as a whole must be limited in some respects, compared to what is conceivable, and so must the transcendent as actual. But the transcendent cannot be a mere fragment of the actual whole. Whatever is actual the transcendent being does possess, whatever could be actual he could possess. His actuality and his potentiality are both inclusive, whereas our actuality and our potentiality are fragmentary. To be possible is to be possible for God, to be actual is to be actual for God; neither statement holds if a non-transcendent individual is substituted for God. You might think that reality as a whole, or the universe, could here be put in the place of God. But then in what sense is reality a whole, or in what sense is the universe an individual? I hold that God is unsurpassably inclusive and also unsurpassably integrated or unified. He is the all as an individual being.

Not only dependence and independence, not only finitude and infinity, but many other similarly abstract concepts permit if not require dual transcendence. Thus 'cause of all' is no more extraordinary than 'effect of all'. You and I can no more be influenced by everything than we can influence everything. We cannot be influenced by (and hence cannot know) our descendants any more than we can influence our ancestors; and our causal independence of remote contemporaries, according to relativity physics, is the exact counterpart of their independence of us.

Take again the idea of God as knowing all things, as the subject for whom all else is object: is it any less remarkable that he should be object for all subjects? No man could be experienced by all other sentient creatures, any more than he could experience them all. But God, being ubiquitous and eternally existent, is always present for any creature to experience. He responds (in his eminent way) to all, but all (in their noneminent way) respond to him. Neither statement holds of other individuals.

The transcendent has been termed immutable, but there can be a transcendent capacity for novelty as well as for stability. To change in and through all changes is as unique a property as to be changeless through all changes. The transcendent has been termed simple, but complexity admits a transcendent form as readily as simplicity. It is true that there can be no absolutely maximal complexity; however, transcendence as such is not properly defined as an unsurpassable maximum of this or that. The transcendent is exalted above all other beings, actual or conceivable; but the exact formula for this is not unsurpassability, but 'unsurpassability *by another*'. Any complexity can be surpassed, but the transcendent complexity can only be surpassed by the being already transcendent. God is surpassable only by himself. This I take to be the religious meaning of 'eminence', which is a word less abused historically than transcendence.

The two sides of the transcendent duality are, as already noted, reconciled by the old principle that the concrete contains the abstract. Indeed, abstractness and concreteness have their transcendent forms. God is at once the most abstract and the most richly concrete of all beings, most abstract in his identifying or essential traits, most richly concrete in his contingent qualities. All other individuals are less abstract in their identifying traits or essences, as well as less richly concrete in their accidents. I could not have been myself with different parents or a different gene structure at birth; but God only has to be unsurpassable or universal in scope to be himself and no one else.

The famous 'coincidence of opposites' affirmed by Cusanus was scarcely an anticipation of dual transcendence; for the abstract and concrete contraries are not coincident, if this means identical or indistinguishable. They are both in God, but they are not the same in him. Tillich's assertion that God is 'beyond the tension' of the contraries is equally vague or unhelpful. The contrast between the poles is not less but incomparably greater in God. Independent of all, dependent upon all, are infinitely different, though both describe God. Had Cusanus meant this, he was able enough to say so, unless possibly he did not dare to attack tradition so sharply.

Dual transcendence sheds a new light on the problem of evil. For that problem is a result of the non-dual view of causation or power. God is cause, the creatures are effects; he is creative, they are created; he is independent, they are dependent; he is active, they are passive. On the contrary, the creatures, in their non-eminent way, are also causes or creators, they are independent and active; while God, in his eminent way, is also creature, effect, derivative, and passive. If God has eminent power, every creature has some degree (above zero) of non-eminent power. It, therefore, cannot be deduced from the eminent power of God that what happens is his doing, since the totality of causal conditions of an event includes all antecedent creatures as well as God. Does this mean that God could not have so acted that the particular evils which occur would not have occurred? No, he could have so acted. But only by opening the door to other evils. For while God could have determined otherwise than he has the limits of creaturely causation or power (as seen in the laws of nature), he could not have eliminated the non-eminent creativity which is the necessary counterpart of eminent creativity. With a multiplicity of creative agents, some risk of conflict and suffering is inevitable. The source of evil is precisely this multiplicity. But it is equally the source of good. Risk and opportunity go together, not because God chooses to have it so, but because opportunity without risk is meaningless or contradictory. God is eminent decision-making power; he is not and could not be the only decision-making power. From particles to man, nothing is simply determined by God. Until this is seen all talk about the problem of evil is an attempt to choose between absurdities.

Some readers will perhaps object that while universal creativity, self-determination by each momentary self, may explain why there must be a measure of conflict and frustration, it does not explain why there must be moral evil, deliberate choice of the lesser good. Could not God establish as a natural law that thinking animals would always make the morally right choice? This implies that thinking animals, capable of ethical principles, could be made infallible in their obedience to these principles. Infallibility, however, is a divine attribute, and an incommunicable one. One must not forget that the menace of natural evils – frustrations and sufferings caused innocently by subhuman creatures, or by human creatures with perfectly good intentions – puts pressures on us to act in our own interest and for our own need, even regardless of the needs of others. To resist these pressures to the ideal extent is to be infinitely good ethically. But to be infinitely good is once more a divine attribute. To suppose that it could be a human one by a law of nature or divine decree seems to amount to supposing that the ideal form of the voluntary could be entirely involuntary. Only God needs no choice to be good – he alone *is* goodness in its ideal form. (Yet even he faces open alternatives of good and good.)

There is also the question, could a rational animal be born rational or must it go through sub-rational infancy? A cybernetics expert has asked whether an artificial adult man could be produced without a duplicate of infancy and youth being produced first. His conclusion favoured the second view. If, as I suspect, something like infancy is necessary for a non-divine rationality, then ethically perfect individuals imply ethically perfect parents and teachers, in infinite regress. An infant is

without moral resources, it cannot meet bad treatment nobly
or in saintly fashion, but must develop resentment and hatred
as basic attitudes. Psychiatry, rather than Augustine, has
enabled us to understand the 'inheritance' of wickedness. And
wickedness here need only mean something less than ethical
perfection. Under great pressure from frustration, which mere
chance suffices to explain, only infinite ethical heroism and
wisdom stand between parents or teachers and some mistreatment of infants.

There might indeed be a better race of thinking animal than
ours and I trust that there are many in the vast cosmos. There
is no reason to guess that we happen to be the best – or the
worst.

The main trouble with this whole matter is that the word
'omnipotence' paralyses thinking. We suppose a sort of magic
which just makes creatures to be what they are. We have no
analogy that gives content for this supposed power. We are
what we are, not simply because divine power has decided or
done this or that, but because countless non-divine creatures
(including our own past selves) have decided what they have
decided. Not a single act of a single creature has been or could
have been simply decided by divine action. In the cosmic
drama every actor, no matter how humble, contributes to the
play something left undetermined by the playwright. What
could it mean, then, to suppose that in the application of
ethical principles to action, an infinitely delicate, difficult
matter, the actors have nothing to decide save ethically neutral
options? Whether or not this is self-evidently absurd, it is not
self-evidently free from absurdity. Hick talks about the possibility of God's giving us a 'character' such that only morally
right choices would be possible for us.[1] But character is a
deposit of past creaturely action; it could not be a mere deposit
in us of something which God has produced just by himself. All
that God can directly give us is the beauty of his ideal for us,
an ideal to which we cannot simply not respond, but to which
our response has to be partly self-determined, and it has to
be influenced by past creaturely responses in our universe.
'Persuasion' is the ultimate power; not even God can simply

---

[1] John Hick, *Evil and the God of Love* (London: Macmillan and New York:
Harper & Row, 1966).

coerce. The contrary idea implies a false analogy with pushing puppets or passive clay about, or with hypnotism mistakenly construed, or with the use of brutal punishments, or more or less irresistible bribes, in the human management of human beings. Right action secured only by rewards and punishments, even were this conceivable, would not be genuine goodness at all, let alone perfect goodness.

If the problem of evil were the greatest difficulty for theism, I should feel happier in my theistic belief than I do. For me it is rather a confusion than a genuine problem. If the existence of evil is logically incompatible with the existence of God, then that existence must be contingent. (For evil is certainly at least possible, and nothing which contradicts a necessity can be so.) But if I have any grasp at all of the meaning of 'existence' in this application, God could not exist contingently. Hence either his existence is impossible, or it is necessary. If it is impossible, then it is incompatible with evil only because it is incompatible with anything you please. If it is necessary, then it is compatible with anything genuinely possible, hence with evil. The analysis of 'unsurpassable power' yields the same result.

Universal creationism will not permit us to say, as so many have, that while God determines particular goods he does not determine particular evils. Rather, creatures determine worldly particulars, good or evil. God wills good as such. Good and not evil is his aim everywhere; but the particularization of this aim at good in the world is left to creatures. For creationism this is the meaning of 'creature'. The particular goods which God himself determines are not in the world, but as Niebuhr says, 'beyond history'. They are the particular responses which God makes to the creaturely decisions, the way in which he makes optimal use of them as data in his own consciousness.

A friend of mine has objected that if God accepts even the most wicked creaturely experiences as immortal data in his life, he thereby shows neutrality between good and evil. I reply: what good would it do the victims of Hitler for God to know and remember them and not know or remember Hitler? And how could God adequately appreciate their innocent and perhaps heroic experiences if he did not also retain Hitler's experiences to which theirs were responsive? It is also argued that if even Hitlers contribute to the divine bliss, they are not really bad after all, and God is a sadist who needs and wants wicked creatures. My view is this: God gets what value he can from Hitler's experiences, and those of Hitler's victims. But he not only did not need these, he could have derived greater value if Hitler, his parents and associates, and everyone involved, had made better use of their freedom. There is no creaturely suffering which God requires for his own satisfaction. Essentially it is creaturely fulfilments that enrich the divine life; creaturely frustrations are misfortunes for God. (Berdyaev says something to this effect.) Like any wise and good person God makes the best use he can of such misfortunes, but he does not choose them or prefer them to creaturely good. Just the contrary. We ourselves derive optimal value from the health of our bodily cells, but we should do the best we can when they are unhealthy. They not only lose nothing by this, they gain something. If we do not make the best of their ills we add to them. So with God and his cosmic body.

How, it is asked, can God feel the sadistic joy of a malicious man without being sadistic? Jesus was not wicked simply because he could perceive the wickedness of others. God feels wicked feelings not as his own feelings but as his creatures'. This is the subject-object duality implied by the Whiteheadian category, 'feeling of feeling', a concept which, in other words, others had already adopted. The first feeling is the 'subjective form' of the experience, the second the 'objective form'. Both are feelings, but the second is the original (and temporally prior), the first is a participation in the second after the fact. Wickedness is in wrong decisions. God inherits our decisions, as ours, not as his. In feeling them he does not enact or decide them; for they are already decided. Similarly, he can share in the pain that goes with being afraid without in the same sense being afraid. For being afraid, as we are, involves belief in dangers to oneself, such as deity could not be exposed to. The courageous adult can sympathize with a child's fears of the dark without sharing in the belief that the dark hides dangers. (God is not in every sense unexposed to danger, as my phrase 'misfortunes for God' implies.) The wise can understand the ignorance of those less wise. The more can contain the less: in A's experience of B's experience, the first subject in principle includes the other and is more than it. What is not possible is that the less can include the more. God can adequately and not merely 'in principle' experience our humbler experiences. We cannot adequately experience his eminent experiences. The ignorant cannot fully understand the wise, nor the cowardly the courageous, nor the wicked the righteous. Only the converse is possible. In this psychological doctrine I am agreeing with a great psychologist, Fechner.

A curious instance of what happens when creationism is not adopted is the argument of James Ross to show that, although God creates the wickedness of wicked men, he is not thereby himself shown to be wicked. For, says Ross, Shakespeare created wicked individuals, and no one considers this a wicked act on his part. But in fact Shakespeare created no individuals, wicked or not wicked. He created striking semblances of individuality, brilliant symbols of good and bad individuals, but no individuals. They lack individuality by two criteria: They are not concrete or definite (what were their gene structures, what were their pubic hairs like, what childhood memories did each have, etc., etc., etc.?); and they are not self-determined. Since they are not self-determined (though they seem to be), they are neither good nor wicked; they merely show us very specific types of goodness or wickedness. But God has definite and hence self-determined individuals as creatures. Therefore, he is not 'omnipotent' in the Thomistic sense, which Ross defines (historically correctly) as the power effectively to choose that any possible world, no matter which, shall be actual. The alleged choices of creatures are then simply itemized portions of God's choices. Why Ross should suppose this to make coherent sense I can only wonder. To me it makes none. It is a pity, for he has a rare capacity to think clearly, and on some issues is brilliantly right where so many in the Thomistic tradition have been wrong (see Chapter XIV).

The necessity of dual rather than single transcendence can be seen from still another point of view. There are dimensions of value which seem not to admit a maximum or upper limit but rather to imply an open infinity. Thus, knowledge measured simply by freedom from error and ignorance (i.e., as infallible) can have a maximum – that is, knowing all that is actual as actual, and all that is possible as possible. But knowledge measured by the richness, variety, harmony, of its objects can have no maximal form. Leibniz tried to conceive a best possible world, a world most worth knowing, so to speak, but he did not succeed. Given any harmonized variety of objects, or, by the standard definition of beauty, any beautiful spectacle, there could be a still greater variety, a more intensely beautiful spectacle. All possible variety actualized together would be sheer confusion, since, as Leibniz conceded, there are incompossibles, things distributively but not collectively possible. What, short of the absurdity, 'all possible harmonized variety', would be the greatest possible one? There is no reason to suppose the question has an intelligible affirmative answer.

What follows? Since value, even the value of knowledge, has an unmaximizable aspect, transcendence cannot consist simply in an unsurpassable good, or sum of possible perfections. God must in every aspect be unsurpassable by any other being, but since in one aspect he cannot be unsurpassable absolutely, we must say that in this aspect he is surpassable by himself only. In all aspects he is exalted in principle above conceivable rivals, and he is capable of being surpassed only by himself and only in those aspects which do not logically admit a maximum. The maximizable aspects, such as infallibility, are as we have seen, abstract.

The concrete aspect of value which admits no final maximum is best indicated by the word beauty, rather than by the words goodness or truth. The transcendent is eternally, independently, and maximally good and aware of whatever is true, but the concrete beauty, the intensity, harmony and richness, of the divine life can reach no final maximum. As a Hindu sociologist and writer on mysticism once said in Chicago, God is absolute and immutable ethically but open to increase aesthetically. Since this had already become my doctrine at the time, I was delighted to have this support from a country in which the world of time and change is supposed to be looked down upon.

The God of religion, as Pascal saw, is not the absolute of philosophy, any more than the richest concrete actuality can be identical with the most abstract of all individual characters. Yet both can form one transcendent being.[1]

---

[1] Recent theological writings by authors whose views seem compatible with the principle set forth in this chapter include:

Ogden, S. M., *The Reality of God* (New York: Harper and Row and London: S.C.M. Press, 1966).

Browning, D. S., *Atonement and Psychotherapy* (Philadelphia: The Westminster Press, 1966).

Hamilton, P. N., *The Living God and the Modern World* (London: Hodder and Stoughton and Philadelphia and Boston: United Church Press, 1967).

Cobb, J. B., Jr., *A Christian Natural Theology, Based on the Thought of Alfred North Whitehead* (Philadelphia: Westminster Press, and London: Lutterworth Press, 1965).

Pittenger, W. N., *God in Process* (London: SCM Press, 1967).

For more traditional metaphysical views see:

Gilkey, Langdon, *Maker of Heaven and Earth: the Christian Doctrine of Creation in the Light of Modern Knowledge* (New York: Doubleday, 1959).

Neville, R. C., *God the Creator: on the Transcendence and Presence of God* (Chicago and London: University of Chicago Press, 1968).

Farrar, A. M., *Finite and Infinite* (London: Dacre Press, 1943).

Faith and Speculation (London: Adam and Charles Black, 1967).

Parmentier, Alix, *La philosophie de Whitehead et le problème de Dieu* (Paris: Beauchesne, 1968), pp. 481–574.

Mascall, E. L., *He Who Is* (London: Longmans, 1943).

For readings, with critical discussions, covering three millennia of theistic and anti-theistic speculation in many countries and religions, see: Hartshorne and Reese, W. L., *Philosophers Speak of God* (Chicago: The University of Chicago Press, 1953).

XII

CAN THERE BE *A PRIORI* KNOWLEDGE OF WHAT EXISTS?

ORDINARY existential statements are contingent: their truth and falsity are equally conceivable. Are all existential statements contingent? No, because some are necessarily false: those containing contradictions. Perhaps, however, all true positive existential statements are contingent. If so, 'something exists', which is true and positive, is contingent. But then the contradictory, 'nothing exists', is only contingently false, and it makes sense to say, 'there might have been nothing'. For reasons pointed out by authors as diverse as Jonathan Edwards, Henri Bergson, Milton Munitz, and myself, this fails to make sense. The possibility of nothing is no more a possibility than the eating of nothing is an eating, or than (Lewis Carroll) being told something by nobody is being told something.

Is it only bare 'something' whose existence is without alternative? In that case, 'exist' and 'exist contingently' say the same thing, apart from the existence of something in general. This seems rather odd. Is it obvious that 'exists' entails 'might not have existed'? I should think, no more than it is obvious or even true that 'there is a prime number between 4 and 6' entails that there might have been no such number. Existing contingently seems to be a distinctive way of existing, not a redundancy. The 'principle of contrast' may be invoked here. Contingency, like all terms with a meaning beyond that of reality as such, and in the vaguest possible sense, must apply negatively somewhere. Also, could it be necessary that something or other exists, or that nothing exists should be false, if of every kind of something it is true that it might not have existed? It seems that there must be a non-contingent kind of something.

If 'something exists' is necessary, necessity must be connected with extreme abstractness; for nothing is more abstract than the bare idea of something. Four further considerations support this conclusion. (1) Our example of the prime number, a number being highly abstract. (2) The impossibility that concrete realities should be necessary unless their abstract characters were also. Since the concrete is more determinate and inclusive than the abstract, to take the concrete or determinate as necessary is to take everything as necessary. (3) The necessary can only be what all contingent possibilities have in common; for that is necessary which is true in any possible case. But the common element of alternative possibilities is the abstract residuum remaining when all specificities distinguishing contingent alternatives from one another have been set aside. (4) God, the usual candidate for the status of necessary existence, is definable in more abstract terms than any other individual being. Take the usual philosophical definitions of God. You will find them to consist of extremely abstract or general terms: cause of all, uncaused cause, unmoved mover, knower of all, such that none greater can be conceived, the being which is not conceivably surpassed by another. I do not say that these definitions are all equally adequate; but I do say that an adequate definition can and must be given in extremely abstract terms. God is the only individual identifiable by abstractions alone. This does not imply that God is a merely abstract entity, but only that what makes him God and no other individual is abstract. The necessity of God, as the Socinians were perhaps the first to see, does not have to apply to his entire reality, but only to his identity as God and no other. We do not identify even ordinary individuals by all their qualities, for in that case we should not know who a man was until he was dead, if then. But except in the one divine case, purely abstract concepts are never enough to identify individuals. The merely relative abstractness of ordinary individual identity becomes absolute in the divine individuality. This is the long missing key to the ontological argument.

I conclude from the foregoing that if anything is necessary, the most abstract truths or entities are so, just as, if anything is contingent, the most concrete truths or entities are so. That the ontological argument could be debated for centuries without these considerations being brought to bear is odd indeed. Findlay, not long ago, used the words 'abstract' and 'concrete' in his famous article on the proof, but who before him? Perhaps I did, but I have found no third person. The term 'predicate' is no synonym for 'abstract'; for only some predicates are abstract enough to be necessarily exemplified. The important difference is not between essence and existence but between two levels both of essence and of existence. Miss that and you miss almost everything. Kant did miss it, as did Hume, Russell, and Ryle.

When Kant said that without sensory intuition we cannot know any individual, he should have said that without such intuition we cannot know any individual which must be identified through the specific or concrete. With all individuals except God this is the case. A man presupposes his parents, 'this man', the world common to him and the speaker who is pointing him out; but God is defined by reference to possibility as such and actuality as such, entirely without regard to any particular actualities. We do not have to say, e.g., that God knows Mao, or that Mao exists; we only have to say that whatever is actual God knows as actual and whatever is possible he knows as possible, and that he could and would know any possible thing as actual were it actual. Thus God is defined through categories alone, whereas Mao must be defined partly through contingent facts. Most logicians hold, rightly, I think, that individuality and existence are inseparable. That God's individuality is definable *a priori* means that his existence is knowable *a priori*. This existence or individuality is a universal principle both of possibility and of actuality, hence neutral to the frontier between what happens to exist and what happens to be merely possible.

Note also that since God as unsurpassable must be non-localized or ubiquitous (this being the optimal relation to space and time) and necessary to any existence whatever, the idea implies a sense in which every intuition has God as object, whatever other objects it may have, and however incapable conscious introspection may be of disclosing this universal object. It is notorious that the universally experienced is not the most obviously experienced. Kant assumes, he does not prove, that there is no intuition of God; the theistic proofs, if they prove anything, prove that there is such an intuition. They do so by a *reductio ad absurdum* of the denial. This, at least, is their implied claim.

The property traditionally supposed to connect God with necessary existence was his unique excellence. The reason this connection can obtain, I suggest, is that the only abstractly definable degrees of value are the minimum and the maximum. These alone are specifiable *a priori*. All values between these extremes must be indicated empirically and concretely: thus, 'better than X but not better than Y'.

Let us consider the minimal degree of value. Would it be simply zero value, or a supremely negative value? This is the question of the 'perfect devil' which has been proposed as a rival to God for the status of necessity. The proposal is in order, provided supremely negative value is conceivable. Various considerations support the contrary view. An unsurpassably bad individual must be completely without integrity, for integrity is a merit. But an individual with zero integrity is a contradiction in terms. Again, moral badness appears as hatred or indifference; the first is partly self-destructive and hence cannot be maximized, and the second reaches a maximum only in death or total unawareness. As the tradition rightly held, to be an individual is already a good. Therefore, there is no *a priori* concept of supreme badness other than nonentity, but complete and infallible integrity is at least not so obviously vacuous. To this extent tradition was correct in using 'perfection' as the unique bridge between individuality and necessary existence.

Yet there is a difficulty. Can there be a maximal good, than which none greater is conceivable? There is no concept of greatest number. How do we know that greatest value makes any better sense? Here is the essential question about the ontological argument, the hard core of the difficulty. If number, quantity, multiplicity, cannot be maximized, then either multiplicity contributes nothing to value, or value cannot be maximized either. There is good reason to think multiplicity does contribute to value. A complex beauty is superior to an ultra-simple one, a symphony to a chord. Happily there is, as we saw in the previous chapter, a way of defining the unique excellence or unsurpassability of deity without positing an absolute maximum of value. One has only to say that God is strictly unsurpassable in whatever respects, if any, value can be maximized, and, in all other respects, surpassable by himself only. In short, he is the being unsurpassable *by another*. The concept 'unsurpassable by another' is purely abstract, without empirical entailments. It shares this feature with Anselm's definition, but unlike that definition avoids commitment to the possibility of an absolute all-round maximum of value.

Please note also that an island unsurpassable by another island is devoid of any clear meaning, and an island unsurpassable by anything else whatever is even more obviously absurd. Island excellence is unmaximizable. The key to the ontological argument is not the mere term 'perfect', which is not even Anselm's word, but the idea of unsurpassability in its purely abstract and general form. Restrict the idea by some specificity, such as island, and the connection with necessity either vanishes, or turns into negative necessity, impossibility. From Gaunilo to Henle people have missed this point.[1]

Anselm did not view the connection of unsurpassability with necessity as due to its abstractness. Rather he argued: contingency is a source of weakness, a deficiency, since it puts a being at the mercy of circumstances which may or may not permit or cause it to exist, may or may not favour its continued existence. This seemed to him a sufficient reason to deny contingency of God's existence. It seems so to me. But the reasoning is still in terms of purely general or abstract conceptions. No empirical fact has to be mentioned. Anselm was also clear, as many seem not to be, that if a thing could not exist contingently, it also could not contingently fail to exist. Thus either the existence or the non-existence of God is a necessary truth. Theism and positivism, or *a priori* theism and *a priori* atheism, are the reasonable options. Empirical arguments pro or con are out of order.

There is another approach to our problem. God may be defined abstractly without using explicit value terms, for example, as the eternal and hence uncaused individual. How could anything eternal be caused, and how could anything uncaused be contingent? We understand contingent things through their causal conditions. But God, by most definitions, cannot be caused to exist. If then he exists contingently, this is the most irrational case of such existence conceivable. He is, he

[1] For Henle, see *The Philosophical Review*, 70 (1960), pp. 93–101.

might not have been, nothing explains or has in any way influenced or helped to bring about his existence. And if he fails to exist, nothing explains or has caused that. Thus an uncaused yet contingent entity is an exception to any usual rule of intelligibility. (By such a rule I do not mean determinism. All events or contingent things are influenced, conditioned by causes, whether or not they are fully determined by them.) Opponents of Anselm keep accusing him of rule breaking. But what about the rule that the contingent must have causal conditions?

There is, of course, no way to avoid making the uncaused a gigantic exception. But the intelligible way to construe this exception is to make it also an exception to the rule that all existence is contingent. The overarching rules remain: something is contingent if and only if it can be caused and is not eternal, or if and only if it is surpassable by another, or if and only if it cannot be defined purely abstractly. That which is abstractly definable is not subject to causes. We need no explanation of why there is a prime number between 5 and 8 beyond this, that there could not not be such a number. But with the assertion of a contingent thing we need an explanation in other terms. With God none such is possible. His existence, unless necessary, is sheer irrational fact. (John Hick says, 'sheer fact'.) Aristotle saw much of this long ago, and accordingly declared: 'with eternal things, to be possible and to be are the same'. Causality is the principle of contingent existence, not of existence in general. To assume it should be the latter, as Kant did in a famous passage, begs the question. The eloquence of the passage has blinded people, as Kant's eloquence often does, to its illogical character. It is irrelevant poetry.

Since 'the eternal God exists' expresses an uncausable situation, then so does 'something exists', which is an entailment of the previous statement. It is also directly evident that 'something exists' could not be caused. For what caused it must either be something existent or nothing existent. Here, too, we see that the necessity of God comes under a principle, rather than being an exception to all principles. The abstract and the uncaused are necessary, the concrete and the caused are contingent.

The necessarily existent abstraction 'something' divides *a priori* into two correlative abstractions, divine or unsurpassable something and non-divine or surpassable something, or creator and creature. Both sides are equally abstract. If, then, abstractness implies necessity, 'God' and 'not God' must both be necessary. However, the necessity applies only to these abstractions as somehow actualized. If we call God creator, then the necessity is that God exist with some creature or creatures, no matter what creatures in particular. In other words, the creator must be, and must be actually, not merely potentially, creative. He must be the God of some creatures or other, but he need not be our God or Abraham's God, since neither we nor Abraham exist by necessity. However, God as in a particular state of creating a particular set of creatures is no less contingent than the creatures.

The difference between the necessity of God and that of creatures is simply that God's necessity, though equally abstract, is individual, whereas the creaturely necessity is merely the impossibility that the most general kind of thing other than divinity should lack instances. The contingency of God is only the contingency of what is to be the concrete state of one and the same unique individual, whereas the contingency of creatures includes both states of individuals and their very individuality.

Why precisely does concreteness entail contingency? The concrete is particular or definite, and the abstract is by comparison indefinite. The definite cannot be necessary for a simple reason: there are mutually contradictory forms of definiteness. Red just here now excludes green just here now. Both are equally positive. If one side of the exclusive alternative were necessary, the excluded side would be impossible, and if possibility determined actuality in this way there would be no contingency at all. How, anyway, could a particular distribution of qualities be the only possible one? Two giants of intellect, Spinoza and Leibniz, tried to find an *a priori* reason for the particularity of the world. They failed, and the sufficient explanation of that failure is that there can be no such reason. The contingency of the concrete is not to be explained away, either teleologically or logically. It must be accepted. But if the incompatibilities between rival possibilities of particularity give the reason for contingency, the absence of such rivalry in the most abstract conceptions gives the reason for their necessity. Instead of red, green; but instead of something, only nothing. Rivalry with nothing is no rivalry, incompatibility with nothing is no incompatibility. On the most abstract level, all intelligible ground of contingency vanishes. Most perversely Kant tried to prove the opposite, that all intelligible ground of necessity vanishes. But the necessary is its own ground, since it is uncaused. And if *caused* has meaning, so has *uncaused*. The uncaused or unconditioned is no paradox; what would be paradox would be a contingent unconditioned.

The particular is contingent; is not God – you may ask – a definite or particular individual? Yes, in one respect. As the God of this actual world, he is indeed particular. But then in this aspect he is also, I hold, exclusive and hence contingent. As merely God of some world or other, no matter what, God is not particular, in the sense in which particularity involves incompatible alternatives. There is no positive alternative to the divine existence, or to God's creating some world or other. The purely verbal and negative alternatives of 'no God', or 'God not creating', have no such relation to the positive as red has to green, but only the pseudo-relation of nothing (or an absurdity) to something. And this is a relation only within language.

In his bare existence, then, God is not particular. After all, he is conceived as the individual with strictly universal functions, knowing all things, creatively influencing all things, present everywhere and always. For him to have this abstract universal role, it is entirely indifferent what particular things are there to be known or influenced. Thus the divine existence is not in rivalry with anything. It is wholly non-exclusive, non-competitive. There is no place that God must occupy which someone else must vacate in his favour. He has no role that others might assume. You or I cannot live without using food and water someone else might use. But God has unsurpassable power to coexist with others, adapt his action or knowledge to them, play his unique role no matter what others may do or not do. The ubiquitous, all-knowing, all-creating individual is absolutely non-competitive in his mere existence.

How, you may ask, can existence follow from the property 'divine' if existence is not itself a property? Answer: existence is not a property of ordinary, particular, competitive sorts of thing. Existential contingency, which is inseparable from particularity, is neutral as to existence. The other side of the very same principle implies that existential necessity is not neutral as to existence, but includes it. The wholly non-particular or abstract concepts include existence and, in the divine form, individual existence. Here alone is existence an individual yet *a priori* property. To assert against this that existence can in no case be a property is mere dogmatizing.

Thought, apart from empirical evidence, has five possible relations to existence. It may:

(*a*) exclude existence – thus absurdities, impossibilities;

(*b*) include existence without indication as to kind of indivi-dual – thus the idea of something, reality in general;

(*c*) include existence of the universal or unsurpassable individual – the idea of divinity, or of the creator, taken purely abstractly;

(*d*) include existence and the universal kind of individual other than divinity – thus the equally abstract idea of surpass-able individuals or creatures;

(*e*) neither include nor exclude existence – thus particular or competitive ideas of creatures or of divine states, e.g., dollars, islands, devils, and God's knowing of these as existent.

Kant, like many of his admirers, fails to see that the key to the meaning of (*e*) or the *a priori* neutral form of existential judg-ment is its place in the fivefold scheme. He does not mention competitiveness as the key to contingency. He proposes a purely phenomenal theory of modality, whereas the ontological argu-ment rests upon an ontological theory. Against this theory Kant has only his general arguments for phenomenalism, for example, the argument from the antinomies. This is too large an issue to be discussed here.

To assume, as so many now do, that modality is merely linguistic is to decide almost every metaphysical issue at once. Hobbes took this position against Descartes. I agree here with Descartes, still more with Aristotle, Peirce, and various others. 'Time is objective modality', as Peirce put it. Eternity is the mode of absolute or abstract necessity and possibility, the past is the mode of conditional or concrete necessity (being necessary, given the actual present), the future is the mixed mode of conditional necessity and possibility. So much for the distinction between necessity *de dictu* and necessity *de re*, logical and onto-logical necessity. The better our language, the more it reflects the real or temporal modalities into linguistic ones.

Our discussion has implied, but not explicated, a distinction between *existence* and *actuality*. Species or properties exist in individuals, individuals exist in concrete events or states. That a property exists means that there is at least one individual with the property; that an individual exists means that there has occurred at least one event constituting a state of the individual. The state is the actuality. To exist is to be somehow actualized, in some individual and state. By 'actuality' is meant the how, the state, of actualization. With all properties except those equivalent to deity, that a property exists only means that there is some individual of the kind in question in some state or other; just what individual being another question, requiring addi-tional information. With all individuals, even God, in what actual state the individual exists is contingent. *Actuality can in no case be necessary*. This is the truth misstated in the dogma, 'exist-ence is never a property'. Existence, being somehow actualized, can be a property; but never actuality, the precise how of actualization.

We may symbolize the problem of the ontological argument as follows:

W for Words (verbal definitions)
E for Essence (consistently thinkable property)
X for Existence
A for Actuality
I for Individual
U for Universal
P for Particular (not universal)

Transitions	1	2	3	4
I. Particular (concrete)	PW	+ PE	+ PX	+ PI	+ PA
II. Universal (abstract):				
a. Ordinary	OUW + OUE	= OUX	+ OPI	+ OPA
b. Divine	DUW + DUE	= DUX	= DUI	+ DPA

'Universal' means non-competitive, excluding nothing positive from existence.

'PX' means that the particular essence exists, i.e., is somehow individuated and actualized.

'PI' refers to particular, existing individuals with the essence.

'PA' refers to particular actual states in which individuals exist.

'UX' means that the universal essence exists in some individual or individuals.

'UI' means that the unique universal individual exists.

'+' means that the transition to the right requires additional evidence.

'=' means that additional evidence is not required because the two expressions say the same thing.

With the most abstract essences there is no alternative to existence.

Note that particular or concrete ideas (I) have the same logic whether they refer to ordinary or divine things, whether to my existence, say, or to God's knowing that I exist. Hence (I) is not divided into the ordinary and the divine forms. Only with purely abstract references to God or ordinary things (II) does the distinctive status of deity affect the logic, and even then the difference is only in transition (3). The three cases of '=' in II are all justified by the same principle that the transition involves no step towards particularity or concreteness (from U to P or P to P), but remains within the purely universal or abstract, or the wholly non-exclusive.

One may have a verbal definition but not an essence or thinkable property, because the words either lack clear meaning (whether universal or particular) or have inconsistent meanings. Transition (1) needs justifying, especially in II*b*. Anselm and Descartes took this transition for granted, or at most gave questionable grounds for it. Leibniz saw this flaw, but failed to find the remedy.

If one has consistent meaning and thus an essence, still, if the essence is particular or exclusive, additional evidence is required to proceed further. Transition (2) is *a priori* only when the essence is purely universal or non-exclusive, as in II. Here there is no real change in logical content, since the distinction between essence and existing essence depends upon the competitiveness of exclusive essences and disappears with non-competitive ones.

Since 'divine – non-divine' is an *a priori* correlation, UX in IIa and IIb really asserts but one thing, the only difference being which side of the correlation is explicit and which is merely implicit. Both sides of the 'creature-creator' contrast must have actualization; but the first side is an extremely indeterminate class of PI's, and the second is the universal individual, UI. Transition (3) in IIa is empirical and only in IIb is it *a priori*. This is the sole unique feature of the proof as applied to God, who alone is abstractly identifiable.

From the foregoing it follows that the proper cosmological argument is not from a contingent fact that there is some contingent world or other; for that this is so cannot be contingent (note IIa(2)). One argues rather from the *a priori* truth that there must be something, which something must be divine, or not divine, or both. The last, one may judge, is the rational view. There must be some particular contingent individuals, PI, and the universal necessary individual UI. Each requires the other, but PI is required only as a class, while UI is necessary in its unique individuality.

The final transition (4) to actual states of individuals is without exception empirical. Individuality is in all cases less determinate or exclusive than actuality, and this contrast, so far from disappearing in divinity, is there incomparably greater than anywhere else, being the whole extent of the gap between universality and particularity. Thus, actuality cannot be a predicate, deducible *a priori*. Existence is or is not such a predicate according to whether the definition of the kind of thing can or cannot dispense with exclusive specifications, empirical references.

The ultimate principle of the foregoing is that the logically stronger or more determinate cannot follow from the logically weaker or less determinate. Particularity is logical strength. From the universal only the universal can follow. But the supreme individual must have strictly universal functions and be identifiable by these alone. Only its actuality is particular and non-deducible. However, since to know that God exists there is no need to know in just what actual state or states he exists, transition (4) is additional to the admission of God's bare existence.

Since in IIb transitions (2, 3) are equivalences, and (4) is unnecessary for the theistic assertion, the basic issue is as to the legitimacy of (1), the admission of a thinkable property corresponding to the definition of God. Positivism is the real alternative, not atheism; or, to speak with Charlesworth, the alternative is *a priori* atheism, not empirical atheism (or empirical theism). Kant and many others blur the distinctions between transitions (1) and (2, 3, 4), or between *a priori* or positivistic objections and empirical ones. Against an *a priori* rejection (denial of transition (1)) other arguments than the ontological are needed. Against empiricism, however, the argument is cogent. Empirical evidence cannot adjudicate the central religious question. To show this, rather than to furnish a sufficient proof of theism, is the main function of the onto-logical argument.

That divine essence, divine existence, and divine individual-ity are the same is traditional, and is correct. But that divine actuality (or how, in what state, God exists) is a further, incomparably richer and contingent reality, is untraditional, and yet is also correct. God is more than any essence whatever, even his own – indeed, especially his own, since the divine essence is the most abstract individual essence of all. This is the true theological existentialism. Only, it is really actualism. That this sounds awkward is just one of those pieces of bad luck that have more effect than one might wish they did.

I submit that the foregoing scheme has a logic which can bear comparison with that of any rival doctrine. It adheres strictly to the equation contingent=competitive (definite, in the sense of excluding something positive). Every addition of exclusive definiteness means additional contingency, a further non-deductive step. In IIa and IIb, however, nothing is excluded until, in IIa, PI is reached, or in IIb, PA.

I await instruction from my professional colleagues. Nothing I have so far found shows the foregoing reasoning to be illogical. Not that it proves the existence of God, but that it exhibits a rational view of the theistic problem. The reason it does not, without qualification, prove the divine existence is that it assumes step (1) and gives grounds only for steps (2, 3). Since step (1) can always be challenged, the ontological argument by itself is not a coercive proof of the divine existence.

To justify the first step other arguments are required. But these other arguments can independently reach the conclusion that God exists. In so far the ontological argument, if cogent, is also in a sense 'superfluous' (Purtill).[2] But it is so at most only for the purpose of giving rational grounds for belief. For another purpose it is not superfluous but invaluable, the purpose of establishing the logical status of the theistic question. For if step (1) is invalid, then it is absurd to look for empirical evidence either for or against the divine existence, since that existence will be meaningless or impossible. If, however, the first step is admitted, then (2, 3) follow, and again empirical evidence is irrelevant. Monolithic empiricism is therefore powerless to adjudicate the central religious question. This is an immensely important truth. Our whole culture has been pervaded by confusion at just this point. The famous problem of evil is an example. The ontological argument shows that there can be no such problem. No observational facts could show the divine non-existence, and the only sense in which they could show the divine existence is that any conceivable facts would also show it. The theistic question is an *a priori* one.

Since the question is *a priori*, any valid theistic argument must be so. There can be no *a posteriori* arguments. Here Hume and Kant are right. But the ontological argument is not the only *a priori* one. Its uniqueness is not in being *a priori*, but in reasoning from the *a priori* idea of God. There are other *a priori* ideas from which one may argue to a theistic conclusion: truth, beauty, goodness, order (see Chapter XIV).

Four final considerations: (1) People are haunted by the notion that if something is necessary, something else must have made it necessary. However, we should rather say, if the non-existence of something was possible, something must have made it possible. Possibility requires a ground if anything does. By contrast, absolute impossibility is a mere privation and needs no cause. The necessity of God is the absence of an alternative possibility. Nothing makes or could make his non-existence possible; so there is no such possibility. God himself is conceived as the ground of all possibility, presupposed by any affirmation, any possibly legitimate negation, any state of affairs, any truth. Either that, or an absurdity.

(2) Those who say that modality is merely linguistic are implying that disposition properties are put into the world by language, that the distinction between past and future, the one

as settled, the other as subject to determination, and all contrary to fact conditionals, are words about words, or about word usages. But every man in practice supposes that there are truths not only about what happens but also about what may happen and might have happened. Yet the Anselmian controversy should teach us that one thing could not merely happen, the divine existence or failure to exist, and likewise the existence of some world or other, or its failure to exist. What can happen (if divinity is conceivable) is only God in such and such a state knowing such and such a world, or God in some other state, or knowing some other world.

(3) Kant's contention that if the individual is denied, its properties can without contradiction also be denied is readily answered. True enough, if 'God' fails to name an individual, there is no question of the properties of this individual. But the argument does not start with a name, assumed to be such, but with a concept which upon analysis turns out to be either nonsense or, though pure concept, yet also a name. If there is no such concept, or it is contradictory, then step (1) is to be rejected. I have admitted that there is a plausible case for this rejection. But if step (1) is admitted, it is too late to say that the word God fails to name an individual. For this denial is contradictory of the concept which has been admitted. Divinity, as a property, is not a subject for contingent realization in an individual. It is self-individuating, and here as everywhere individuality and existence are inseparable. Had I not existed there would not have been a non-existent Charles Hartshorne, but just no Charles Hartshorne. Had deity not existed – but this implies that 'divine' has no intelligible consistent meaning; for here alone property and individual are coincident. 'God' and its equivalents are the only purely conceptual names. If they are not that, they connote less even than a concept. Talk about divinity is, willy-nilly, talk about God, or else about nothing coherently conceivable.

(4) If – I say if – the self-individuating power of divinity cannot be expressed in terms of Russell's theory of definite descriptions, so much the worse for the claim that that theory covers all cases. The refusal to take seriously the possibility that God might be a logically unique case is only one form of the refusal to take theism seriously. For, by definition, God is

radically unique, exalted above all else, actual or possible, and this requirement is so abstract that, to say the least, it cannot be obvious that logical machinery designed to accommodate other things must also accommodate the idea of God. 'All else, actual or possible' is on a level comparable in generality with the terms that formal logicians use as principal tools. Logicians are required to make room for the idea of God, not conversely; unless atheism is to be made an *a priori* dogma. They have not made room for it, at least not explicitly and obviously. I do not see that this is a fatal objection to the idea. Logic has a future as well as a past and present.

XIII

IDEAS OF GOD: AN EXHAUSTIVE DIVISION

SINCE the existence or non-existence of God must be known, if at all, *a priori*, his essential nature or 'defining characteristic' must be knowable in the same way. This will include his relation to creatures as such, but not to any contingent species of creature except by deduction from the essential nature plus the empirical fact that the species in question exists. Thus that God loves man is not in his essential nature, but that he loves all creatures whatever may be. If so, then since man exists, God loves man. Taking the unique excellence, eminence, or transcendence of deity to mean that he surpasses all possible others (and, in some respects, himself), it follows that if a loving being is superior to a non-loving one – and this is to me intuitively evident – God must love eminently. I can only suppose this to mean that he loves or cherishes all creatures for their actual and potential qualities. To say that God loves creatures regardless of their actual or potential qualities makes no sense to me, no matter what some theologians have said. It would imply that a man is no more to God than a sparrow. This is very different from saying that God loves sinners. Sinners have both actual and potential qualities denied to a sparrow. Even men, if they are good naturalists, in a weak sense love all creatures for what they are and can be, and God must do so in a strong sense.

That God surpasses all is implied – as Anselm, following Plato, Philo, and Augustine, maintained – by his being the proper object of worship. If he could have a rival we should not know whether to worship him or some other. But the idea of an all-surpassing being arises logically, with or without religion, simply by thinking freely about the relation, superiority. The series of more and more superior beings either can or cannot have an upper limit. If the criterion of superiority is ethical, why should not a being be incapable of acting except with due regard to all interests concerned? It would then be ethically unsurpassable, by this criterion. But suppose the criterion is aesthetic or hedonic, a matter of beauty or happiness. We can verbally speak of 'absolute beauty' or absolute happiness; but as soon as we seek criteria for the maximal degree of beauty or happiness we find difficulty. To be free from ugliness or suffering is not enough. A musical chord is the one, a contented oyster may be the other. Aesthetic criteria must be positive, something like intensity, variety or scope of contrasts, completeness of integration or harmony (see Chapter XVI). But just as no number is the greatest possible, so no actual variety can be the greatest possible. And what can be meant by unsurpassable or absolute intensity? We thus have good reason to take aesthetic value to be without upper limit. It follows that in aesthetic enjoyment even God must be surpassable. However, it is another question whether he could in this respect be surpassed by another than himself. If the beauty of the entire cosmos is bound to be fully appreciated by deity, while anyone not divine can enjoy but a fragment or partial glimpse of this beauty, then, though the cosmos may grow in beauty and God's enjoyment with it, no one else can ever be his rival in this respect. Thus God may be the 'greatest possible' by those criteria which make this conceivable, and the greatest actual, yet without possible rival, by other criteria. Either way, as beyond rivalry, he is worthy of worship.

It may seem that God cannot surpass others in all respects. Thus he cannot be as sharp as a knife, as fast-flying as a bird, as noble in facing death as a man. However, since all actual intrinsic value is in satisfaction, harmonious experience, and since God can participate, by his omniscience, in all such experience whatever, he surpasses all others in actual intrinsic value. He also surpasses all others in extrinsic value, by sustaining laws of nature without which nothing could be useful to anyone. Note too that the 'participation' spoken of above is the essential element in what I at least mean by 'love'. Given adequate participation, adequate benevolence follows; without it, benevolence is bound to be inadequate and more or less inappropriate, as 'do-gooders' often demonstrate, in spite of themselves. I personally see no difference between knowledge or awareness in the ideal form and love in the ideal form. And apart from awareness and love we have no analogy for conceiving supreme worth. Here all religions agree rather well.

God cannot face his own death, whether nobly or ignobly; but he can face any and every real death threat with full participation in the sufferings of those whose death is in question. I agree heartily with Berdyaev and Whitehead in their repudiation of a mere spectator God who surveys creaturely sufferings and fears with 'mere happiness' (Whitehead), i.e, without participation. But this would be only an abstract and inadequate knowledge of the creatures. The denial of divine suffering is 'a profanation', as Whitehead implies. God knows fully and feels fully (for only feeling can know feeling) what our unhappy fears are like for us, and this without being afraid *for himself*. (If this is a paradox so is any idea of adequate knowledge.) Christianity, with its symbol of the cross, together with the doctrine of the incarnation, seems to point to the truth of divine suffering, in spite of official denials by theologians, and whatever the difficulties of the doctrine in question. Other religions tend to make God mere spectator, or else to deny the reality of suffering. In this, in my opinion, they are philosophically less profound.

The great tradition, all over the world, in conceiving the transcendent form of love or other excellence is to employ certain metaphysical contraries, such as absolute-relative, necessary-contingent, infinite-finite. I have elsewhere shown how the first contrast yields nine ways of conceiving deity, of which one way alone seems self-consistent and intelligible. I shall here do the same for the essentially equivalent second contrast. Let capital letters stand for the eminent or transcendent forms of a category and small letters for the ordinary or non-eminent forms. Let N or n stand for existing necessarily and C or c for existing contingently or (in the eminent case) having some contingent properties. Since the transcendent is a unitary being or individual while the non-transcendent is a class (all non-transcendent or non-divine beings), n, unlike N, allows the individuals to which it applies to exist contingently, and requires only that the class, non-divine beings, necessarily exists, i.e., has some members or other. Thus the difference between eminent and non-eminent necessity is definite, for it is the difference between individual and non-individual necessity. The difference between C and c is that C is not existential but only qualitative contingency, and that divine contingent qualities are best taken as cosmically inclusive, summing up the entirety of contingent values, while non-divine contingent qualities must be partially exclusive, representing but fragments of the total value of contingent reality. Assuming provisionally that transcendent reality and non-transcendent reality are both non-vacuous, nine possibilities are to be considered, in terms of their necessity-contingency, or modal, status. The method of elimination from an exhaustive division can then be employed, using the following principles of criticism.

(*a*) *The principle of contrast.* 'Existing necessarily', like any concept, gets its meaning through contrast, and hence there must also be something existing contingently; conversely, to say, 'exists contingently', is to imply that 'exists necessarily' also has a use.

(*b*) The principle of *contingent concreteness.* The concrete differs from the abstract by decision among positive but mutually exclusive possibilities. Thus the concrete is not merely coloured, say, but red and therefore not green, or a certain pattern of red and green and therefore not some other pattern. Hence the merely necessary must be extremely abstract. If either God or the world is entirely necessary, it is an empty abstraction.

(*c*) The principle of *divine freedom.* God is conceived as effecting a transition from indeterminate or abstract possibility to concrete actuality, i.e., as creating freely. This implies that there must be contingency both in him and in the world. His creative act could have been otherwise and so could the world it produces. Many theologians have taken it for granted that if God is free to create this or that he must be free to create nothing at all, i.e., not to create. But this is, to me at least, counter-intuitive. For a creative being not to create at all is for it not to exist as creator. At most it would be potentially creative. But the reality of creativity is the very basis of possibility or potentiality itself. Moreover, since any world is better than none at all (there is no value in nonentity), it would be wrong or foolish of God not to create. But God cannot do wrong or be foolish. I conclude that not only does divine freedom imply contingency both in God and in the world, but that if there is necessity in God there is also necessity in the world. (Otherwise, too, principles (*b*) and (*c*) would give the same results.) In scoring the nine cases under the principle of freedom I shall therefore first put plus or minus according as *C* does or does not occur, then according as *c* does or does not occur, and finally as *N* occurs, if at all, with or without *n*. (Thus *N* or *NC* should always be combined with *n*.) So three signs will be needed in scoring the six forms involving *N*.

One might argue that the absence of necessity in God is also incompatible with divine freedom, or at least with divine power. Only beings defective in power, as Spinoza and Scotus insisted, could fail to exist. But if this is allowed, then all but the last of the nine forms are ruled out by the freedom requirement alone. Then, too, the requirement that there be divine necessity is covered by the classical principle (below). So I shall not take the freedom requirement in so strong a sense. (The stronger our principles, the stronger the opposition to them. One hopes this is an overstatement!)

(*d*) The principle of *divine inclusiveness*. Anything whatever, divine or otherwise, is either a constituent of the total reality or is itself the all-inclusive reality. Since the inclusive reality cannot be less than what it includes, though it can be more, God is either inclusive or he has a rival or superior. I hold therefore, not only with Spinoza but with Whitehead, Berdyaev, Ramanuja and many others, that God must be all-inclusive. But since in modal logic the purely necessary cannot include the contingent (the conjunction of a necessary truth and a contingent one is contingent), there must be contingency in God if anything in the world is contingent. Hence *c* entails *C*. I score a view plus if it conforms to this requirement.

(*e*) The *Classical principle*. I here appeal to an approximate consensus in the history of theology, at least in the West: that there is a sense in which God contrasts to the world as the necessary to the contingent. Often this was thought to imply that God is exclusively necessary and the world exclusively contingent. But so interpreted it conflicts with several of the other principles, and it also then represents a less universal consensus. Hence I define the principle to mean only that necessity applies to God and contingency to the world, whether or not the contrary modality also applies in either or both cases.

Listing the nine possible combinations of N, C, n, c, and noting their agreement or disagreement with the five principles by plus or minus, and partial agreement or disagreement (considering the relevant factors, taking capital letters first) by two or more signs, we have the following:

(Omitted letters are to be considered negated.)

	contrast	contingent concreteness	divine freedom	inclus.	classical
1. N, c	+	– +	– + –	–	+ +
2. N, n	–	– –	– – +	+	+ –
3. N, cn	+	– +	– + +	–	+ +
4. C, c	–	+ +	+ +	+	– +
5. C, n	+	+ –	+ –	+	– –
6. C, cn	+	+ +	+ +	+	– +
7. CN, c	+	+ +	+ + –	+	+ +
8. CN, n	+	+ –	+ – +	+	+ –
9. CN, cn	+	+ +	+ + +	+	+ +

Thus nine reasonable requirements are fully met only by No. 9.

It is interesting that Spinoza's view, No. 2, has the smallest number (three) of plusses. No wonder theologians were so shocked by it. However, one can also explain why it appealed not only to Spinoza but to many others. It is a simple view; it enables God to be inclusive (and therefore to have knowledge of all things) without the modal absurdity of trying to make the necessary include (or know) contingent things. It also avoids the paradox of a creator able not to be such. In addition it agrees with one part of the consensus that God must be necessary and the world contingent, the part concerning God. Finally it conforms to the deterministic, rationalistic prejudice of early modern science and metaphysics, that there must be determining reasons or causes for things being 'as they are and not otherwise'. ('Sufficient Reason' in its strongest form.) Several centuries were required to overcome this prejudice, this ultra-simple view of causality, by recent philosophies of process, creativity, and freedom, which hold with Peirce that even in inorganic nature, causal regularities are relative and statistical, not absolute and strict for individual cases.

It is perhaps harder to understand the wide appeal of No. 1, the classical view in its extreme form. Still, it does meet more requirements than No. 2 or No. 5. Also the principle of contingent concreteness was not clearly formulated until recently. The principle of inclusiveness was easily mistaken for the necessitarian or Spinozistic form, besides conflicting with the simplest way of construing divine 'perfection' or worshipful superiority. And the requirements of divine freedom are easily overlooked. The two views most widely held until recently, Nos. 1 and 2, are the simplest views, apart from two others: C, n, which completely violates the classical principle (the profound intuition that, while we might not have existed, God exists by no lucky chance nor as conditioned by a cause that might have failed to produce him); and C, c, which violates the principle so far as God is concerned. Simple views tend to be preferred until difficulties force us to more complex ways of thinking. As Bunge has suggested, simplicity, while convenient, is if anything a mark of error rather than of truth.[1] Are relativity physics, quantum mechanics, current genetic theory, simpler than the views which preceded them? Whitehead's 'seek simplicity – and mistrust it' packs more wisdom than most metaphysicians and theologians have had.

If instead of Contingency we take Relativity or Dependence and instead of Necessity we take Absoluteness or complete Independence, using A, R, a, r for the four forms, we get the same results. Unqualified independence is by no conceivable test different from unconditioned necessity (in spite of Hick's attempt to deny this) and qualified or creaturely independence is the same as conditional necessity, and that is the same as contingency from an ultimate point of view. And just as the necessary cannot include the contingent, though the contingent can include the necessary, so the independent cannot have dependent constituents though the dependent can have an independent constituent. The positive can include the negative (absolute means non-relative, 'necessity' is the denial that there is a possible alternative); the negative cannot include the positive, as the lesser cannot include the greater. The model for this in modal logic is the *contingency of the conjunction* of a necessary with a contingent proposition; the model in non-modal logic is the *truth of the conjunction*, p and not q, as the only way to state

---

[1] Mario Bunge, *The Myth of Simplicity* (Englewood Cliffs, N.J.: Prentice-Hall, 1963).

the total situation expressed by all positive and all negative propositions. (To deny a conjunction is to fail to say which member is false. The inclusive act must be assertion, and a double negative is in this application only symbolically different from simple assertion.) The 'negative theology' could only be an account of something partial or abstract in God, and this applies to a purely necessitarian theology, or a purely absolutistic or non-relativistic or infinitistic theology.

Two views, Nos. 6, 7, the first omitting only the necessity of some world or other, the second omitting only the necessity of God, each score but a single minus. Should they not have been more popular than it seems they have been if they are so close to the truth as expressed in our principles? But by that reasoning No. 9 should have been the most popular of all. Rather, history shows that the full truth is too subtle for easy assimilation. However, as some interpret Thomism, it is really No. 7, provided that the contingent factors in God are not supposed to be dependent upon the world, but to result wholly from divine *fiat*. But then we have given up the equivalence of necessity with independence and of contingency with dependence, and this to my mind ruins one of the best of the Thomistic insights.

Our five principles are not the only tests we can apply to the nine forms. As for No. 6, it implies that though the supreme cause or creative power could fail to exist, the class of creatures could not be empty. One would think that any necessity in the world must be grounded in a necessity in God, and this is indeed one form of cosmological argument.

It is plausible that No. 6 also conflicts with divine freedom. For if God could fail to exist and if he makes choices as to his concrete state (contingent concreteness), perhaps he could choose not to exist? But this seems absurd. Or, does the contingency of his existence mean that he could be, or have been, prevented from existing? But this too seems dubious. Eminent freedom implies eminent capacity to adapt to any state of the world; hence none could exclude God. One may also argue that the principle of contrast is not adequately met by admitting a modal contrast in the world while denying it in God. Finally, one can propose an additional principle, *the non-invidiousness of the metaphysical contraries*. Deity is not identical with some abstraction, such as necessity or absoluteness, nor yet with contingency or relativity. The contrast between the transcendent or eminent and the non-transcendent is not to be collapsed into that between necessity and contingency, as in classical theism, No. 1, or between pure necessity and mixed necessity and contingency, as in No. 3, or between pure contingency and mixed modalities, as in No. 6, or mixed modalities and pure contingency or necessity, as in Nos. 7, 8. Eminence is in *how* a being is contingent and how it is independent or necessary. It is suspiciously easy to distinguish the transcendent merely by the categories applying to it or failing to apply to it, without any consideration of how, in what eminent way, they do so.

It is hardly obvious that eminence or worshipfulness is identical with necessity, contingency, or both together. If the principle of non-invidious categories is applied to the table, the superiority of No. 9 will be immediately apparent. It is the only principle, and No. 9 is the only one of the nine cases, that forces us to conceive two forms of each side of the metaphysical contraries. Eminence thus acquires a dignity superior to that of the categories, showing us how they are to be applied. True, one might claim that N, n and C, c avoid using the categories invidiously. However, they achieve this avoidance only in the sense of not really using the categories. For, since necessity and contingency are in essential contrast, N, n and C, c both imply that the omitted contrasting pole is unreal or mere appearance, and this is taking the contrast as in a quite radical sense invidious. Or if there is no contrast, then what is being said? Evidently the principle of contrast and that of non-invidiousness are closely connected and scarcely more than two ways of formulating one intuition. Neither the Western traditions nor the Hindu traditions seem more than ambiguously compatible with either principle. I can only view this as a defect in both. I believe that Buddhism (the 'Protestantism of Hinduism') is closer to the balanced view. It tends to affirm both the relative and the absolute as in principle (not in particular details) correlative, rather than related as real and unreal.

The non-invidiousness of categorial contrast does not mean that the contraries are in all respects equal. Such complete symmetry is not what we should expect (Chapters VI, X). One pole is abstract and exclusive, the other concrete and inclusive.

But the contrast between concrete and abstract is real at both ends (Chapter IV). The contrast between real and unreal is not 'quite' an ultimate metaphysical contrast (Whitehead). Eminent knowledge is not subject to mere appearances, and the lowest creatures can scarcely achieve indulgence in 'mere fancies'. They feel their environments very inadequately, but not wrongly. Doctrines of the unreality of the empirical world will be considered presently.

Since No. 2, or Spinoza, differs more in its scoring from No. 9, sometimes called 'panentheism', than from any of the seven remaining views, it is apparent how utterly crude 'pantheism' is when used to cover all doctrines which hold God to be inclusive. Yet defenders of classical theism, No. 1, have often defended their doctrine by assuming that the only alternative (apart from a hopelessly finite God) is something like Stoicism or Spinozism. The distinction between pantheism and panentheism is not only more than a literary flourish; it is a logical difference greater (six minuses compared to none) than that between classical theism and panentheism (four minuses compared to none).

Note too that if *c* provides room for divine freedom it does the same for creaturely freedom. Nothing in the schematism entails that the contingencies of the world are wholly determined by contingent divine decisions or creative fiats. All that is implied is that free divine decision making is the eminent form, and this by the principle of contrast, generously interpreted, implies that there is also non-eminent free decision making, indeed non-eminent creativity, and that the world is somehow a joint product of the two forms of creativity, and is not uniquely or unilaterally determined by either. Furthermore, this duality is not itself a divine choice but is a logical requirement of metaphysical necessities, or of the eternal essence of deity, which any divine option presupposes.

The key to the problem of evil is here. No single power, not even God, has decided the concrete details of the world. They were not intended by anyone. They were in no sense necessary. They are accidents. But that accidents, some accidents or other, happen is itself neither an accident nor anyone's choice. It inheres in existence as such, any possible existence. This is not opposed to the ideal power of God, but is an aspect of that power and of power as such, which is by its essential meaning power over those who also have power, or it is deciding which leaves to others the final concreteness of their own decisions. The idea of X making Y's concrete decision or fully determining Y's action or change is merely verbal, says nothing consistent. I say this over and over because (*a*) I am as sure it is true as of anything in metaphysics, and (*b*) many philosophers seem not even to have heard of the idea, let alone to have carefully considered its grounds and consequences. It is the most definite and important addition which modern philosophy has made to Job's problem. To be is to create. An agent who alone created would create only itself.

Since the contingent can include the necessary, CN does not imply two Gods, but one God contingent in concrete properties (he could have other concrete properties, but the class, divine concrete properties, could not be empty) yet necessary in abstract essence. The essence is, without possible failure, concretized somehow, the particular how being contingent. The necessary or universal is (Aristotle, Whitehead) real only in the contingent or concrete.

Though No. 9 is in an obvious sense a symmetrical view, it does not violate our axiom of the primacy of asymmetry. As we have seen, N and C are different in principle from n and c, and there is a one-way relation of inclusion between the first pair and the second. Moreover, since the contingent can include the necessary but not *vice versa*, the modal contrast itself, apart from the question of eminence, is asymmetrical. C includes N and also includes n and c. God in his contingent concreteness, that and nothing else, is all-inclusive. Is this what Tillich meant by 'being itself'? True, by being aware of God we include him, but as the awareness is deficient so is the inclusion. God includes us without loss, he has our full value; this is not how we include him. If this is paradox, then, so far as I can see, so is any form of theism.

If we allow transcendence to be vacuous (or to lack categorial status) and allow the world the same option, we have the following additional cases:

10. O, *c*	13. *N*, O	16. O, O
11. O, *n*	14. *C*, O	
12. O, *cn*	15. *CN*, O	

The principle of contrast counts against Nos. 10, 11, 13, 14. No. 16, generalized for related categories, such as independence and dependence, implies that neither deity nor anything else is rationally describable. The principle of contingent concreteness counts against Nos. 11 and 13. No. 12 seems the most acceptable form of atheism. But it involves several paradoxes (see Chapter XIV). Thus, though each individual in the world exists contingently, the class of non-divine individuals cannot be empty (the reasonable meaning of n). Theism alone can ground this necessity in the necessary existence not of a class but of a being, in some sense one individual. This takes us back to No. 9 or No. 3. Of the three acosmic forms of theism, only No. 15 fulfils the requirement of contrast. But it and the other two forms imply that the supreme creative power produces no creatures, the supreme cognitive being has nothing to know but its own knowing.

The collapse of all contrast into that between eminent reality, Brahman, and unreality, Maya, is especially popular in Asia. On good authority I have been told two things about the doctrine of Maya: it cannot be understood except by one who has been disciple to a Guru; it must be conceived by analogy with dreams. I have not had a Guru, and I believe the dream analogy (*the* analogy in Vedanta, it has been said) is badly misused not only by Vedantists but by Descartes, and even by Husserl, if not by most modern western philosophers, including Kant. First, a dream really occurs; as an event it is as real as any other event. Its having in fact occurred cannot be 'annulled' or cancelled out. Second, in the dream, as Bergson says, we experience processes actually going on in the physical world, at least inside our own skins, as when we dream kinesthetic sensations and are having them, at least from movements connected with breathing. We also dream the lack of kinesthetic sensations, as when we try to run from danger and our limbs do not move, when this is physically the case. When we dream colours, the retina, some experts believe, is active.

In certain forms of Asiatic mysticism, e.g., in Zen Buddhism, the reality of concrete particulars is affirmed.

Hindu writers often use the following argument: the real is at least the permanent; illusions are detected by the non-permanence of their supposed objects; but nothing is absolutely permanent except the eternal One. There are two assumptions here. One is that changing things rather than events are the final units of empirical reality; the other, that events are as transitory for the universe as they are for our memories, perceptions, and recording devices. In this book both assumptions are rejected. Events are the units – the final singulars; and these, though not eternal, are strictly permanent, for 'the moving finger writes, and having writ, not all your piety or wit can lure it back to cancel half a line'. In other words, becoming is cumulative.

In some forms of Buddhism, 'sunyatta', or nothingness, is said to be the universal principle. What seems to be meant is not only the lack of permanence but the lack of self-sufficiency, whether of things or events. Nothing is what it is in its own terms but always (partly) in terms of other things – causal conditions, e.g. Thus only the unimaginable whole is real. Plurality is not ultimate. I hold that *if* all relations are taken as symmetrically internal the argument has cogency. But they should not be so taken.

I do agree with Buddhism that there is a mysterious unity not obvious in ordinary experience. Relations to their predecessors are constitutive of events, and ordinary memory and perception do not distinctly disclose this complete summation of an event's origins. Only divine memory and perception could possess this distinctness. But it would not abolish external relations looking forward in time. It would make these as definite as the internal relations looking backward. Thus the distinction between events and their predecessors would not be cancelled out. If my memory of the vague states of mind in which I anticipated my career as a teacher of philosophy were perfect and also my memories of the later definite experiences as such a teacher, then the difference between the earlier anticipatory experiences and the later fulfilling – or frustrating – ones would be only the more apparent. Therefore, I cannot agree with those who argue that absolute memory would abolish temporal distinctions. Absolute memory and absolute anticipation of detailed experiences would indeed do this, but not the first by itself. Not at all.

The foregoing is the best I can do to meet East Indian or Buddhist acosmic doctrines.

All the forms from No. 10 to No. 15 seem to employ one side of the contrast eminent-non-eminent while rendering the other vacuous, conflicting with one application of the principle of contrast. We see that No. 9 is still on all counts the most intelligible view, at least if transcendence is conceivable at all.

I have spoken as though Buddhism and Hinduism were concerned with God, as though they were forms of worship. This is of course very questionable, and some would say false. In much of Buddhism, what is worshipped seems to be Buddha, or some other quasi-human figure; in Hinduism perhaps even the Guru, or a pantheon of deities. On the other hand there is at least some analogy between worship and the attitude towards the eminent reality, access to which is often held to be intuitive rather than conceptual, recognized in most non-theistic Asiatic doctrines. If it is not worship, it seems to take the place of worship as the supreme human response to life.

The foregoing reasoning not only selects one among the categorial possibilities for conceiving deity but also gives some reason for favouring theistic over non-theistic views. To that extent it anticipates the subject of the next chapter.

XIV

SIX THEISTIC PROOFS

ARISTOTLE discovered the principle of the golden mean. He saw that the moral good is one but the bad is two. Individuals deviate from the goal not in a single direction but in two opposite ones. The principle holds not only in ethics but in many other spheres. Concerning 'proofs for the existence of God' there are two extremes which seem equally mistaken: (1) the proofs, and even the search for proofs, are vain; (2) the proofs are completely satisfactory and coercive. The first extreme is now fashionable; the second was the fashion in the Middle Ages. I shall propose a view intermediate between the two.

To say that there can be a completely satisfactory and coercive proof for theism is to say that some formally correct inference could have universally convincing premises and a theistic conclusion. I concede at once that given any proof for theism either the premises will not be acceptable to all or there will, at least in the judgment of some competent logicians, be a formal fallacy. However, to say that the search for proofs is vain is to go far beyond this; for it is to say not only that any arguments will fall short of being universally convincing, but that they will convince no one not already convinced by other means. Arguments are useful only if they convince some who otherwise would not be convinced. But obviously between 'convincing to all' and 'convincing only to those already committed to the conclusion' there is ample room for intermediate possibilities. (I owe this point largely to George Mavrodes.)

Kant seems to me to have done much less than justice to the foregoing considerations. As for his contention that proofs (apart from the moral argument, which he did not term a proof) are quite unnecessary for belief, I feel entitled to reply,

'Speak for yourself'. I am clear in my own mind that he was not speaking for me.

That a formally valid proof of theism is possible seems obvious. Thus, to state a proof which I do not find persuasive as it stands: 'If there is change there is something absolutely unchanging, but there is change, therefore . . .; also, only deity could be unchanging, therefore deity exists.' Of course many will deny the connection asserted in the first premise between change and strict immutability, or the connection asserted in the second premise between such immutability and deity. But some will admit these connections, and while it is easy to assert that they will be only those who would believe without any such argument, it is less easy to justify the assertion. Also, as we shall see, there are better arguments.

Rejection of an argument is always possible, on pain of rejecting one or more of the premises. Thus a proof establishes a price for rejecting its conclusion, and in this way clarifies the meaning of the latter. It helps to measure the gap between belief and disbelief. The more formally correct proofs we have, the clearer we can be concerning the issue under discussion. The difference between believing and disbelieving is finally measured by the totality of possible proofs or disproofs.

Note that I say, 'possible proofs'. Hume and Kant, especially Kant, and many others, overlook the importance of this qualification. Kant claimed to have exhausted possible proofs. (This is one of many mistaken claims proffered by this rather dogmatic writer – dogmatic in the plain sense, not in his own somewhat self-serving one.) In fact, Kant gave rather poor versions of each of four theistic arguments, neglecting at least two others, though one of the two is close to the surface in the first *Critique*.

In Kant's four I include his moral argument. The two he omits, or at most hints at, can also be viewed as normative, or arguments from value, the values of truth and beauty. I think this is nothing against them, and indeed I take the 'primacy of practical reason' even more seriously than Kant himself. All the arguments are phases of one 'global' argument, that *the properly formulated theistically religious view of life and reality is the most intelligible, self-consistent, and satisfactory one that can be conceived.* (This was essentially what Peirce meant by his 'neglected' argument from 'musement'.)

'Properly formulated' implies, among other things, a serious divergence from Kant and many other notable writers. Kant claimed to have defined the one and only philosophically legitimate 'ideal of reason' or idea of God, and even calls it an 'ideal without a flaw'. I hold that he here fell into a trap set for him by the one-sidedness of the Greek philosophical heritage. The *ens realissimum* is not simply indemonstrable – even (as Kant admitted) as barely possible – but it is indeed demonstrably impossible. It is also not what 'God' as a religious term ought to mean.

God is not the immutably perfect being, the idea of which Christianity derived from Greek thought. Rather, as Fechner said a century ago, God's perfection is his ideal form of perfectibility. He is not absolutely unsurpassable and hence immutable; rather he is in certain aspects surpassable, but by himself only. Unsurpassability *by another* (from which it can be deduced that all are surpassed by God, who surpasses himself as well) is the religious idea of perfection. There can be no rival to deity. Immutability in some respects, but not in all, follows from this.

Kant's favourite notion (which deeply corrupted his epistemology) that the divine intuition must be wholly active, and produce rather than accept its content, is not entailed by the definition of deity just given. Rather, divine intuition or perception must be universally and adequately receptive of its objects, whereas ours is only locally and deficiently so. True, deity is eminent creativity. But, as in Lequier, Bergson, Sartre, and Whitehead, creation is first of all self-creation, and this is the process of emergent synthesis whereby each actuality takes into its own unity the self-creative experiences of antecedent actualities. God changes us by changing himself in response to our previous responses to him, and to this divine response to our response we subsequently respond. Creation is modelled in dialogue, wherein each recreates himself, and thereby helps others to recreate themselves. All of this is a far cry from Kant. It is closer to Buber and close to Berdyaev. It is not what Kant criticized as rational theology. But it is, I believe, what religion at its best requires. This idea of God implies an ideal form of passivity as essentially as it implies an ideal form of activity. Our passivity, like our activity, is nothing like ideal or unsurpassable.

According to Kant two of the proofs, the arguments from

design (or from the order of the world) and from the world's contingent existence, have empirical premises. The ontological proof starts, on the contrary, from the mere conceivability of a certain definition. My own view is that no theistic proof should be taken as empirical in the sharp sense defined by Popper, that its premises could conceivably conflict with observation.[1] Thus, e.g., to say, something contingent exists, therefore God exists as its non-contingent cause is not an empirical argument. For what conceivable experience could contradict the premise? To consult experience to see if in it something is observed is silly. In any experience something must be observed. And in any experience, I am prepared to argue, the something must have contingent aspects. The cosmological argument is thus *a priori*. And I have known a Catholic priest, no mean philosopher, who independently came to this conclusion. The design argument is empirical only if put in the weak form which Hume and Kant sufficiently discredited. To hold that we find the experienced world, as compared to some conceivably experienced world, so well ordered that it must be divinely created is to suppose that there are two classes of possible worlds, those God could create and those he could not create. But this is theistic nonsense. God is the ground of the possible and of the actual. What he could not create must, from the theistic point of view, be taken as not coherently conceivable. Any world order must require the divine orderer.

And as for a mere chaos, that could not be experienced and is mere verbiage. In so far as Kant's point was that no empirical argument for God can be valid, I agree with him. I agree also that no empirical argument for the divine non-existence is possible.

That the ontological argument is not empirical Kant saw. But he failed to distinguish clearly and systematically between two radically distinct objections to the argument: that it is formally invalid, and that its premise, 'God is at least consistently conceivable', is false. One may urge either or both of these objections, but only confusion is caused by failing to make clear at any given point which position is being taken. Kant's

---

[1] John Hick holds, if I understand him, that theism is empirically confirmable but not disconfirmable. This is hardly what I mean by 'empirical'. See his *Faith and Knowledge: A Modern Introduction to the Problem of Religious Knowledge* (Ithaca, N.Y.: Cornell University Press, 1957). See also *Evil and the God of Love*.

discussion is muddled in this respect. Furthermore, Malcolm, Findlay, and I, among others (also Koyré and Barth), have shown that the essential issue is independent of the question: Is existence in general a predicate? That existence is a predicate in the unique divine case is a conclusion, not a premise, of the inference. And to declare that the general rule, existence is not predicative, can have no exception is to beg the question. Anselm gave definite reasons why deity must be an exception to the rule. God is not just another being. The chief of these reasons are not even mentioned by Kant.

Is Kant's moral argument empirical? I should deny this. For no experience could show the negative, could show that there was no moral law or lawgiver. A merely sub-rational experience could not put the question, and a rational experience could, if Kant is right, only answer it affirmatively.

If all the arguments are *a priori*, are they not all coercive? Not at all. One may not be able to see the premises as indubitable. Human rationality is rather weak and dim. Even the mathematicians differ sharply concerning infinite sets. Yet how could empirical observation settle *that* issue? Only trivial *a priori* truths are obvious to all, as in finite arithmetic.

An argument, considered as a premise and a formally implied conclusion, can be rejected by those who disbelieve the premise. 'Not p or q' is then the choice before one. But since there is always more than one elementary proposition in the total premise, it is more illuminating to consider a proof not as a dilemma but as at least a trilemma. One chooses between two (or more) non-theistic views and the theistic one. For my purposes what Kant thought of as theism is non-theistic, and I shall sometimes so treat it in what follows. What he was taking as the conclusion of theistic proofs is for me and a good many others but a form of idolatry.

There is no reason to suppose that there is only one right way to formulate a given proof as a trilemma, or perhaps tetra-lemma; rather, there seem to be various possibilities in each case. Mathematicians will not be surprised at this statement, I imagine. Even in mathematics, an element of arbitrary choice is irreducible. Spinozists like Blanshard may be left to struggle with this indication (among many) that sheer 'necessity' is a long way from being *the* key to truth or rationality. Rather, it is necessary that there should be all sorts of contingencies, contingency as such being among the *a priori* ideas which could not fail to have instances, even though each such instance might very well not have been. That accidents happen is itself no accident. That there are arbitrary choices is not itself arbitrarily chosen.

A formally valid proof is a set of options: (*a*) reject premise p, (*b*) reject premise q, (*c*) reject premise r, (*d*) reject two or all of the premises, (*e*) accept the premises and the conclusion. I shall state the proofs in the form of possible rejections enabling one to avoid the conclusion. Thus I shall list (instead of p, q, r) not-p, not-q, not-r, labelling them A1, A2, A3. (A for antitheism.) Anyone able to accept one or more of these will then, at that price, be entitled to reject the theistic conclusion, which I shall label T (for thesis or theism).

The form of the arguments is, then, that the rejection of T involves one in a trilemma or tetralemma, a forced choice among allegedly unattractive possibilities. That they are unattractive is outside the formal scheme, a matter of intuitive judgment, except that of course other arguments, in similar or different form, could be used against them. If the proofs are stated in standard form as inferences, the premises are the falsity of A1, A2, A3. . . .

One argument may support another. Thus the cosmological or design argument may be used to combat the suspicion that deity is not even conceivable, this conceivability (the falsity of A1) being a premise of the first or ontological proof, by showing that apart from deity we cannot construe the modal structure of reality. All the proofs except the ontological may be interpreted as showing that the idea of God, taken as true, is required for the interpretation of some fundamental aspect of life or existence. Kant underestimates the complexity of the proofs and hence oversimplifies their interrelations. The aspect of the ontological which the cosmological needs for its own cogency is the strongest aspect of the former, and *vice versa*. The arguments thus help one another at their weakest points. I find this not surprising or especially paradoxical.

Kant is right that the arguments must form some sort of system, and he is right that his own system of ideas makes a proof of God impossible. But then his system rests upon arguments which are, to some of us, a good deal less impressive than the kind of system which more carefully formulated theistic proofs do fit. And even Kant's system suggests a proof (argument IV below) which he never considered, though the system must be revised drastically to make the proof really work.

I first consider three proofs corresponding loosely to the three in Kant's *Critique*. They are arguments from modality and order ('design').

REVISION OF THREE CLASSICAL ARGUMENTS

Ontological

I   A1   Deity cannot be consistently conceived.

   A2   Deity can be consistently conceived, equally whether as existent or as non-existent.

   A3   Deity can be consistently conceived, but only as non-existent, as an unactualizable or regulative ideal or limiting concept.

   T   Deity can be consistently conceived, but only as existent.

Cosmological

II   A1   Nothing exists.

   A2   What exists either (*a*) has no modal character or (*b*) is wholly contingent.

   A3   What exists is wholly necessary.

   A4   What exists is partly contingent and partly necessary, but nothing is divine.

   T   What exists is partly contingent and partly necessary and something is divine.

Design

III   A1   There is no cosmic order.

   A2   There is cosmic order but no cosmic ordering power.

   A3   There is cosmic order and ordering power, but the power is not divine.

   T   There is cosmic order and divine power.

In all three cases, I, II, III, I find A1, A2 . . . not only unacceptable as true but absurd, not genuinely conceivable. Hence I conclude that T is necessarily true. It is intrinsically the least paradoxical position, so far as my intelligence grasps the options. If I am mistaken – and I am not infallible – the error is logical, not empirical; I have failed to understand my own ideas. 'Necessarily true' thus does not mean, 'Certainly true'. The necessity spoken of is ontological. It rules out empirical evidence as irrelevant, but non-empirical mistakes are always possible in human thinking. One has only to think of finite arithmetic, which is a much easier case.

Contra IA1. This option is, I grant, not *obviously* wrong. And I also grant that if there were not other theistic proofs I should remain in great doubt at just this point. It still stands that the absurdity or non-absurdity of the idea of deity is a non-empirical matter. If absurd, it could not have made sense; if it makes sense then, since – as I have explained at length in several books – A2 and A3 are (in my judgment) absurd, T is necessarily not just empirically true. And it can be deduced directly from the idea of deity that no observable state of affairs could show God not to exist, since God is defined as having unsurpassable power to exist, no matter what else does or does not exist, also as having unlimited capacity to know truth, so that to suppose it possibly true that he did not exist would be to posit a possibility whose actualization God could not know. But then God, so conceived, is surpassed by another, the God whose power of knowing has no such limitation. If this is not conceivable, then, as can be shown, we are back at A1.

IA2 is open to a long list of objections. It makes God a possible existent either with causal conditions of his existence or without them. But, by the causal principle, 'possible' in this contingent sense implies causally 'conditioned', and a conditioned existence contradicts the idea of deity. There are many other bridges from 'divine' to 'not capable of contingent existence'.

In principle and in many details I agree with James F. Ross's brilliant discussion of what he and I independently call the 'modal proof' – much as I disagree with the theological determinism embodied in his Thomistic definition of 'omnipotence'.[2] I agree also with his rejection of the Principle of

---

[2] See Ross's *Philosophical Theology* (Indianapolis and New York: Bobbs-Merrill, 1969), chs. 1–4, 7. For a formalization of one of my forms of ontological proof see Purtill's article in the *Review of Metaphysics*, 21 (1967), pp. 297–309.

Sufficient Reason as necessarily false, but I think that 'Principle E' which he substitutes for it is in one aspect too weak, in another too strong. Contingent things must *always* have real (not merely, as Ross says, conceivable) causal conditions, the absence of which would have *prevented* the thing from existing; but no set of conditions uniquely determines any concrete outcome, which is *always* in some degree self-determined or creative. Nothing concrete is *made* to exist (even by God) just as it does, but anything concrete could have been prevented from existing. And, as Ross quotes Scotus as writing, nothing could prevent the existence of God (which, as I have often argued, is not in itself concrete) any more than anything could cause that existence. To take God's existence as contingent contradicts even the most circumspect version of the causal principle.

IA3. The idea of God is not something we are trying to actualize yet can never fully attain to. Any non-divine knowledge is separated by an infinity from omniscience. We cannot approach closer and closer to being immortal, or ungenerated. Deity is not analogous to 'perfect lover', or 'perfectly righteous judge' in the human sense.

Contra IIA1. Both atheists and theists have argued that 'there might have been nothing' is either mere verbiage or a contradiction. The term nothing has a use only in a relative sense, nothing of some specified sort or for a given purpose. Apart from this relativity the word is meaningless. (See J. Edwards, Bergson, M. Munitz.)[3]

IIA2. If A1 is *impossible*, then something is necessary, at least the falsity of A1. Also the necessity that at least something should exist is not intelligible apart from the idea of a being which exists necessarily. Finally the principle of contrast is poorly satisfied by A2 (*b*). Basic abstractions must apply both positively and negatively.

IIA3. The paradoxes of Spinozism are well known. All true propositions become equivalent, mutually implicative, the principle of contrast is flagrantly violated, becoming is explained away.

IIA4. The necessary aspect of existence is, as Kant admitted,

[3] Milton Munitz, *The Mystery of Existence* (New York: Appleton-Century-Crofts, 1965), pp. 142–59.

positively intelligible, if at all, only as the existence of deity.

Discussion. According to Kant, this proof starts with an empirical fact, the falsity of A1. But this falsity is *a priori*. We do not have to commit the fallacy of arguing from a contingent premise to an unconditionally necessary conclusion (the divine existence must be unconditionally necessary, not necessary on some contingent condition).

Also according to Kant, we do not know that A3 is false, since everything might be necessary. He assumes here that the principle of contrast is without validity, and that the necessitarian view of becoming makes sense.

Note that nothing is said in the proof about explaining why specific features of the world 'are as they are and not otherwise'. It is contradictory to admit contingency and then explain it away as a hidden form of necessity, whether this be called logical, metaphysical, or teleological necessity. Contingency means chance, the absence of any ultimate reason, whether in cause or purpose. The world consists of a mixture of chance and necessity. Again we find use for the principle of contrast. God as necessary is required not so that chance may be shown to be illusory, but so that there may also be a contrasting factor. God is the creative ground capable of producing various sorts of contingent worlds, bound to produce something contingent, but not the particular contingent world that exists. There is no 'why' for particulars, which are free creations. Concrete realities are non-deducible. For a theist to suppose otherwise is for him to fall into the Spinozistic trap and forget the meaning of divine and creaturely freedom.

Contra IIIA1. A merely chaotic world must be unknowable; for no knowledge could exist in it. One could not distinguish IIIA1 from IIA1. Neither could be true.

IIIA2. Being is in principle free creativity, limited only by antecedent acts of freedom. Any order is infinitely threatened if the free agents include no supremely influential one. A committee with no directive and no chairman is a weak instance of the potential chaos this implies.

IIIA3. We have some insight in experience into the power of agents over other agents. A man as conscious being sways his bodily constituents (cells, etc.). He is incomparably the most powerful agent in his psychophysical system. He is also, we all in effect assume, incomparably the most important and valuable. His experience sums up what is going on in the system vastly more than any events involved in the other agents, taken individually. By analogy we conceive the cosmic ordering power as the supreme or eminent form of awareness.

Discussion. Kant and Hume assume that the specific character of the cosmic order, as known empirically, must be a premise of the proof. Not at all. Any cosmic order is intelligible theistically, otherwise a mere mystery. To argue from empirical facts is to imply that had the world been less well ordered, God could not have been its orderer. A world not basically ordered (how if not by an orderer?) is without clear meaning. This has nothing to do with the requirement that the order prevent any evils from occurring, or suit some blueprint of a best possible world. Such notions all imply the attempt to turn contingency into necessity, or the bizarre idea that eminent freedom could have as creatures not agents with lesser degrees and forms of freedom but agents with zero freedom. Free decisions whose precise interactions can only be matters of chance cannot possibly be subjected to an absolute order, exclusive of danger. Risks are the price of existence. What God is needed for is to make opportunity possible, and indeed even to make risk possible. For in chaos there is nothing definite, even definite risk.

The second triplet of proofs might be called normative, since they turn upon truth, goodness, and beauty. Arguments from ideals or values may be met by the contention that the desirability of something does not guarantee its reality. Perhaps, it may be urged, there is no truth or reality except such as can be adequately realized in human knowledge, no supreme aim for the future beyond death, no unity of value other than that which we actualize in our social experiences. Wishful thinking is not knowledge. I reply that although the goodness of contingent possibilities does not imply the actualization of these possibilities, with eternal necessities the question is quite different. There is virtue in facing ugly contingencies, and there are bound to be such. But ugly eternal necessities are nonsensical. They could not be faced at all, for neither pragmatic nor contemplative benefits could result. And if in the long run nothing is important, it cannot be important for us to face the 'fact' that nothing is important. The argument against wishful thinking applies only to contingent goods and evils. William James never made this distinction, and this is why his Will to Believe is so unsatisfying. Absolute necessities, whether indispensable ideas or ideals, cannot be desirable or undesirable; for desire pertains to possibilities. They can, however, have beauty, give satisfaction to those contemplating them. Indeed they must do so. The neutral or repellent is contemplated only because it is not merely neutral, or merely repellent, or because if repellent it also is or might have been avoided by someone. But the flaws in reality implied by the absence of deity would be in principle unavoidable altogether. No one could have prevented them. No limit can be set to the absurdity of life (Sartre, Camus) on the atheistic assumption. And this absurdity can in no reasonable sense be viewed as accidental.

Kant held that a value argument for God justified belief but did not constitute knowledge. Yet he asserted the primacy of the practical reason. I accept the latter point but fail to see its consistency with the former. And in any case I think he was mistaken in supposing the value arguments to be more cogent, as such, than the theoretical arguments. It has turned out more and more that those who reject the latter as readily reject the former also. Kant's moral argument, to be sure, is weak, but it can be made stronger. And the same is to be said for the theoretical arguments as he formulated them.

THREE NORMATIVE ARGUMENTS

Epistemic or Idealistic

IV A1 Reality (or truth) is in no way dependent upon knowledge.

A2 Reality is actual or potential content of non-divine knowledge

A3 Reality is potential content of divine knowledge (what God would know if he existed).

T Reality is actual content of divine knowledge.

Moral

V A1 There is no supreme aim or *summum bonum* whose realization a creature's action can promote.

A2　There is a supreme aim, which is to promote the good life among some (or all) creatures during their natural life spans.

A3　There is a supreme aim, which is to promote the good life among creatures after death or in heaven.

T　There is a supreme aim, which is to enrich the divine life (by promoting the good life among creatures).

Aesthetic

VI　A1　There is no beauty of the world as a (*de facto*) whole.

A2　There is a beauty of the world as a whole, but no one enjoys it.

A3　There is a beauty of the world as a whole, but only non-divine beings enjoy it.

T　There is a beauty of the world as a whole and God alone adequately enjoys it.

Contra IVA1. As Royce, among others, well argued, we can explain 'reality' or 'truth' only in terms of some form of experience or knowledge. Given truth we can define reality, or given reality we can define truth (Tarski's definition assumes the difference between real and imaginary 'grass'), but to define either apart from some notion of evidence is impossible.

IVA2. The paradoxes of making our type of knowledge the measure of reality are well known. Above all, consider how the concept of the real past tends to become blurred. What we could not know about the past did not happen. Or does one persuade oneself that there is nothing past we could not know? Every moment each of us has experiences that in their concrete specificity will never be known to anyone else, and eventually we shall not know them either, even in the limited sense in which we ever did know them from memory. Or again consider the array of events in galactic space. No animal explorer will ever have more than a vanishingly small fraction of this array in his consciousness.

Also all our knowledge, even of the most obvious events, is approximate at best.

IVA3. If God does not exist, one thing is true which he could not and would not know if he did exist, namely his own non-existence. Hence it is impossible that all reality or truth is even potential content of divine knowledge, if the non-existence of God is among the realities or truths.

Discussion. This proof is a version of Kant's implicit proof from the contrast between appearance and reality. The former differs from the latter, according to Kant, as the content of our sensory intuition differs from the content of a non-sensory intuition. Since the idea of such an intuition is an insoluble problem for us, we cannot make the distinction between appearance and reality save in a problematic way, to prevent us from claiming to know that appearances-to-us are the whole story. But, after all, even the truth about appearances escapes us radically.

Royce contributed a brilliant insight to this proof. He saw that to define omniscience we need not assume an independent notion of 'all reality' or 'all truth'. Instead of saying that eminent knowledge is that which knows everything, we can say, 'everything' is simply the entire content of eminent knowledge, defining the latter without reference to 'reality'. Our knowledge is non-eminent because of internal characteristics: confusion, inconsistency, doubt, inconstancy of beliefs, and, above all, a lack of concepts adequate to interpret our percepts and of percepts adequate to distinguish between false and true concepts. Defects of cognitive experience are in principle internal defects. Otherwise we should never have talked about a partly inaccessible 'reality' or 'truth'. Suppose, then, an experience perfect in the specified respects. It would have nothing to do with any reality except that which it adequately perceived. Phenomenalism, thought limited to appearances, is perfectly in order for an ideal perceiver and thinker. 'The world is what I perceive' is a truism if I am God; otherwise it is a paradox. Royce made many mistakes, but his contentions that the criticism of knowledge is internal and therefore knowledge as such defines reality, yet not just any knowledge, finally; that eminent knowledge alone can distinguish between reality partially glimpsed and reality *simpliciter* or without qualification – these were great ideas, not yet sufficiently appreciated.

The above argumentation is entirely *a priori*. Experience is used, but as in arithmetic, not as in physics, to furnish ideas, models of meaning. Any non-divine consciousness, in any world, would face the Roycean problem and have good reason to solve it somewhat as he did. No peculiarity of human beings, no special law of nature, is assumed.

Contra VA1. If there is no supreme aim, there is no reasonable idea of comparative value or importance. Even Dewey comes close to stating a supreme aim, which he calls variously 'growth', 'release of human capacities', 'freedom'.

VA2. This is intended broadly so as to include both egoistic and altruistic versions, both tribalistic and universalistic. There are two difficulties: death and the multiplicity of beneficiaries. Since both individuals and species are mortal, or cannot be known to last for ever, the long-run prospect is of the total fading out of any good achieved. The aspect of multiplicity is less obvious, but equally serious. If one seeks only one's own good, and takes others as mere means to this, one is unethical and indeed more or less inhuman. If one does include others, then one loses the one advantage of the self-interested person, namely the unity of the beneficiary of his efforts. Good is good *for* someone. How is the welfare of A plus the welfare of B a greater good than that of either alone? The sum of happinesses, for whom is this a happiness? Yet we feel that it is more important that two should be happy than one. Furthermore, my happiness yesterday is one thing, my happiness today, another. Yet we feel that it is more important that a life should be steadily happy than that there should be a moment or two of happiness during its course. What 'does it all add up to' is thus a problem, even apart from death and within a single individual's life.

VA3. There is the obvious objection that we not only do not know our individual immortality, but there are *a priori* arguments against it. Immortality is a divine trait, why should it be ours? We are limited spatially, why not temporally? Also only a minority of human beings have been able to believe in their own immortality while clearly disbelieving in deity. But, on the other hand, since immortality puts us in rivalry with deity in one respect, it is a dubious matter to make God the means to our ultimate fulfilment, as Kant did, rather than taking our fulfilment as means to God's, who can appreciate the value, the beauty, of our lives as even we cannot possibly do.

Contra VIA1. If this were true, the world would be either a chaos or a mere monotony. Neither is possible, the first for the same reason as holds against IIIA1, the second for the reason that order implies a contrasting element of disorder, and also because reality is essentially active and free and all radical monotony is secondary and artificial. (On earth man creates what we find of it.)

A2. Even in thinking 'the world as a whole', we enjoy a glimpse of its beauty, or we should not have this thought. There is no experience and no thought absolutely without aesthetic fulfilment.

A3. Our enjoyment (or that of any localized or non-divine being?) is utterly disproportionate to the beauty in question. This disproportion would be an absolutely basic flaw in reality, such as never could be eliminated. It must always have obtained, and it could not be merely contingent, but must rather be an eternally necessary yet ugly aspect of things. Always God ought to have existed to enjoy his creation, and always he failed to exist. To think such an eternal deficiency is to form a thought without intrinsic reward. Nor has it any pragmatic value, either. It is just a drooping of spirits, not a genuine concept. Its real meaning is as an experiment to bring us to the realization that the beauty of the world could not fail to have its spectator.

It will, I trust, now be clear in what sense I claim to have rational arguments for theism. The arguments consist in making explicit what the denial of theism implies, so that people will know the price tag on the denial. I have believed for most of a long lifetime in the theistic view because I have been unable to believe in any logically possible alternative. And I have made great effort to discover what these alternatives are. A formal proof could not, in the nature of the case, do more than exhibit the alternatives for individual acceptance or rejection. To say that this is not worth doing, and doing carefully, seems at best a form of 'blocking the path of inquiry', and this is objectionable even if a Kant indulges in it.

A philosopher seeking arguments for a position is under obligation as a rational being to experiment also with arguments against it. Schopenhauer scolded Kant for neglecting to do this. And in fact the doughty Koenigsberger contented himself with assuring his reader that disproving theism is as impossible as proving it.

The pro arguments, as I have formulated them, are convertible into contra arguments if one can show the greater credibility of A1, A2 ... as compared to T. Kant almost reveals, but does not state, the superior credibility of IA1 to T *if* deity is defined in the classical way Kant adopts. For, as he says, positive or good qualities can conflict; hence deity as lacking no possible excellence is impossible, an absurdity like greatest number. Kant's scepticism at this point can, I hold, be turned by good arguments into definite disbelief. But the same arguments will not work against 'neo-classical theism'.

Another negative argument is Findlay's, also an argument from impossibility. On the one hand, he reasons, God must, as Anselm held, exist without possibility of non-existence, i.e., necessarily, since contingency is a defect implying other defects and making a being unworthy of worship. On the other hand, he thinks existence cannot be necessary. Thus IA1 and IIA2 are correct and IT, IIT absurd. Here again, as I have explained elsewhere, neo-classical, but not classical, theory can fairly meet the challenge. Concrete *actuality*, even in the divine case, is always contingent, but *existence* is more abstract than actuality, and divine existence is, in the relevant sense, completely abstract and hence can be the common element of all possible actualities, adding nothing to the content of our most abstract concepts but merely making the content explicit. Since writing his famous essay Findlay has partly reconsidered his position to take this point into account.[4]

A challenge more difficult to meet comes from relativity physics. A self-surpassing deity must have something like a settled past and an open future, some sort of divine time or super-time, as Berdyaev hints and Whitehead more than hints; but it is not at all easy to relate this requirement to the structure of ordinary time as discussed in physics. This difficulty I take seriously, but there are at least two ways of meeting it, neither of which I can see clearly to be impossible.

It might appear that a conflict between theism (as truth about the necessarily existent) and an empirical scientific

---

[4] J. N. Findlay, 'Can the existence of God be disproved?', *Mind* 57 (1948). Reprinted in Findlay's *Language, Mind, and Value* (London: Allen and Unwin, 1963). See the preface of that book. For some more recent thoughts by Findlay on this topic see his 'Reflections on necessity' in: Wm. L. Reese and Eugene Freeman (eds.) *Process and Divinity* (La Salle, Ill.: Open Court, 1964).

theory could not occur. But the necessary must be compatible with any *possible* contingency; hence if relativity physics is even conceivably true, a contradiction between it and theism would be fatal to the latter. That the scientific theory may be false is irrelevant. All that matters is whether it makes sense or not.

Another antitheistic argument is N. Hartmann's that omnipotence would make man's moral freedom impossible; from which it follows that argument V should be taken as a disproof! If our purpose is to conform to an all-powerful purpose, we cannot be morally free agents. It does not seem to occur to Hartmann that 'omnipotent' is a problematic concept even within theism. I learned from my Episcopal father long ago that worshipping God was one thing and worshipping a cosmic power-monopoly or decision-making monopoly quite another. Not that God must fall short of some ideal degree and kind of power (as 'limited God' suggests), but that sheer monopoly of power or decision-making in one agent is a nightmare – strictly speaking an absurdity – not an ideal.

Finally we must mention the disproof from the evils of the world. Against a theist claiming empirical evidences for his position such evils are relevant and cogent grounds for rejecting the claim. Here I side with Hume and Kant. But against the position that the entire question is *a priori*, so that observation in any possible world, or else in no possible world, would 'declare the divine glory' for those able to interpret the observation, there can be neither argument nor counter-argument which is empirical in the significant (Popperian) sense. Not the actual existence of evils counts against such a position; for their mere conceivability would be enough to refute it if all-surpassing power and goodness could not coexist with evils. For whatever is incompatible with something genuinely conceivable must be contingent. But God cannot be contingent. And the existence of evil is conceivable. Hence either theism is an absurdity or God's existence is compatible with the existence of evil.

As I have often explained, I hold to the second horn of the dilemma, and this for a reason already hinted at in the answer given above to Hartmann. Monopolistic power able to guarantee universal harmony is a hopeless misconception of the divine 'majesty'. It betrays a pitiful human weakness that this has not been clear all along. Ordinary rulers delegate decision-making, some too little, some too much; deity delegates it precisely in the right degree. And no decision making can be without risk of conflict with other decision making. Parents, teachers, neither can nor, if they are good and wise, do they wish to deprive their pupils of self-determination. Strictly speaking, the absolute degree of this deprivation is simply the non-existence of the pupils. Short of that, we have their truncated existence. It is the glory of Franco-American philosophy, with powerful help from the Anglo-American Whitehead, to have generalized this insight so that it applies not just to man or angels but to creatures as such. A creature is a derivative creator, a creator on a non-divine level. This is not an empirical but a logical truth, since it elucidates the meaning of 'creature' .

To be is to act, to be as individual is to act individually, and this is taken merely verbally, not insightfully, if thought to mean that the individual's act may merely reiterate, or be a portion of, some other individual's act, no matter if the other individual is deity.

The history of the problem of 'second causes', i.e., causes other than God as First Cause, is a scandal. The scandal came into the open with Malebranche. Only the first cause, he held, acts, is really a cause. The others may think they are causes. But how can they think causality, if they and other creatures are not causes? The whole theory is semantic jugglery. And so is the classical problem of evil. It cannot be that the details of cosmic history are divinely decided. Countless cooks made the historical broth, not just the Unsurpassable cook. Huxley's query, why did not God create beings without freedom, really means, why did he create? To that, neo-classical theism has an answer: because God enjoys his creatures as he could not enjoy a vacuum of no creatures, or his own knowing of his own knowing of his own knowing.

Since I have praised French and American, or Anglo-American philosophy, I will remark that Locke and Crusius, as well as Descartes, resisted the traditional philosophical bias in favour of determinism – the notion that causal possibility is coincident with what actually happens, instead of setting a range of potentiality less determinate than what happens, leaving some room however slight for the self-determination of each present reality. True, these thinkers took this view only so far as the human individual is concerned. But Fechner, with some help from Schelling, made the generalization referred to above. And so the advance in question is international, however, with special credit due to France and my country. No future philosophy of religion will amount to much if it misses this achievement. Everything else has been tried *ad nauseam*, except only the concept of creativity as metaphysical ultimate. God's creating is creativity's eminent or unsurpassable, but not its sole form, and man's creativity is merely the rational-animal form, a quite special kind of creaturely freedom, infinitely far from exhausting the non-divine possibilities.

The dozens of essays which I have read trying to show that moral freedom is compatible with a total absence of creativity or causal indeterminacy seem to me to show nothing which a believer in creativity needs to deny. Of course moral freedom is, as these writers keep saying, not only compatible with, but requires, the universal validity of the causal principle. That is not the issue, which is, rather, how the causal principle is to be conceived. According to determinists, 'causally possible' coincides with 'causally necessary'. According to indeterminists, what is causally necessary is always less definite than what happens, which is thus shown to have been causally possible, but not shown to have been causally necessary. The real issue is within the causal idea, not between it and its negation. Maxwell, Peirce, Poincaré, and Boutroux understood this long ago, most physicists have some understanding of it now. But cultural lag is always to be reckoned with in philosophy, not necessarily because its practitioners are lazy, still less stupid, but because what is expected of teachers of philosophy is almost more than human energy can make even a decent pretence of accomplishing.

None of the six arguments is empirical, from mere facts; all are arguments from the requirements of concepts, concepts so general or abstract that they cannot be simply rejected, though they may, of course, be left implicit while only more special concepts are explicitly employed. The first argument is from the modal structure of the concept of deity itself; the second, from the modal structure of the concept of existence; the third, from the concept of order or the mutual compatibility of elements making up a cosmos, any cosmos and any conceivable state of affairs. The fourth explicates the concept of reality or truth in relation to the concept of knowledge; the fifth, the concept of *summum bonum* (one of Kant's greatest discoveries), meaning the supreme or inclusive aim (valid against any rational objection and for all rational beings); the sixth, the concept of the *de facto* inclusive reality (as such, any thinkable inclusive factual whole) in relation to the concept of beauty and aesthetic enjoyment. Against the objection that inferences from concepts are hypothetical only, that is, they assume that the concepts have application, the defence is that the distinction between empty and non-empty conceptions has meaning only with reference to specific or non-metaphysical concepts, those whose negative application could be vouched for in some conceivable experience. But the concepts upon which the six proofs turn are all metaphysical. So at last it is made clear that the divine existence is entirely metaphysical, non-contingent, and no factual matter at all – in the normal meaning of 'fact', i.e., contingent state of affairs. Tillich's polemic against talking about the 'existence' of God is justified if he means that we are not, in putting the theistic question, asking what happens to be the case but rather, what could not thinkably fail to be the case.

If the divine existence follows from extremely abstract concepts, must not God be a mere empty abstraction? This was Findlay's objection, in the stronger of the two forms which he gave it, the other being that modern logic has shown that existence cannot be necessary. My answer turns entirely upon distinguishing between the divine actuality, or *how*, in what contingent state or other God exists, and the mere proposition that he exists *somehow*, in some state or other expressive of his not by others conceivably surpassable excellence. This distinction is nothing particularly odd, but is one we can make in regard to any individual's existence, though only in application to deity does the distinction make all the difference between contingency and unconditional necessity. The necessity that deity be concretized somehow is not itself anything concrete. Only the *how* would introduce concreteness. To know anything at all about *that* one must have empirical knowledge. And indeed for a theist all science tells us empirical truths about God. For if science knows a contingent truth T, then it is true of God that he knows that truth. Since T is contingent, it is only contingent that God knows it. Were it not true, God would know whatever would then be the case. But in asking, Is theism true or false, we are only asking, What is necessarily true of God? Science is not the adjudicator of that question, as most scientists realize. But then there should be an end of search for empirical proofs and disproofs concerning theism. It is science which searches for empirical truth, not philosophy, except perhaps so far as it is truth too close to the individual's own uniqueness for science to handle that is in question. Existentialism or phenomenology may have something neither metaphysical nor quite within the scope of science to contribute. I leave that question open.

Fully developed, each of the arguments points not simply to the theistic conclusion, but to the neo-classical form of this conclusion. This is made explicit in the formal statements of the proofs only in V. Clearly we could not 'enrich the divine life' if this is conceived in the classical terms of immutability and impassibility, or as in every sense and aspect absolute and self-sufficient, or as an absolute maximum which even God himself could not surpass. I hold that all reasons for God are weakened if not contradicted by this classical view. Thus the 'Findlay paradox' – the necessary is the abstract – refutes the ontological proof as classically employed quite apart from any question about the predicative or non-predicative status of 'existence'. Indeed it refutes the sheer identification of deity and necessary being. God's existence can be necessary but not his entire reality or actuality. Only neo-classical theism can make this distinction. Similar remarks could be made about the other proofs, in relation to the two forms of theism.

One may prefer mystery to an idea as definite as that of God. Or one may find this idea so little definite as to constitute a mystery equal to any. In either case one will distrust arguments for the idea. To this extent, at least, there seems to be an irreducibly personal element in belief or disbelief.

Those who find that in each of the six cases one or more of the A options seem more credible than T will have 'refuted' the proofs, so far as they themselves are concerned. (Or they may find that the options are not exhaustive, and that a neglected one is the most credible.) But this will be a long way from having refuted the proofs for all of us.

If there are no universally convincing proofs, there are also no universally convincing disproofs. So far Kant was right. But in his claim to have refuted all possible proofs (and all possible disproofs) for mankind at large he deluded himself. Rather, each man must take his own stand on the proofs he knows, and run his own risk of missing important insights into truth and the meaning of life. Belief is a privilege. To scold or think ill of those who are unable or refuse to avail themselves of this privilege is inappropriate. To persecute them is monstrous. But there is also little need to congratulate them. Nor perhaps are they wise to congratulate themselves.[5]

[5] For anti-theistic argument, depending in my judgment on the assumption that theism must be empirically testable, or upon a failure to comprehend the metaphysics of universal creativity, see:

Michael Scriven, *Primary Philosophy* (New York and London: McGraw Hill, 1966).

A. G. N. Flew, *God and Philosophy* (London: Hutchinson, 1966).

E. H. Madden and P. M. Hare, *Evil and the Concept of God* (Springfield, Ill.: C. C. Thomas, 1968).

More circumspect discussions are:

John Wisdom, 'Gods' and 'The Logic of God', the first reprinted in A. G. N. Flew (ed.), *Logic and Language* (first series) (Oxford: Basil Blackwell, 1951); the second in J. Hick (ed.), *The Existence of God* (New York: The Macmillan Company, 1964).

M. K. Munitz, *The Mystery of Existence* (New York: Appleton-Century-Croft, 1965).

XV

SENSORY QUALITIES
AND ORDINARY LANGUAGE

THERE is a doctrine confidently accepted by many philosophers and psychologists for which, however, no firm evidence has ever been given. This is the doctrine that the qualities given in sense experience – sweet, painful, blue, etc. – are, in themselves as given, value-neutral, free from anything like emotional tone, although in some way values, feeling-tones, are often connected with them, probably through association by contiguity. The doctrine is enshrined in the classical distinction between 'secondary' and 'tertiary' qualities, the 'primary' being those of spatio-temporal configuration and motion. Some philosophers (Berkeley – especially in his *Commonplace Book* – Bradley, Whitehead, Croce, e.g.) and psychologists (Dashiel, Spearman, and others) have rejected the doctrine. (However, I learned about their view only years after reaching a firm conviction to reject it myself.) My first book was an attack upon it. The arguments in the book, like those of Berkeley, Spearman, etc., on the point, have been largely ignored. Apart from admitting faults in details, I still hold the position with much the same confidence. The idea of a sheer difference in kind between secondary and tertiary qualities is a blunder, and a very destructive one for philosophy. In this chapter I wish to consider some evidence from ordinary language bearing on the question.

Consider the following:

secondary quality	tertiary quality, emotional tone
sweet	sweet, sweetly, 'my sweet'
sugar	'Sugar'
bitter	bitter, bitterly
sour	sour, sourly, tartly

spicy	variety is the spice of life
pain	painful, painfully
pleasure (physical, e.g., sexual)	pleasant, pleasantly
hot	hot, hotly, heatedly
cold	cold, coldly
blue	'blues'
bright	bright, brightly
dark	dark, darkly
black	black (black mood)
dim	'a dim view of . . .'

In the above cases language assumes, and successfully assumes, that the tertiary as well as the secondary use of the above adjectives or adverbs will be intelligible to everyone. If the basis of this is association, then not the slightest personal differences seem to have affected communication. The reason is simple: the basis is not mere association. Horses and children find sugar pleasant, and they need no learning for this. It does take some learning to get to like very bitter things, and this is like the pleasure of being frightened in the theatre, or in reading a thriller. It is a paradoxical or two-layered emotional tone.

Are the 'associations' a cultural matter? If so, let the cultural differences be exhibited. They have not been, so far. A favourite candidate used to be the Chinese use of white in funerals. This usage does indeed reflect a cultural difference, but the difference is, as I show in my book, irrelevant to the present argument. (The Chinese have different feelings, not about white, but about the meaning of death and the way to do honour to ancestors. Their feelings, incidentally, are in some ways more intelligent than ours.)

In the above double list, auditory qualities may seem to be missing, except in the case of the 'blues'. But in fact 'sweet' is instantly understood of sounds as well as of tastes and smells. And 'he spoke coldly' or 'brightly' also offers no difficulty.

In a recent book, a musician offers, not apparently intentionally, strong support for the view that emotional qualities inhere in auditory qualities as such.[1] He gives massive evidence for the

---

[1] Deryck Cooke, *The Language of Music* (Oxford: Oxford University Press, 1959).

view that certain intervals and other simple musical elements have fixed emotional characters. Thus, for example, a fall in pitch is relaxing. Why not, when the physiological fact is that low pitches mean diffuse rather than concentrated activity in the cochlea? The primary datum of experience is the body, and the immediately conditioning physiological facts are directly given in experience, even though not necessarily in consciously detectable fashion. But the concentrated intensity or sharpness of high pitches is detectable, as is the diffuse massiveness of low ones.

The primary data of experience are at once physiological and emotional. They have spatio-temporal structure and feeling-tone. Their utilization to get knowledge is what is tertiary. Before we 'know' anything about an extremely bitter or foul-smelling substance we have begun to reject it. This built-in relation to feeling and action is the primitive substratum of all experience. The mind is not a camera, merely recording facts to which another function is added, reacting to facts and bestowing value upon them. The primitive facts are value-facts already. The mere camera idea is a relic of the old faculty psychology, as Whitehead charges. There was 'cognition, volition, and affection'. But the best interpreters of this triad knew that *mere* cognition would be nothing at all.

Are we then experiencing only our own feelings about the world, not the world? No, we are experiencing a world composed at the very least of feelings. These are not in the first instance ours, but belong especially to creatures making up our bodies. Certain cells have already rejected the bitter substance, if you will, disliked it, and their feeling becomes ours. This is why it seems to be *there* in the mouth. It really is there. The 'ocean of feelings' (Whitehead), each with some self-determination and some participation in previous feelings, is reality itself.

Because of the question of racism, black poses a special problem. It is a complex problem. (1) I have yet to see a literally black skin, or a literally white one either, though some skins are a very light pink or gray, and some a very dark brown, or tan, or gray. (2) Where light shines on a smooth dark surface, brilliant glints qualify the colour experienced. (3) Both black and white furnish enriching contrast to whatever lighter, or darker, colours are also involved, as in clothes, hair, etc. (4) Though black, like white, is an extreme in one of the three dimensions of colour (brightness), in the dimension red-green it is strictly neutral or intermediate, while in the dimension yellow-blue, white is intermediate but closer to yellow, and black is intermediate but closer to blue. (5) No evidence has been shown that the darker peoples of Asia, for example, have different aesthetic feelings about colour from those that Nordics have. I am convinced that this question is essentially not a racist one. When the North American Indians called Europeans 'pale faces', they suggested a deficiency of richness, of saturation, in the pigmentation of their visitors. And indeed mere white, or mere black, is neutral (and so in a sense deficient) with respect to the emotional contrasts red-green, yellow-blue.

Mark Twain, in India, delighted in the rich browns of the skins and felt that those he had left behind in North America were lacking in this respect. But all such reactions are on a more complex level than the tertiary qualities this chapter is concerned with. Some people like more bitter candy than others, but this does not mean that they fail to sense the contrast, sweet-bitter, as essentially positive-negative. It means that they do not want *mere* pleasantness, but rather the more complex and sophisticated experience of the 'bitter-sweet'. 'Parting is such sweet sorrow' suggests an analogous complexity. The sensory-emotional life is inexhaustibly subtle and complex. But mere sensation, in my view, is that part of the feeling content of experience which is localized in phenomenal space and directly conditioned by the sense organs. Liking for someone is not localized in this fashion. We have feelings *about* our sensory feelings. This genuine duality is the source of the pseudo-duality of feeling and mere sensation. The latter is a fiction.

The Egyptians who worshipped the sun were dark skinned, but the sun was anything but dark to them. Coleridge, speaking of the rising sun, 'nor dim nor red like God's own head' was reacting to the sun's beauty (according to Goethe, the most beautiful object we see on earth) essentially as Ikhnaton did. And Wordsworth, feeling that the moon 'doth with delight look round her when the heavens are bare' was not being influenced by the colour of anyone's skin. There is a more primitive layer of feeling here than association theories know how to deal with. In what sense association comes in is considered with some care in my book.[2] There may well be association built into the sense-organs themselves through millions of years, but it has nothing to do with associations formed in historical times, and is fully compatible with the emotional theory of sensation.

[2] *The Philosophy and Psychology of Sensation* (Chicago: The University of Chicago Press, 1934; out of print).

XVI

THE AESTHETIC MATRIX OF VALUE

VALUES may be considered under three heads: acting rightly, thinking correctly, and experiencing well or satisfyingly. In other words, goodness, truth, and (in a generalized sense) beauty. But, as Peirce held, the order is wrong. The basic value is the intrinsic value of experiencing, as a unity of feeling inclusive of whatever volition and thought the experience contains, and exhibiting harmony or beauty. If we know what experience is, at its best or most beautiful, then and only then can we know how it is right to act; for the value of action is in what it contributes to experiences. Thinking, Peirce held, is one form of acting, and hence logic as a normative science is a branch of ethics. Both presuppose aesthetics, in a generalized sense: the study of what makes experiences good in themselves. C. I. Lewis accepted this Peircean view.

Remarkably enough, Whitehead independently arrives at nearly the same conclusion. He does have much more to say about what the generalized aesthetics comes to. Beauty (as an intrinsic value) is, in his words, the 'mutual adaptation of the elements of an experience'. Beauty of objects is instrumental, it is an organization of, or in, things experienced such that the experiences tend to be of the sort just defined. Mutual adaptation or harmony is not, however, a sufficient condition of great value. There must also be intensity. And intensity depends upon contrast, the amount of diversity integrated into an experience. Thus aesthetic value is found in diversified, harmonious experiences. This agrees with the old formula, beauty is unity in variety.

To the obvious objection that every experience has both unity and variety – unity as one experience, and variety as involving objects diverse both from the experience and from each other – the answer is that this only insures that there will be at least minimal aesthetic value. And of course there will be. Absolute aesthetic failure simply means no experience at all. The question is what measures values above the bare minimum. In the absence of sufficiently diversified stimuli an animal goes to sleep. If there is no dreaming, there is then no experience and no actual value. But an animal may also lose consciousness from shock, from too strong a diversity through time. There are then two notions of minimal value, not one. Either the degree of contrast or the degree of integration may be barely sufficient. Beauty in the emphatic sense is a *balance* of unity and variety. Given a certain complexity, beauty is the diversification of that complexity just to the extent that the aspects of unity, or similarity, are no more, and no less, impressive than the aspect of diversity. Thus it is with a rhyme scheme of abab, for instance. To have aaaa is monotonous, the off-balance is towards mere unity; to have abcd is, in so far as rhyme is concerned, mere diversity. Too much repetition of consonants or vowels is monotonous, too little tends to make verse as unmusical, unappealing phonetically, as prose.

The essential point of the seemingly so empty formula, 'unity in variety', is thus that while the ideal of success is single, the possibilities of failure are dual, and opposite to one another. This is the old Aristotelian principle of the golden mean: in the middle is the desirable quality, undesirable are the two extremes – e.g., rashness and timidity, compared to courage. So in aesthetic value. For each level of complexity there is a balance of unity and diversity which is ideally satisfying. What we spontaneously call beautiful exhibits this balance. Discord, diversity not integrated by unifying factors, is not very good; but a too tame harmony or unity, not sufficiently diversified with contrasting aspects, is not very good either. And at the extreme limit, one form of aesthetic failure is as bad as the other; for in either case experience becomes impossible. To be bored to death is no better than to be shocked to death. And both can happen, as probably most doctors would admit.

Though beauty is the ideal aesthetic value, it is not the only one. For deviations from the mean still have value if they are not hopelessly far from the mean. Also, the very contrasts between cases of ideal beauty and distortions towards either extreme of un-unified diversity and undiversified unity can themselves, taking life as a whole and memory of other cases into account, enrich the total beauty of experience.

Moreover, there is at least one other dimension besides that of unity vs. diversity, and that is the dimension of complexity or profundity vs. simplicity or superficiality. A musical chord is equally unified and diversified, hence it is beautiful. But it is too simple to count heavily, just in itself. Its beauty is superficial, not profound. However, for a tiny child such things may perhaps be profound enough. And a bird song that seems trivial to us need not be trivial to a bird. For us it may be beautiful but not profound; for the bird perhaps it is both beautiful and profound and as near a sense of the sublime as that creature can get. It is apparent on reflection that ordinary speech makes the distinctions we have been discussing. Superficially beautiful things are 'pretty' in English, *hübsch* in German. If the beauty is very profound, 'sublime' or 'magnificent' may be more appropriate adjectives.

There is also the ridiculous. This involves discord, but one not taken as profound enough to be tragic, or merely horrible.

The following is a diagram of these relationships. (I am indebted here to Max Dessoir [émigré from Nazi Germany] and to a former student, Kay Davis Leclerc.)

THE DESSOIR-DAVIS CIRCLE

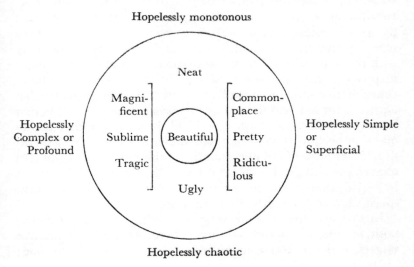

Outside the circle there is no value, everything inside has some value. For different organisms the circle could be conceived to move farther towards the right or the left, according to various capacities to assimilate complexity. For a bird, a symphony is hopelessly profound; for a human being, some bird songs are almost hopelessly superficial. The 'diameter' of the circle as well as its location of course also may vary greatly, when organisms with small or large scope are considered.

Diversity in time means unforeseen novelty. Indeed completely foreseen novelty is a contradiction, for the new would have been there before in experience and so would be not new. It is an aesthetic law of experiencing that without the unforeseen there can be no experience. This is an aspect of the creativity inherent in experiencing as such. Unlimited foresight is not even a valid ideal. Bergson and Whitehead have grasped the full import of this. Most philosophers have not. The popularity of determinism is enough to show that.

Creativity guarantees a minimum of value to every actuality. Always there is the unity of an experience; always there is novelty and genuine contrast, not only with what went before, but with what could have been anticipated. As artists know, but some writers on aesthetics seem to deny, predictability beyond a certain point is a negative value. Yet I know an astronomer whose only reason, he said, for being a determinist was aesthetic, In this, he betrayed aesthetic ignorance. Determinism is a theory of cosmic monotony, not of cosmic beauty. The very sense of intensity in scientific activity is essentially bound up with the unpredictability of future discoveries and the frequent surprises in experimental results. (The more the environment comes under human control the more the attempt to predict nature is turned into the partly hopeless problem of predicting future inventions and future political decisions. Science makes many important things less predictable, not more. No generation has ever faced the uncertainties of this one! Such a result of science could indeed in general terms have been predicted but was not, thanks to the extent to which intellectuals have succumbed to the myth of determinism.)

In my own study of birdsong, a striking discovery was the positive role of unpredictability. There are highly repetitive singers, which reiterate many many times a single little song;

there are also singers with great 'immediate variety', that is, after singing A (possibly several times quickly) they go on to B, and then to C, then perhaps back to A, then to D and E, perhaps back to B or C, and so on until the 'Repertoire' is exhausted. In this versatile type of singing, the next item is in principle unpredictable, apart from statistical preferences for some items or some sequences. The more highly developed the song, i.e., the more extensive the repertoire, the less predictable will be the next item. Thus the evolution of singing is towards maximizing unexpectedness, though always within limits, since the repertoire is essentially fixed in maturity, and since there is a general similarity of style. 'Theme with variations' is a very natural phrase in describing many songs. In the first or repetitive style of singing, there is also (usually) unpredictability; but it is extra-musical. After singing A the bird does not *immediately* repeat; rather, he pauses for a time much longer than the song, and longer than there is any reason to think the bird has vivid retention or memory. So what is unpredictable in such cases is what non-musical activity will follow the song. The general principle covering both types is that pause lengths and immediate variety of singing vary inversely, the versatile singers generally having much shorter pauses.

Of the 4000 birds in the world called technically Oscines or Songbirds because they possess specialized muscles for sound production, I know something about the songs of perhaps 1500. Scarcely a single extreme exception to the foregoing rule has turned up. Outside the sub-order of Songbirds there are some species which seem insensitive to monotony (chiefly barbets, nightjars, and rails). I assume that these are less interested in sounds as such and are singing largely mechanically, by comparison with the species more specialized in singing. But the great majority of birds of all types (example, the rooster) that have something anyone wants to call a song, do conform to the 'anti-monotony principle', or they avoid crossing the 'monotony threshold'. They limit the predictability of their actions.

I believe that the basic idea of beauty as integrated diversity and intensity of experience is metaphysical, valid for any possible state of reality. There is nothing whatever of anthropomorphic specificity about it. Value could not not be this sort of thing and actuality could not not have value. This is Plato's

Good which is the key to being. God himself enjoys harmonized contrasts, and so do micro-organisms. An organism or individual is a functioning unity in diversity, so long as it endures at all.

Life, in all its phases, can be valued aesthetically, in terms of contrasts and harmonies in experiencing various states and activities. A good tennis player experiences a harmony between intention and execution more often than a poor player does. And his intentions themselves are more complex and diversified.

The value of truth is in part a form of aesthetic value, since the more truth one knows, the more one can order and also diversify one's ideas and make them fit one's perceptions. But there are also harmonies between elements of imaginative experiences. Aesthetic value is thus the broader category. It is more illuminating to take truth as a form of beauty than beauty as a form of truth. Truth also has instrumental value as we act upon it.

Ethical value, goodness, is not the value of experiences themselves, but rather the instrumental value of acting so as to increase the intrinsic value of future experiences, particularly those of others than oneself. However, the good will, the will to enhance the value of future experiences generally, is itself, as experienced, an element of present harmony, just as hatred is a kind of discord. So the good will is twice good: it enriches one's own present experience and in its consequences tends to enrich future experiences, not necessarily one's own. Goodness is the self in its purposes transcending the personal future and making itself trustee for others (according to religion, finally, trustee for God). In this transcendence of the personal there is a kind of 'peace' or 'Nirvana', an escape from the agonies of egotism. This peace is the only essential reward of virtue. It is in the present and is not a looked-for reward in the eventual future. Rather, so long as one's own future is taken as *the* important matter, there is no peace.

Since the intrinsic value of experiences is by definition aesthetic value, and since goodness is the disinterested will to enhance the value of future experiences, ethics presupposes aesthetics.

Another way of showing the primacy of aesthetics is the following. All animals experience harmony and discord; all react to unity and variety. A newly-caged wild animal is in a state of discord, trying vainly to escape. A resigned caged animal is in a stage of at least mild boredom much of the time. It is not necessarily suffering, but is not fully alive either. Young animals find plenty of diversity in life, for so much is new. Old animals tend to find too little diversity, so much is old. They look on mildly bored while the young eagerly play. This gives, I seriously believe, the ultimate reason for death, and for me makes the idea that death is essentially or in principle an evil a sheer mistake. Death at a certain time, or in a certain way, may be a great evil, but death as such is a good. 'Glad did I live and gladly die, and I laid me down with a will' makes excellent sense to me.

All animals are subject to aesthetic good and evil, but not to ethical good and evil. For this requires that one consider future consequences not only for oneself and mate, offspring, or other herd members, but impartially for individuals generally, and even in principle for species generally. Other terrestrial animals can be intentionally useful to others of their kind, or even to a member of another species, but only man can be ethically good.

The ethical good is not only inapplicable to some animals, but it is not applicable in the same sense to deity. God, I hold, is an artist fostering and loving the beauty of the creatures, the harmonies and intensities of their experiences, as data for his own. This love is in every way more than our goodness, not less. Yet it involves no transcendence of God's own future good, analogous to our ethical transcendence of our future good. For this transcendence of ours is only the refusal to compound aesthetic weakness – our inability eventually to enjoy all future goods resulting from our actions – with moral weakness, the over-valuation of our own importance. How could God over-value his own importance? His aim could not transcend his future good and have any content, for this future good is all-inclusive. God alone inherits all the harvests for which he, or anyone, sows the seed. To forbid him to enjoy the harvest, since that would make him selfish, is one of the oddest confusions into which sentimentalists have ever fallen. 'Selfishness' has meaning only in application to a partially ignorant, more or less apathetic (or perhaps malicious), and mortal creature whose usefulness to others cannot be guaranteed to bring proportionate future benefits to itself. Omniscience and immortality make the whole issue irrelevant. God cannot benefit another without benefiting himself. In his case self-interest and altruism are indeed coincident, but not because he is clever enough to do us good so as to satisfy his own egoistic desires. He has no egoistic desires, if words are properly used. He wants only to enjoy creaturely good, seeking for the creatures the happiness they seek for themselves.

The aesthetic value of good will, of aiming at the general aesthetic good, is in God ideally complete, and is the same as his righteousness. What is not and could not be complete, and is not mere righteousness, is the aesthetic value of God's enjoying the actual aesthetic good of the creatures. For this enjoyment can reach no final maximum, but is endlessly capable of increase, since the divine capacities for aesthetic enjoyment are strictly infinite, and any totality of actual creatures must in some respects at least be finite. So God can be endlessly enriched aesthetically; he can endlessly increase in achievement, though not in the rightness of his aim. The rightness is always perfect.

It is to me pathetic that man has come so far as he has in power and skill and yet, even today, has scarcely begun to reflect rationally upon life as an aesthetic problem for which death is in principle the proper solution. The only death that could not be good in principle is the 'death of God'. But fortunately that death does not make sense. What does make sense, all too easily, is that man as a species might prematurely end, or terribly maim itself, before having unfolded anything like its full potentialities, especially potentialities for wisdom, philosophic maturity.

Goodness, truth, and beauty overlap in important ways. A kind of goodness is required for science, the co-operative search for truth. And good intentions, when they do not include a resolute will to face truth and acquire as much truth as is relevant to decisions, can be futile or worse. In the United States many well-meaning persons, who may be in Northern cities as well as in the South, have never faced the truth about the unimportance of mere race as such. These persons are destructive and dangerous, because they think they know what in fact they do not know, and because what they do not know Negroes on the whole, and most of mankind, do know. It is a frightening form of provincialism.

The beauty of life includes, we have seen, that of good will as such and also that of the search for and finding of truth. All values can contribute to the diversity, and hence to the intensity and valuable harmony of experience. For the scientist, a good theory has beauty, and the sense of not yet discovered beauties drives his search for better theories. Our teaching about science has been far too prosaic. Science is a romantic adventure, a means of widening the horizon of beauty. All can see the ocean waves, but as to the 'waves' governing particles, only many centuries of ingenious inquiry have made these 'visible' to a few. What is needed most of all is to give the study of man himself more of this appeal. Somehow we must inspire a greater love of the beauty to be enjoyed in understanding our own natures. Here I believe the ethologists – e.g., Lorenz and Ardrey – can help.

We need one more principle, not made sufficiently explicit so far, the principle of *positive incompatibility*. Aesthetic discord is not essentially a clash between good and bad, or positive and negative, but between good and good, positive and positive. Berdyaev and Whitehead are the philosophers who have seen this most clearly. Those who do not see it will never understand life. Fanaticism and cruelty often spring from this blindness. Life is full of choices between good things, often about equally good things. Being a scientist is good, being a musician is good, but the same man cannot in the fullest sense be both. Sonnets have many possible rhyme schemes, each of which is good, but each of which in a given case excludes all others. This conflict of positive values is at the root of both contingency and tragedy in existence. Between positive values there can be no necessary or uniquely right choice. And always some goods must be renounced. A person lacks sense who aims to enjoy 'all the good things of life'. We are all willy-nilly ascetics, doing without some very good things. But some ascetics deliberately choose their renunciations to a greater extent than others. They are the most free.

The principle of incompatible goods, together with that of creativity, or the self-determination of each moment of existence in and by the reality of that moment, furnishes the ultimate reason for suffering in the world. It is only luck if the various partly free or creative beings pursue mutually compatible goals.

Freedom and the incompatibility of goods are enough to make a purely harmonious world impossible. And if the objection is that then there ought to be no freedom, the answer is: existence and freedom are two aspects of the same thing. There could not not be freedom, the only question is, how much and what kinds of freedom. Moreover, even the least freedom means a probability of conflict. If the probable conflicts are trivial, so are the probable harmonies or goods. The price of one good is the renunciation of others; but the price of a world in which only compatible goods were in question is the price that cannot be paid, for there would not then be a world.

The failure to see the aesthetic matrix of all value has had many unfortunate consequences besides the failure to arrive at a rational view of death, or of the ground of suffering. It has also prevented us from having a really illuminating treatment of sexual ethics. Promiscuity and short-term relations have often been condemned as contrary to divine or human law, as hindering the proper care of offspring, as exposing people to disease or unwanted pregnancy. I shall not discuss how far these reasons still have force. Rather I wish to present some aesthetic considerations against the practices in question. The discussion will be very incomplete; many factors must be passed over. First, and obviously enough, physical pleasure alone is not human fulfilment. Man seeks beauty in his overall experience, harmony and intensity not just of sensations but of emotions, purposes, and intellectual interests. Physical or sensory pleasure is our participation in harmony among our bodily members. It is not in an absolute sense non-social. But harmony with other persons is aesthetically on a higher level. Inter-personal relations are presupposed in language itself, which is the distinguishing mark of humanity. There are many kinds of such relations, all subject to aesthetic criteria.

There are relations to inferiors, such as the non-human animals, infants who are scarcely as yet persons, small children, or adults of really feeble intelligence. Relations to inferiors are at their best with several inferiors, rather than just one. For otherwise there is lack of balance. One child confronted with an adult feels overwhelmed and threatened; several children give each other support. (Since the falling death rate makes ever smaller – or else fewer – families desirable, we have one more difficulty created by technology. However, an empirical study of the 'only child' problem did not show that such children are inferior. The greater attention they get from parents partly makes up for their deficiencies. Also it is a fair question whether there ought not to be fewer families with any children. Some persons ought not to be parents.)

Think of God with just one creature! This is a picture that, so far as I know, has never been found attractive. But if relations to inferiors ideally involve more than one of the latter, they also (given human limitations) involve the sacrifice of the full measure of attention to any one of the inferiors. So the supreme human inter-personal relation is not with inferiors.

The most complete and intimate purely human relations must be between equals, in pairs. (They need not be in all respects equal. Hamlet and Horatio were not politically equal, but still Horatio did not feel especially inferior.) When relations between equals are happy or harmonious, they may be termed friendships. The beauty of friendship is in its harmonizing, in an intimate and concrete way, felt by both parties, of the deep contrasts which are more or less inevitable between two human individuals, that is, members of the earthly species in which individual differences are almost infinitely greater than in any other earthly species. (The folly of racism, by the way, is chiefly in its unwitting or deliberate failure to reckon with this truth. Non-negroes are treated as individuals, Negroes as Negroes.)

A friend is not simply another with whom one has good things in common. This was the Aristotelian idea. The only reason this was plausible was that inevitably two persons have differences, and so the only question might seem to be, are they sufficiently alike? But on that basis identical twins should be the most happy of all in their relationships. I have not observed this to be so, and would be astonished if it could be supported by much evidence. 'Birds of a feather flock together' is poor ornithology, as could easily be shown. In any case, herd or flock behaviour is not friendship. Friendship is selective sociability, selective of individuals, not of mere fellows in a species. And one can observe over and over again that deep contrasts as well as close similarities are involved in the more intense and richer friendships.

Since friendship is the most complete inter-human relation, and since it presupposes difference without inequality, the ideal of social equality has a good basis. But this ideal has to take its chances with several others. One is that each individual shall have opportunity to make the best possible use of innate powers. That these powers are in numerous important ways highly unequal seems reasonably certain, in the present state of our genetic knowledge. If well-endowed and poorly-endowed individuals (note I say individuals, not races) have equal opportunities to do their best, the result will not be a society of equals in the sense required for friendship. All the more is this true if competitiveness is needed to induce individuals to exert themselves. It must be borne in mind, too, that, since very early training and exposure is the most important of all, even equally-endowed infants will not have equal opportunity unless their parents, nurses, parental substitutes, age-equals, are comparable. Thus to get from a society of unequals to a society of equals in even a number of generations is scarcely possible, regardless of genetics.

Another ideal is that of liberty. Anything like strict equality of opportunity would have to result partly from coercion, since those who have advantages are likely to strive to retain them for themselves, or for relatives or favourites. Thus the ideal of a friendly and therefore equalitarian society cannot be given an absolute right of way without sacrificing other ideals, that seem as well-founded. Nevertheless in some societies, including ours in the United States, inequality has in some respects, especially economic, gone to fantastic extremes – especially so far as the citizens of African (or partly African) origin are concerned. In this respect we cannot suppose that a mere continuation of present conditions is tolerable or likely to be tolerated. This is a challenge for statesmanship and good citizenship.

Sex contrast is additional to all other possible ones. Women, like men, can be artistic, scientific, or politically activistic; they can be interested in butterflies rather than birds or birds rather than butterflies, or plants more than animals; they can be vivacious or phlegmatic, etc., etc., through all the personality differences. It follows that the greatest possibility for contrast in friendship is between persons of opposite sex. Moreover, the sex difference, by its very nature, tends more to unite than to divide, to harmonize more than produce discord. Thus this relation is potentially, though often not actually, the supreme form of harmony between equals. Can they be equals? In principle, yes. Science finds no demonstrable overall inequality between male and female children or young adults. Thus the inequalities of adult achievement are essentially effects of culture, custom, law, religion, and other non-innate influences, plus the biological necessity that most women must put substantial parts of their lives into having and caring for children, and the near necessity that they should do most of the housework. But technology is continually reducing the extent of these necessities, e.g., by lowering the death rate and hence the desirable birth rate. Ideally at least, equality between men and women is possible. But the ideal cannot even be approached in the near future unless men are willing to help women to balance the inequality deriving partly from custom and only partly from biological necessity.

The double standard of our ancestors took inequality for granted. It allowed the risks of promiscuity to fall chiefly upon women. But to some extent this is bound to be so. It certainly is at the present time, as the abortion rate in all the advanced countries is enough to show. It is women who are biologically almost compelled to take the long view of sexual relations. The act of a moment can, and statistically speaking must, for them often have consequences for life, in a sense in which only custom and law causes the same to hold for men.

But there is an aesthetic argument for the long view, apart from the biological necessities. To realize to the full extent the possibility of friendship, the entire personality must be involved. Human beings look ahead, plan for a lifetime. To commit oneself to another is to commit one's life. Less than one's life is less than one's self. A similar argument holds against polygamy, as Kant said. Polygamy is a relation between the whole woman and a part of the man. It is less than friendship, for there is no equality of commitment.

Caring for small children is a human task, since we do it on a level impossible for the other animals. Still, much of the mother's mind is scarcely utilized in this task. If men are to help women overcome their traditional and partly built-in handicaps, they too must try to take the long view and must make certain sacrifices. Such sacrifices should be balanced against the thought that not to have a wife able to enter into a genuine friendship with her husband is itself a very substantial privation. But many women need to change their ideas, also, and to form a better conception of their life problem than that of getting a nice man with a nice income.

Psychiatry has shown us how difficult it is to fit our instinctive nature into civilized – and now more and more automated – societies. I see no easy answers. But it seems to me that we might be better off if we had an ethics adequately aware of the fundamental problem of beauty, i.e., harmony and intensity of experience, especially in the relation between two persons and two lives contrasting in sex as well as in other stimulating, intensifying ways. To share memories from the distant past and hopes for the distant future is no small portion of the value of such a relationship. Fidelity is not merely obedience to a moral command, or contribution to the welfare of children or the stability of society, it is the enjoyment of a high privilege not lightly to be renounced.

Perhaps the hardest question, however, is how loyalty to family can be reconciled with loyalty to the larger needs of mankind. Here is where religion, at its best, is especially needed. The ultimate loyalty is not to any human person, including oneself. Perhaps it is not even to the totality of mankind, still less to a nation, class, or party, but rather to that cosmic something or someone relation to which, or relation to whom, must ultimately embrace *all* our values, and which or who is above our narrow prejudices, and stands for the truly common or universal good of all creatures. Without an aim beyond self, and even beyond any merely human good, life on this temporary planet seems as absurd as Sartre says it is.

We need to feel relation to a superior as well as to equals and inferiors. The notion that there is something humiliating in relation to a superior arises, I believe, from confusion, in so far as it is better than unthinking egoism. A human being who assumes unqualified superiority over us is offensive because human excellence has too many dimensions, some of which are too difficult to estimate in particular cases, for such an assumption to be justified. In the very act of claiming superiority, a man may demonstrate moral or other inferiority. But to feel that there is something radically superior to *any* human being is hardly humiliating. We are born, we die, our very sanity is constantly at the mercy of chemicals that may get into our bodies, we have just enough knowledge to know that what we can ever know is vanishingly small compared to what there is to know. How ludicrous to feel threatened by the idea of a cosmic superior! How could there not be a superior to mere man? Of course, if the cosmic reality is not really conceived as cosmic, but as a 'magnified non-natural man' (Arnold), then indeed we may feel threatened. But we do not have to conceive the cosmic Reality just as some theologians conceive it or him. We are free to face the cosmos for ourselves. We know that conventional Christianity is not alone in the religious world. There are many attempts to conceive the superhuman. We can even make our own attempt.

Sartre's contention that man must give himself meaning in a universe itself as a whole devoid of value seems to be Bertrand Russell's Free Man's Worship over again. My contention has always been that if we have no value for the cosmos, we have no value – period. On the other hand, we do have value. We cannot but feel value in living; indeed living is realizing value, however poor or less than ideal this value may be. The philosophic task, as Schweitzer says, is to harmonize our view of reality with this irreducible value-affirmation. It is ideas of the cosmos that are on trial, not our essential value-sense. Sartre and Russell have it upside down. Particular cosmologies are dispensable, not the affirmation of worth that is life itself. The idea that the universe is absurd or meaningless is itself absurd or meaningless. It expresses a living creature trying to deny its aliveness.

It is necessary to forestall one misunderstanding. I admit that the universe has no such 'meaning' as those have in mind who ask, Why should the universe or God cause me, or some pitiful child, to suffer? I do not believe that evils are merely disguised blessings, or divinely imposed chastisements, or anything like that. The evils are not fulfilments of any cosmic purpose. The cosmic reality contains the evils, but it does not intend or cause them. People may cause them, bacteria may cause them, not the cosmic reality. Yet I believe that there is cosmic purpose and meaning. The evils are in spite of this meaning, not because of it.

With the pragmatists, and many not so called, I hold that

ideas must be livable, expressible in action. Knowledge is chiefly of the past, but our view of the past is integral to our making of the future. How we look backward is how we decide forward. But today technology produces changes so fast that it seems impossible to assimilate the relevant past fast enough.

Before assuming responsibilities in South-East Asia, we should have known something of the history of that region. But who did? How many of us even now have much conception of Buddhism, for instance? Yet it is the greatest international alternative to our Judeo-Christian tradition.

How many scholars have assimilated the change from a science which, for centuries, was based on the idea of absolute causal order to a science which, apart from mere talk, is based on a probabilistic conception of causality, not just in microphysics but in biology, sociology, etc.?

This has relevance for action. If order were absolute, it seems there could be a wholly beneficent order, a Utopia, in which everyone was so conditioned that universal harmony obtained. But conditioning only alters probabilities.

Nature, including man, is a mixture of order and randomness. Also, as some quantum physicists have long realized, it is active individuals, whether atoms or human beings, which evade absolute order. And they do this in proportion to the degree of their individuality.

Man is by far the most highly individuated of species, hence only gross statistical regularities can be expected in human affairs. If people manage to harmonize their purposes together this is good luck as well as good management, and some bad luck is inevitable.

Science, by magnifying the scope of human choices, increases the risks inseparable from these. It also increases the need for social change. But we must distinguish between mere utopian dreams and feasible ways to better our society. Modern cities cannot survive very many weeks of civil and economic disorganization without terrible evils and losses. And the major revolutions of this century produced the two statistically most murderous of all tyrants, plus some minor ones.

The underestimation of randomness in life results in the scapegoat idea that haunts both Right and Left. Someone is to blame. But no one intends events as they happen.

All are caught in a web of mixed intentions, blind necessity, and chance. Who intended the population upswing that has caught our educators unprepared to deal adequately with the new masses of students?

Like the New Left, I am disgusted with what we have done and not done about race. No major philosopher has, in any reasonable sense, been a racist. Royce said some fine things about this evil. Yet far more should have been said and done. It ought to have been a truism that persons are above all individuals, that within physically identified groups variations in abilities are enormous.

The criterion of being human is the 'symbolic power', centring in language; any group – say women – that can use language with elaborate skill is thoroughly human.

Another way in which scholars have erred is in the conception of science as 'prediction and control'. These two functions are not only different; carried to the limit they exclude each other. One does not predict his own future because each moment life consists in controlling that future, deciding bits of it for the first time. Nor can we predict future scientific and technological discoveries, so important for our lives.

We predict most where we control least – thus an eclipse. The more nature comes under human control, the less predictable will some things be, for the more prediction must reckon with human choices, as yet undecided.

An excuse for us all is that human freedom is so great, and resulting elements of order in disorder so complex, that life is a bewildering affair. A touch of tolerance and willingness to see good in various groups might help.

At the same time, the young agitators have a strong case against merely continuing our social and political arrangements. These must, they will, change. But only great care can prevent them from changing for the worse.

Right action is that which is taken in the light of relevant facts and truths. The following considerations seem relevant to our choices.

We are mortal.

There is no independent self or ego, always simply identical with itself, always simply non-identical, non-overlapping, with others. (Hence taking self-interest as the absolute motivation is irrational.)

There is no definitive rational aim short of the good of humanity (at the very least) so far as we have power to promote that good.

There is no inequality of racial groups known to be innate, rather than caused by culture, fortune, circumstance.

Artificial birth control has not been shown to be a greater interference with 'natural law' than our fantastic modern hygiene is such interference. And it is mathematically demonstrable that nature is not in principle a going concern without either a substantial increase in the present death rate or substantial decrease in the present birth rate.

Access to means and knowledge of birth control will not suffice, so long as traditional ideas of women as wives, mistresses, mothers, and little more remain widely accepted by both men and women. If women are socially rewarded only as parents they will of course have an unneeded number of children.

The Malthusian problem is not confined to food. Pure air and water, various minerals, are also in limited supply. Our standard of living concept – ideally, luxury for all – is in contradiction to our attitude towards offspring, together with our demand for hygienic protection. We have never really faced the implications of the tragic deprivation in much of Asia, the Southern Hemisphere, and some parts even of our own country. Bringing all up to our level has not yet been made anything like a practical programme. The hippies are partly right in rejecting our combination of luxurious, wasteful living and humanitarian ideals.

The unlimited (terrestrially speaking) destructive power of technology, together with the unbalance in birth-death rates, are threats so vast that they should humble the pretensions of us all when promoting merely personal or partisan concerns. The concept of humanity, and of this globe, as one, must be made much more real to people.

The experience of this century does not support the view that peace is attained by unilateral pacifism in part of the world. Hitler viewed French and British pacifists as allies, and they did help him to conquer France. Similarly, Russian or Chinese expansionism will not stop merely because we look weak or confused. Lack of patriotism in one place is no cure for the wrong kind of patriotism in another.

We have some notion of the rational ideal. But we are all, much of the time, inclined to entertain irrational goals. The ideal cannot, in any simple, absolute way, be institutionalized. But in relative ways, suitable to time and place, it can be institutionalized, so that, as Kant put it, man's social sense works against rather than for his wickedness and folly. This is the task of religion and social reform. It has not been shown that psychedelic drugs are a short cut to the self-conquest and wisdom without which reformers are likely to be chiefly destroyers.

However all this may be, the aesthetic value of life is realized in relation to other individuals and to the cosmos. Moral value is realized in adopting aims for the future that transcend personal advantage. Life is enjoyed as it is lived; but its eventual worth will consist in the contribution it has made to something more enduring than any animal, or than any species of animal. The final beauty is the 'beauty of holiness'.

INDEX OF NAMES

INDEX OF SUBJECTS

materialism, xvi, 27, 50, 112, 132, 143f., 161, 220; methodological, 54
mathematicians, 92
mathematics, xvii, 32f., 44, 193
Matter, 48, 101(15a), 114ff., 220; as blindly obedient, 8; as 'stuff' inherited from the past, 117; insentient, 72, 160f.
Maya, 177, 272
Meaning, criteria of, 20f.; empirical, 20f.; general, 21; pragmatic, 81; of the universe, 317
Meaning postulates, 23
Mechanism, 129
Memory, 2, 7, 60, 105, 218; absolute, 273; 'impersonal', 109; mistakes of, 79, 91f., 217; 'natural' view of, 88f.; as paradigm of experiencing, 75, 218; and personal identity, 182; secret of, 127
'Meroscopic', 130
Metaphor, xiv, 128
Metaphysical abstractness, 57; contrarieties, 99–130; error, 69; insight, 98; mistakes, 20; principle, xii; statements, 19; systems, xvi; truth, 37
Metaphysicians, criteria for evaluating, 41
Metaphysics, xiii, 19–56, 132, 162f.; classical, 43, 48; 'general' and 'special', 39; twelve definitions of, 24, 33; method of, 69–98; neoclassical, xv, 40; revisionist, xix
Middle, *see* 'excluded'
Mind, 27, 72, 220, 300; as fountain of existence, xi; as free, 8; not inextended, 8; and matter, 51, 111, 145; and possibility, 115f.
Mind-body relations, 107; *see* 'interaction'
Minds (experiences), their causal relations, 113
Modal logic, *see* 'logic'
Modal theory of time, 134; *see* 'time', 'future', 'futurity'
Modality: applied to idea of God, 263–74; as linguistic, 132, 258; phenomenal theory of, 253; objective, 24, 29, 61, 107, 133; ontological theory of, 138, 253; essentially temporal, 133f.

Molecules, 6, 161
Momentary: experience, 128; self, 199
Monism, 8, 95, 216; most radical, 177
Monopolistic power, 292
Moral argument for theism, 286f.
Moral badness, 248
More can contain the less, 241
mortality, 202
Motive, strongest, 3, 6
'Musement', 276
Mysticism, Asiatic, 272

'Natural law', 320
nature: as a chaos, 83; a vast tautology, 83
Necessarily non-empty universe or class, 23, 47, 101f.(11), 102, 144f., 162, 256, 270, 272
Necessary: being, 47, 170, 296; existence, 47; 'and sufficient', 102, 105, 223; statements, 21; *see* 'truths'
Necessity: as abstract, 246f., 249f.; asymmetrical, 101; generic and particular, 103; of God, 250; retrospective, 103f.
Negative anthropology, 155
Neo-classicism, 128
Neural process, 117, 220
Nirvana, 308
Nominalism, 25, 61
Nominalist, complete, 66
Nominalistic argument, 59
'Non-duality', 17
Non-existence not in all cases conceivable, 146
Non-restrictive, 37, 159–72
Normative, *see* 'arguments', 'logic'
Nothing, 228; alleged possibility of, 21, 34, 57, 245, 283
Nothingness (in Buddhism), *see* 'sunyatta'
Novelty as inclusive, 89
Number, 27, 32, 108; no greatest, 38

Object for all subjects, 236
Objective form, 241
Objectivity as intersubjectivity, 108
Object-language, 133

trast'); of divine freedom, 264f.;
of divine inclusiveness, 265; of
inclusive contrast, 89f.; of general-
ity, 90ff.; of least paradox, 88f.;
of positive incompatibility, 311;
of non-invidious contraries, 269f.;
the classical principle, 265; the
absolute principle, relativity as,
52f.
Privation, perception of, 79
Probabilities, 16
Probability, as guide of life, 202f.
Process philosophy, xv, 63, 68
Progress, unlimited, xi
Promises, 198
Promiscuity, 312
Proofs, theistic, 247, 275–97; not co-
ercive but important, 275f., 279f.;
see 'arguments'
Proportionality, rule of, 101
Providence, 66
Psychiatry, 239, 316
Psychicalism, 9, 54, 81, 129, 141ff.;
see 'individuals', 'panpsychism',
'singulars'
Psychical terms, 49, 154ff., 224
Psychological: laws, 2; predicter, 5
Psychologists, 298
Psychology, 2, 5
Punishment, 200
Purpose, and language, 87; cosmic,
317
Purposes, 198; as efficacious univer-
sals, 66f.

Qualities: abstracted from in science,
27; continuum of, 66; of particulars are particular, 64; 'secondary'
and 'tertiary', 76
Quality, 24, 33, 205
Quanta of becoming, 123
Quantity, not maximizable, yet
applies to God, 248
Quantum mechanics, 123

Race, racist, 300, 319
Randomness, 318
Rational: aim, 198; animal, 294;
inquiry, 98; *see 'summum bonum'*
Rationalism, xvi; critical, xviii
Rationality, 98, 199

Rationalist, 36
Realism, 108, 110, 168; and nominalism, 61; moderate, 68
Reality, general idea of, 140f.; as of
now, 118; protean, 67
Refutation in philosophy, 130
Relation, to be is to be in, 114
Relations: of comparison, 215; between events, 15; external and
internal, 52, 82, 100, 167, 226;
interpersonal, 312; rules governing, 147; symmetrical and asym-
metrical, 205–26
Relative: determinism, 204; self-
centredness, 201f.
Relative, the: 205; includes the
absolute, 100 (1r, 3r), 168
Relativity: as the absolute, 46f., 52,
120; of becoming, 26–7; as
directional, 53; of events, 53;
physics, 17, 53, 87, 115, 124f.;
supremacy of, 55
Religion, xviii, 39, 55; task of, 316,
321
Religions: of Judaic origin, 88; love
exalted in all, 81
Religious issue, 40
Reminiscence, 122
Remorse, 199
Repentance, 199
Response, 5f., 50, 78; divine, 12
Responsibility, 198f., 202
Restrictive statements, 159
Ridiculous, the, 305
Right action, 303, 319
Risk, 55, 318
r terms, 100f., 127
Ruler, God as, 12
Rules, in metaphysics, 101, 158

Schema, 29, 71, 137
Scholasticism, 45
Science, 4, 9, 39, 51f., 54, 306; a
romantic adventure, 311; and
philosophy, 57; history of, 70;
and language, 71
Second causes, 293
Self, xx; future, 191
Self, present, and past, 199
Self-activity, 50
Self-created, 3
Self-determination, 190